"An important read for anyone in ⎯⎯⎯⎯⎯⎯⎯⎯⎯⎯⎯⎯⎯⎯⎯⎯
informative and offers a new and innovative way to look at mental disorders.
I recommend it to everyone who wants to know more about themselves and
how their minds work."

　　　—Dr. Frederick Dembowski, president of the International
　　　　Association of Organizational Innovation

"*Nine Dimensions of Madness* is wonderfully written. It is a fascinating volume that will challenge what you think you know about mental disorder,
what we decide is 'normal' or 'disordered,' and how we treat psychiatric illness. In this well-researched, thought provoking and courageous volume,
Robert Gallon argues that how we address the treatment of people we see
as having a mental disorder needs to change. He questions what is really
disordered, and argues instead for a biopsychosocial model that presents
an integrated view of the dimensions of dysfunction. He encourages us to
be more critical of the apparent biological basis to mental disorders and
methods of treatment. Most importantly, Gallon argues for a new solution to our declining trust in a system that overprescribes mood altering
drugs as a quick fix for what are often normal human responses to crisis
and suffering."

　　　—Penny Spikins, PhD, author of *How Compassion Made Us Human:
　　　　the Evolutionary Origins of Tenderness, Trust & Morality*

"A comprehensive, innovative, and provocative work that challenges many of
the medical establishment's assumptions. In addition to medical personnel,
the general public will find this book a fascinating, readable new approach to
mental health issues and treatments for a wide variety of disorders including
ADHD, depression, and even internet addiction."

　　　—Allan D. Currie, MD, FACP, former Chief of the Medical Service,
　　　　Eastern Maine Medical Center

Nine Dimensions of Madness

REDEFINING MENTAL HEALTH

Robert L. Gallon

North Atlantic Books
Berkeley, California

Published by
North Atlantic Books   Cover and book design by Suzanne Albertson
Berkeley, California

Printed in the United States of America

Nine Dimensions of Madness: Redefining Mental Health is sponsored and published by the Society for the Study of Native Arts and Sciences (dba North Atlantic Books), an educational nonprofit based in Berkeley, California, that collaborates with partners to develop cross-cultural perspectives, nurture holistic views of art, science, the humanities, and healing, and seed personal and global transformation by publishing work on the relationship of body, spirit, and nature.

North Atlantic Books' publications are available through most bookstores. For further information, visit our website at www.northatlanticbooks.com or call 800-733-3000.

MEDICAL DISCLAIMER: The following information is intended for general information purposes only. Individuals should always see their health care provider before administering any suggestions made in this book. Any application of the material set forth in the following pages is at the reader's discretion and is his or her sole responsibility.

Library of Congress Cataloging-in-Publication Data

Gallon, Robert L., author.
    Nine dimensions of madness : redefining mental health / Robert Gallon.
        p. ; cm.
    Includes bibliographical references and index.
    Summary: "This book challenges the current medicalization of mental disorders by proposing a system of viewing mental problems as varying dimensions of dysfunction, rather than as pathological, thus encouraging people to become active participants in their own lives and empowering them to cope with life›s difficulties"—Provided by publisher.
    ISBN 978-1-58394-926-9 (trade : alk. paper)—ISBN 978-1-58394-927-6 (ebook)
    I. Society for the Study of Native Arts and Sciences, sponsoring body. II. Title.
    [DNLM: 1. Mental Disorders—etiology. 2. Mental Health. WM 101]
    RC454
    616.89—dc23   2015003833

1 2 3 4 5 6 7 8 9 UNITED 20 19 18 17 16 15

Printed on recycled paper

*I dedicate this book to my grandchildren,
Jacob, Zoe, and Kate, who are my posterity and who,
I hope, will read my book someday.*

Contents

Acknowledgments

I had, of course, been thinking of writing a book for many years, but I never got around to doing it. Then Professor Richard Borden of College of the Atlantic persuaded me to teach a course called "Abnormal Psychology" and told me he was writing a book for North Atlantic Books. Rich told me that the founder of the press, Richard Grossinger, had a home in a neighboring town, and he said he would introduce me if I wished. I got together some materials, then spoke to Richard at length. Initially, Richard was very discouraging, but he warmed to the idea, and I was committed. I thank him for his support, because I never would've written it otherwise. I also very much appreciate the support I received from the editors at North Atlantic, starting with Tim McKee, who gave me extensive advice through the developmental phase, then to Leslie Larson, who took charge of the editing, and to my copy editor, Jennifer Eastman.

I taught material this book is based on at Acadia Senior College several times, and these classes, mostly composed of retired professionals, were a very helpful sounding board. One of my favorite students, Julius Krevans, MD, Emeritus Chancellor of the University of California at San Francisco, read the entire book, made insightful comments, and encouraged me. His wife, Pat, also read sections.

Other people who read all or most of the book were Howard Ehrlichman, emeritus psychology professor, and Frederick Dembowski, emeritus dean of educational leadership. My long-time neuropsychological testing assistant, Linda Currie, also read the book and offered her comments. Finally, my wife, Rita, has read it and supported me throughout the long process. All of these people were extremely helpful but are not responsible for any of the contents.

Preface

We are a psychiatric nation. As University of Chicago anthropologist Tonya Lurhmann put it, "psychiatric knowledge seeps into culture like dye from a red shirt in hot water."[1] Psychiatric disorders are as familiar to us as the names of movie stars. Every difficulty we may face in life has a psychiatric label to explain it. Psychiatric drugs are constantly marketed to us on television and in magazines as the cure for all that ail us. They are routinely prescribed by our physicians and taken by a great many of us—they're said to be the solution to our troubles.

The marketing of psychiatric explanations and treatments has become been so successful that we almost never ask some basic questions. Are mental disorders legitimate medical diseases that can be diagnosed and treated? Has giving people these psychiatric labels helped them lead better lives? Has reliance on psychiatric drugs been a blessing or a curse? And, in general, are we heading in the right direction for good mental health, or are we merely increasing the power and income of mental-health professionals and pharmaceutical companies?

Psychiatric notions aren't only an American story; they have spread across the globe. The giant international drug companies and American psychiatrists have combined to push the medical ideas of psychopathology around the world. Journalist Ethan Watters tells an anecdote that demonstrates this. The Japanese had a name for people who are extremely incapacitated by symptoms that we might term *depression;* they called it *utsubyo,* but it was extremely rare and highly stigmatizing. They had another term, *jibyo,* for a prolonged sadness. *Jibyo* was considered a personal hardship that made people stronger. When the drug company GlaxoSmithKline wanted to market the antidepressant Paxil in Japan, they found that there were not enough people with *utsubyo* to make it a hit. So the company organized a conference in Japan, ostensibly to discuss cultural beliefs in mental illness. The real purpose was to turn *jibyo* into depression. The psychiatric expert they sent to Japan observed, "What I was witnessing was a multi-national pharmaceutical corporation working hard to redefine narratives about mental health. These changes have far-reaching effects, informing the cultural conceptions of personhood and how people conduct their lives. And this is happening on a global scale."[2]

The way we conceptualize our problems has enormous consequences for the way we live our lives. Psychiatric diagnoses change the way we think about ourselves and where we look to solve our problems. They also influence what we consider "medical" and what we think is appropriate medical care. Psychiatry looks at people's mental problems through a narrow lens. They are medical illnesses that can be specifically diagnosed and treated. They are biological in nature, a matter of chemical imbalances and faulty brain functioning. We, in turn, believe that many of our problems are caused by mental disorders and should be treated with medication.

This manner of conceptualizing our difficulties might be acceptable if it did more than merely pathologize human woes and foibles. We would cheer if psychiatric diagnosis and treatment actually decreased the burden of mental disability and made people happier and more productive. This has not occurred.[3] It would even be useful if psychiatry had developed an objective and reliable means of categorizing people's problems more precisely. Instead, it has given us an even ever-increasing number of terms for disorders that exist only in the opinion of mental-health professionals. There has never been an objective scientific basis for any psychiatric diagnosis. As the psychiatric critic Thomas Szasz has said repeatedly, the term *psychopathology* is a contradiction in terms because *pathology* indicates a condition of the body and not of the mind.[4] True mental diseases, like Alzheimer's, are neurological, not psychiatric.

This book is about an alternative to the psychiatric way. I will present a human-ecology view of people's mental and behavioral problems. The ecological perspective sees us and the world in which we live through a broad lens. We are the product of multilayered and complexly interactive forces. To put it simply, these forces can be divided into biological, psychological, and social ones. Our problems are not discrete medical disorders but are the result of our individual biological makeup, as molded by our psychological experiences, and playing out on a complex social stage. We come into this world as biological human beings with our own temperaments, talents, and limitations. We then must adapt to the physical and social world we live in, as well as to ongoing changes in our bodies. At any specific time, we must cope with the challenges and opportunities life presents, to the best of our abilities. When a person runs into difficulties, it is because he or she is struggling to adjust; it is not a disease process.

A major theme of this book is the question of how we should describe and categorize the kinds of problems people have. If not "mental disorders," what should we call them? I see the categories of problems we have as human-made types, like categories of literature or furniture, not as objective scientific terms like the names of chemical elements. I call them *types of dysfunction*. They are descriptive labels only.

These types are not discrete entities, but exist along dimensions:[5] I call them *dimensions of dysfunction*. Each dimension illustrates characteristic kinds of deficiency from least to most. I will use terms such as *schizophrenia* or *autism* as types of dysfunction that describe a certain degree of life difficulty on one of my dimensions. The number of such dimensions is somewhat arbitrary and open for discussion. I have delineated nine dimensions that I believe capture most of the problems that the field of psychiatry describes as *disorders*.

I have written this book for the intelligent layperson. The issues I raise here go beyond the mental-health profession to society as a whole. Psychiatric diagnoses influence much more than just medical treatment. They impact how we administer justice in our legal system and how we educate our children in schools. They help determine who receives disability payments and who is hospitalized. They affect how we treat our children, spouses, and parents when they are troubled, as well as how we expect to be treated ourselves. Psychiatric diagnoses even determine whether or not we have a right to own a gun. In my state, judges must warn patients they commit that they've lost the right to own a gun. We all have a stake in this, and none of us should see the issues as irrelevant to our own lives and future.

Part I of the book begins with my own history and a description of how I came to conclude that a new paradigm was needed for the mental-health field. Then I proceed with a brief history of how madness, as I call it, has been perceived through the ages up to the origins of modern psychiatry. I trace the development of the psychiatric diagnostic system through successive revisions of the psychiatric bible, the *Diagnostic and Statistical Manual.* I then discuss the psychiatric medical model and my alternative ecological model. I describe a dimensional typology that I propose should replace the idea of mental disorders.

Part II describes each of the nine dimensions of madness in turn. I discuss the types of dysfunction found within each dimension with an emphasis on the biological, psychological, and social roots of these dysfunctions.

Part III addresses a variety of related issues in the context of my model. I discuss the forms of treatment, including psychotherapy, psychotropic drugs, and psychiatric hospitalization. Then I turn to a critique of the current mental health system and ask whether it has been effective in relieving suffering and reducing mental health disability. I end with a look at what a future mental health system might be. In order to maintain the confidentiality of patients described in this book, I have changed their names and certain identifying information.

PART I

HISTORY OF MADNESS

1

Introduction and Some Definitions

I have often viewed myself as a poorly socialized psychologist. That is because I wasn't part of the prevailing mental-health culture of my time. In the 1960s in New York City, it seemed that most of the people I knew were "in analysis." It is hard to appreciate at this remove just how much psychoanalytic beliefs dominated the thoughts and wallets of the intellectual class of New Yorkers. I was skeptical and even somewhat appalled. Where was the science in it? Was psychoanalysis really improving people's lives?

In college, my imagination was captured by Skinnerian Behaviorism.[6] The behavioral model teaches that all learned behavior is shaped and directed by the pattern of rewards and punishments it produces. Early on, behaviorists made the decision to study only what could be objectively observed. Anything that went on inside the creature—call it *mind* or *brain*—occurred in an unobservable black box. Conjecturing about mental activities was unscientific and unnecessary. This was much more conducive to my way of thinking. Stop trying to read people's minds and focus on their behavior.

In graduate school, I came to see behaviorism as rigorous and valid, but sterile. The black box did matter, and we did have new ways to look inside it. The brain was important for understanding behavior. Besides, for egocentric reasons, I had a particular interest in one species, my own.

My studies turned to biopsychology with an emphasis on how the brain controlled behavior. At the time, this was called *physiological psychology* and has now developed into the field of neuropsychology. The methods we had were crude, with no brain scans or other refined techniques to study the human brain. We were, however, beginning to learn a lot about the damaged brain and how that damage related to human impairment. It appeared that we might soon learn a great deal about the relationship between the brain and mental illness.

This was at the beginning of the psychiatric pharmacological revolution. The theory was that mental illness was a matter of abnormal brain chemistry and that the miraculous new drugs promised a cure. I knew little about the history of failure of medical treatment in psychiatry, but I, like the rest of the country, believed what we were being told about a psychiatric miracle. Away with psychobabble!

Psychiatry was at odds with itself during those years. In an attempt to be more in line with medicine, it had created a manual that attempted to define psychiatric problems, the *Diagnostic and Statistical Manual of Mental Disorders*, commonly known as DSM. While I was in graduate school, a new DSM came out that described itself as giving clear, operational definitions for each diagnosis. It remained psychoanalytic in orientation, however, and did not reflect any of the new biological advances. To me, it continued to be opinion masquerading as medical science.

After graduate school, I got a position teaching biopsychology and thought little of the issues of psychiatry and mental disorders. While I was teaching, however, I was given the opportunity to engage in clinical-psychology training at a local mental-health center. I was assigned to a substance-abuse program and began to see firsthand the ravages of addiction. We were an early methadone-maintenance clinic, and I was able to observe both the benefits and drawbacks of methadone treatment. I was also beginning to form what I was later to understand as a biopsychosocial approach to clinical psychology.

In 1973, I undertook a formal postdoctoral internship in clinical psychology at a large Veterans' Administration (VA) psychiatric hospital. This was before the movement to treat mental health patients in community-based settings emptied the psychiatric hospitals, and there were almost two thousand patients in my hospital. Some of them had been there since World War II, and some had had prefrontal lobotomies. This was my first extended contact with people labeled *schizophrenic*. In fact, my assigned office was right in the middle of a locked ward of some of the most chronic patients

4

in the hospital. I still vividly recall one toothless old gent who always lay motionless on the marble floors of the hallway. The only time he seemed to pay attention to anything was when anyone walked by, and he would yell, in his guttural voice, "Get any lately?" Because of my unusual background, I was given two assignments. I was put on an experimental behavioral unit run by a wonderful woman not much older than I was. The unit was run as a "token economy"; we tried to use positive reinforcement to teach some extremely chronic patients adaptive skills that might allow them to function outside the hospital. This was my first exposure to attempting to manipulate social factors to alter the behavior of people deemed hopelessly psychotic.

My other assignment was to the biofeedback lab. The idea of monitoring a biological function, such as brain waves or muscle activity, and feeding the information back, so that the patient might learn to consciously control it, was new. I did not find biofeedback to be effective with our patients, because it was hard to get them to attend to anything like that. I did learn a great deal about biofeedback, however, which I was able to apply in my next position.

One miscellaneous memory from that era is of an old German psychiatrist who had been trained in the days of the German Gestalt psychologists. He had become a believer in the disease model of schizophrenia to such an extent that he thought schizophrenia was a communicable disease. He would allow patients into his office for consultation, but after they left, he would wipe down the chair with antiseptic. He also believed that Thorazine was the cure, and he gave it to patients by the water glass. Of course, his patients were tremulous zombies, shuffling around in a trance. I couldn't help but think, *Is this what psychiatry means by "cure"?* It reminded me of an old adage: with psychoanalysis, psychiatry had no brain, but biological psychiatry had lost its mind.

After my internship, I took a position at Jefferson Hospital and Medical School in Philadelphia. My clinical job was in the Psychosomatic Medicine Clinic, where we used psychological techniques to treat people with physical complaints. Many of these problems concerned pain, and one of my contributions was to develop a defined Headache Treatment Program. This was a fifteen-session program of biofeedback, visual imagery, home practice, and home completion of a psychophysiological diary. As I documented at the time, the results were very successful. Immediately after the program, 84 percent of our patients were either greatly (50 percent) or moderately (34 percent) improved, and 75 percent of those who benefited remained improved three months later. The key to success was a patient's active participation. Those who were not prepared to work hard on themselves dropped out.[7]

I published that data in a book I edited that grew out of a conference that I organized at Jefferson called Recent Advances in the Treatment of the Psychosomatic and Related Disorders. One of the keynote speakers was Herbert Weiner, MD, professor of psychiatry and neurosciences at Albert Einstein College of Medicine. His ideas put things together for me. He argued that all human disease was a combination of biological, psychological, and social factors. I had already been observing this in my clinical practice, where I realized that just prescribing biological treatments to people with somatic (bodily) complaints was making no one better and many worse. I came to realize that effective treatment required recognizing and changing the social factors that maintained the illness and teaching and strengthening psychological skills, as well as addressing any biological deficiencies. The psychiatrists around me were all psychoanalysts trying to graft the new biological psychiatry onto their old beliefs. I saw this as a play to maintain their ascendancy, because they knew their patients wanted the miracle drugs. I, on the other hand, was becoming disillusioned with the psychiatric medical model. I sought out a new model that did not depend too much on either talk or drugs. At that time, my mother worked for a psychiatrist who was a colleague of Alexander Lowen, MD. Lowen was the founder of a therapy movement called Bioenergetics.

Although a psychoanalyst, Lowen believed in the intimate connection between the mind and the body. "The feeling of identity stems from a feeling of contact with the body," he wrote.[8] Our emotions are bodily emotions, and "the neurotic ego dominates the body, the schizoid ego denies it, while the schizophrenic ego dissociates from it." While I could not accept all of Lowen's theory, the idea that the perception of our physical body was psychologically important appealed to me. It was in line with my growing belief that mental disorders were not medical diseases, but something else.

When I moved to Maine in 1979 to become head of psychology at Eastern Maine Medical Center, my background in psychosomatic medicine led to my being asked to consult on a large variety of hospitalized patients. Many of them had been hospitalized for physical complaints, but medical treatment was not making them better. Their doctors wanted to know if there were psychosocial factors that accounted for their illnesses.

It was my practice to get as complete a history as possible of the past and current lives of these patients. Detailed examination frequently revealed the role that physical complaints played in these patients' lives. Many of them had learned to be ill from childhood, because it solved emotional problems for them. Others had significant reinforcers in their current lives that made being sick advantageous. What became clear was that these nonbiological factors had to be addressed before there could be any effective medical treatment.

One of the major concerns in any large medical center is chronic pain. Acute pain, of course, often is a signal that a person has a serious medical condition. In that case, tracking down the cause of pain may lead to accurate diagnosis and treatment. But what are we to make of chronic pain? The experience of pain is nature's warning, but what could pain that lasts for years be warning us of? There were a huge number of chronic-pain patients who had received a variety of physical diagnoses and a great number of medical treatments, but they were no better. Many were addicted to pain medications, but the drugs did not lessen the pain. A different approach was needed.

I, along with physical-medicine doctors, anesthesiologists, and physical therapists, formed a multidisciplinary chronic-pain program. Our plan was to address the psychological and social factors of chronic pain as well as the physical ones. We focused on functional restoration rather than cure.

Based on the many hundreds of chronic-pain patients we saw, I developed a classification system. We estimated the relevant proportion of biological, psychological, and social factors that seemed to be involved in a given patient's pain, and I used that to create a chronic-pain typology. That is, we attempted to group patients into different types, and we based our treatment on the type rather than a diagnosis. I will explain this typology in some detail in chapter 10.

A new expansion of my perspective on mental conditions came about twenty-five years ago, when I was asked to be an examiner for court commitment hearings. In my state, before a mental patient can be held involuntarily, the hospital must petition the court. An independent examiner is appointed to evaluate the patient, and the examiner and a hospital psychiatrist testify before a judge. The patient may testify as well. The hospital must prove to the judge that the patient is dangerous to himself or others or is unable to care for himself by reason of mental illness. As an examiner, it is my role to testify first and offer my opinion as to whether a patient meets the requirements for commitment and, if so, how long the commitment should be.

This is a big responsibility. An individual's liberty is at stake, and I take it very seriously. Over the years, I have evaluated several thousand patients, and I remain conflicted about the process. The problem is mental illness. I soon recognized that the term cannot mean every label in the psychiatric diagnostic manual and must be more than just saying that a person is socially disruptive. Of even more significance, I saw that the diagnostic process was subjective and somewhat arbitrary.

What I came to conclude was that mental illness was a dimensional concept, not an absolute one. The people I was seeing had attributes that were dysfunctional to a greater or lesser degree. There were no discrete disorders that could be separated one from another. I could characterize patients as different types, as I did with chronic-pain patients, but my real challenge was to determine whether a particular patient was so dysfunctional as to be unsafe if not committed.

At about the same time that I began to do commitment evaluations, I was asked to join the State Forensic Service. My job is to evaluate defendants in the criminal-justice system when mental-health issues are raised. Mostly at the request of defense attorneys, judges order psychological evaluations to help determine defendants' competency to stand trial and/or their criminal responsibility. Accused persons cannot be considered criminally responsible if they were able to appreciate the wrongfulness of their alleged actions due to mental illness or defect.

The State Forensic Service assigns cases to me, specifying a specific issue in each case. My role is to do a thorough psychological evaluation and offer my opinion. The crucial question concerning criminal responsibility is whether the accused suffered a mental illness at the time of the offense. It cannot be because the defendant is a psychopath or was intoxicated at the time. In my terms, to be not criminally responsible, the defendant must have been mad and not just bad. Madness, though, is a matter of degree. I consider it my job to determine whether a person was mad enough not to know right from wrong.

The sum of my experiences has led me to conclude that we need a new mental-health paradigm. The model of discrete mental disorders is artificial and does not work. In this book, I will argue that mental disorders are not diseases, but types that can be seen as falling on different dimensions of dysfunction.

A Matter of Definition

An author writing a book about the problems people have in their lives needs to find a word or phrase to define the subject matter. Many psychologists use the term *abnormal behavior.* The idea that some forms of behavior, emotion, or thinking are abnormal seems reasonable to most of us. But what does it mean? Who decides what is normal?

If *normal* means *desirable,* that is a value judgment. We would define many creative, nonconforming, and original thinkers as abnormal. Such a definition of *abnormality* dominated Soviet psychology; people who expressed anticommunist beliefs were diagnosed as schizophrenic.

Normal can also mean *average,* but that would indicate that there are as many abnormal people who are better than average as there are below. It does not make sense to suggest that people can function too well. Finally, *normal* may be interpreted as *ideal.* But even if we could define the ideal, we would recognize that no one meets the criteria. We would be left with the absurdity that we are all abnormal.

Psychiatry's term for abnormality is *mental disorder.* Their assumption is that by carefully describing sets of attributes, they have defined medical conditions. Mental disorders become medical diseases to be diagnosed and treated. *Mental* becomes equivalent to *physical.* I will discuss whether there are psychiatric diseases just below.

I prefer the term *madness*. This is an old and venerable term and does not suggest anything about the cause of the problem. *Madness* does imply a certain form of dysfunction that is not physical in nature but is the result of maladaptive thinking, feeling, and behavior. We all exhibit madness in one form or another and to one degree or another. To the extent that our madness is more severe, it interferes with our ability to cope with the world we must live in.

There are different forms of madness that I conceive of as falling into different dimensions of dysfunction. These dimensions form a continuum, but they can be clustered into types based on similar attributes. I will use mental-disorder terms (like *psychotic*) to describe these types, but when I do so, I am not suggesting that they are discrete diseases. The dimensions range from a little dysfunction to so much that people cannot live effective lives in the complex social environment of the modern world. Although there are no real breaks in the continuum, we may be justified in calling the seriously mad *mentally ill.*

In the world of mental health, the most dysfunctional people are labeled *psychotic.* Clinical terms such as *schizophrenia, mania,* and *major depression* are used to characterize people who are psychotic. Common to all psychoses is that they reflect serious distortions in people's perceptions of reality. They are mad. We do not usually think of people we describe as *neurotic* as mad, but they too are responding to a distorted picture of reality. So we all have some degree of madness, and we cannot easily divide ourselves into the sane and the mad.

Disease and Illness

The great evolutionary biologist E. O. Wilson wrote, "Western science is built on the obsessive and hitherto successful search for atomic units with which abstract laws and principals can be derived."[9] Disease mechanisms are the atomic units that modern medicine is built on. The goal of medicine is to build a scientific taxonomy in which all bodily ills can be placed on a medical version of the phylogenetic scale or the periodic table of elements.

In disease theory, disease mechanisms or causes form the base of a hierarchy of increasingly more specific diseases. For instance, infectious diseases are caused by biological pathogens. A pathogen might be determined to be bacterial and then narrowed down to a particular species of bacterium. Medicine is at its most successful when a doctor can fully describe the mechanism causing a patient's objective signs and subjective symptoms and then prescribe a specific course of treatment for it.

Interestingly, the basic formulation of the disease concept was first introduced in 1858 by the German pathologist Rudolf Virchow. Virchow proposed that the basis of all disease was injury to the smallest living part of the body, the cell. This was called the *cellular theory of disease.* Today, there is some controversy as to how broadly we can interpret the disease concept, but there is agreement that a disease must be objectively defined. *Dorland's Illustrated Medical Dictionary* describes a disease as "a definite pathological process having a characteristic set of signs and symptoms."[10] Disease should not be a matter of opinion or political expediency. People have diseases when they are shown to have an anatomical or physiological injury.

Acting sick is not the same as having a disease, no matter how convincing. One notable illustration of this came from the practice of the famous nineteenth-century neurologist Silas Weir Mitchell. Mitchell was called to consult on a woman who could not rise from her bed and appeared to be dying. After examining her, Mitchell asked all the anxious doctors to leave the room and then soon came out himself. He was asked if the woman had a chance to survive, and he replied, "Yes. She will run out of the room in two minutes. I set her sheets on fire."[11]

If acting sick does not define *disease,* neither does feeling sick. People feel sick or in pain for many reasons, and only some of the time do they have a true disease. Descriptions of sickness and pain may guide a doctor in looking for a disease, but such subjective symptoms may also represent emotional distress. On the other hand, we are all well aware that we can have a serious disease with no experience of sickness until it is too late.

There are two major criteria that we can use to define a true disease: (1) diseases are identified by objective data that every observer can agree on, such as laboratory tests, scans, or, if you are unlucky, postmortem tests; and (2) a disease is a discrete condition you either have or do not have. You may be more or less sick, but a disease is all or nothing. This does not mean a doctor can always specify a disease, because there are many gaps in medical knowledge. But it can be assumed that if all relevant information were available, diseases could be uniquely classified.

There is a word that we can use to describe the experience of being sick. That word is *illness.* Today we tend to treat *disease* and *illness* as synonyms, but that blurs an important distinction. *Disease* describes the objective, third-person world, and *illness* describes the subjective, first-person experience. I will use the terms in this manner.

2

How Madness Became Medical

Early History of Madness

Attempts to understand madness can be traced to antiquity. The earliest writings show madness as demonic possession or punishment by the gods. An Assyrian text of 650 BC describes the treatment of what we might now call epilepsy this way: "If at the time of possession, his mind is awake, the demon can be driven out. If at the time of possession, his mind is not so aware, the demon cannot be driven out."[12] The Old Testament quotes Moses as saying, "The Lord shall smite thee with madness."

Interestingly, in many ancient cultures and even in the Middle Ages, possession was not always seen as a bad thing. If the symptoms of madness appeared to have a religious or mystical significance, the sufferer might be treated with awe. Such people had supernatural powers. They could be holy innocents or prophets.

At the beginning of the Christian era, the emperor Constantine officially aligned the church to a supernatural understanding of madness. The church's view was that the Holy Ghost and the Devil battled for a human's soul, and if the Devil won out, the person was punished with madness. Ministering to lunacy was left to the clergy. In the Middle Ages, the mad were often treated kindly. Priests would perform mild forms of exorcism to expel the Devil. These included the laying on of hands, touching relics, and prayer. Sometimes, the exorcist tried to strike a blow to the Devil's pride by insulting him and cursing him.

As the Middle Ages progressed, the church's treatment of the mad became increasingly brutal and barbaric. Madness became a diabolic scheme of Satan, and witches and heretics were his henchmen. The witchcraft frenzy overtook Europe in the sixteenth century and peaked about 1650. It is estimated that over two hundred thousand people, mostly women, were executed during the witchcraft craze.

As the body count grew, so did public skepticism of possession as the cause of madness. During the Age of Reason, physicians began to speak out against the superstitious beliefs of the church. One early dissenter was Johann Weyer, who, in 1563, wrote a treatise called the *Deception of Demons*. He offered a step-by-step rebuttal of the theory of demonic possession. He argued that many of those condemned for witchcraft were really sick in body or mind, and great wrongs were being committed against them. He was too far ahead of his time, however, and his work was banned by the church.

Others took up his cause. In 1584, Reginald Scott wrote, "these women (witches) are but diseased wretches suffering from melancholy, and their words, actions, reasoning and gestures has affected their brains and impaired their powers of judgment."

In 1603, there was a famous case in which the English physician Edward Jordan was called to testify during the trial of one Elizabeth Jackson, who was accused of bewitching a woman named Mary Glover. He observed that Mary suffered "fittes so fearful that all that were about her supposed that she might die," but he denied that her problem was supernatural. She had a disease he called "suffocation of the mother," by which he meant her womb. This idea harked back to the early Greek physician Galen. Galen had postulated that irregularities of the womb bred vapors that wafted through the body. These vapors induced physical disorders in the extremities, the abdomen, and even the brain. He considered this a "natural" explanation, and it is the origin of the term *hysteria*, from the Greek word for "womb," *hyster*.

By about 1650, doctors and philosophers had turned against religious explanations of madness in favor of either individual sickness or "mass hysteria." Many even pointed out the similarities between religious fanatics and lunatics. Both groups displayed glossolalia (speaking in tongues), convulsions, and weeping and wailing. Slowly, explanations of religious madness and supernatural intervention were replaced by psychopathology. Doctors took over for the clergy in the handling of the mad.

The idea that madness might be a disorder of the nerves arose in eighteenth-century England. In the 1720s, a physician named Nicholas Robinson described "a very learned and generous gentlemen" who had lost his reasoning and believed he was a hobby horse. He demanded that visitors "must mount his back and ride." Dr. Robinson reported, "I could not dispose him of this conceit, 'till by application of generous medicines, I restored the disconnected nerves to their regular motions and by that means, gave him the sight of his error."

Growth of the Mad Hospital

Beginning in the late Middle Ages, those deemed mad and "village idiots" began to be formally segregated from society and put in asylums. Initially, this was viewed as an act of Christian charity. Then, in the seventeenth century, a movement started in France that became known as the Great Confinement. The mad, the poor, and other undesirables were incarcerated in state hospitals. But this was seen as a police measure, not as a form of asylum or treatment.

The first mad hospital in England was created by Henry VIII and was called St. Mary of Bethlehem, a name that was shortened to "Bedlam," which quickly became synonymous with noisy chaos. It was open to the public as a kind of freak show, where the healthy could come face-to-face with the mad. The stated purpose for this was for an edifying lesson in the wages of passion, vice, and sin, which were thought to cause lunacy. Inmates were often sent out into the streets to beg for their food. Shakespeare described the scene in *King Lear:* "Bedlam beggars, who with roaring voices ... sometime with lunatic bans, sometime with prayers, enforce their charity."

In the late eighteenth century, a system of private asylums, called *mad houses,* were developed and run by "mad doctors." Mad doctors were subsequently renamed *alienists* and then *psychiatrists.* The methods of the mad houses were often barbaric. Treatment called "taming" was the therapeutic answer for madness, which included confinement, restraint with straightjackets (and the like), bloodletting, and purges.

In America, the idea that the mad should be hospitalized and given medical care was introduced in 1751 by the Quakers of Philadelphia. Oddly enough, Ben Franklin petitioned the Colonial Assembly for such an institution: "It has been found by experience of many years that above two thirds of the mad people received into Bethlehem Hospital and there are treated properly, have been perfectly cured." These efforts resulted in the founding of the first mad hospital in America, Pennsylvania Hospital, in 1756.[13]

While the original impetus for Pennsylvania Hospital may have been compassionate, Philadelphians expressed a second purpose. They believed that there were too many mad men in the city: "Going at large [they] are a terror to their neighbors, who are daily apprehensive of the violence they may commit." The purpose that prevailed in the early Pennsylvania Hospital was public protection more than treatment.

The mad hospital was the beginning of the comingling of medical care for the mad and society's perceived need to both protect the public and to punish people who were unruly. What hospitalization meant was that twenty to thirty male and female inmates were put together in foul-smelling cells of about ten square feet. They were ruled over by keepers with whips. If inmates got out of control, they were restrained with handcuffs and ankle-irons that were bolted to the walls and floor. Or they were forced into "mad-shirts" (straightjackets) that "left the patient an impotent bundle of wrath." As in Bedlam, inmates became a spectacle for the public, who came to taunt and enrage them.

Much of this was to change when the humanitarian doctor Benjamin Rush came to Pennsylvania Hospital in 1783. Rush is now considered the father of American psychiatry. By 1796, he had a special hospital wing built for insane patients, and he insisted they be made comfortable and given a variety of activities. He treated them with kindness and respect.

Rush was a doctor of his time, and he followed the teachings of the best European physicians, but their methods were often barbaric. From them he learned that madness was caused by "vitiated blood," a circulatory disorder that could be cured by systematic bloodletting. He had another up-to-date cure: he believed that "terror acts powerfully upon the body, through the mediation of the mind, and should be employed in the cure of madness."

Over the next decades, the therapeutic techniques of Rush and other mad doctors came to be seen not as kind and medical, but as torture. A new type of treatment had emerged in France in 1793 while the French Revolution was still raging. The physician Philippe Pinel was sent to oversee the Paris insane asylum by the new government. He found the institution run by a lay governor, Jean Passin, who was treating the inmates with kindness and getting good results. Pinel came to conclude that the mad behaviors usually seen in such places were "primarily antics of protest over inhuman treatment." He observed that under Passin's guidance "even extravagance and disorder were marshaled into order and harmony. I then discovered that insanity was curable in many instances, by mildness of treatment and attention to the state of mind exclusively, and when coercion was indispensable, that it might be very effectively applied without corporal indignity."

Pinel developed a new treatment program in which he actually talked to patients and listened to their complaints. He named his approach *traitement moral*, "moral treatment." In his 1801 treatise, Pinel concluded that madness was unlikely to be a "physical lesion of the brain" but was the result of the "adverse shocks" in the patients' lives. Pinel expressed an attitude toward his patients that would seem unbelievable in the world of today's mental hospital: "I have never met, except in romances, with fonder husbands, more affectionate parents, more impassioned lovers, more pure and exalted patriots, than in the lunatic asylum, during their intervals of calmness and reason. A man of sensitivity may go there every day of his life and witness scenes of indescribable tenderness to a most estimable virtue."

In England, a different form of moral treatment was introduced by the Quakers. Quakers believed that all people were equal before God and that all were guided by an inner light. They mistrusted doctors, especially after one of their own died of ill treatment in a mad asylum in 1791. The Quakers opened their own small retreat in 1796 that was guided by their religious values rather than by any medical wisdom. Paramount was the needs of those cared for, not the needs of the managers. Their philosophy was that of Aeschylus two thousand years before: "Soft speech is to distemper'd wrath, medicinal."

The approach of both Pinel and the English Quakers was contrary to that of the European medical establishment. They were not wild animals needing to be tamed by terror and cruelty. A patient should be treated "as much as possible in the manner of a rational being as the state of his mind will possibly allow." Recovery lay inside the person, and the institution's job was "to do little more than assist nature."

The moral therapy movement was brought to America in 1817, once again by the Philadelphia Quakers. It soon spread to religious and private asylums in New England. In 1833, the first public moral-treatment asylum for the insane poor opened in Worcester, Massachusetts. By 1841 there were sixteen private and public hospitals of this type in the United States. They followed a similar pattern: they were relatively small, with up to 250 patients; they were located in the country, where patients could enjoy fresh air and working in the gardens; and they were governed by father-figure superintendents who would eat with the patients and know each of them well. The superintendent's job was to guide his patients along the path of reason.

Patients would spend their days in recreational and educational activities to divert their thoughts from their delusions. Restraints were rarely used, and patients were rewarded for good behavior. For instance, those whose behavior was good got preferred rooms and extra liberties. The disruptive ones were placed in rooms farther from the social center. The method of treatment, as the superintendent of the Hartford retreat described it, was "to treat (the mad) in all cases as far as possible, as rational beings."

In the early years of the moral-therapy movement, the asylums were able to stick to this kind, gentle, and decidedly nonmedical approach. And the results were extremely good. Bloomingdale Asylum in New York reported that it had admitted 1,841 patients between 1821 and 1844, and 60 percent were discharged as improved or cured. In 1843, the superintendent of Worcester Hospital wrote, "I think it is not too much to assume that insanity is more curable than any other disease of equal severity; more likely to be cured then intermittent fever, pneumonia or rheumatism."

This treatment philosophy was soon to come crashing down. The moral-therapy asylums posed a significant threat to physicians. The superintendents were often not medically trained, and one of them admitted that he and like-minded people "were so prejudiced against medical measures, as to object to the election of physicians to their boards, being fearful they might affect some innovations." The movement was undermined from within in 1824, when the physician superintendent of the Hartford retreat complained that the Quakers had "placed too little reliance on the efficacy of medicine in the treatment of insanity, and hence their success is not equal to other asylums in which medicines are more freely employed."

Doctors began demanding that physicians be appointed as superintendents of all new public asylums. They made asylum medicine a specialty and in 1844 formed the Association of Medical Superintendents of American Institutions for the Insane. They said they were combining moral and medical therapies. And what was their medical treatment? They applied mild cathartics, sometimes bloodletting, and drugs (mostly narcotics as chemical restraints). As asylums got more crowded, they even returned to physical restraints, including putting disruptive patients into claustrophobic cribs at night—those patients would fight to get free until they collapsed from exhaustion.

The prevailing medical theory became that mental illness was the result of irritated or worn-out nerves that transmitted faulty impulses in the brain, causing mad behavior. Moral treatment was recast as medical treatment, because it soothed and restored the irritated nerves.

Ironically, much of the downfall of moral-therapy institutions can be traced to the reformer Dorothea Dix, who had benefited from moral-therapy treatment as a young woman. In the 1840s and 1850s, she lobbied states to build more mental hospitals to protect the mad from abuse in society. The result was that the number of mental hospitals jumped from 18 in 1840 to 139 in 1880, and the number of patients in them increased from 2,561 to 74,000 in state institutions alone. Hospitals became huge, and it was impossible for any superintendent to know his patients and guide them toward wellness. The staff wages were extremely low, and as one superintendent put it, employees "had to be drawn from criminals and vagrants," who were unlikely to provide any moral treatment. Legislatures were not interested in expensive treatment for the indigent insane and hired superintendents who managed budgets wisely. Other appointments were due to political patronage.

The final blow came from the new medical specialty of neurology, which developed during the Civil War to treat soldiers with traumatic brain injuries due to gunshot wounds. After the war, these neurologists opened private clinics and considered themselves experts in nervous disorders. They were certain that mental illness was caused by lesions of the brain. They sneered at the old-fashioned asylum doctors, whom they considered charlatans who knew nothing about "the diagnostic pathology and treatment of insanity." By then, the now completely bureaucratic hospital directors could not fight back and had to give in, promising a new direction. In 1892, they formally named their association the American Medico-Psychological Association. As the superintendent of McLean Hospital (one of the original moral-therapy institutions) said in 1895, "the best definition of insanity is that it is a symptom of bodily disease. Thus it is that psychiatry is shown, more than ever before, to be dependent upon general medicine."

On to the Twentieth Century

The history of psychiatry in the twentieth century is dominated by the thinking of two nineteenth-century men. Both were German-speaking physicians born in 1856. One, Sigmund Freud, is a name familiar to all of us. The other, Emil Kraepelin, is known to almost nobody. Freud, the father of psychoanalysis, was the psychiatrist of the consulting room, who often treated the wives and daughters of the rich and prominent. He was the doctor to the neurotics, and he named mental conditions such as *anxiety neurosis* and *obsessive-compulsive neurosis*. His ideas ruled academic psychiatry and popular culture through much of the twentieth century.

Kraepelin was the psychiatrist of the asylum, where the poor and the undesirable were confined. Where Freud talked about the unconscious and reactions to life's conflicts, Kraepelin believed in mental diseases. While Freud's psychoanalytic theories dominated the European and American imagination for most of a century, Kraepelin's medical beliefs remained the prevailing wisdom of the mental hospital. By the century's end, Freud had become something of a Woody Allen joke, and psychoanalysis a cult activity. Kraepelin's ideas about psychiatric diseases became almost universally accepted, though his name was forgotten. Today, it is the rare psychiatrist who challenges the notion that psychiatric disorders are true medical diseases. Let us examine the two men and their theories.

Freud (1856–1939) finished his medical studies in 1881 and then had to make a living, which was difficult for a young doctor in nineteenth-century

Vienna.[14] First he tried the academic world as a neurologist, and in that role he did some significant research on the neuronal theory of the brain. But he was unable to succeed in that career path, so he opened a private practice as a neurologist; he got few patients.

In 1885 he was twenty-nine years old and still living in his parents' home. He decided to go to Paris for four months to study with the famed neurologist Jean-Martin Charcot. Charcot had gained his great reputation by discovering the brain lesions that connected abnormal behaviors with diseases such as syphilis. By this time, Charcot had turned to the study of hypnotism and the "disease of hysteria." Charcot was a showman and something of a charlatan, who ran the Hospice de la Salpetriere, where he put on dramatic displays of hypnosis with hysterical patients before large audiences. As one historian observed, "the most striking feature of the treatments employed is their theatricality: scenes and spectacles are staged.… These treatments were, to use the phrase of the period, pious frauds; deceptions to take advantage of the gullibility of an individual for his own benefit."

Freud was very impressed and admired Charcot's doctrine that "the work of anatomy was finished and that the theory of organic diseases of the nervous system might be said to be complete: What had next to be dealt with was the neuroses." Freud changed his career path. Psychopathology was real disease that could be studied and treated. He did abandon hypnosis as his treatment method after a time and substituted a semi-hypnotic process called *psychoanalysis*. The rest, as they say, is history.

Freud's psychoanalytic theory was a deterministic system just like the rest of medicine, or so he thought.[15] Mental symptoms such as neuroses were the product of natural forces, not supernatural or religious ones, and they were not the product of free will. The only difference between neuroses and physical diseases was that these natural forces were not pathogens, but unconscious conflicts. The person's symptoms were a reaction to these conflicts and an attempt to defend against them.

Freud posited that there were elemental forces of the mind that developed and changed over time in stages. These forces were the instinctual energies of *libido* and *thanatos*,[16] which that demanded satisfaction. These were unconscious, and their repository was called the *id*. The ego, or conscious problem solver, develops to get the id's needs met in the real world. But this brings the infant into conflict with other people (especially parents), who discourage the expression of these drives in their raw form, and these prohibitions are internalized as the superego.

The ego has to mediate the conflict between the id and the superego. This often means trying to suppress, alter, or rechannel drives in some way. Freud saw the ego's methods as defenses that might be more or less effective. Some psychoanalytic theorists see a hierarchy of defenses that become increasingly pathological. There are *mature defenses* that are healthy, such as humor, altruism, sublimation, and even suppression (or putting off paying attention to drives). At a lesser level of effectiveness are *neurotic defenses,* which lead to neurotic symptoms and include denial or disassociation, intellectualization, and repression. Next there are *immature defenses,* which lead to even more serious dysfunction. These include schizoid fantasy, projection, hypochondriasis, passive-aggressive or sadomasochistic behavior, and acting out. Finally, when all else fails, the ego resorts to *psychotic defenses* like delusional projection, psychotic denial, and distortion. The breakdown of the ego results in what we might consider madness.

Freud's psychoanalytic therapy, of course, had nothing to do with the rest of medicine and was nothing like what doctors usually did. Freud's basic idea was that if you could help a person bring his conflicts into conscious awareness, he would gain insight into his defenses and be able to handle these conflicts in a more mature way.

Freud believed that the conscious mind was only the tip of the iceberg and that most of what we actually do is controlled by the submerged unconscious. The unconscious mind "determines" behavior, so nothing we do or say is random or accidental. Slips of the tongue (Freudian slips), forgetting, accidents, dirty jokes, hallucinations, and, above all, dreams reveal the working of the unconscious and can be analyzed.

Although most of Freud's theories have now been relegated to the psychiatric dust bin, psychoanalysis made some significant advances that should not be discarded. One is that we cannot really be divided into diseased and healthy people, but there is a continuous range of people struggling with the same forces, more or less effectively. Although Freud insisted all of this was in the province of medicine, it really was not. There are no real diseases in psychoanalysis, just "reactions" to human mental forces. These reactions are treated by talking and understanding, not drugs and hospitals.

Also, Freud's psychoanalysis can be seen as an early form of an explanatory model that we will discuss later as the biopsychosocial model. This model suggests that a person's personality and behavior are determined by the activity of biological forces (Freud's *id*), psychological forces *(ego)*, and social forces *(superego)*.

Emil Kraepelin (1856–1926) was a hospital psychiatrist whose goal was to place psychiatry beside what he considered the "hard" medical sciences of neurology and pathology.[17] He wanted to cast out the embarrassing influences of mesmerism (hypnosis) and spiritualism. His most significant contribution was to collect the case studies of thousands of hospitalized patients, distill them into the core signs of mental diseases, and describe the course of each. He was uninterested in how or why people might develop mental disturbances. He wished to categorize them into discrete diseases. For him, mental disorders were "disease entities," and patients were "symptom carriers."

After Kraepelin got his MD in 1878 and, like Freud, began working in a brain research laboratory, trying to discover the origins of psychiatric illness under a microscope. He had trouble with his eyesight, however, and could not participate. He became interested in the laboratory psychology of Wilhelm Wundt and went to study with him.

In 1884, Kraepelin was in the same circumstances Freud would be two years later. He needed to make a living. He was lucky, with a professorship in psychiatry in Estonia. Then, in 1890, he went on to head the psychiatry clinic at Heidelberg University.

Kraepelin's plan was to classify psychiatric patients on the basis of the course of their illness over many years. He had his residents fill out an index card on each patient and put them in a "diagnosis box." When the patient was discharged or died, Kraepelin would enter his revised diagnosis. He wrote, "in this manner we were able to get an overview and see what diagnoses had been incorrect and the reasons that had led us to this false conception."

He began entering his diagnostic conclusions in the fourth edition of his textbook of psychiatry in 1893. He had published the first edition of this textbook in 1883 to make some money. Each new edition was eagerly awaited by psychiatrists, as he reshuffled his file cards. In his fifth edition, he abandoned grouping psychiatric disorders by their clinical presentation. He wanted to reveal their true nature "as manifest in their course and outcome." His sixth edition, of 1899, was to provide the basis for psychiatry's *Diagnostic and Statistical Manual of Mental Disorders,* published fifty years later.

In 1907, Kraepelin made this prediction for what the future held for psychiatry: "Judging from our experience in Internal Medicine, it is a fair assumption that similar disease processes will produce identical symptom pictures, identical pathological anatomy and an identical etiology." Once psychiatry worked these three things out, "we would have a uniform and structured classification of mental diseases." In other words, they would be understood just as infectious diseases were.

From his case studies, Kraepelin concluded that there were only two forms of major mental disease, each associated with a different type of brain pathology. The first he labeled *dementia praecox,* characterized by mental deterioration or senility that began at an early age. He grouped together a number of illnesses that had previously been considered separate illnesses, including *catatonia, hebephrenia,* and *dementia paranoides,* all of which were considered to have a poor outcome, and said that they were manifestations of the same disease, one with an irreversible deterioration from which no one could ever recover. It is interesting to note that Alois Alzheimer was a colleague of Kraepelin's. Alzheimer's studies of senile dementia, now named after him, may have contributed to Kraepelin's *dementia praecox* conception. He concluded that *dementia praecox* was a metabolic disorder, just like thyroid psychosis and neurosyphilis.

He labeled the second core mental disease *circular insanity,* which he later renamed *manic depressive illness.* This was an episodic illness in which periods of abnormal mood were followed by normal functioning. He had become convinced that all forms of mood disorder were "really just manifestations of a single disease process." Having just two kinds of insanity simplified diagnosis.

Kraepelin's view of mental patients was decidedly negative. He used pejorative terms like "atrophy of emotions" and "vitiation of the will" to describe their condition. He also implied that the mentally ill were moral perverts without the basic ingredients of humanity. He was highly pessimistic about their fate; they were without hope of cure. He believed hospital psychiatrists functioned mainly as gatekeepers protecting society from the insane.

Kraepelin's theories dominated institutional psychiatry in the early twentieth century. The asylums had been filling up with patients since the late nineteenth century. The eugenics movement had been gathering force and had the notion that the mentally ill carried defective "germplasm." They were a degenerate human strain and were breeding rapidly. In America, the Eugenics Record Office was keeping track of the burden such misfits placed on society. One of its advisory groups concluded that 10 percent of the population was defective and needed to be sterilized. Included in these defectives were the *dementia praecox* patients now called *schizophrenics*.

Based on Kraepelin's theories, chronic mental patients were deemed incurable, so no treatment was offered them. Despite this, a 1927 British textbook of psychiatry painted a rosy picture of mental asylums. It said, "the peace and quiet of a mental hospital, the orderliness and discipline, the tolerant and understanding attitude of those in charge, and the simplification of life, may at once produce a most gratifying change" in the patients. This description was, of course, far from the reality of mental hospitals. In time, the terrible abuses that occurred in mental hospitals, including prefrontal lobotomy and insulin shock treatment, became widely known.

After World War II, it was learned that leading German psychiatrists (followers of Kraepelin) had sent seventy thousand mental patients who had "lives not worth living" to the Nazi gas chambers. This ended the good name of Kraepelin, and, for a time, his ideas about mental disease went underground.

3

The Rise of Psychiatric Diagnosis

The Classification of Mental Disorders

Kraepelin's idea that all madness could be described by a very small number of discrete diagnoses with medical causes was actively resisted—at first. The prevailing view was that there were a large number of different clinical presentations of madness. Writing about an earlier attempt to classify madness, the German psychiatrist Hermann Emminghaus wrote in 1878 that this "pigeonhole system ... is unable to accommodate certain more complex psychopathological entities and, although they do exist in fact, the system has to ignore them or treat them as irrelevancies."[18] Even Kraepelin himself expressed his misgivings, in 1920, about whether there were discrete psychiatric diseases that could be adequately diagnosed. He recognized that there were many cases in which "despite the most assiduous observation, it is impossible to reach a diagnosis. The experience that we cannot significantly reduce the number of misdiagnoses has a crippling effect on one's job satisfaction."

Despite the obvious difficulties correctly shoehorning many types of people into a few categories, the Kraepelinian idea was too appealing to be ignored for long. In the early twentieth century, the approach had a simplifying effect that seemed in line with emerging scientific medicine. The sea change began with the 1911 publication of Eugen Bleuler's book *Dementia Praecox or the Group of Schizophrenias.*

Bleuler was a Swiss psychiatrist, born just a year after Freud and Kraepelin. Unlike Kraepelin, Bleuler actually liked his patients and was interested in what they had to say. He was greatly influenced by psychoanalysis, and in

1910 he wrote a letter to Freud, telling him, "I certainly do not underestimate your work. One compares it with that of Darwin, Copernicus and Semmelweis."[19] He also greatly admired Kraepelin's work and wanted to expand and clarify it. First, he thought the term *dementia praecox* was misleading, because the patients he saw in his hospital were not necessarily mentally deteriorated, nor did they necessarily become ill at a young age. He coined the term *schizophrenia* (from the German *schizein*, "to split," and the Greek *phren*, "mind") to point to the splits in the psychic apparatus of the personality of these patients.

Bleuler believed, with Kraepelin, that his schizophrenia was a unitary form of madness, probably caused by some yet-to-be-discovered cerebral disease. Unlike Kraepelin, he gave schizophrenia a theoretical structure in which there were primary symptoms that characterized all people with it and secondary symptoms that were "psychogenic" and distinguished different types of schizophrenia.

The inner unity of schizophrenia consisted of what, in English, became known as the "four A's." First, there was a loosening of *associations,* so that the stream of thought was no longer coherent; this is now known as *thought disorder.* The second was *ambivalence;* the patient could hold extremely contradictory emotions and attitudes at the same time. The third was *autism,* which involves the withdrawal from the social world to an inner fantasy world.[20] The last was inappropriate *affect;* the patient displayed emotions incongruent with his or her circumstances or thoughts. Paradoxically, Bleuler believed some of the phenomena that are viewed as cardinal symptoms of schizophrenia today, like hallucinations and delusions, where secondary symptoms that could vary with the individual.

Another distinction between Bleuler and Kraepelin was that Bleuler believed one could understand the content of schizophrenic thought even though it did not make sense. He believed that the thinking was generated by "unconscious complexes," just as Freud described neurotic symptoms. This was music to the ears of the newly emergent psychoanalysts.

Before we leave Bleuler, there is one further distinction between his thinking and Kraepelin's. As Bentall put it, "whereas for Kraepelin, the mad were subjects of scientific interest and scrutiny, for Bleuler they were full human beings engaged in the same existential struggles as the rest of humanity, struggles that were made more difficult by their illness."[21] This theme was picked up by the existential psychiatrist R. D. Laing in the 1960s and by Peter Breggin in the 1990s. It seems to have been lost by modern-day psychiatric classifiers.

Medical Madness

Following the work of Kraepelin and Bleuler, academic psychiatry turned almost exclusively to the issues of classification and causes of madness. Treatment was seen as hopeless, and the mad were left to the institutions. Neurotics were the domain of the psychoanalysts in their consulting rooms, not in the medical schools.

The most prominent of the proponents of the new approach to psychiatry in the early twentieth century was Kurt Schneider. Schneider led a group of like-minded psychiatrists at the University of Heidelberg in Germany. He followed the "method of empathy," which featured a psychiatrist studying a person's life trying to understand it. When a psychiatrist's empathic readings failed, and meaning could not be discerned, the psychiatrist would conclude that there was a pathological process that had disrupted "the meaningful cohesion of the personality."[22]

Using the method of empathy, Schneider came up with a group of first-rank symptoms that marked schizophrenia. He said that he picked them not because they were all necessary to the diagnosis but because they were convenient. When the symptoms were seen "we speak clinically in all modesty of schizophrenia." Some of his eleven first-rank symptoms included audible thoughts, voices heard commenting on one's actions, thought withdrawal (a person's belief that thoughts are being taken out of his or her mind), and delusional perception.

When Schneider's textbook, *Psychopathology*, became known to English-speaking academics, it became hugely influential. His strategy was taken as a way to identify real cases of schizophrenia from more general personality problems. By 1965, psychiatrists began using the term *Schneider-positive schizophrenia* to identify patients showing first-ranked symptoms. Schneider's first-rank symptoms, which emphasized hallucinations and delusions, contrasted sharply with Kraepelin's emphasis on dementia and Bleuler's fundamental symptoms. However, Schneider was also a pragmatist who rejected the idea that schizophrenic diagnoses had a common cause.

There were early dissenters from this rush to psychiatric diagnosis. The most prominent was Adolf Meyer, a Swiss-born psychiatrist who was chair of the Johns Hopkins department of psychiatry from 1910 to 1941. He began his career as a confirmed Kraepelinian but later rejected that methodology for a holistic approach. He equally supported Freud's psychoanalysis and John Watson's behaviorism. He believed that biological, psychological, and social factors were of equal importance in understanding psychiatric disorders. This represented an early version of the biopsychosocial model that I will develop in this book.

Meyer did not think that psychiatric diagnoses did justice to people's problems or that a diagnosis could lead to any kind of specific treatment. He was quoted as saying, "we should give up the idea of classifying people as we do plants." Instead, he thought psychiatric treatment should be based on the individual history and the social circumstances of the patient.[23]

It is important to take a moment to review what happened in response to the Kraepelinian movement in psychiatry. First, in the late nineteenth century, eugenics movements sprang up in both England and the United States. The apparent increase in the number of insane people, imbeciles, paupers, and criminals meant there was defective germplasm on the loose in the land, and it needed to be controlled. Defectives could not be allowed to breed. This was contrary to democratic principles, but if it could be couched in terms of science, something could be done about it.

In 1904, Andrew Carnegie gave money to a biologist named Charles Davenport to study human inheritance in a way that would support eugenics. Davenport set out to prove by Mendelian genetics that social misfits and immigrants from some parts of Europe inherited defective genes. In 1910, he established the Eugenics Record Office to document the number of "cacogenic" people in America. A doctor at Kings Park State hospital in New York, working with Davenport, tried to show a genetic link for seventy-two insane patients in his hospital. Unfortunately, only forty-three relatives of these patients had ever been psychiatrically hospitalized, and that number was much lower than his calculation predicted. To fix this discrepancy, he redefined mental illnesses and came up with 351 "neuropathic" relatives. For Davenport, this was enough to show insanity was inherited.[24]

The eugenics movement ushered in the darkest period of psychiatry. The insane were being sterilized to prevent reproduction and segregated from society in barbaric asylums for extremely long periods. In the 1930s, shock therapies were introduced, including a practice of repeatedly putting asylum patients into deep insulin comas. It was believed that killing brain cells could help cure schizophrenics. As late as 1942, one American psychiatrist told the American Psychiatric Association that this sadistic treatment liberated patients from their "unconscious sense of guilt."

Also in the 1930s, a new form of treatment for brain damage was inflicted on the insane, the prefrontal lobotomy—the surgical destruction of the front part of the brain . It was such a heralded psychiatric treatment that its inventor, Egas Moniz, was awarded a Nobel Prize in 1949.

The decline of eugenics and the end of Kraepelin's reputation began after World War II, when the massacre of the mad in Nazi concentration camps sank into America's consciousness. For a time, Kraepelin's ideas went underground, only to resurface twenty-five years later. People had slowly begun to recognize the inhumane treatment of patients in mental hospitals.

A Crisis in Psychiatry

In the early twentieth century, medical science was rapidly advancing and an increasing number of diseases could be accurately diagnosed. Psychiatry felt it was being left behind. So, despite Meyer's admonition that classification was unhelpful, the American Psychiatric Association determined it must make a psychiatric contribution to the *Standard Classified Nomenclature of Disease*, published in 1933. The diagnoses they offered were based on the clinical descriptions of institutionalized patients by the asylum psychiatrists.

A crisis occurred when American doctors attempted to use this diagnostic system with soldiers during World War II. Almost 10 percent of all discharges from the military were on the basis of psychiatric illness, but the available diagnostic system was found to be inadequate to describe the kinds of problems presented by the veterans. Soon, the Army, Navy and the Veterans Administration each invented its own methods for psychiatric diagnosis. Chaos reigned. In response, in 1948, the American Psychiatric Association (APA) formed a task force to create a new, standardized system of diagnosis.

Thus, in 1952, the *Diagnostic and Statistical Manual of Mental Disorders* was born. The British psychologist Richard Bentall describes this DSM as "a triumph of the doctrine of truth by agreement."[25] After consulting the opinions of mostly academic psychiatrists, the APA officially adopted it by voice vote. The DSM consisted of sixty-six different disorders; each was given a simple description and a thumbnail sketch. The World Health Organization incorporated the DSM in what was now called the International Classification of Disease.

The response of practicing psychiatrists was underwhelming. Most ignored it, and it was never even officially adopted in the United States. Despite the tepid response, the APA did not make another attempt to define psychiatric disorders until 1968, when DSM-II was published, which included "operational definitions." That is, it presented rules that were to be followed in order to make each diagnosis.

Psychiatry was still falling further and further behind the rest of medicine. Both DSM-I and II were heavily psychodynamic, because Freudian theory had come to dominate academic psychiatry. All the disorders were considered reactions to environmental events, and there were no sharp distinctions between normal and abnormal. Everybody was more or less abnormal. The big division was between psychosis and neurosis. Psychoses were defined by a break with reality and severe symptoms, while the neuroses were mostly characterized by anxiety and depression. Diagnoses were considered unreliable by many and more like myth-making than science.

None of this was good for the psychiatric enterprise, which was becoming less and less credible as a medical science. In the 1960s and 1970s, there was a large group of psychiatrists who, like Adolf Meyer, wanted to abandon the practice of diagnoses, because it was meaningless and dehumanizing. They were countered by a group of conservative psychiatrists who thought the problem was that the psychodynamic approach was neither rigorous nor medical. They saw psychoanalysis as ineffective and out of step with modern medicine. Led by Robert Spitzer, this group wanted to adopt a completely biological approach to mental disorders.

In 1972, Gerald Klerman coined the term *Neo-Kraepelinian* to describe the new attitude. In 1978, he threw down the gauntlet with the psychiatric manifesto that still rules psychiatry today. Here are some of its edicts:

- Psychiatry is a branch of medicine.
- Psychiatry treats people who are sick and who require treatment for mental illness.
- There is a boundary between the normal and the sick.
- There are discrete mental illnesses. Mental illnesses are not myths. There is not one, but many mental illnesses. It is the task of scientific psychiatry, as of other medical specialties, to investigate the causes, diagnoses, and treatment of mental illness.
- The focus of psychiatric physicians should be particularly on the biological aspects of mental illness.
- There should be an explicit and intentional concern with diagnoses and classification.[26]

A New DSM

The Neo-Kraepelinians beat back the Freudians in the APA. Led by Robert Spitzer, a group of six hundred psychiatrists developed a new diagnostic system with rigorous definitions for mental disorders. In 1980, APA published DSM-III. It was very different from the preceding two. For one thing, it was five hundred pages long and contained many more diagnoses. It discarded any reference to *reactions* or other Freudian terminology. It was considered to be empirical and objective. That is, it gave specific rules as to the kind and number of symptoms needed to diagnose a specific disorder.

The growth in the use of the "revolutionary" psychiatric drugs was an important part of the development of DSM-III and the "remedicalization" of psychiatry. It was assumed that these drugs, which were marketed as antipsychotics, antidepressants, mood stabilizers, and anxiolytics, specifically treated different mental illnesses, which reinforced the idea that there were distinct psychiatric diseases to be treated. In 1975, Spitzer asserted this conclusion when he wrote, "the superiority of major tranquilizers in schizophrenia, electro-convulsive therapy in psychotic depression and more recently of lithium carbonate for the treatment of mania" demonstrated the legitimacy of the medical diagnostic process.[27]

The relationship between psychiatry and the pharmaceutical industry was important to both groups. Drug companies wanted the immense profits to be had from the new miracle drugs, but the Food and Drug Administration demanded that the drug companies specify the diseases their drugs were designed to treat. Vague and un-medical Freudian reactions would not do. Meanwhile, for the psychiatric establishment, having drugs that treated real diseases was necessary to propel it toward being a proper medical specialty.

Another incentive for psychiatry and the other mental-health professions was that the 1970s saw the rise of medical insurance. Insurance could be used to pay for mental-health treatment, but insurance companies wanted medical diagnoses and wanted the APA to establish objective criteria to describe them. The APA was happy to oblige.

An important quality of any classification system is reliability. The people using it should be able to agree on at least the broad category something belongs in most of the time. Reliability had become an embarrassment in psychiatric diagnosis over the years. Studies were consistently demonstrating that even under ideal circumstances, diagnostic reliability was not reaching desired levels. For instance, in 1972 a large cross-cultural study was done comparing diagnostic patterns in New York and London for the most significant psychiatric disorders. Examining matched groups of patients, New York psychiatrists diagnosed 62 percent of them with schizophrenia. London psychiatrists diagnosed only 34 percent of similar patients with schizophrenia and were much more likely to use terms like mania, depression, or neurosis.[28] DSM-III was supposed to end this disorder in psychiatry. The Neo-Kraepelinians crowed that field trials demonstrated that they now had a reliable system of diagnosis, even while research psychologists noted that these trials were beset by problems.

The response to this kind of criticism was to increase the number of diagnoses. Less than three years after the publication of DSM-III, Spitzer began the process of making minor adjustments to it. The result was published in 1987 as DSM-III-R, which altered half the diagnostic criteria and created thirty entirely new diagnostic entities. Within a few years, the APA created another task force to create DSM-IV, which came out in 1994.[29]

In order to increase reliability and make it more "grounded in empirical evidence," DSM-IV increased the number of diagnostic categories again. They also made the diagnostic system more complicated. For instance, DSM-IV divided schizophrenia into five subtypes and added "severity and course specifiers." It grouped all the diagnoses into sixteen "major diagnostic classes," but offered no theoretical explanation for the purposes of these classes or the relationships between members of each class.

Furthermore, DSM-IV adopted a "multi-axial assessment" process. That meant that the clinician was to describe the patient on five axes for "capturing the complexity of clinical situations, and for describing the heterogeneity of individuals presenting with the same diagnoses." The first two axes described the patient's mental disorders—one for the majority of "clinical disorders" and the second for personality disorders and mental retardation. The third axis is for medical conditions that might affect mental health. The fourth axis is a social one, in which problems such as poverty, family disruption, and educational problems are listed. The fifth axis is an attempt to define the severity of a patient's problem from worst (0) to best (100) on a "Global Assessment of Functioning Scale."

DSM-5

The development of the newest DSM has been an extremely divisive and exceedingly protracted process. It was originally set to be published in 2010 and finally appeared in print in 2013. Its development was a highly political process that was more like the Academy Awards than a scientific deliberation.

One of the reasons that it was so controversial was that there are so many stakeholders that have interests in what is defined as a mental disorder. There are an estimated four and a half million Americans receiving mental-health treatment at any one time, and whether they have a mental disorder or not matters a lot. Insurance companies paying for treatment, pharmaceutical companies selling and doctors prescribing drugs, and individuals receiving disability payments all depend on an official diagnosis.

The DSM is a product of the American Psychiatric Association, which makes huge profits from its sale and has complete control of its contents. The development of DSM-5 began in 1999 and was shrouded in secrecy. The APA appointed twenty-seven psychiatrists to a task force that oversaw the process. They, and all members of their working groups, were required to sign nondisclosure agreements. Two of the most prominent psychiatrists in the country—Robert Spitzer, the editor of DSM-III, and Allen Frances, the editor of DSM-IV—have been prominent critics of the lack of transparency, as well as of the product.

The APA, in turn, has attacked Spitzer and Frances, both of whom were excluded from the DSM-5 working groups. A hired spokesman for the APA described Frances as a "dangerous" person for "trying to undermine an earnest academic endeavor."[30] Other task-force members suggested that Spitzer and Frances have financial motives, because they receive royalties from DSM-IV-related publications.

Spitzer and Frances have joined many other critics in expressing concern over ties between the APA and the pharmaceutical industry. Sixty nine percent of task-force members reported receiving money from drug companies, although they were limited to $10,000 annually, excluding research grants.[31] Drug companies also fund the APA's conventions and psychiatric research. The issue is that drug-industry ties bias the definitions of psychiatric disorders and compromise the integrity of the classification process.

Frances has been particularly forceful in his attack on DSM-5, which he calls "deeply flawed" and "containing many changes that seem clearly unsafe and scientifically unsound." He warns potential patients: "be deeply skeptical, especially if the proposed diagnosis is being used as a rationale for prescribing medication for you or your child." He writes, "except for autism, all the DSM-5 changes loosen diagnosis and threaten to turn our current diagnostic inflation into diagnostic hyperinflation."[32] Frances highlights ten changes that he considers particularly dangerous, summarized in the following box:

Frances's Worst Diagnoses

- A new diagnosis, Disruptive Mood Dysregulation Disorder "will turn temper tantrums into a mental disorder."

- Major Depressive Disorder will now include grief "thus medicalizing and trivializing our expectable and necessary emotional reactions to loss."

- Old age forgetfulness "will now be misdiagnosed as Minor Neurocognitive Disorder, creating a huge false positive population of people who are not at special risk for dementia."

- Adult Attention Deficit Disorder will become a new fad diagnosis "leading to widespread misuse of stimulant drugs."

- The new diagnosis of Binge Eating Disorder turns "gluttony … into a psychiatric illness."

- Changes in autism definitions that will lower rates, break DSM-5's promise to "have no impact on rates of disorder or service delivery." Although he believes autism has become a fad diagnoses, he contends that "school services should be tied more to educational needs, less to a controversial psychiatric diagnosis created for clinical (not educational) purposes and whose rate is so sensitive to small changes in definition and assessment."

- The new substance-abuse category will lump "first time substance abusers … in with hard-core addicts."

- The new diagnostic category of Behavioral Addictions "can spread to make a mental disorder of everything we like to do a lot," leading to diagnoses of internet and sex addiction.

- New definitions of Generalized Anxiety Disorder obscure the boundary with "worries of everyday life," which can create "millions of anxious new patients and expand the already widespread practice of inappropriately describing addicting anti-anxiety medications."

- New PTSD definitions have further "opened the gate … to the already existing problem of misdiagnosis of PTSD in forensic settings."

Paradoxically, despite the uproar, DSM-5 is very much like DSM-IV. There are added diagnoses and alterations in some definitions, but no change in the mental disorder paradigm or the approach to diagnosis. The biggest changes involve trying to make the system more dimensional and describing some disorders as spectra.

Dimensions and Spectra

In an effort to improve reliability and credibility, the editors of DSM-5 eliminated some features of DSM-IV and added a dimensional feature. First, they eliminated the axis structure. All relevant information is now included in one scale. Now, however, clinicians will have to rate each diagnosed disorder on a scale of mild to very severe. There are also two new suicide scales, one for adolescents and one for adults, to administer. Mood disorders will require an anxiety rating from 0 to 4, as well as a suicide rating.

The most controversial change is the introduction of spectra. The several schizophrenia subtypes are eliminated and replaced with Schizophrenic Spectrum Disorders. Previously separate diagnoses of Autism, Asperger's, and Childhood Disintegration Disorder now become part of the Autism Spectrum Disorder. Another group of disorders are lumped into Anxiety and Obsessive-Compulsive Spectrum Disorders.

The Pluses and Minuses of the DSM System

To conclude this chapter, let us consider some of the positives and negatives of DSM mental disorders, beginning with the positives:

- DSM provides a language to describe people's problems. Without a descriptive language, we cannot begin to understand and investigate these problems.

- Diagnoses give patients a non-moralistic and (mostly) welcome label for their problems. Some of these diagnoses have become popular, if not with the patients, at least with their families. Mental disorders appear to provide an objective cause for a person's condition and take responsibility for behavior off his or her shoulders.

- Mental disorder classifications have a long history and represent the consensus of a large number of experts and the collective wisdom they bring to the table.

- The DSM diagnostic system plays a prominent and perhaps necessary role in many social institutions. It forms the basis for disability and medical insurance payments, eligibility for many social services, determinations in criminal and civil law, and many educational decisions.

On the other hand, there are significant negatives:

- Mental disorder diagnoses are based on subjective information, not objective data. There are no medical tests or scientific markers for any mental diagnosis. Any time a possible psychiatric disorder is convincingly shown to be caused by brain pathology, it is reclassified as a neurological disease.

- The type of information used to classify a mental disorder is inconsistent. Many disorders are diagnosed on the basis of what a patient reports. The clinician has no way to verify a patient's experience. Other disorders are based on what a clinician observes, whether the patients agree they have a problem or not. The disorder is determined by the clinician's judgment. Finally, some diagnoses are made on the basis of what a clinician learns about a patient from outside sources. For instance, Pedophilia and Impulse Control Disorder are disorders of reputation.

- Diagnoses are all or nothing. A person either has a mental disorder or not. A clinician may judge the severity of a disorder or say it is in remission, but a person should not have just some parts of a disorder and not other parts.

- The DSM is intentionally nontheoretical. That means there are no real organizing principles or hierarchies other than the new spectra. Although diagnoses are grouped into sections, there is no attempt to show how they are related. There is no indication the diagnoses that are grouped together have like causes or any causes at all. It is more like a shopping list.

In one sense, the DSM can be viewed as a part of psychiatry's marketing campaign. Often the most successful marketing plans are when the public does not even know it is being marketed to. Colleges have been extremely successful at this type of marketing, and psychiatry has been equally successful with its product. The public has accepted mental diagnoses and the drugs used to treat them. It is up to us to decide if there is real value to the product.

4

An Alternative Model

The Concept of Mental Disorders

Psychiatry follows a medical model, and the foundational concept of medicine is disease. Psychiatrists assume that most or at least the most significant disorders are true diseases. Psychiatrists use analogs such as diabetes and heart disease to describe chronic mental illness. The DSM does not use the term *disease*, but continues to use the opaque term *mental disorder* to describe its subject matter. However, it uses the language of medicine, as if it were describing cancer. Disorders are diagnosed into discrete medical categories. They have symptoms and signs and prognoses. Disorders are treated with medications, and if a case is severe enough, the patient is hospitalized. These are all terms applicable to diseases.

Disorders are considered abnormal, and the DSM's implicit assumption is that trained clinicians can use it to distinguish the disordered from the normal. Although unstated in the manual, the prevailing psychiatric theory of the cause of mental disorders is a "chemical imbalance." That is, there is either too much or too little of a specific brain chemical, called a *neurotransmitter.* Psychiatry suggests that the medications they use redress this imbalance and treat the underlying disease process. Unfortunately, despite years of trying, no one has been able to come up with a medical test that objectively defines a disorder, and no one has proved a chemical imbalance.

So, what is a mental disorder, according to the manual? DSM-IV does not really say. In fact, the editors state up front that "it must be admitted that no definition adequately specifies precise boundaries for the concept of mental disorder." In fact, they see the term as unfortunate, because it "implies a distinction between 'mental' disorders and 'physical' disorders." Despite these caveats, they go on to give a definition that states, "Each of the mental disorders is conceptualized as a clinically significant behavioral or psychological syndrome or pattern that occurs in an individual and that is associated with present distress ... or disability ... or with a significantly increased risk of suffering death, pain, disability, or loss of freedom. In addition, this syndrome or pattern must not be merely an expectable and culturally sanctioned response to a particular event, for example the death of a loved one."

There is more. Editors freely admit that "in DSM-IV there is no assumption that each category of mental disorder is a completely discrete entity with absolute boundaries dividing it from other mental disorders or from no mental disorder. There is also no assumption that all individuals described as having the same mental disorder are alike in all important ways." They acknowledge that the DSM's disorders are "types based on criteria sets with defining features."[33]

The Problem with Mental Disorders

Of course, no one really reads the introduction to the DSM. If disorders are not discrete conditions and cannot be defined by objective data, they are not mental diseases. If they are types, they are a matter of opinion—expert opinion, perhaps, but not the sort of classification we expect from medical science. Types are human-made constructs we use to facilitate communication. We describe types of furniture or literature. When we say *chair* or *novel,* we have a picture of a certain type of object. Experts may make many subtle distinctions, but types are never absolutes. Indeed, types are usually elements of dimensions. Chairs and sofas are part of a range of furniture objects.

DSM-IV states that it considered a dimensional approach, but rejected it. It agrees that "dimensional systems increase reliability and communicate more information," but "they also have serious limitations and therefore have been less useful than categorical systems in clinical practice and in stimulating research." This may be so, but equating types of mental disorders with medical diagnoses has had serious societal ramifications. The British psychiatrist Joanna Moncrieff puts it this way, "The transcription of deviant behavior into medical conditions serves important functions. It authorizes certain actions such as the incarceration and restraint of the disturbed individual and the dedication of funds for care and maintenance of the economically dependent. It also conceals value judgments that are imbedded in these actions. The concept of mental illness therefore facilitates a disguised form of social control."[34]

Because mental disorders have no boundaries, they are expandable and political. The consequences are particularly troubling when mental disorders are assigned to children. Children have no say in the matter and are increasingly subjected to psychiatric medications. One striking illustration is the growth in the diagnosis of attention deficit hyperactivity disorder (ADHD), especially in boys. As reported in the *New York Times* in 2013, the Centers for Disease Control and Prevention found that almost 20 percent of high school boys in the United States had been diagnosed with ADHD.[35] The overall rise in the rate of diagnoses over the previous decade was 41 percent. Further, about two-thirds of diagnosed kids were prescribed stimulant medication. Despite the fact that these drugs are similar to amphetamines and cocaine, one famous ADHD psychiatrist, Edward Hallowell, MD, once described them as "safer than aspirin," although he recently said he regretted the analogy. It could be that the rapid growth of ADHD represents better diagnosis, but the article quotes one prominent ADHD researcher as saying, "there is no way that one in five high school boys has ADHD."

There has been a similar increase in the diagnosis of bipolar disorder in children. Stuart Kaplan, MD, a child psychiatrist and the author of a book on bipolar disorder, summarized his experience in a *Newsweek* article.[36] He notes that before 1995 bipolar disorder was rarely diagnosed in children, but "today nearly one-third of all children and adolescents discharged from child psychiatric hospitals are diagnosed with the disorder and medicated accordingly." He believes that there is no scientific evidence that bipolar disorder occurs in children. In addition, "when a child is misdiagnosed with pediatric bipolar disorder ... he or she will likely be given dangerous adult medications with no known effectiveness for children and plenty of known dangers." He called it a fad diagnosis and noted that it was supported by "lucrative opportunities" offered by pharmaceutical companies to promote pediatric bipolar disorder. I applaud Dr. Kaplan, except for one detail of his argument: he thinks that most of these children actually should be diagnosed with ADHD and put on stimulants.

The proliferation of mental disorder diagnoses affects not just children, but people of all ages. The effect of this is discussed by Marcia Angell, MD, (who is a former editor of the *New England Journal of Medicine*) in one of a pair of essays she wrote for the *New York Review of Books*.[37] She described a large, randomized study of adults that was sponsored by the National Institute of Mental Health and conducted between 2001 and 2003. The study found that an amazing 46 percent of American adults met psychiatric criteria for a mental illness in four broad categories: anxiety disorders, mood disorders, impulse-control disorders, and substance use disorders—and most of those people met the criteria for more than one. She asked, "What is going on here? Is the prevalence of mental illness really that high and still climbing?" I would add that any system that diagnoses half the population as mentally disordered must be flawed. As psychiatry expands the number of mental disorders, as it does with each new DSM, will the number of disordered rise to 75 percent or to 90 percent?

Angell noted that most psychiatrists now consider themselves "biological" psychiatrists (that is, focused on brain chemistry) and "treat only with drugs." Despite increasing drug treatment, psychiatric disability keeps rising. In the two decades between 1987 and 2007, the number of mentally disabled people in this country has increased nearly two and a half times. The number of disabled children has increased an astounding 35 times over the same period. She asked, "are we simply expanding the criteria for mental illness so that now nearly everyone has one?"

It is time for us to consider whether the concept of mental disorder has outlived its usefulness. We cannot continue to escalate opinion diagnoses without any firm scientific basis. We need a different paradigm for describing the difficulties that people face in life, if for no other reason than that we cannot afford the cost of treating them as medical conditions.

Childhood Disorder

Almost any condition of life can be made into a mental disorder. You just have to use enough psychiatric and pseudo-medical terms. Jordan Smoller proved this in a spoof research article that demonstrated why "childhood syndrome" should be included in a new DSM.[38]

There are five core features of the disorder that Smoller is certain will be included in the DSM: (1) congenital onset, (2) dwarfism, (3) emotional lability and immaturity, (4) knowledge deficits, and (5) legume anorexia. Biologically, childhood runs in families and is very prevalent, although some countries have a much higher rate than others. In twin studies, the concordance rate is extremely high especially for identical twins. When one twin has the condition, almost invariably the other will have it too.

There are significant social implications for childhood. The vast majority of children are unemployed, and children represent one of the least educated segments of society. When emotional lability and immaturity are the only criteria used for the diagnosis, otherwise normal adults may suffer the stigma of being labeled a child.

Treatment of childhood disorder is complex. Institutionalizing the patients in schools has been largely ineffective. Freud, of course, thought that childhood disorder was treatable by analysis of their dreams, but people have lost faith in that approach. Recent studies, though, show that childhood has an excellent prognosis given enough time. Ten-year follow-up studies on such measures as the Vegetable Appetite Test and metric height show marked improvement.

When DSM-5 was in the early planning stages, the leaders of the APA and the National Institute of Mental Health (NIMH) sat down at a series of conferences to discuss what could be done to create a more scientific DSM. From these meetings, the APA published *A Research Agenda for the DSM-V.* In the introduction, the editors announced, "All these limitations in the current diagnostic paradigm suggest that research exclusively focused on refining the DSM-defined syndromes may never be successful in uncovering their underlying etiologies."[39] A new, as yet undefined, paradigm was promised.

This paradigm shift never occurred. The expected advances in neurobiology that would allow mental disorders to become psychiatric diseases never materialized. The humiliating truth is that there are no true diseases in psychiatry. There has never been reliable evidence that a mental disorder is caused by a chemical imbalance. There are no scientifically validated brain abnormalities to differentiate one disorder from another. Recent genetic studies have shown a large number of genetic risk factors for psychiatric disturbances, but not one of them is "specific to one of the traditional diagnostic categories."[40]

These facts were brought out into the open in 2004 by the University of Chicago psychiatrist Donald Luchins. First, he reported (as have many others) that despite "extensive … study of brain chemistry,… there is [no disease] established." He went on to note, "no doubt mental or psychiatric illnesses involve the brain. But the term brain disease is already used to describe neurological illnesses…. Mental or psychiatric illnesses generally are disturbances of feeling, thinking, or behaving with basic brain function intact." On the other hand, a number of neurological diseases "manifest with syndromes indistinguishable from psychiatric ones."[41] For instance, fifty percent of people suffering from stroke exhibit the symptoms of major depression.

It is likely that many new brain diseases are yet to be discovered. Some of these diseases may explain the symptoms now attributed to psychiatric disorders such as schizophrenia or autism. They will then become neurological diseases. We just do not know which ones and what kinds of diseases they will be shown to be. They will not be mental disorders.

When the diagnostic model and drug management of psychiatry is challenged, the reaction of many psychiatrists is defensive. Rather than offer a rational justification, they attack their critics and deny that there are alternatives.

For example, Ronald Pies, MD, writing on the eve of the publication of DSM-5, attacked unidentified adversaries for opposing psychiatric diagnosis and creating a "myth of medicalization." He asserts, "so long as the patient is experiencing a substantial or enduring state of suffering and incapacity, *the patient has disease (dis-ease)."* He contends that this definition does not "medicalize normality" but "affirms what physicians have recognized as an ethical imperative for millennia: the need to relieve the misery of their patient."[42]

This is a specious argument in several ways. Disease does not equate to a lack of ease any more than disorder is a lack of order. Medicine has come a long way in establishing an objective theory of disease. We would be discontent if doctors diagnosed diseases solely on perceived "suffering and incapacity" or "a general concept of enduring and significant departures from health." We would lose confidence in medicine if opinion were not bolstered by valid medical tests.

From the other side of the ledger comes a startling observation that was made by one practicing psychiatrist. Sally Satel ruefully addressed the uproar over DSM-5 in this way: "many critics overlook a surprising fact about the new DSM: how little attention practicing psychiatrists will give to it." Why is that? "This is because psychiatrists tend to treat according to symptoms.... Simply naming a mental illness does not necessarily point the way to effective treatment. That is why patients often qualify for more than one diagnosis and many have a poor response to medications."[43] In other words, Satel is admitting that a diagnosis does not necessarily benefit the patient.

Another prominent psychiatrist, S. Nassir Ghaemi, MD, professor of psychiatry at Tufts School of Medicine, accuses the APA editors of the previous DSM editions of "pragmatism," which he defines as "making practical judgments about what is best for the psychiatric profession, first of all, and then for social, economic and other reasons." This tradition, where science is the last consideration, carries on with DSM-5. Ghaemi makes a serious charge: "When the DSM leadership—whether in the 3rd, 4th, or 5th revision—gerrymanders psychiatric definitions for professional purposes, *nature* will not follow suit, and our biology, genetic, and pharmacological studies will be doomed to fail, as they have in the past three decades."[44]

This dismissive attitude toward DSM diagnoses is also taken up by none other than the current director of NIMH. Writing in his Director's Blog just prior to the publication of DSM-5, Thomas Insel, MD, rejected DSM-5 as unscientific. He wrote, "That is why NIMH will be reorienting its research away from DSM categories." His criticism is that these diagnoses lack validity because "unlike our definitions of ischemic heart disease, lymphoma, or AIDS, the DSM diagnoses are based on consensus about clusters of clinical symptoms, not any objective laboratory measure. In the rest of medicine, this would be equivalent to creating diagnostic systems based on the nature of chest pain or the quality of fever. Indeed, symptom-based diagnosis, once common in other areas of medicine, has been largely replaced in the past half century."[45] To sum up Dr. Insel: psychiatric diagnosis is not medical.

The British Psychological Society has also voiced its opposition to the DSM-5 diagnostic system. Its division of clinical psychology issued a statement saying, "psychiatric diagnosis is often presented as an objective statement of fact, but is, in essence, a clinical judgment based on observation and interpretation of behavior and self-report, and the subjects of variation and bias." The report also called for a "paradigm shift." A spokesperson for the society, Lucy Johnstone, commented that psychological issues were not illnesses with biological causes; "on the contrary, there is overwhelming evidence that people break down as a result of a complex mix of social and psychological circumstances."[46]

In the following pages, I will first present a dimensional approach to classification as an alternative to the DSM categorization. Then I will describe an ecological model that explains these dimensions as the interaction of biological, psychological, and social factors.

A Dimensional Approach

We may fairly conclude that the biomedical model of mental disorders has failed. It has not produced meaningful advances in our understanding of the human condition, which is the first requirement of a scientific model. By objective standards, no one can show that biological psychiatry has been successful in curing people of their ills or in reducing the burden of mental disability. Yet people do suffer from emotional distress and behavioral impairment. We need to find some way to characterize and understand the problems people have. If we abandon the medical model, what do we replace it with?

There are two issues that we must address in a new approach to psychological and behavioral problems: classification (we do need to label the kinds of problems people have in order to discuss and organize them) and our understanding of the causes of those problems. In this section, we will deal with classification.

The system I propose does not divide people between the diseased or disordered and the supposedly sane. It places people's problems on continua, with no dividing lines between normal and abnormal. People have more or less of different kinds of difficulties—though this is not to minimize the seriousness of some people's problems. This approach leads to a different philosophy of treatment and a way for people to perceive their problems as other than diseases. In my view, this approach is much more in tune with true science and is much more conducive to civil liberties. I call this system a *dimensional typology.*

There are two kinds of classification systems in science. Mature sciences create taxonomies, which are objective systems of classification based on scientific theory. Taxa are discrete categories with clear rules for what belongs in each one. They are not matters of opinion or consensus. The periodic table of elements and the phylogenetic scale are examples of scientific taxonomies. Medicine aspires to a taxonomic system and the theory of disease is a specific type or kind of taxonomy called a *nosology,* in which diseases are classified by cause. For instance, one class of disease is infectious disease, which can further be classified by whether it is bacterial or viral. Mental disorders do not meet this standard.

Another form of classification, typology, is based on opinion and subjective description. Typologies are very useful and employed by experts in every field to label their subject matter. We create typologies in political science, art, literature, and the social sciences in order to communicate effectively about the subject. What we're attempting to do is group objects by their perceived similarities, not by taxonomic standards.

Pruritus Ani

Types remain common in general medicine. I recently read a doctor's column about pruritus ani, which is extreme anal pain and itching. This is a label that tells nothing about the cause of the itching but merely describes the condition by location and experience. There can be many causes of it, some known and some not. It is not a diagnosis, but a type. It is useful because it leads the doctor and the patient toward possible causes and solutions.

Types are created by expert opinion. They are human-made labels, not objective descriptions of nature. Experts may argue about how to make these classifications until they reach some consensus. We judge a good typology by how well it groups the elements of the field into a small and consistent number of concepts.

To grasp the distinction between a typology and a taxonomy, think of a library. The Dewey Decimal System (for those of us old enough to remember) and the Library of Congress System are multilayered, intricate classification systems that arrange books by types and subtypes. They are useful if you wish to browse the library on a topic or get a specific book.

It is no more than a typology, because it offers no additional information. It is not like the periodic table of elements, which is built on scientific theory and makes many useful predictions. A typology just labels things by similar characteristics.

Mental disorders are types dressed up in medical terminology. They are metaphorical diseases—matters of opinion, not facts of nature. The DSM classification system has a lot in common with the Dewey Decimal System. It consists of a large number of categories divided into lots of subtypes identified by numbers.

Just as John Dewey described and numbered the topics, so has official psychiatry labeled and numbered mental disorders. Clustering people's patterns of dysfunction into types can be just as useful, but it doesn't make them medical. There are no discrete and objective mental disorders.

There are many psychological classifications that form dimensional typologies with anchors at both ends of the spectrum. For instance, we can describe styles of social behavior on a dimension ranging from introversion to extroversion. We may call a person an introvert, but this is a relative descriptor. We do not diagnose a person as an introvert. Similarly, intelligence is a dimension that we can divide into relative types based on an attribute called IQ. The term *mentally retarded* used to be used as a descriptor, but we were not saying that a person was part of a categorical state of being. We were using an artificial cut-off in a conceptual dimension to describe a type.

Extend this idea to something more related to health. We understand that there is a dimension of body types related to weight. When we call someone *obese*, we are describing a conventional partition in a fatness dimension. We would consider obesity a type that is a matter of expert medical opinion. Obesity may be disabling, a precursor to disease, or a product of disease, but it is not a disease itself.

Now take depression. If we say someone is depressed, are we not implying that his or her mood can be described on a dimension? A happy person is at one end, but no one is perfectly happy. A depressed person falls toward the other end of this dimension, but it is a type, not a category. It is impossible to define how much depression a person must exhibit to be called categorically depressed.

In the classification system I propose, I identify nine functional domains. Each domain includes a spectrum of deficits and deficiencies that I will call *dimensions of dysfunction*. These dimensions encompass a range from no or minimal difficulty to severe dysfunction. I contend that all the kinds of emotional, behavioral, and cognitive problems that are considered in the realm of mental health fall on one or more of these dimensions.

I stress again that there are no true dividing lines along these dimensions, but it is important for a clinician to characterize both the type and severity of a person's problems. Our focus must be on functioning, and people who occupy the lower end of each dimension have the most difficulty living productive and satisfying lives. I do not believe that where people's difficulties lie on a dimension is static. People change over time and under different circumstances. The degree, and perhaps even the type, of dysfunction a person exhibits today might be very different tomorrow. Sometimes this change is gradual, but sometimes it is precipitous and dramatic, as life stressors themselves change. It is always the job of a therapist to help a patient move up the scale to less dysfunction.

I will occasionally use the language of mental disorders to describe the different types of problem I'm discussing. I am not enamored with this language, but it is the only terminology we currently have. It strikes me that if we turned all the effort used in trying to categorize mental disorders toward an adequate dimensional typology, we could have a much more satisfactory classification system. We would also be doing less harm to people than we do by trying to separate them into "normal" and "mentally ill."

An Ecological Model

Classification is only a first step in understanding psychological problems. The more important issue is why people are or become dysfunctional. If we discard a simple disease model, we need to consider an alternative one. There is such a model, but it will not fit on a bumper sticker like *chemical imbalance*. It's called the *biopsychosocial model*, and I liken it to an ecological model.

This model was first proposed by psychiatrist George Engel in 1977. He argued that psychiatry—and, indeed, all of medicine—was in crisis due to "adherence to a model of disease no longer adequate for the scientific tasks and social responsibilities of either medicine or psychiatry." He recognized that mental disorders were much more than biological brain diseases. Conceiving of mental disorders as somatic (bodily) aberrations "leaves no room within its framework for the social, psychological, and behavioral dimensions of the illness." Separating the physical from the functional derives from an outdated "mind-body dualism" that had now become psychiatric "dogma." He concluded that a "Bio-Psycho-Social model provides a blueprint for research, a framework for teaching and a design for action in the real world of health care."[47]

This characterization of mental disorders is complex. It posits that one's mental condition at any time is the result of the interaction of biological, psychological, and social forces. It is ecological because, like the environment, all the forces work as an integrated whole. Change one of these factors, and the whole changes in important ways.

The ecological metaphor is apt, because mental disorders represent adaptations to a biopsychosocial environment. We are all doing the best we can to thrive—and sometimes just to survive—in the complex and particular world in which we live. We each have individual talents, attributes, and preferences that enhance or limit our adaptive abilities. We each have had different experiences and learn different ways of coping with life stresses. Mental disorders do not strike us down like cancer or polio; they represent deficiencies in our adaptive capacities. The point of view in this book is that true mental-health treatment involves helping people alter these biological, psychological, and social factors, not curing them of disease.

Biological Factors

Each person's brain is unique, yet built on the same plan. By analogy, consider your face. As humans, we inherit the same component parts, and we never look like dogs or elephants. Yet each of our faces is individual, and the sizes and shapes of the individual components vary widely. To a large extent, our faces resemble the faces of our parents. This is inheritance. Sometimes, by genetic accident or illness, however, parts of our faces are misshapen or even missing. The shapes and coordination of a face has ramifications for both our psychological development and on how the world treats us. Some of us may be considered homely, and this will strongly influence, but not determine, what becomes of us. Some may develop low self-esteem and behavioral patterns that are dysfunctional. And still others may learn to use their homeliness as a distinction and succeed despite it. Think of Abraham Lincoln.

Now use this same logic for the brain. Seeing the structure and activity of a living brain is much more difficult than looking at the components of a face, but many of the principles are similar. The architecture of every human brain follows a consistent plan— none of us behaves like a chimpanzee. But we each have an individual brain, and that influences how the component parts interact. Sometimes, by genetic flaws or brain accidents, brains are misshapen or poorly functioning. More commonly, however, life's experiences subtly change the way our brains work, just as life etches our faces.

The brains we inherit are the foundation of all our behavior, but not the determinant, just as a sculptor's medium, the marble or the clay, sets limits and direction, but does not determine the work of art that results. Our brains start developing shortly after conception, and the process continues throughout our lives. A striking fact is that the human brain starts with far more neural connections then we need. Early in brain development, experience begins eliminating unneeded connections by the principle "use it or lose it." The neuronal connections that are used strengthen, while the unused wither and die. The Nobel laureate Gerald Edelman discovered this process, which he called *neural Darwinism.*[48] Additionally, groups of neurons that activate together form closer bonds. As Edelman put it, "neurons that fire together, wire together." As this process continues, our brains become more individual, shaped by our own experiences as we face life's demands. The current concept of the brain is more like an ecosystem than a machine. Our many brain elements are in constant competition with one another throughout our lives. Each neural network strives against others for feedback from both the outer and inner world. Genes can set this developmental process in motion, but they cannot determine the outcome.

Genetics and Susceptibility

A lot is made of the inheritance of mental disorders, so we should look at what that means. Heredity is a statistical measure that tells us nothing about causes or mechanisms. For instance, twin studies find that identical twins—who share the same genes—have a 48 percent probability that if one twin is diagnosed with schizophrenia, the other will be as well. This is called the *concordance rate.* In contrast, fraternal twins—who on average share half their genes—have a concordance rate of 17 percent, and non-twin siblings (who develop in different psychosocial worlds) have an 8 percent rate.[49]

Just what is inherited, however, is a mystery. The data say that there is a genetic factor in the diagnosis of schizophrenia, but only half the time. What happens to the other 50 percent of identical twins, who do not appear to be seriously disturbed? Something other than genetics is at work here.

To understand data of this sort, we can invoke the concept of *susceptibility.* Something as complex as the human brain is prone to disruption. Based on individual differences that may occur through genetics, injury, or other factors, we have differing degrees of vulnerability to disruption in different areas of functioning. When vulnerable individuals are exposed to life stresses that overwhelm their coping capacities, they become symptomatic. That is what we mean by *susceptibility.*

A good analogy is the medical disease mesothelioma, a lung disease associated with exposure to asbestos. People do not develop mesothelioma unless they are both susceptible and exposed to asbestos. The susceptibility may be genetic, but the disease is not. People who are exposed to asbestos but are not susceptible never get the disease; nor do people who are susceptible but are never exposed to asbestos. We can say something similar about mental disorders. People who are genetically susceptible are likely to break down mentally if exposed to stressors, but genes do not condemn them to a mental disorder.

Executive Brain

The human brain has an estimated one hundred billion nerve cells (neurons), each of which may connect to up to ten thousand of its fellow neurons. Such a complex mechanism would seem impossible to study except that we can divide it up into systems and subsystems that are generally located in different regions of the brain. We are far from fully understanding the intricate workings of the brain, but we know enough to begin to speculate on how brain functioning relates to what we call *mental disorders*. It is worth our time to take a glimpse at what we know about the world's most complicated structure. We will focus on three brain systems most significantly associated with behavioral and emotional dysfunction. These are the executive systems, located in the prefrontal cortex; the motivational and emotional systems, located in the limbic system of the midbrain; and the memory systems, which originate in the hippocampus and then are distributed throughout the cortex.

The most advanced part of the brain, the part that humans rely on most, is the *cortex* (or bark) of the brain. In general, the *posterior* (back) part of the cortex is concerned with perception, while the *anterior* (front) is the action part. Then there is the very front of the brain, called the *prefrontal cortex*. It amounts to almost a third of the cortex. The human prefrontal cortex takes up twice the space in the brain as the prefrontal cortex of a chimpanzee does. Dog lovers, you should note that dogs have about twice as much prefrontal cortex as cats.

The prefrontal lobe does not have one specific duty. It is the leader and coordinator of the brain. We call what it does *executive functions*. It is the physical location of our personality, our sense of self, and, indeed, even what we consider "mind." All the unique achievements of our species are due to the rapid evolution of the prefrontal cortex over the past few hundred thousand years.

The neuropsychologist Elkhonon Goldberg likens the prefrontal cortex to the conductor of an orchestra, the general of an army, or the CEO of a corporation. It is the brain's command post, and how well it functions is crucial to success in every human endeavor. As Goldberg says, "The prefrontal cortex plays the central role in forming goals and objectives and then in devising plans of action required to attain these goals. It selects the cognitive skills required to implement the plans, coordinates those skills and applies them in correct order."[50]

It is easy to see that inadequacy or malfunctioning in the executive systems can have profound effects on human functioning. This is especially true when other people need to be considered and social situations evaluated—in other words, in almost everything we do in our complex modern world.

Drives and Emotions

Feelings are the conscious manifestation of drives and emotions. They occur when the frontal cortex brings them to awareness as part of our narrative of self. Awareness, however, is an after-the-fact process that occurs only part of the time.

Drives and emotions are generated in structures deep in the brain. These subcortical structures were labeled the *limbic system* by Paul McLean in 1952 and we will use this as a general description of these areas. The words *motivation* and *emotion* are both connected, etymologically, to the word *movement*, and action is what the limbic system impels. These are the basic survival mechanisms that drive most of our behavior and that we share with mammalian kin. Most of the time, the actions generated by the limbic system are automatic and unconscious. Neuroscientist and neurologist Antonio Damasio characterizes the distinction between emotions and feelings: "Emotions play out in the theater of the body. Feelings play out in the theater of the mind." Damasio says, "we have emotions first and feelings after because evolution came up with emotions first and feelings later. Emotions are built from simple reactions that easily promote survival of an organism and thus could prevail in evolution."[51]

Our most studied emotional response is fear, and psychologist Joseph LeDoux has detailed how it works. A part of the limbic system called the *amygdala* has the responsibility for monitoring the world for threats. The amygdala has different regions. One part of it scans input from the senses for signs of danger. If danger is detected, a signal goes to the central area, which immediately initiates the bodily changes and behaviors that characterize fear. A neutral input (say, a clump of grass rustling slightly) only causes a brief and mild activation, which is quickly inhibited. But if the neutral stimulus is followed by something perceived as threatening (a growling lion leaping from the clump of grass), the amygdala creates a strong response, marking the initial stimulus (the rustling) as dangerous. That emotional tag is how the amygdala learns to generate a fear response to an experience that may have been associated with danger in the past.

The memory area of the brain, the hippocampus, provides the amygdala with information about the context of a potentially dangerous situation. Context is a sort of on-the-spot memory about various factors involved in an emotional situation. This context information goes to the basal nucleus, which controls the response of the central nucleus. For instance, we see a lion, and the lateral nucleus signals danger. The basal nucleus receives context as to whether the lion is behind bars or not. If it is, a fear response is suppressed (for most of us). All of this occurs instantaneously and before any information goes to the cortex for considered action.[52]

Damasio offers a clinical description of what happened with a young woman whose amygdalae in both hemispheres were completely calcified and could not function (Urbach-Wiethe disease). She was "excessively and inappropriately forthcoming.... It was as if negative emotions such as fear and anger had been removed from her affective vocabulary, allowing the positive emotions to dominate her life." She was unnaturally positive toward all people and had been frequently taken advantage of by people she trusted. Intellectually, she knew what fear was, but she could not learn "the telltale signs that announce possible danger and possible unpleasantness." She could not read the expression of the fear in another person's face or even mimic the facial expression of fear.[53]

There is another brain layer between emotions and feelings, the *anterior cingulate gyrus*. This acts as an executive secretary to the frontal lobes. It also considers information from the environment and the limbic system and gives that information an emotional rating. It tells the frontal lobes which information it should attend to and with how much intensity. For instance, if we wake in the middle of the night and see a shadow, the amygdala signals *threat*, and we become frightened. Then the anterior cingulate appraises the situation. If it determines that the shadow is only a clothes rack, it signals the prefrontal cortex that the situation is unimportant, and the frontal cortex puts the entire experience into perspective and calms the danger response.[54]

The final stage of emotional processing lies in the frontal lobes, where emotions become conscious feelings. This is not a global and ambiguous statement about mind because different areas of the frontal lobes have different functions in controlling our emotional responses. We know this because damage to different parts produces different forms of emotional dysregulation. Two of these syndromes, *dorsolateral syndrome* and *orbitofrontal syndrome*, have been extensively studied.[55]

Dorsolateral syndrome is the result of damage in that part of the frontal cortex. Patients with this damage exhibit extreme inertia. They may lie passively in bed without eating or drinking or engaging in any spontaneous activity. They appear depressed, though they aren't, and hence the syndrome has been called *pseudo-depression*. They have no mood and are indifferent to either good or bad things.

Elkhonon Goldberg reported the case of a man named Vladimir who had suffered a severe head injury when hit by a train.[56] The damage (and the subsequent surgery) was mainly on the dorsolateral parts of both frontal lobes. Goldberg reported that he spent most of the day in bed staring into space. Trying to activate him might result in a brief string of profanities or a thrown chamber pot.

Goldberg was able to engage him in little experiments, during which Vladimir would "follow [his] instructions in a detached, zombie-like fashion." What was particularly interesting was that when Vladimir did initiate a task, he would never end it. Goldberg told him a little children's story and asked him to recall it. Vladimir gave an endless rendition of it. Goldberg said, "[he] continued his monologue until I turned off the tape-recorder and left." Vladimir was like a "Newtonian body"—when at rest, he remained at rest, and when in motion, he remained in motion.

The second type of frontal lobe damage is *orbitofrontal syndrome*, which causes a loss of emotional control and has been called *pseudo-psychopathic syndrome*. These patients are emotionally and behaviorally disinhibited. As Goldberg described it, "Their affect is rarely neutral, constantly oscillating between euphoria and rage, with impulse control ranging from poor to non-existent. Their ability to inhibit the urge for instant gratification is severely impaired."

Goldberg reported the case of a man named Charlie, who was found unconscious by the side of the road following an automobile accident. Damage to his brain was largely in the orbitofrontal region. Following recovery, Charlie "embarked on an idle, vacuous existence. He spent his days watching television, drinking beer and taking drugs." He occasionally worked menial jobs, but he couldn't hold them for long, and then he would "hit the road." On one occasion, when he ran out of money, he held up a convenience store and was caught within two hours.

Charlie finally was put in a long-term rehabilitation program, where Goldberg interviewed him. Charlie "proceeded with a jolly delivery of his life story, dwelling on its more delinquent details with particular relish, and sprinkling his narrative with casual profanities. This left the uncanny impression of a tipsy teenager in the body of a middle-aged man."

Both Vladimir and Charlie demonstrate the overall importance of emotional processing in executive functioning. Further studies show that emotional control can be different in the two frontal lobes. Damage to the left frontal hemisphere tends to cause negative emotions, which appear much like depression, with pathological crying. Right frontal damage tends to produce euphoria, with pathological laughter and a nonchalance that has been termed *la belle indifference*, "the beautiful indifference."

Evidence for this hemispheric division of emotional labor has been found in experiments using brain imaging.[57] When subjects were presented with pleasant imagery, such as happy movies, they exhibited activity in the left frontal cortex. Conversely, when shown unpleasant or sad imagery, activity was predominantly in the right frontal cortex.

These findings also suggest that individuals have a dominant emotional style. Goldberg writes, "People with an optimistic, sunny disposition constantly exhibit the preponderance of activation in the left prefrontal regions. By contrast, gloomy, habitually dysphoric and brooding types given to depression consistently exhibit a preponderance of activation in the right prefrontal regions.... The remarkable consistency exists across lesion studies and studies of normal states in both children and adults, all pointing to a profound and dichotomously specialized role of the frontal lobes in emotional control."

The amygdala and a prefrontal cortex act in reciprocal fashion. Animals with lesions in the medial prefrontal cortex display an exaggerated fear reaction. The role of the prefrontal cortex seems to be to inhibit fear, and pathological fear is seen when the amygdala is unchecked. Conversely, when the prefrontal cortex has the opportunity to weigh all aspects of a situation, it can suppress the amygdala's fear response. Put another way, cognitive information processing in the prefrontal cortex regulates the emotional responses of the amygdala.

Drives can be distinguished from emotions. Drives are responses to needs that are recurrent. Parts of the limbic system, such as the hypothalamus, perpetually monitor the state of the body and are charged with keeping conditions as constant as possible. Deviations (such as low blood sugar) generate a motivational signal that impels goal-directed behavior (getting a meal). This process is known as *homeostasis*. Emotions are based in an evaluation of the external world, but can be quite drive-like. For example, maternal behavior, curiosity, and boredom may each be considered an emotion or a drive.

In addition to fear, there is a suite of primary emotions that appear to be innately wired in our brains. Many researchers agree on the four basic emotions—fear, anger, sadness, and joy. Antonio Damasio adds surprise and disgust. Damasio additionally describes a palette of secondary or social emotions, including embarrassment, jealousy, guilt, and pride. The social emotions are largely the product of life experiences, although they may have genetically determined components. All of these emotions are evoked automatically and then incorporated into a sense of self by the prefrontal cortex.

These emotional states, either singly or in combination, form our prevailing mood. So *depression* is primarily sustained sadness, with elements of anger and guilt and a suppression of joy. *Mania* is likely to be joy, with some anger possible and the suppression of most other emotions. *General anxiety* is derived mostly from fear, with the likely addition of some anger and guilt. Many psychiatric and recreational drugs affect mood states to our benefit or detriment.

Our emotional and motivational systems ordinarily work in a seamless and effective manner in response to our needs and the external environment. It is the job of the executive system to coordinate and control all these systems. In large part it does so by incorporating these responses into a sense of self and storing that persona in memory as a narrative of self-consciousness. What is important for our purposes is what happens when this intricate system operates poorly or breaks down.

Panksepp's Theory of Emotions

To complete this review of the brain's emotional systems, I will present psychobiologist Jaak Panksepp's comprehensive theory of seven evolutionarily determined affective (that is, emotional) systems in the mammalian brain. Panksepp's formulation is particularly intriguing because it relates so closely to the kinds of mental dysfunction I will be discussing for most of this book. Panksepp's first book on the subject, *Affective Neuroscience,* revolutionized the way many people looked at emotions.[58] I will refer to these emotional systems frequently in subsequent chapters.

Panksepp describes the seven emotional systems as the source of "affective valuations of world events in the form of nonverbal feeling states. These seven are consistent throughout all mammalian species (as far as we know) and are hard-wired in ancient subcortical areas of the brain." He labels these SEEKING, FEAR, RAGE, LUST, CARE, PANIC/GRIEF, and PLAY.

SEEKING, alternatively called *expectancy,* is the reward system that is "characterized by persistent exploratory inquisitiveness."[59] It motivates animals (human and nonhuman) to seek out and acquire what they need in order to survive. It pushes us to explore and engage in the world. It creates the feelings of excitement and anticipation that comes prior to the act of consummating a pleasurable activity. Panksepp describes it as "a general-purpose system for obtaining all kinds of resources that exist in the world, from nuts to knowledge."

The primary brain chemical of the seeking system is dopamine. Drugs of abuse like cocaine and amphetamines are addicting precisely because they mimic the brain's dopamine system and arouse this system. Overstimulation of this system seems to lead to suspiciousness and paranoia and may play a role in paranoid schizophrenia and mania. We will discuss this further in chapter 5, "Reality Misperception."

The FEAR or anxiety system is engaged when an animal senses danger, and it promotes the wish to escape. It is wired into the brain to warn us of stimuli or events that caused our species pain or danger in the past. As a raw emotion, fear is intensely negative and highly motivating. When it is overstimulated, the FEAR system can become hyper-sensitized and become the objectless fear of chronic anxiety. FEAR arouses the autonomic nervous system to produce bodily effects like trembling, a racing heart, and freezing in place. When FEAR stimulates the SEEKING system, animals flee to seek relief. FEAR provides the emotional substrate for the many dysfunctions we will discuss in the anxiety chapter.

The RAGE or the raw anger system is dedicated to striking out when we perceive threat or offense. RAGE, like SEEKING and FEAR, is a primary emotion that doesn't have a specific object, but it can be turned into secondary emotions like anger, jealousy, and hatred, which do. These feelings can be turned into thoughts and actions like blame, revenge, and vengeful fantasy. Panksepp notes that human anger always tends to increase in times of increasing frustration. RAGE plays a large role in social pathologies such as interpersonal aggression, explosive behavior, and mass murder. It is also a significant part of chronic irritability as well as some forms of paranoia and depression.

LUST is Panksepp's term for the primary emotional system underlying sexuality. One doesn't have to be a Freudian analyst to understand that eroticism is in the background of a great deal of our psychological and social lives. It is one of the two emotional systems in which there are significant gender differences—CARE being the other.

In males, puberty increases the production of testosterone by the testicles and brings on an awakening of intense sexual interest. Testosterone in the lust system is associated with male sexual aggression and social dominance. When LUST in men is over-aroused, underregulated, or frustrated, it can produce antisocial behaviors, from unwanted sexual advances to downright predatory sexual behavior. When combined with RAGE, LUST can lead to violent or vengeful behavior.

In females, puberty comes with the production of estrogen and progesterone, which prepares a girl for sexual receptivity. These steroids promote the production of oxytocin, which is the key to the female LUST system. Oxytocin strengthens affection and the vigor of the female orgasm. According to Panksepp, oxytocin also sensitizes the female SEEKING system, which increases a woman's responsiveness "to a variety of life challenges, including stress, hunger and drugs of abuse." The hormone also promotes socially positive behaviors, such as confidence and trust.

CARE is the emotional system for nurturing love. The arousal of the CARE system is a necessary component of the bond between parents and their young. Without it, raising the offspring would be nothing but a burden. We typically associate care with maternal love, but fathers exhibit this love as well. Panksepp sees the CARE system at the root of general human empathy, and we can imagine that deficits in the CARE system are the source of indifference toward others.

The two brain chemicals most closely associated with the CARE system are oxytocin and the endogenous opioids (the brain's natural narcotics). These are the chemicals of good feeling, generated by all positive social experiences. They inhibit tendencies toward aggression and irritability and tend to offset the aggressive effects of testosterone. Panksepp sees the CARE system as vital to good interpersonal relationships. People we call *psychopaths* are likely to have marked deficiencies in oxytocin and endogenous opioids.

In his next emotional system, Panksepp combines PANIC and GRIEF. The model he presents is called *separation distress*. When the youngster of any mammalian species is separated from its mother (or other caregiver), it first responds with acute distress or panic. If this panic is not relieved by the youngster reuniting with its parent, the baby lapses into something much like persistent depression. In Panksepp's view, when a child suffers excessive PANIC/GRIEF (shortened to simply grief) in the first six months of life, the system becomes sensitized, leaving the child vulnerable to chronic anxiety and depression in later life. He writes, "their lives are more likely to be full of separation distress, resulting in chronic feelings of insecurity, sadness and the inability to express pleasure."

The GRIEF system appears to be related to physical pain in that both are regulated by "pleasure chemicals" such as endogenous opiates and oxytocin. Both physical pain and "psychic" (that is, emotional) pain can be immediately relieved by the administration of narcotics. Endogenous opiates are naturally released when an infant is reunited with its mother. There is an inverse relationship between the GRIEF and the CARE systems. Activating the CARE chemicals diminishes GRIEF, while the GRIEF system produces stress hormones that decrease the comfort chemicals.

Panksepp's final primary emotional system is PLAY. PLAY is a positive emotion that "brings all young mammals great joy." It probably exists to promote physical skills like hunting and foraging, as well as the social capacities that underlie courting, sexual behavior, and parenting. It is also essential for developing both cooperative and competitive behaviors. As Panksepp sees it, thwarting a child's opportunity to engage in vigorous physical play may lead to maladaptive social behaviors like ADHD.

Chemically, the PLAY system leads to the release of endogenous opiates in the brain. In fact, administering low doses of narcotics in animals enhances playfulness and social-dominance play. On the other hand, administering psychostimulants like amphetamines markedly diminishes play. This fact has been noticed by parents whose children received these stimulants for ADHD. Panksepp believes that "perhaps ADHD in children is sometimes an indication of a play-starved or especially robust [PLAY] system, rather than psychopathology."

Memory

The third brain system we will consider is memory. Memory is complicated and incompletely understood. We will focus on two types of long-term memory: *episodic* and *semantic*. *Episodic memory* is what is employed when we remember events from the past. It is autobiographical. *Semantic memory* is the memory of facts, words, and categories. It forms our knowledge base.

As we understand it now, both types of memory begin in the hippocampus of the limbic system. The hippocampus does not store memories, but it is what psychiatrist John Ratey calls "an intelligent collating machine, which filters new associations, decides what is important and what to ignore or compress, sorts the results, and then sends packets of information to other parts of the brain."[60]

What is important is that memory is not a true recording, but a reconstruction. When a memory is conscious or explicit, the stored pieces of information are called up to the virtual desktop of the frontal lobes (called *working memory*). If it is an episodic memory, it is usually a verbal narrative, although it is colored by recalled perceptions and emotions associated with the narrative. It is the job of the frontal lobes to try to make the narrative coherent and consistent with other autobiographical memories. Our executive system then makes decisions and plans based on these reconstructions.

Most of the time, these narratives are useful to us and benign. They help us act effectively and successfully. Sometimes, however, they have a negative effect. Memories we construct may lead us to poor decision making and dysfunctional behavior. Instead of positive and successful memories, we remember things in ways that cause us emotional distress or encourage us to behave in destructive ways. Dysfunctional memories do not have to be explicit narratives. They can also be implicit or unconscious and not tied to autobiography. For instance, we might learn to react automatically to certain people or situations in a fearful or angry manner, even when it is not beneficial to do so.

As we examine the different dimensions of dysfunction in this book, we will look at the interaction of stored memory, emotional and motivational responses, and the executive system as the biological basis of these dysfunctions. Much of this must be speculative, because research has not looked at our psychological problems in quite this fashion. It will, however, offer up with some ideas about the reasons we function well or poorly in the real world.

Brain Chemistry

The role of neurochemicals has become important in modern psychiatry, and we will now attempt to understand why. In all the billions of neural connections in the brain, very few neurons actually touch each other. Generally, there is a little space between neurons called a *synapse*. When a message signal (called an *action potential*) reaches the end of one neuron, a little packet of neurochemical (called a transmitter substance) is deposited into the synapse. This neurochemical migrates over to the next neuron and stimulates it, either positively or negatively. The synapses act like little processors, and the sum of all the transmitter substances available at any given moment determines whether the next neuron fires an action potential and sends the message further on in the brain. So the brain is really a machine that works on biochemistry.

There are many transmitter substances, and the different brain systems each utilize one or more of them. A few of them are well-known to many of us because psychiatric drugs are based on them. We hear frequently about serotonin in connection with antidepressants, dopamine with both stimulants and antipsychotics, GABA (gamma-amino butyric acid) with anxiety and sleeping aids, and endorphins with pain medications.

The main work of the brain is accomplished by the transmitter substance glutamate. It is the principal excitatory transmitter and is found all over the brain. Glutamate works in conjunction with the principal inhibitory neurotransmitter, GABA, which dampens the effect of glutamate. Alcohol, sedatives, and anxiety drugs work by potentiating GABA, calming us and putting us to sleep.

Both glutamate and GABA act quickly and are eliminated once their work is done. Other transmitter substances are slower acting and are more limited in action to certain regions of the brain. These are called *neuromodulators* and include dopamine, serotonin, norepinephrine, and a class of neurotransmitters called *endorphins*. The main purpose of these neuro-modulators is to alter synaptic transmission, not to directly initiate it. Like many other neuromodulators, serotonin-creating neurons begin with cell bodies deep in the brain and then send nerve fibers to almost every part of the brain.

We know of the transmitter substance dopamine as the "pleasure" chemical. Drugs that elicit a sudden surge of dopamine produce the feeling of exhilaration that we call a *high*. On the other hand, antipsychotic drugs, which block dopamine, produce a state of joylessness and a loss of motivation. When dopamine levels get too high, people appear manic or otherwise psychotic.

Dopamine is much more than a pleasure maker. It is the basis for much of our drive and motivation. Elevated dopamine creates the focus and goal-directed behaviors necessary to accomplish many life tasks. Research suggests that it is essential to long-term memory, linking new objects to old memories so we can identify them. Dopamine may also establish a link between experiences that give pleasure and the memory of those experiences.

Psychiatric theory has postulated that a "chemical imbalance" of too much dopamine in the frontal lobes causes schizophrenia. This dopamine theory began when it was discovered that the first generation of antipsychotic medications (called *neuroleptics*) acted by blocking the receptors for dopamine. It has been known since 1974, however, that there is no such surplus of dopamine in the brains of people diagnosed with chronic schizophrenia. Although many psychiatrists would agree with fellow psychiatrist E. Fuller Torrey that "supporting research evidence is sparse," they continue to believe, as he does, that "an excess of dopamine is one of the causes of schizophrenia."[61]

The function of serotonin is more ambiguous. Low levels of it have been associated with depression, anxiety, and obsessive-compulsive behavior. But this conclusion is based mostly on the fact that psychiatric drugs deemed effective for these problems increase the effect of serotonin in the synapses. Ratey called serotonin "the brain's brake and policemen; it prevents the brain from getting out of control from fear or worry. It has a calming effect that helps us to assure ourselves that we are going to survive and elevates mood and self-esteem."[62]

Nevertheless, the case for boosting serotonin may not be so rosy. Lower serotonin levels may have important biological functions, according to the anthropologist and love researcher Helen Fisher. Low serotonin levels may be an important part of being in love. One study cited by Fisher compared groups of people in love, people suffering from obsessive-compulsive disorder, and a control group, who were not in love nor otherwise distressed. The lovers and the compulsives both had low serotonin. Fisher thinks that low serotonin might be responsible for "the lover's persistent, involuntary, irresistible ruminations about a sweetheart."

Fisher also sees a reciprocal relationship between serotonin and dopamine (along with norepinephrine). When serotonin increases, dopamine production (or its effect) appears to decrease. The result is that a person's sexual drive and interest is inhibited and emotion dulled. She believes that this state may "imperil your ability to appraise suitors, choose appropriate mates and form stable and lasting partnerships as well."[63] We might conclude that serotonin and dopamine brain levels must balance appropriately for different circumstances. There are times for low and high levels of each one.

There is a multitude of other modulating biochemicals that affect our functioning and are now being studied by neuroscientists. Among the ones we have some knowledge of are testosterone, a hormone connected to sexual attraction, aggression, and masculine behavior; oxytocin and vasopressin, related to social bonding, attachment, and sex; epinephrine and cortisol, stress hormones involved in the fight-or-flight response and fear; and endorphins, which create feelings of well-being and reduce pain.

Before we leave brain chemistry, we should note that psychiatric drugs do not balance the neurotransmitters in the brain. What they actually do will be discussed later in this book. For now, let us consider what Peter Breggin, psychiatrist and persistent critic of biological psychiatry, has to say: "Psychiatric drugs don't correct biochemical imbalances—they cause them.... Probably, drug manufacturers would rather discover and market drugs that do correct chemical imbalances, but this cannot be done because no chemical imbalances have been identified in the brains of patients with diagnoses such as anxiety disorders, depressive disorders, bipolar disorder, or schizophrenia."[64]

Psychological Factors

One thing special about human beings, compared with all other animals, is the extent to which our life experiences alter us. Some of these alterations involve the slow accretion of learned patterns of behavior. From the moment we enter the world, we begin to adapt and learn in order to meet the demands of the world around us. As we mature, these demands become increasingly complex and social. We continuously develop our behavioral repertory, based on our abilities and deficiencies. We do not have to be Freudians to understand that at each stage of life, we must develop new coping mechanisms to meet new challenges.

The patterns of behavior, thinking, and feeling that we develop are what we call our *personalities.* As we go through life, our personalities have strengths and weaknesses. Some of our personality characteristics help us successfully meet our needs, but others may be maladaptive and lead to chronic dysfunction. Since we are such highly social creatures, many maladaptive personality patterns leave people unable to form satisfying interpersonal relationships. Other personality patterns leave us vulnerable to anxiety or depression.

Maladaptive personality patterns and other dysfunctions can also create a psychological susceptibility to sudden breakdown. Most people are resilient; they have developed adequate coping skills and a firm sense of self and can quickly recover from stressors and conflict. It is likely, however, that each of us can break down and become symptomatic if the stress is too great. People who suffer personal losses may become depressed, and people who are threatened by events they cannot control may develop anxiety-related symptoms. Otherwise well-functioning people may even lose their grip on reality and become psychotic if the threat to self is too intense. Some personalities are rigid and subject to catastrophic psychological breakdown, called *decompensation.* Severe dysfunction of this kind may be labeled schizophrenia, major depression, or panic disorder.

Relevant to this discussion of psychological factors is cognitive behavior theorist Albert Bandura's theory of "self-efficacy." In Bandura's model, perceived self-efficacy is central to a person's psychological functioning. It is a conception of one's sense of control, or what he calls *personal agency*. Bandura formally defines *self-efficacy* as "beliefs in one's capabilities to organize and execute the courses of action required to manage prospective situations."[65]

It is not so much the objective reality of mastery that matters, but what a person believes to be his or her ability to control life events. As Bandura puts it, "efficacy beliefs influence how people think, feel, motivate themselves and act." There is now a great deal of research to show that this is the case. These efficacy beliefs develop over our lives in response to personal and social experiences. Bandura identifies three major sources of influences: *mastery experiences, vicarious experience,* and *social persuasion.*

Mastery experiences give us "the most authentic evidence of whether one can master whatever it takes to proceed." Successes enhance a sense of efficacy, while failures diminish it. Easy success, however, does not build a strong sense of efficacy. Bandura notes that "a resilient sense of efficacy requires experience in overcoming obstacles through perseverant effort." In other words, the more confidence people build in ultimate success, the less susceptible they are to functional disruption.

The second mechanism for building efficacy, *vicarious experience,* involves the lessons learned from watching people whom we believe to be similar to ourselves. If we see such people work hard to overcome obstacles and succeed, it increases our own mastery beliefs. But if those people fail despite their efforts, it undermines our confidence and motivation.

The third influence is *social persuasion.* If people of importance to us persuade us that we can succeed if we make enough of an effort, it can boast our sense of self-efficacy, and we will try harder and attempt to develop the skills necessary to succeed. This kind of social persuasion is of obvious importance in effective parenting, education, and therapy. Conversely, the persuasive message that we lack capabilities and that we should dwell on our personal deficiencies and self-doubts has the opposite effect. Good mentors are very important in helping us develop the skills to become well-functioning people, while poor ones do the opposite.

Bandura describes an additional source of influence in determining our judgment of our capabilities: our appraisal of our own physiological and emotional state. How we feel in terms of mood, stress, or physical symptoms affects how competent we believe we are to handle life challenges. If we find ways to improve our mood, decrease our stress, and ameliorate our physical ills, we increase our sense of our own efficacy.

Unfortunately, efficacy is a two-way street. A diminished sense of efficacy makes it more likely that perceived failures will make us despondent or anxious, will increase stress, and will cause us to dwell on or misinterpret physical symptoms. Bandura writes, "People who have a high a sense of efficacy are likely to view their state of affective arousal as an energizing facilitator of performance, whereas those beset by self-doubts regard their arousal as a debilitator."[66]

I find Bandura's conception of self-efficacy extremely useful in understanding the psychological component of dysfunction. I will refer to it as I discuss the dimensions of dysfunction in part 2. His ideas are also the cornerstone of what is referred to as *cognitive behavior therapy*. His ideas provide a framework for teaching the skills that help patients succeed, that teach them how to decrease their own distress. We will focus on this in chapter 14, "Dimensional Treatment."

A theme I will develop throughout this book is the power our beliefs, how the ways we think about ourselves influence the way we behave and feel. Maladaptive thinking and false assumptions are a major source of dysfunction. Analysis of the ideas people form about themselves, the consequences of their actions, and the relationship that these thoughts have to distress have been the focus of a remarkable group of psychological thinkers collectively grouped under the label *cognitive behavioral therapists*. I will have a great deal more to say about them in succeeding chapters.

Social Factors

The power of situational forces to influence our actions, thoughts, and even our beliefs is vastly underestimated. We have a strong bias toward attributing our behavior to "dispositional forces," that is, our personal qualities. When we look for causes of other people's behavior, we invoke genetic makeup or personality or mental illness. But we are social animals, programmed by evolution to respond to and be shaped by the social forces around us.

Social psychologists, such as Philip Zimbardo, have been demonstrating the power of situations to dominate people's behavior for decades. Zimbardo's recent book on what he calls the *Lucifer effect* details the power of social forces to produce evil behavior, as occurred in Nazi Germany or in the prison at Abu Ghraib in Iraq.[67] His famous Stanford Prison Experiment of the 1970s showed (to his own horror) that he could turn average college students into cruel prison guards or sheep-like prisoners. All he did was create a role-playing situation with certain social rules and symbolic trappings and attitudes, and the participants' behavior followed suit.

Students randomly assigned to be "guards" or "prisoners" fell into their roles within a day, without any real awareness of what they were doing or why. Zimbardo said, "the power that the guards assumed each time they donned their military-style uniforms was matched by the powerlessness the prisoners felt when wearing their wrinkled smocks with ID numbers sewn on their fronts." Even kindly and liberal Professor Zimbardo unknowingly took on the role of prison supervisor and was blind to the abusive world he had created. The experiment was terminated only when the woman who was to become Zimbardo's wife confronted him with an outsider's perspective on what he was doing.

The power of situational forces to determine what an individual thinks, feels, and does is as powerful in the mental-health field as it was in the Stanford Prison Experiment. The behavioral context is of equal importance to personal attributes—such as a mental disorder—in any attempt to understand the level of dysfunction a person exhibits. Behavioral context includes the rewards, punishments, social norms, and expectations the person is subject to. These factors can be protective when they boost people's self-esteem and lead them to believe they can overcome their problems. They can be destructive and increase dysfunction when they reinforce disability.

My experiences with such social factors have given me additional reason to be extremely skeptical of psychiatric diagnosis. I have done extensive reviews of patients' records as part of my evaluations for lawyers, courts, and workers' compensation insurers. I have often found multiple clinicians making diagnostic pronouncements without the least idea about their patients' life circumstances. They seem to be so focused on fitting a patient's complaints to the diagnostic criteria for mental disorders and coming up with a label that they pay no attention to the facts of a person's life that they do know. Such clinicians seem unable to step back and take an objective look at their patients.

I recognize that it is difficult to get context information in an interview setting. But the clinicians who do not even ask the questions sound like partisans, and their opinions are unreliable. We need to learn as much as we can about the situational circumstances of a patient's life and be modest and circumspect in our labels.

PART II

DIMENSIONS OF MADNESS

5

Reality Misperception

The first dimension we will consider is reality misperception, which has two concepts associated with it: *reality testing* and *thought disturbance*. Reality testing is the ability to organize and evaluate information from the outside world and to distinguish it from our imagination and thought. Thought disturbance is the consequence of the breakdown of reality testing.

Humans are natural scientists. Through our experiences and from what we learn from others, we make sense of the world around us and of our own minds and bodies. In order to function effectively, we must have a pretty good grasp of these two realms: external and internal. We must test reality in order to differentiate our own internal dialogues and images from what is generated by the world about us. We can use our subjective feelings to read others and their intentions, but we must also be able to separate our own minds from the world of other people.

Objective reality is a pretty slippery concept, especially in an age when physicists question whether reality even exists. What we believe to be reality changes from time to time and place to place. So, the reality that matters (from the perspective of day-to-day functioning) is not truth, but consensual reality—reality determined by human consensus. For example, we can now appreciate that a rainbow is a perceptual illusion of water droplets and sunlight. If only I see it, it might be a hallucination. But if others see it with me, the rainbow is a consensual reality. It is this kind of reality testing we require to function independently in the social world. The more idiosyncratic our beliefs and perceptions, the harder it is for us to thrive or even survive.

The breakdown of reality testing has been fundamental to psychiatry since the days that Kraepelin described dementia praecox. For the past hundred years, the extreme end of the reality dimension has been schizophrenia, which, in our culture, is almost synonymous with mental illness.

Today, there is a great push to erase the stigma of mental illness, but a mental illness is not like a broken leg. A mental illness is seen as incapacitating that part of us that we see as most human: our minds. By implication, being mentally ill is being not quite human, and a diagnosis of schizophrenia allows society to take away some basic human rights. We can hospitalize people against their will if they are labeled schizophrenic by psychiatrists. In many states, including my own, testimony by a psychiatrist can cause a judge to order involuntary psychiatric medication. Being labeled schizophrenic, then, has huge consequences.

It is important to all of us to examine whether schizophrenia is a valid concept and whether it can be uniquely applied to a certain set of people. Is there one schizophrenia or many? Until recently, psychiatry has held that there are several types of schizophrenia that can be separately diagnosed. The most recent DSM, however, concludes that subtypes are not reliably differentiated. The American Psychiatric Association now believes that the characteristics that were said to mark a patient's subtype often change—thus potentially shifting a patient to a different subtype—and they are also shared by other categories that are not schizophrenia.

The question, then, becomes whether there really is a mental illness called *schizophrenia*. Oddly, the new DSM posits something called *attenuated psychosis syndrome*. This is supposed to designate people who exhibit "minor versions of relevant symptoms" of schizophrenia. The idea is to "identify individuals with an increased risk for developing a psychotic disorder," but the APA admits this diagnosis requires further study to determine whether it can be reliably identified.[68]

What Is Schizophrenia?

When confronted with people whose thinking and behavior is far from our everyday reality, we perceive them as alien to us. Freud once wrote, "I always find it uncanny when I can't understand someone in terms of myself."[69] Psychiatrists Daniel Javit and Joseph Coyle expressed a similar sentiment: "schizophrenia conspires to rob people of the very qualities they need to thrive in society: personality, social skills and wit."[70]

Taking Care of an Embryo

When I became a psychology intern at FDR VA Hospital in 1973, I was assigned two patients of my very own, whom I saw in therapy every week. One was Mr. Cooper, who was then fifty-six years old. Mr. Cooper had been in the hospital since World War II—about thirty years. He had been a truck driver and had been in the Army, so at some point in his life, he had functioned fairly well. I knew he had been born on Nassau in the Bahamas and had lived in Harlem in New York City, but I never learned much more about his background. I didn't know what he experienced in the Army, but at some point he broke down, or "decompensated," and was hospitalized. He never left the hospital; it was now his only home. He was diagnosed as schizophrenic.

When I first met Mr. Cooper, a husky black male with a shaved head, he said little and appeared to have a menacing look. I soon learned, however, that he was a shy, withdrawn man who was rather sweet and gentle. As I got to know him, he became increasingly open with me, and we even formed some kind of relationship. He had an elaborate and fixed delusional system that preoccupied him. One day, he wrote me a summary of it: "in the center of my chest, there is a large embryo, and I have tried to dislodge the embryo by putting my finger on my chest."

The embryo was female and made many demands on Mr. Cooper. He had to roll up his pants' legs and the sleeves of his shirt. He had to "exercise" the embryo by throwing his arms out and bellowing. He would do his exercises on the ward and out in front of various buildings on the hospital grounds. They were seen as bizarre.

Our goal for Mr. Cooper was to try to prepare him for life outside the hospital, so he could make a successful transition to independent living. We used the token economy on our unit to reward and punish his behaviors. We knew that he had to learn to control his odd behaviors, so we fined him tokens for displaying them. We also needed to reestablish basic living skills, so we rewarded him with tokens for functional engagement.

We started by taking him on bus trips to the nearby town. At first he resisted doing this, but finally he agreed to go if I took him. On one such trip, he used a pay phone to call the ward. He was pleased with himself and said it was the first time in thirty-five years that he had used a phone. Over the next several months, he learned to go to town by himself; he always called the ward to tell us he had gotten there.

Mr. Cooper insisted that, if he were to leave the hospital, he would find an apartment in Harlem. Of course, the Harlem he recalled was not the Harlem of the 1970s, but we had to agree with this plan. He began taking the train to New York City, and eventually we found him a room. The first crisis came when his neighbors complained that he was bellowing and masturbating with his door open. We convinced him to keep his door closed. Unfortunately, the experiment ended when he returned to the hospital terrified. He said he had been chased by a pack of wolves. We wondered if this was a metaphor for some bad experience he had had on the streets of Harlem.

The big question is, did Mr. Cooper have a mental illness that made him completely different from the rest of us? Or was the real problem that his ideas and behaviors were too odd for society to handle, but otherwise he was not so different from you and me. Most of us have odd fantasies at times, and we may even behave bizarrely, but we are able to control these things and remain in society. Was Mr. Cooper categorically different?

Given the central role that reality perception plays in our sense of self, people who lack it perplex and frighten us. In an earlier age, such people were often said to be possessed by Satan. Modern psychiatry describes them as having a brain disease. As one of its most prominent spokesmen, E. Fuller Torrey wrote, "schizophrenia is firmly and unequivocally established to be a brain disease, just as multiple sclerosis, Parkinson's disease and Alzheimer's disease are established as brain diseases."[71] But what kind of disease? We know a good deal about the neuropathology of the three diseases Torrey mentions, but we have no such pathology for schizophrenia. Even Torrey admits, "although there are numerous abnormalities in brain structure and function, there is no single thing that can be measured and from which we can say: yes, that is schizophrenia."

The closest psychiatry has come to formulating a disease theory of schizophrenia is that there is an excess of the neurotransmitter dopamine in the brain. At one time, the dopamine hypothesis was seen as established truth, and to this day, many psychiatrists use it to tell patients they have a chemical imbalance. The history of the dopamine hypothesis and its relationship to the development of psychiatric drugs has been told in detail in many places. I will briefly recount it.

The French surgeon Henri Laborit was trying to find a medication that would calm his surgical patients and prevent them from going into shock. One of the compounds sent for him to try in 1951 was known to have a sedative effect. He found that it not only calmed anxiety, but left patients detached and indifferent to their surroundings. He thought the drug might be useful in psychiatry and offered it to Jean Delay and Pierre Deniker, who began using it with their psychotic patients, with apparent success. The drug was chlorpromazine, marketed as Thorazine in America.

The French doctors called chlorpromazine and similar drugs *neuroleptics,* which comes from Greek roots for "take hold of the nervous system." In England and America, they were called *major tranquilizers* to distinguish them from the minor tranquilizers used to treat anxiety. These drugs were not initially thought to have any specific antischizophrenic properties, but according to Delay and Deniker, they produced a vegetative state they called "hibernation therapy." The first North American psychiatrist to test chlorpromazine, Heinz Lehman, hoped it would be a substitute for lobotomy. At that stage, psychiatrists agreed that it made their patients apathetic, sluggish, and vacuous. In 1954, the English psychiatrist Joel Elkes noted that the drugs worked by hindering brain functioning, but they did not actually affect the psychosis: "the schizophrenic and paraphrenic patients continued to be subject to delusions and hallucinations, though they appeared to be less disturbed by them."[72]

Neuroleptics very quickly became standard in psychiatric hospitals, in part because it made patients quieter and easier deal with, and in part because they seemed much more humane than lobotomy and insulin shock therapy. In 1954, after the FDA approved Thorazine, the drug company Smith, Klein and French (now part of GlaxoSmithKlein) launched a massive marketing campaign, and the psychiatric establishment touted the new wonder drug.

In 1964, NIMH published a major study of neuroleptics in the treatment of schizophrenics and concluded that the drugs improve "all the symptoms and manifestations of schizophrenic psychoses" and that they deserve to be called "antischizophrenic" drugs.[73] At the same time this study was going on, a Swedish pharmacologist named Arvid Carlsson found that neuroleptics block the action of dopamine in a specific kind of dopamine receptor, called D2. Based on these findings, researcher J. M. Van Rossum posited that "overstimulation of dopamine receptors" was part of the cause of schizophrenia.[74]

Over the next decade, this dopamine hypothesis came to be seen as an increasingly plausible explanation. In 1973, psychiatrist S. Matthysse introduced the idea of a chemical imbalance, writing, "it may be that a system inhibited by or inhibiting dopamine neurons is deficient in schizophrenia and the dopamine blocking actions of antipsychotic drugs restores a balance."[75] Several years later, psychiatrists Herbert Meltzer and Stephen Stahl stated, "The evidence for a role of dopamine in the pathophysiology of schizophrenia is compelling, but not irrefutable."[76]

Unfortunately, there has never been any real evidence that there is an excess of dopamine activity in the brains of people labeled schizophrenic. In fact, some of the typical characteristics of schizophrenia (such as apathy and reduced movement) are directly the opposite of what one would predict if there were too much dopamine. Other chemical-imbalance theories are still floating around the psychiatric literature, such as an excess of dopamine in one part of the brain and a deficiency in another, an imbalance between dopamine and serotonin, or a surge of dopamine causing the onset of a psychotic experience, but not schizophrenia itself. None of this has been shown to be true.

Symptoms of Schizophrenia

Neither chemical imbalance nor any other medical explanation for schizophrenia has ever panned out. The evidence is abundant that schizophrenia
is not a specific condition that can be diagnosed with any certainty. It has no
clear boundaries and no unique symptoms. It cannot be determined whether
the term *schizophrenia* denotes one concept or many. In a striking admission
in 1998, Nancy Andreasen, then editor of the *American Journal of Psychiatry*
wrote, "someday in the twenty-first century, after the human genome and the
human brain have been mapped, someone may need to organize a reverse
Marshall Plan so that Europeans can save American science by helping us
figure out who really has schizophrenia or what schizophrenia really is."[77]

What the term *schizophrenia* really describes is a set of observations made by
clinicians. Most of these characteristics were established in the early twentieth
century. Psychiatry calls these characteristics *symptoms,* but they are not true
symptoms, because patients rarely complain of them. There is general agreement that there is no symptom found only in schizophrenia and that an individual diagnosed with schizophrenia will not have all of the usual symptoms.

The current DSM says that a person has schizophrenia if he or she exhibits
two or more symptoms listed. These characteristics are divided into "positive"
and "negative" symptoms, indicating the addition of things that should not
be there and the absence of things that should. Symptoms that are considered
"positive" include delusions, hallucinations, disorganized speech, and disorganized or catatonic behavior (which means highly unusual motor behavior).
"Negative" symptoms include such characteristics as emotional flattening,
decreased productivity of thought and speech, lack of initiation of behavior,
social isolation, and loss of cognitive function.

Earlier I mentioned that people we perceive as mad *seem* alien, but is there
really a separation between them and us? Is there a true disjunction between
schizophrenic symptoms and what the rest of us experience? Or do these
symptoms only identify the extreme end of the continuum that includes all
of us to one degree or another? Let's look at some of the characteristics that
are typically described as pathognomonic signs of schizophrenia and see if
they are as specific or unusual as they seem.

Hallucinations

Hallucinations are usually the first thing we commonly associate with schizophrenia. Until this modern era, when people walk around talking on their phones via earbuds and a microphone, a person walking down the street talking to himself would be seen as mad. People who appear to be responding to internal stimuli obviously appear disturbed. For the most part, these unreal perceptual experiences are auditory—"hearing voices"—but they can occur in any sensory modality. Here are some that I have encountered: Paul related, "God said my wife was organizing my mind and sending me here"; John said, "he (God) told me how to make people good"; and Anna saw her baby as a dog.

How do we know that a voice heard inside the head is a hallucination rather than a normal articulated thought? Outside of bizarreness, the only distinction is that hallucinating people do not hear the voice as their own, but as someone else's. When we hear a voice that is not our own, we naturally place it outside our own heads. In order to correctly distinguish between a thought and a voice, our executive brain must form a perceptual hypothesis about the source and test it against other sensory data and memory. There are many times when this is difficult to do. We all make errors of attribution when we are in a hypnagogic or near-sleep state, intoxicated by cortex-suppressing drugs (like alcohol), or suffering from a high fever.

The phenomenon of hearing voices outside of any of these states is much more common than we would expect. In the late nineteenth century, the philosopher Henry Sidgwick conducted a study for the Society for Psychical Research, asking seventeen thousand men and women if they had ever heard a voice when no one else was there. He excluded anyone who appeared mentally unstable and found that 3.3 percent of normal people had experienced a vivid auditory hallucination at least once. This study was replicated in 1991 by Allen Tien, who found an even higher percentage: 11 to 13 percent reported they had hallucinated at some time in their lives. Two-thirds of these people were undisturbed by the voices and did not plan to seek professional help.[78]

A study of 375 college students found that 39 percent reported they had heard a voice speaking their thoughts aloud. A surprising 5 percent of students admitted that they held conversations with their voices.[79] In line with this, an evangelical religious sect was recently in the news because they explicitly trained their adherents to hallucinate, with apparent success.[80] The sect teaches that its members must have a literal relationship with God as a friend. They learn to sit down with God at the kitchen table, pour him a cup of coffee, and ask for his advice. They are taught how to recognize when it is God speaking and not their own voice.

Smith Family Hallucinations

In his book *Muses, Madmen, and Prophets,* Daniel Smith tells the story of his father and grandfather. His father, a lawyer, had begun hearing voices at age thirteen, and the voices had commanded him to do certain things. These were not disturbing or bizarre commands, but simple things like "move a glass from one side of the table to another." He kept these voices a secret for twenty-five years, both because he was ashamed and because he feared being called insane. They were constantly present and tortured him. They were a sign of pathology to him, but he did learn to live with them.

In his late thirties, his secret became too much for him. He had a breakdown and admitted himself to a psychiatric hospital, where he was diagnosed with major depression with psychotic features. His law firm let him go, due to mental unfitness, and he feared his wife would leave him. The happy outcome, however, was that he regained his mental equilibrium, his wife did not leave, and he resumed his law practice.

Fast forward ten more years. Smith's grandfather wrote a memoir, which Smith and his brother edited and self-published.[81] In it, his grandfather wrote a brief section entitled "voices." The grandfather revealed that he had always heard voices. They mostly appeared when he had to make a decision, and he learned to listen to them. He wrote, "listening to the voice and interpreting the correct choice in what you are thinking becomes a habit and in time, your awareness can almost always help you decide an issue."

When he read this, Smith's father was enraged. He felt a great injustice had been done to him, because he had never known that his father also heard voices. He flew to Florida to confront his father and demand an explanation.

The moral of this story is that hallucinating of voices does not have to be a sign of mental illness. It depends on social context and how the person interprets them. For the grandfather, the voices were a welcome guide. For the father, they were a malignant and unwelcome force that almost destroyed his life.

Delusions

By DSM definition, delusions are "erroneous beliefs that usually involve a misinterpretation of perceptions or experiences." This means beliefs that are idiosyncratic and not held by mental-health professionals (usually). DSM does understand that bizarreness of belief can exist in the eye of the beholder, especially across cultures. But it insists that if beliefs are implausible or outside the understanding of the clinician, they are delusional. The DSM acknowledges that it can be difficult to distinguish a delusion from "a strongly held belief," but it asserts that an idea is delusional if it is held with a high degree of conviction "despite clear contradictory evidence."

Here is some delusional material from the patients John and Anna. As is common, their delusions have a strong religious content. I have taken some liberties with their language to make it more comprehensible. John said, "I am Christ. Most people are against me, and the devil is leading them. I'm the force of God. The forces of evil are trying to overcome me by telepathy." Anna told me, "I thought God was coming down to hurt me if I stared at the cross too long. After I fell asleep, I pictured him hurting me."

Delusions are typically grouped by their predominant themes. Persecutory themes are the most common; people believe they are spied upon, controlled, or otherwise tormented by outside entities. Persecutory delusions often take the form of what are called *ideas of reference*, in which people believe random things—newspaper headlines or song lyrics—refer specifically to them.

Another delusional theme is grandiosity. Deluded people may believe that they are Christ or Napoleon or that they have incredible wealth or power. Some people have told me that they own the hospital where they are patients or that Bill Gates is their father.

Another common delusional theme is somatic, which involves odd beliefs about the body or body functioning. This may be expressed as the belief that a person's internal organs have been removed by aliens and replaced with some other being's organs. I have seen several people with the fixed belief that they were infested by bugs or parasites. One pleasant lady fumigated her apartment with ten cans of Raid and almost killed herself. She excoriated her scalp so severely to get rid of her bugs that she had to be medically hospitalized.

Other delusional themes are labeled erotomanic and jealous. Erotomanic delusions involve the fixed belief that another person is in love with that person. We occasionally see news stories about celebrities stalked by people who think the celebrity loves them or that they must rescue the celebrity from danger. The jealous types believe their lover has betrayed them and will find all sorts of evidence (ideas of reference) to support their convictions.

According to DSM, bizarre delusions are enough to diagnose schizophrenia. These include "delusions that express a loss of control over mind or body." These may take the form of "thought insertion" or "thought withdrawal"—a person may express the conviction that aliens or other malevolent forces are either putting thoughts into his or her mind or stealing them.

It is fair to say that a great number of people hold beliefs that many of us would consider false and even bizarre. Some might consider them delusions. It surprises me when people who otherwise seem rational hold convictions that I consider mad. A Gallup poll found that 25 percent of people surveyed think that ghosts are real and 15 percent think that UFOs are. Of Canadians surveyed, 18 percent reported dreams that they believe predicted the future.[82] I am certain that I hold convictions that you might consider mad if you could get me to admit them. The major difference between delusions and the beliefs you and I hold is that we (though I don't know about you) either do not strongly express them or do not act on them.

The distinction between religious beliefs and delusions can be particularly hard to differentiate. A 1999 English study compared psychotic inpatients to members of two new religious movements (druids and Hare Krishnas) who did not seem in any need of psychiatric treatment. Using standardized measures of delusional beliefs, they could not distinguish between the two groups. Both scored higher than ordinary people.[83]

As with hallucinations, we can conclude that false beliefs form a continuum from benign to extremely disruptive and dysfunctional. At the extreme end that we call schizophrenia, these beliefs may be bizarre, but there is no bright line dividing ordinary odd beliefs from delusions. Even the majority of people who describe common delusional ideas to their doctors have no history of psychiatric disorder, nor do they wish any treatment.

Thought Disorganization

While hallucinations and delusions are seen as disturbances of thought content, abnormalities of language and communication are considered a disturbance of thought processing. Thought disorganization is implied by the certain peculiarities of speech that people characterized as schizophrenic exhibit. A primary characteristic of thought disorganization is a loosening of associations—expressed ideas do not follow each other in logical sequence. Sentences can become so disconnected that you cannot follow the person's train of thought; what she says makes no sense.

At the extreme end of disorganization, speech disintegrates into "word salad." Paul said something like this:

> Troubles started when I had no business. I had no money. Second job with life, doing well. Had a baby during the summer. Then cried myself to sleep because I was afraid wife would die when the baby was born. I used to get annoyed with my wife and she with me. I failed the exam, then I ran around trying to get the money. One, two, three, my cigarette, my wife's cigarette, my mother smokes Viceroy. The day it happened, October 15, I was going to work. Realized I passed a gas station I wanted to stop so I made a U-turn like I'm making one now. Come on, laugh.

In addition to loose associations, thought disturbance may involve eccentric generalities and clichés that seem to communicate little. John said that eyeglasses were good and evil, because "your glasses, black-rimmed, red in them, made of two different lenses and they are bifocals and you can change your perception of things and see good through the upper lenses." Paul constantly said, "twenty-two eyes of blue, I am as sick as the rest of you." Abstract association becomes difficult for people with disorganized thought. Asked to describe how a tomato and a beet were alike, Anna said, "a beet is a vegetable, but a tomato could be a lot of things—could be a girl."

Just how uncommon or specific are disorders of thinking? Using a rating scale, Nancy Andreasen found that incoherent speech existed on a continuum, with patients diagnosed with mania more incoherent than those labeled schizophrenic. People diagnosed with depression displayed a moderate degree of incoherence, and "normal" people showed much more of it than expected.[84] One study rated the speech of the people of Dunedin, Scotland, and found about 18 percent exhibited disorganized speech.[85]

Negative Symptoms

A final category of characteristics in the DSM schizophrenia classification are called *negative symptoms*. These include *affective flattening, alogia,* and *avolition. Affective flattening* means that the person seems emotionally unresponsive; emotional expression is diminished most of the time. Although this kind of emotional blunting may seem striking in people labeled schizophrenic, it is also characteristic of any sort of person who is socially disengaged and focused on internal preoccupations.

Alogia means "poverty of speech," but again, this can be seen in almost anyone who does not wish to engage socially. If you can get schizophrenic people to engage on their own terms, they can be quite talkative, although you may not understand what they are saying. Finally, *avolition* is what others see as a lack of motivation to undertake or persist in meaningful activities. Such people may sit still and smoke (when they are still allowed to) or pace the halls with no interest in participating in activities. This, too, should not be too surprising in the case of people who are just not interested in doing what the clinicians think they should. It is also something we might expect to see in people who are depressed or preoccupied.

We all vary greatly from time to time in the degree to which we relate emotionally, speak, or engage in purposeful behavior. Outside of the context of other reality-distortion behaviors, it is hard for me to see these negative symptoms as pathological signs. They appear to represent the end of a continuum of social engagement with the world in general.

Reality Dimension

On the heels of Kraepelin's descriptions of the discrete mental illnesses that we now call *schizophrenia* and *bipolar disorder,* some psychiatrists grappled with how to classify people who seemed intermediate between normal and mad. The German psychiatrist Ernst Kretschmer invented the terms *schizothymic* and *cyclothymic* in 1925 to describe them. Most psychiatrists, however, were too focused on the genetics and other biological causes of schizophrenia to pay much attention.

Then, in 1962, the psychologist Paul Meehl reviewed the inconsistent findings of genetic research and concluded that people inherited a predisposition to schizophrenia rather than the illness itself; he called this predisposition *schizotaxia.* Most such people would not develop schizophrenia unless exposed to stress, but they would exhibit eccentric beliefs and magical thinking. He labeled such people *schizotypal personalities.*

In 1975, Seymour Kety and his colleagues studied adopted children in Denmark who were assessed as schizophrenic. When they examined the biological relatives of these patients, few were found to be schizophrenic, but Kety and his coauthors did determine that many of them showed eccentric personality characteristics. They concluded these relatives demonstrated a subclinical form, which they called *schizophrenia spectrum disorder.*

When the authors of DSM-III were attempting to define types of maladaptive personalities in a system that would run parallel to the main body of psychiatric diagnoses (they called it *axis-2*). They labeled these *personality disorders,* because they were "enduring patterns of perceiving, relating to, and thinking about the environment and oneself." In an apparent attempt to reconcile the distinction between a schizophrenic disorder and a schizo-phrenic spectrum disorder, DSM-III described several almost-schizophrenia personality disorders, including schizotypal and borderline.[86]

At about the same time, but on an alternative track, the controversial psychologist Hans Eysenck was developing a theory of personality based on dimensions that he believed were rooted in genetic factors. The first two dimensions he described were *neuroticism* and *introversion-extroversion*. In 1976, harking back to the work of Kretschmer, Eysenck proposed a third dimension that he called *psychoticism*. Psychosis (for example, schizophrenia) lay at the extreme end of this dimension.

With this history in mind, I suggest that the term *schizophrenia* describes a type or types that lie at the extreme end of a reality-misperception dimen-sion. What that means is that people labeled schizophrenic are not different from the rest of us in kind, only in degree. They do not have a special mental illness that has stolen their minds. We all occupy places along that reality dimension, and as with any other attribute, some of us are more realistic and some are very impaired. Furthermore, our places are not static; our reality abilities vary with time and circumstances.

Looking at them through a dimensional lens, we can attempt to place rel-evant mental disorders as descriptive types along the reality-misperception dimension. The psychiatric diagnostic system was not designed for this approach, so we cannot be precise, and many disorders overlap dimen-sions. Nevertheless, I have sorted most of the mental disorders along the nine dimensions, and in this chapter, I have selected ones that involve reality distortion. Placed this way, the disorders form a continuous dimension, with one disorder merging into another.

At the mild to moderate end of this dimension, there are four patterns of personality that represent four aspects of reality dysfunction—the paranoid, schizoid, schizotypal, and borderline. These reflect long-standing deficien-cies and seriously impair a person's ability to make effective interpersonal connections and lead a satisfying life.

The paranoid personality is marked by suspiciousness and pervasive dis-trust of others, hypersensitivity, and a strong tendency to project feelings onto others. The psychiatrist George Vaillant characterized these people as "many of life's least lovable character types—the bigot, the injustice collector, the pathologically jealous spouse and the litigiousness crank."[87] Paranoid people's main reality distortion is their assumption that other people's motives are malevolent and they are out to harm them, though there is no or little evidence to support this. Others are seen as plotting against them, and they have doubts about the trustworthiness of the people who are supposed to be their friends. They develop ideas of reference—a casual comment is seen as having a hidden and hostile meaning or is a sly attack; honest mistakes are deliberate attempts to cheat them; and small things they think they observe mean a spouse is unfaithful.

Vaillant points out that a paranoid personality's worst demons are people who resemble themselves. He observes that Hitler and his inner circle looked much more like the Jews they hated than the blond, blue-eyed Aryans he wanted to rule the world. Vaillant likens this strange ambivalence to "querulous spinsters" who will allow no man to come close to them but "are desired by imaginary lechers beneath their beds."

What differentiates paranoid personalities from more dysfunctional types is the absence of fixed delusions, hallucinations, and disorganized thinking. Even though their view of the world is biased and egocentric, they usually have enough control and reality testing to survive in it. They may be cold, distant, and hypersensitive, but they can succeed in situations that demand little intimacy and where they can acquire the power to control their circumstances.

The second personality type is the schizoid person, who is socially withdrawn rather than paranoid. They are perceived as eccentric, isolated, and lonely and seem unable to display any warm and tender feelings. Vaillant describes them as having a tendency to "engage in imaginary relationships," and they get little if any pleasure from interactions with others, including from sex. They seem bland and superficial and socially inept. They seem incapable of experiencing strong emotions such as anger and joy.

Schizoid persons do not usually lose the capacity to recognize reality, but they live in a world of excessive daydreaming and fantasy. Vaillant says that they deal with most threats, real or not, with "fantasized omnipotence or resignation." When exposed to more stress than they can tolerate, however, they may experience brief episodes of psychosis and even become delusional.

The schizotypal personality is closely related to the schizoid, but while the schizoid appears ordinary, the schizotypal person is strikingly odd and strange. Like schizoid people, they display social anxiety and acute discomfort with close relationships. Like paranoid people, they interpret interpersonal external events as having personal meaning, but they do not view these events with suspiciousness or hostility. Instead, they think magically, having many superstitions and beliefs in paranormal phenomena. They can believe they have magical control over others or the power to read people's minds. They do not exhibit formal thought disorders or incoherence, but their speech is often idiosyncratic, digressive, or vague.

According to R. D. Laing, schizotypal people are *ontologically insecure*—insecure in their very being. They "cannot take the realness, aliveness, autonomy, and the identity of [themselves] and others for granted." Laing calls them "unembodied," detached from their own bodies. In order to protect their fragile inner selves, these personalities develop a façade or *false self.* Unlike an ordinary person, "his false self does not serve as a vehicle for fulfillment or gratification of the self." Instead, the true person "may remain hungry and starved in a most primitive sense." The false self is a means of self-preservation that "arises in compliance with the intentions or expectations of the other, or with what are imagined to be other's intentions or expectations." Laing conceives of this false self as a product of intense anxiety. He gives the example of a young man who suddenly broke off an argument saying, "I can't go on. You are arguing in order to have the pleasure of triumphing over me. At best you win an argument. At worst you lose an argument. I am arguing to preserve my existence."[88]

Paranoid, schizoid, and schizotypal personalities are all odd and eccentric people who find it difficult or impossible to form emotional bonds with other people. A fourth personality type, with perhaps more reality impairments than the others, is called the *borderline personality.* Borderline persons seem the polar opposite of the other three. Their interpersonal relationships are not cold and distant, but intense, unstable, and extreme. Psychologist Jerold Kreisman described such people as having a "weak sense of identity, fear of abandonment, rapid mood swings, impulsive self-destructiveness and violent outbursts."[89]

According to Vaillant, borderline personality has frequently been described in the psychiatric literature as occupying the borderland between neurosis and psychosis. In 1941, psychoanalyst Gregory Zilboorg called them *ambulatory schizophrenics;* in 1942 Helen Deutsch described them as *as-if people* because their emotional being seemed parasitic on the feelings of other people; and in 1949, psychiatrists Paul Hoch and Philip Polatin coined the term *pseudoneurotic schizophrenia.* Similar references to an almost-schizophrenic type continued up until the 1970s, when psychiatrist Otto Kernberg redefined the concept to *borderline personality organization* to highlight the same condition as a personality defect.

Whatever term is used, the pattern of behavior, thought, and emotion exhibits serious distortions of reality. Borderline personalities see others as either all good or all bad, as people to become dependent on or as hateful figures who are threatening them with abandonment. They vacillate between extremes and often act with anger and violence toward the very people they are closest to. Borderline personalities often cut themselves and make multiple suicidal gestures, and they behave in other dangerous and self-damaging ways, like having unprotected and indiscriminate sex, binge eating, reckless driving, and substance abuse. They also display huge and rapid mood swings (called *affective instability*) with periods of intense misery, irritability, or anxiety.

I Want My Dad

Joni was a tall thin young woman who was involuntarily hospitalized after taking a handful of pills and leaving a suicide note saying she was constantly worried and paranoid. Her reason was that her ex-boyfriend had made threats against her and her current boyfriend. She had been psychiatrically hospitalized once before for an intentional overdose, and she had also been admitted to a crisis-stabilization program twice because she was using unprescribed anxiety pills for panic attacks.

Joni had a dysfunctional life history. She had a history of opioid dependence and had been in an inpatient substance-abuse program three years before. She had been in two long-term relationships with drug-abusing men, whom she described as abusive and controlling. She told the hospital that she was "scared of everything" and that she had been depressed for a long time. She said she had been having back pain ever since she had a stillborn baby a few years ago and was using narcotics to treat her pain. The hospital diagnoses were mood disorder, not otherwise specified; opioid dependence; and posttraumatic stress disorder.

I evaluated her five days after her admission. She walked down the hall very slowly and came in wrapped in a blanket, sobbing and acting terrified. When I tried to explain why I was there, she acted perplexed and repeatedly said, "I want my dad on the phone. I don't understand." She did tell me she had been hospitalized "because I took a bunch of pills." She would not tell me any more, and she only said, "I want to go to a nursing home."

In my view, Joni was best described as a borderline personality. She had a chronically distorted picture of reality, but no evidence of hallucinations, delusions, or thought disorganization. She had a history of highly dysfunctional relationships, with dependence on abusive men. She was a drug abuser, made suicidal gestures, and was emotionally volatile. When I saw her, she was dramatically distraught and fearful and acting in a regressed (infantile) manner.

Further down the dimension of reality distortion is a type called *delusional disorder*. As the name implies, this kind of person exhibits prominent delusions of one or more of the kinds described earlier. What distinguishes these people from those with more dysfunctional reality perception is that their beliefs are implausible, but not bizarre. These are things that could possibly happen, but no amount of evidence can convince such people they did not happen. Delusional people may appear quite ordinary when they are not talking about or acting on their fixed beliefs. When they cannot control themselves is when they come into conflict with family, employees, or the law.

At the severe end of the reality-dysfunction dimension we come to those people labeled schizophrenic. As we have been discussing, psychiatry has not been able to settle on whether there are many schizophrenias or just one, with different patients showing different mixes of symptoms at different times. A number of distinctions used to be made between different forms of schizophrenia, but they seem to have gone by the wayside. One of these was called the "process" versus "reactive" distinction. The term *process schizophrenia* was used to describe a slow march of deterioration, beginning in the teen years and ending in a high degree of incapacity. *Reactive schizophrenia* meant a more sudden and generally later onset and a more variable course. A second distinction was "paranoid" versus "non-paranoid," with the paranoid having a better prognosis than those who were not. I continue to believe there is some utility in these distinctions, because they help us place different types along the reality-dysfunction dimension.

The Amazing Mr. Weiner

Mr. H. had been psychiatrically hospitalized many times over the previous thirty years, and when he was not in the hospital, he lived in group homes. I evaluated him twice, three years apart, to help the court determine whether he required involuntary hospitalization. When I saw him the first time, he had become agitated and extremely paranoid and was reported to have threatened to kill staff. What appeared to have set him off was that he learned that the group home where he had been living comfortably and peacefully would be closing. When I saw him the second time, in 2012, he had again been taken from his group home after becoming threatening.

He came to the interview walking briskly. He carried a cane, but he seemed to use it merely for effect, because he did not rely on it as he walked. He was neatly dressed, in a sports jacket and presented himself like a man of importance. He immediately asked me if I had any medical credentials and whether I had read all his records (all nine volumes of them). When I said no, he demanded, "Why is it you are coming here without knowing what the argument is?" I began thinking that this was unreasonable, but not bizarre.

He then said, "You know what the issue here is. I am pregnant, and a political opponent wants to end it. I am Sen. Charles Weiner of New York. The name has changed several times." There was a real representative Weiner from New York who was forced to resign after sexting pictures of his penis to a woman.

I have made it seem as if designating an individual by disorder type and where he or she sits on a particular dimension is a straightforward process. It is not, as reflected by the DSM system's use of many different terms like *almost-schizophrenia* or *schizophrenia-like pictures*. People with short or first-time episodes of reality disturbance may be labeled as having a *brief psychotic episode*, a *psychosis not otherwise specified* or even a *schizophreniform disorder* (a disorder "in the form of schizophrenia"). When there is a component resembling mania or depression, a person is as likely to said to have a *schizoaffective disorder* or *bipolar disorder as schizophrenia*. The amazing Mr. Weiner was diagnosed as *paranoid schizophrenic* in some hospital records and as *bipolar, manic* in others.

Biology of Reality

There is a growing body of research suggesting that various kinds of insults to the brain can increase a person's vulnerability to severe reality dysfunction. Although most of these studies use the term *schizophrenia* to describe their results, they are really only referring to the observed characteristics we discussed above, not a definable disease process. Nonetheless, these insults are intriguing hints as to the kind of things that can disrupt our brain functioning.

Many older studies have shown a heritability component to who gets labeled schizophrenic. Family studies reviewed in 1990 showed that if the parent was diagnosed schizophrenic, offspring had a 12 percent chance of having the same diagnosis, as compared to 1 percent of the general population. Similarly, if an individual is labeled schizophrenic, 8 percent of his or her siblings and 5 percent of the parents are so labeled.[90] That risk, though, is not specific to schizophrenia, but to reality misperception in general. Another study showed that family members also had an increased rate of being described as having schizotypal or paranoid personality disorder or schizoaffective disorder, but not other kinds of mental disorders.[91]

One particularly clever study that tried to parse out the influence of family genetics versus family environment was done by a team led by Finnish psychiatrist Pekka Tienari.[92] Finland has a national database of adoptees. Tienari started by identifying a group of adoptees whose biological mothers were described as schizophrenic and a comparison group of adoptees whose mothers were not. His team then did extensive interviews of the adoptive families and classified their patterns of interaction as healthy or disturbed. They wanted to know if disturbed families increased risk for their adoptive children and if healthy families helped protect them from schizophrenia? What they found was that the children who came from schizophrenic mothers had a higher risk of schizophrenia or other forms of reality dysfunction than the children of non-schizophrenic mothers, but only if they were raised in disturbed families. Adoptive children's outcomes were no different if they were raised in healthy families, no matter what kind of mother they were born to. The conclusion, again, is that genetics may raise the susceptibility to reality disturbance, but it does not cause it.

More recent studies have more directly investigated the relationship between reality dysfunction and genetics. In one such study, professor of psychiatry and behavioral sciences Wendy Kates and her team found a group of people who had an abnormality called a *deletion* in a small section of chromosome 22.[93] This deletion causes the condition *velocardiofacial syndrome*, involving defects in the structure of the heart and face. About 32 percent of patients with this deletion go on to be diagnosed with schizophrenia or a related psychosis. Kates performed MRI scans on the brains of adolescents with this syndrome and found that there were progressive deficits in the volume of the temporal cortex.

Another study showed a connection between the brain and the later diagnosis of schizophrenia. Professor Andrew McIntosh and his team studied a group of young people who had family members who had been diagnosed with schizophrenia. Over a ten-year period, McIntosh examined his participants with psychiatric evaluations and brain MRIs. He found that there was a correlation between those in the group who were later assessed as schizophrenic and the progressive reduction in the size of their frontal lobes.[94] Studies like these show that there is a relationship between genetics, the brain, and the development of psychosis, but they are far from showing a direct biological cause.

And genetics is not the only factor. Both prenatal maternal viral and bacterial infections and childhood viral encephalitis have been shown to be risk factors for various psychotic disorders. HIV infections and infectious hepatitis have also been associated with the diagnosis of schizophrenia. But there is one result that is especially surprising. Psychiatrist Brian Miller and his team found a strong association between urinary tract infections and acute psychosis.[95] Specifically, 35 percent of patients admitted to a hospital and diagnosed with acute schizophrenia had urinary tract infections, twenty-nine times more than in control groups, including stable outpatients diagnosed with schizophrenia. The implication is that even something as seemingly benign as a urinary tract infection can disrupt brain functioning in a vulnerable person.

What are we to make of all this? Schizophrenia, especially in its acute form, is primarily a breakdown in the coherence of self. Self is a product of executive systems of the frontal lobes, so events that disrupt the functioning of the frontal lobes may lead to a disorganization of self. There is evidence supporting the connection between reduced frontal lobe activity and schizophrenia. Severely reduced frontal lobe activity *(hypofrontality)* has been demonstrated in brain imaging studies of people diagnosed as schizophrenic.[96] This is supported by neuropsychological test data. Schizophrenic patients do particularly poorly on problem-solving tasks designed to assess frontal-lobe functioning.[97]

Just as humans vary in myriad other aspects of our being, we vary in our frontal-lobe functioning. Our ability to create a robust self and, with it, our ability to separate self from nonself is variable. We should expect that people's grasp of consensual reality differs among us. This ability has taken on increasing importance as we cope with an increasingly complex and demanding social world.

There is more than genetics and biological injury to consider in understanding frontal-lobe dysfunction. For one thing, executive systems in humans are extraordinarily complex and interdependent. Any system with this many interacting parts is vulnerable to disruption. It's a miracle that it works at all. Whether this disruption is biological or involves psychological factors based in memory and affective systems, the result can be a cata-strophic breakdown of self that we call *acute psychosis*. Alternatively, these psychological factors can produce the characteristic types of chronic reality dysfunction I have described earlier.

Psychology of Reality

In 1976, the Princeton psychological theorist Julian Jaynes produced a bril-liant and still controversial theory of consciousness.[98] In his conception, consciousness (what I have been calling *the self*) is an organization of brain functioning that is relatively recent in human history. Jaynes's hypothesis is that self-consciousness emerged in humankind less than three thousand years ago.

Jaynes amasses evidence that for tens of thousands of years, up through the period of the *Iliad* (and early books of the Bible, such as Amos) the human mind was bicameral, or two-chambered. One mind, mediated by the left cortical hemisphere, was all about the practical and routine. For the bicameral human, "the world would happen to him and his action would be an inextricable part of that happening with no consciousness whatever." Achilles of the *Iliad* seems more like an automaton than a feeling, thinking human being we can identify with. Most of his common actions were attrib-uted to *thumos*, "motion" or "agitation." A wild ocean has *thumos*. When a person stops moving (dies) the *thumos* leaves his limbs. The character Dio-medes says that Achilles will fight "when the *thumos* in his chest tells him to and a God rouses him."

The other chamber of the mind, mediated by the right hemisphere, was the god hemisphere. In Jaynes's conception, the right hemisphere stored the remembered voices of fathers, priests, and objectified gods. These voices were called up to guide the person when he was confronted by a decision. Jaynes wrote, "volition, planning, and initiative is organized with no consciousness whatever and is told to the individual in his familiar language, sometimes with the visual aura of a familiar friend or a father figure or single 'God,' or sometimes as a voice alone," and the individual obeyed.

Today we call these voices *hallucinations,* and they frighten us, but they were vital to the ancients. The bicameral mind system was extremely effective over the millennia, but started to break down under the enormous pressure of events in the second millennium BC. Geological catastrophes and wars left half the population as refugees, and civilizations collapsed. As people mixed, so did their gods. The voices of the conflicting gods weakened, and so did their authority. Literacy also weakened the auditory voice of the gods.

The resolution of the bicameral crisis was the creation of a new mind, a conscious one. The integration of the two minds was accomplished by creating a metaphor, an "analog I," representing the self and moving around in a metaphorical mind-space. Jaynes wrote, "subjective consciousness is an analog of what is called the real world. It is built up with a vocabulary or lexical field where terms are all metaphors or analogs of behavior in the physical world." This metaphorical world is what we now construe as our personal reality.

Under the Jaynesian hypothesis, there was not and could not have been the kind of madness we now call *schizophrenia* until the advent of modern consciousness. In order to distinguish between external reality and self, there must be a self, and self-consciousness has only been in existence about three thousand years. Before then, everyone did what we would call *hallucinating.* But without an "analog I" acting in a metaphorical mind-space, there could be no such thing as hallucinating. Jaynes saw schizophrenia as the erosion of the "analog I" and a frightening reversion to the bicameral mind state. Jaynes wrote, "with the loss of the analog I, its mind-space, and the ability to narratize, behavior is either responding to hallucinated directions or continues on by habit. The remnant of self feels like a commanded automaton, as if someone else were moving the body about."

Jaynes finds that in the literature and art of civilization prior to consciousness, there is no evidence of the idea of madness. There are references to idiocy, but not insanity. Even after consciousness arrived in ancient Greece, madness was seen in bicameral terms. He quotes Plato as calling madness "a divine gift and the source of the chiefest blessing granted to man." The earliest mention of insanity as an incapacitating condition occurs around 400 BC, when the self became a firmly established creation of Western culture.

Understood from a Jaynesian perspective, then, schizophrenia (or any other form of reality distortion) is not the acquisition of an illness, but the breakdown of a relatively recent way of conceptualizing a personal homunculus performing in mind-space. This is important only because everyone around such a person is operating as if they had an inner self. We are probably all vulnerable to a deterioration of self, either for brief or extended periods of time. Biological factors such as heredity and various kinds of disease may affect our resistance to such a breakdown, but in no sense are they the causes of it. The causes lie in the psychological realm of life events that we typically summarize as *stress*.

Given that we are variably vulnerable to the breakdown of unified consciousness, we can consider the kinds of psychological stressors that can lead to this breakdown. The psychiatrist Peter Breggin characterizes people who become psychotic as in the midst of a *psychospiritual crisis*, a "crisis of identity, values and perspectives." As Breggin puts it, "so-called schizophrenics, especially during their initial crisis, almost always are preoccupied with the meaning of life, God, love, and their own personal identity, often with cataclysmic implications about the end of the world or the disintegration of their own personalities." He terms this state *schizophrenic overwhelm*.[99]

The psychotic's position is similar to that of the mystic, in that they are both on a journey that is "mysterious and perilous," but the mad are failed prophets, according to Breggin. He quotes Arthur Dykeman, who wrote in 1971, "both the mystical and psychiatric states have arisen out of a situation in which the individual has struggled with a desperate problem, had come to a complete impasse and given up hope and abandoned the struggle in despair."

For vulnerable individuals, the origin of an integrated-reality breakdown may lie in traumatic past events, such as unresolved physical, sexual, or emotional abuse. People may suppress their feelings about these events until they break down. Breggin notes that mad people often express their outrage and anger at their parents in a "seemingly irrational fashion, as agents of the devil, the FBI or other feared authorities."

.Breggin also observes that schizophrenia is often diagnosed in the teenage years. This is a time of identity struggle and "unleashed passions" that can make a young person seem mentally unstable. Breggin believes that what may help teens through these years without being characterized as mentally ill is "the love, patience and tolerance of the adults who surround them."

Breggin sees a psychological vicious cycle in operation that drags susceptible youngsters into chronic despair and helplessness. Such children express their anguish and anger by attacking their parents in bizarre and outrageous ways, and the parents respond by rejecting any responsibility for the emotional suffering and by trying to "crush dissent" with psychiatric treatment.

Over time, the overwhelmed person suffers shame and humiliation and tries to strike back in anger and hatred. In Breggin's view, "many of the symptoms associated with so-called schizophrenia are blatant attempts to compensate for humiliations experienced while growing up." For instance, grandiose delusions may be a way to bolster self-esteem in the face of a profound sense of worthlessness. Paranoid delusions may be a way of striking back for earlier humiliations. Breggin concludes that "people undergoing psychospiritual crises express the most intense degrees of shame and humiliation I have ever witnessed."

My conclusion is that no matter what the source of stress, it is relatively easy for the executive function that normally creates a unity of self to disintegrate. With this breakdown comes the loss of reality perception, which can lead to what we see as the signs of psychosis. It would seem that people with warm and open families, people who live in societies more accepting of mental deviance, and those who receive treatment that helps them live through their crisis without suppressing it are all better able to reintegrate their personalities.

Emotional Trauma

There is a large body of evidence that early emotional trauma either leads to vulnerability to or directly causes reality dysfunction. Manfred Bleuler (son of Eugen Bleuler, who coined the term *schizophrenia*) performed a series of five studies with a total of 932 people who had been diagnosed with schizophrenia.[100] He found that they had suffered loss of a parent before the age of fifteen at a rate of 31 percent, which is much higher than for the general population. Childhood abuse is also very common among patients who are diagnosed schizophrenic. For instance, one study of adult outpatients found that 35 percent had suffered emotional abuse as a child, 42 percent physical neglect, and 73 percent emotional neglect.[101] A number of other studies have shown a significant association between childhood sexual abuse and incest and adult symptoms of hallucinations and delusions.[102]

. The role of family dynamics in the creation of reality dysfunction is extremely controversial and little emphasized today. But they are very important, and the scientific literature strongly supports Breggin's concept of psychospiritual overwhelm. While it is very painful for many families to confront, studies show there are specific family characteristics that are predictive of madness along the reality-dysfunction dimension.

An early model of maladaptive family communication in the genesis of schizophrenia came from the behavior therapy group of Gregory Bateson, Don Jackson, Jay Halley and John Weakland. In 1956, they described how conflicting family messages could make it impossible for family members to get clarity or respond effectively.[103] Their interest was not to blame anyone, but to focus attention on intergenerational patterns of family dysfunction. In a later article, Bateson and his colleagues wrote, "the group prefers an emphasis on circular systems of interpersonal relations to a more conventional emphasis upon the behavior of individuals alone or single sequences in the interaction."[104]

Over the years, there have been many studies showing the effects of what came to be called *communication deviance.* By 1992, psychologist David Miklowitz and coauthor had found twelve studies that showed significantly higher levels of communication deviance in the parents of people labeled schizophrenic than among people having other psychiatric diagnoses or considered normal.[105] More recently, Dr. M. Annet Nugter and her colleagues found communication deviance in 73 percent of families with schizophrenic patients.[106]

Correlational studies can bring us only so far in understanding the relationship between family dynamics and reality disturbance. What are needed are prospective studies—studies that first document the characteristics of families thought to be susceptible and then perform follow-up assessments at later times to judge the outcome.

A fifteen-year study that attempted this kind of analysis was called the UCLA Family Project.[107] The project began by assessing the parents of sixty-four adolescents who were troubled, but who had not shown any signs of psychosis at the start of the study. The study was primarily designed to assess a parental style it referred to as *expressed emotion* (EE), a euphemism representing three components of parental interactional styles. One component assessed was *hostility,* which was a global measure of expressed criticism and rejection. Another was *criticism,* negative comments toward what the child does, thinks, or feels. The third was *emotional over-involvement,* which assessed things like overprotectiveness, self-sacrifice, and intrusiveness. Families were rated as high EE or low EE.

Fifteen years later, the researchers examined the diagnoses that the children (who were now adults) had been given. Of the children of low EE parents, 6 percent were given diagnoses somewhere along the reality distortion dimension *(broad-spectrum schizophrenia),* while 0 percent exhibited neither signs typical of schizophrenia *(narrow-spectrum schizophrenia)* or a definite diagnosis of schizophrenia. On the contrary, if both parents were labeled high EE, 73 percent of the offspring had been diagnosed with broad-spectrum schizophrenia, 45 percent with narrow-spectrum schizophrenia and 36 percent were actually diagnosed as schizophrenic.

A number of other studies used the EE concept to assess the effect of dysfunctional parenting style on relapse rates for children who were hospitalized for schizophrenia.[108] Over a period of nine to twelve months, children of low EE parents were rehospitalized at a rate of 21 percent, but at a rate of 48 percent for those with high EE parents. After two years, the rates were 27 percent for low EE and 68 percent for high EE families.

The UCLA Family Project also looked at two additional measures of parental style and their effects on future reality disturbance: the *communication-deviance* measure (of conflicting family messages) and a measure called *affective style,* which has components of personal criticism, guilt induction, and intrusiveness. The results for these measures were very similar to the ones for EE. For instance, only 4 percent of the once-troubled teens were later diagnosed with a schizophrenic-spectrum disorder if they were from benign affective-style families, compared to 56 percent from negative affective-style families.[109]

Taken as a whole, all of these studies lead to a very clear conclusion. Early life events, either episodic like trauma or continuous like negative family patterns, are the root cause of reality dysfunction. When we use a label like *schizophrenia,* we are categorizing the results of a psychological disruption, not a straightforward biological disease. Significant psychological stressors break down the sense of self or "analog I" and the distinction between the outside and subjective worlds that we ordinarily, so easily, take for granted.

Social Context

Madness exists in a social context, and the expression of reality impairment is greatly affected by the responses of family, institutions, and the community in general. Until maladaptive behaviors become so ingrained that they cannot be changed, the level of dysfunction displayed can be altered by social forces. When people are undervalued or regarded as outcasts or as less than complete human beings, it should not be surprising when they think and behave in an incompetent and socially inappropriate manner. Add treatment that is coercive, unwanted, and unpleasant, and people act increasingly withdrawn, helpless, or enraged. On the other hand, when even seriously impaired people are valued and are expected to act responsibly (within the limit of their abilities) and to fit into a social structure, it is amazing how well they can do.

Evidence that the social rehabilitation of the mad can work can first be found in the nineteenth-century moral therapy movement (discussed in chapter 2). The treatment of the mad was cruel and brutal by contemporary standards until the Philadelphia Quakers opened the first institution based on the creed that personal transformation was possible for all people. Robert Whitaker described the guiding principles and history of the moral therapy movement in his book *Mad in America.*[110]

The lesson to be learned from the moral therapy movement is that madness is not a biological illness that has to be suppressed by medical means. Arranging a social environment conducive to sane behavior made a huge difference in the functioning of people who might be seen as hopelessly psychotic today. The drawbacks were that the process took a great deal of time, required extensive resources, and cut the medical profession out of the loop. As the moral asylums filled and the hospital psychiatrists asserted their power, this grand experiment met its end.

Another way to understand the social context of reality dysfunction comes from cross-cultural studies of people diagnosed with schizophrenia. In 1992, the World Health Organization conducted such a study in twelve sites around the world.[111] They concluded that the incidence rate for schizophrenia did not vary (although that interpretation was suspect, because there were statistically significant differences using a broad definition of schizophrenia). But there were major differences in the course and outcome of the disorder. In underdeveloped countries, 37 percent of patients had only a single episode and only 16 percent showed impairments of social functioning throughout the follow-up period. In contrast, in industrialized countries, only 16 percent had a single episode, and 42 percent had impaired social functioning. English psychologist Richard Bentall concludes that "the evidence that madness is more benign outside the industrialized world is quite compelling."[112]

A more recent study on cultural differences in the experience of schizophrenia was done by anthropologist Tonya Luhrmann and colleagues.[113] They looked at how people diagnosed as schizophrenic evaluated the voices they heard (auditory hallucinations) in different cultures. The subjects came from San Mateo, California; Accra, Ghana; and Chennai, India. The voices heard were broadly similar in most characteristics, including both good and bad voices and religious or sexual contents. But there was a large cultural difference. Most of the African and Indian subjects found hearing these voices to be mostly positive experiences, but not one of the Americans did. The U.S. subjects mostly perceived their voices as "violent and hateful and evidence of a sick condition." The others, particularly the Indians, often felt they were being spoken to by family members or elders, and many times the voices were seen as playful or entertaining. Most of the Americans did not identify who was talking to them and usually perceived them as threatening.

Luhrmann's explanation highlights the cultural differences between different peoples. In the West, people tend to define themselves as separate individuals, and the voices are "an intrusion and a threat to one's private world." In other cultures, "people imagine the mind and self as interwoven with others and defined by relationships." Those people "were more comfortable interpreting their voices as relationships and not as the sign of a violated mind."

What these data suggest is that while a breakdown in reality perception occurs in all cultures, how well a psychotic person fares is very much dependent on the social factors of the culture.

6

Depression and Mood Dysfunction

From a neuropsychological perspective, our brains have a number of very important emotional mechanisms that motivate and guide our actions, thoughts, and feelings. As Antonio Damasio describes them, "emotions are part of the bioregulatory devices with which we come equipped to survive."[114] They are a group of rapid-reaction mechanisms and operate below the level of consciousness to quickly appraise a situation and react to it.

Mood is built from sustained emotions and is a defining characteristic of the human experience. We see displays of emotion in other animals, but it is harder to find evidence of mood. Recently, there have been observations of grief in other mammals, such as apes, porpoises, and elephants, usually seen in the interaction between a mother and a dead infant. Otherwise, there does not appear to be the type of sustained emotional state we call *mood* in other animals. Perhaps this is because the sort of narrative memory that is the hallmark of a conscious self is a human innovation. It is the self that creates the feelings that characterize mood.

As important as mood is to our psychological well-being, it is difficult to define adequately. Mood is based in emotion but is longer-lasting, less specific, and less closely tied to any specific event. Emotions are a direct response to something, but mood is more of a color. Moods generally have a positive or negative valence that affects how we interpret the world around us and react to it.

In general, our moods tend to follow our appraisal of the quality of our lives at any given time. When our mood is positive, we usually say we are happy, and we respond to the world with energy and optimism. When we are down, we are sad, unmotivated, and pessimistic. We usually perceive and act on things in a manner congruent with our current mood. For instance, people in a down mood tend to look for the negative and behave accordingly. Conversely, happy people tend to see the world positively and act that way.

Mood is most functionally associated with our social circumstances. You are sad when someone close to you dies or you lose your job, and you are elated and energized when engaged in something fun or when someone you really like returns your interest. We are constantly appraising our social environment and our place in it. Based in our desires and past experiences, we have expectations about what will or should happen in that environment. We make emotional investments in some parts of it, less so in others. How all this plays out in our lives and our fantasies strongly affects our mood.

For most of us, mood varies frequently, but within fairly narrow limits. There are some people, however, whose moods are often or mostly very low, and we call them *depressed*. People who have periods of sustained elation or excitement are called *manic*. Others exhibit swings of extreme moods, with both sustained highs and lows, whom we describe as *bipolar*.

So, we have a dimension. At one end there are people who are generally calm and composed. When they get sad or happy, it never seems extreme or prolonged. People further down the dimension of dysfunction are more emotionally unstable, and their emotions seem less related to their circumstances. At the bottom are people who become so high or so low that they can't function in the world of reality, and they may be described as *psychotic*.

We shouldn't think that a negative mood is always damaging. There is a theory called the Negative State Relief Model, which suggests that people have a desire to relieve negative moods through mood-elevating actions, such as helping or altruism.[115] Altruism repairs mood both by the positive reward of gratitude and by internalized self-gratification. A negative mood, then, can be socially useful when it leads to helping others in order to reduce our own bad feelings.

Melancholia and Depression

The term *depression* is a renaming of the ancient term *melancholia*. The Greek physician Hippocrates described *melancholia* as resulting from imbalances of four vital forces (or humors): blood (which was the liquor of vitality), choler (which was bile or gastric juices), phlegm (which included sweat and tears) and melancholy or black bile (which was invisible, but darkened other bodily fluids). Melancholia was the accumulation of black bile in the *hypochondrium* (upper abdomen). It was "seen as part of a developing picture of a chronic form of insanity without fever that was commonly focused on a fixed obsession."[116]

Until the early nineteenth century, melancholia was not a mood but a condition characterized by an "intensity of idea" or a fixed delusion.[117] The term *melancholia* was used to describe "a rag-bag of insanity states whose only common denominator was the presence of few (as opposed to many) delusions." By mid-century, it came to mean something like low mood and inhibition. *Depression,* as applied to psychiatry, is a late nineteenth-century term that grew out of a transformation of *melancholia*. Why melancholia was renamed *depression* is an interesting story.

Early in the nineteenth century, people with heart disease were described as having a depression of cardiac functioning. As an analogy, people who suffered low spirits as a result of any disease were characterized as having mental depression. Physicians began to prefer the term *depression* to *melancholia*, because it seemed more physiological. By century's end, *melancholia* was defined as "a state of mental depression in which misery is unreasonable."[118] The final step was to drop the word *mental,* and the analogy became the thing. *Cardiac depression* had been transformed into a *depressive mood state*.

Depression was not considered a major psychiatric concern, however, until well into the second half of the twentieth century. Prior to that, depression was considered infrequent, and occurring in only two types of conditions. One was part of Kraepelin's original conception of manic-depressive psychosis. The other was a severe depression of old age called *involutional melancholia*.[119]

Kraepelin divided manic-depressive insanity into three subcategories, one of which was called *depression-only*—what is now called *major depression*. In 1921, Kraepelin concluded that sufferers of manic-depressive psychosis had generally positive outcomes: "Usually all morbid manifestations completely disappear, but where that is exceptionally not the case, only a slight, peculiar psychic weakness develops."[120]

Kraepelin studied the outcomes of 450 depressed-only patients who had been psychotic enough to be kept in his psychiatric hospital to recuperate. He reported that 60 percent of them had only a single episode of depression and only 13 percent had three or more such episodes. This was without any treatment other than being in an institution.

Hospitalization for depression remained relatively infrequent, and prospects for full recovery were considered very good even up to the 1970s. In 1964, Jonathan Cole of NIMH wrote, "depression is, on the whole, one of the psychiatric conditions with the best prognosis for eventual recovery with or without treatment. Most depressions are self-limited."[121] As late as 1974, Dean Schuyler, the coordinator of NIMH's Depression Section, wrote that most depressive episodes "will run their course and terminate with virtually complete recovery without specific intervention."[122]

However, this limited conception of depression began to change with the psychopharmacological revolution and the advent of drugs called *antidepressants*. After the success of Thorazine (chlorpromazine), drug companies searched for a new psychiatric miracle drug and a new disease to treat. Depression became a disease for them to promote, and it quickly increased in popularity as a diagnosis. A 1962 ad by Pfizer touted its new antidepressant as a "specific treatment for depressive illness," and Roche described its new drug as a "potent anti-depressant."[123]

A new disease and a lucrative drug treatment were born, and psychiatry supported and defined a new family of depressive disorders. One classic British textbook of psychiatry did not introduce the new conception of depression as a specific category of psychiatric illness until its ninth edition, in 1962.[124] From that time to this, the scope of depression expanded, along with the number of people who suffered from it. In 2008, a Johns Hopkins university study reported that fifteen million American adults suffered from depression, and of those, 58 percent were "severely impaired."[125] Much of the increase is due to the expansion of the range of conditions we call *depression*.

Today the word *depression* is used so ambiguously that almost all of us have experienced it in one form or another. *Depression* has become as difficult to define as *pornography*. Is it what people say about what they feel or how they behave? Does it describe any sort of misery or is it more specific than that? Is it what people feel when they suffer the consequences of bad decisions? *Depression* is used so generally that it has lost all specific meaning. At times, I think the term should be left to represent a hole in the ground or an economic downturn and discarded from mental health.

The distinction I believe we must make is between suffering from depression and having a miserable life. We do not help a person who acts self-destructively or who repeatedly makes poor decisions in life by calling him or her *depressed*. Such people need to learn to evaluate the consequences of their actions, not process their losses.

The Business Tycoon

Mr. W was the picture of a successful and influential man. He was an Ivy League MBA with a financial-advising practice. He was respected in the community and had a wife, grown children, and grandchildren. Such a man does not seek out a psychologist unless he has a secret, and indeed, Mr. W did.

He initially told me that his wife was upset and concerned because of his financial troubles. He had undertaken a large business venture involving building subsidized housing, and it wasn't working out well. He was having difficulty making his payments. After a couple of sessions, he admitted that he had borrowed a good deal of money from his mother-in-law to maintain his ventures. Unfortunately, since he managed her money, she knew nothing about it. His wife had learned what he was doing, and she was furious. Then he told me that he had been robbing Peter to pay Paul. Unfortunately, Peter was the U.S. government, and Mr. W expected to be indicted.

Over the course of several months, I tried to convince him to bring all the facts out on the table and have a frank discussion with his wife, but he never was willing or able to do that. He kept digging his hole deeper. Perhaps it was pride or magical thinking, but he never would talk to his wife, his grown children, or the authorities. Once his wife joined us for a session and expressed her intense shock and anger, but still Mr. W would not come completely clean. His son called me, sobbing, because of what he feared would happen to his father, but there was little help I could give at that point. I remember thinking that this cascade of bad decisions and secrecy had ruined his life.

A session or two later, Mr. W came in and told me he had been to see a psychiatrist, who told him he was depressed and prescribed an antidepressant. He was going to continue seeing the psychiatrist. As I said goodbye and wished him good luck, I remember thinking, *Of course you're depressed. Should you be happy? Perhaps if you had had the courage to deal with these issues six months ago, you would not be in the position you are in now. You will soon be going to prison. How are antidepressants going to undo any of that?*

A few months later I read in the papers that Mr. W had been indicted and later that he was on his way to a federal penitentiary.

In order to preserve the term *depression*, we need to give it a specific psychological meaning, and that is to equate depression with grief. There is really no way to separate the two.

Is Depression Another Name for Bereavement?

In 1972, a group of research psychiatrists led by John Feighner formulated a set of descriptive "symptoms" for diagnosing depression.[126] They argued that if psychiatry used these as objective criteria to evaluate patients, it could more reliably diagnose major depressive disorder. Depression was characterized by complaints of persistently low mood, inability to enjoy activities that were usually enjoyable, difficulty falling and staying asleep, daytime fatigue, inability to concentrate or make decisions, and poor appetite.

The authors of DSM-III adopted the Feighner criteria (as they came to be called), but they had a dilemma. The criteria for depression applied equally well to people who had recently lost a spouse. In a groundbreaking study, Paula Clayton and colleagues had evaluated more than two hundred widows and widowers.[127] About 35 percent of them met all the criteria for clinical depression a month after the death of a spouse, and a third of those continued to be depressed after a year. For such people, depression and bereavement were indistinguishable. Grief, however, is recognized as a normal response to loss, and the DSM did not wish to pathologize it.

The resolution to this paradox was a political solution, not a scientific one. The authors of DSM-III concluded that "a full depressive syndrome is a normal reaction to the death of a loved one," but it is not depression.[128] As a compromise, they decided that uncomplicated bereavement could last for two months. After two months, it could morph into major depression. This was known as the *bereavement exclusion.*

Meanwhile, evidence mounted that people's reactions to other major life stressors, such as the loss of a job, often triggered the same psychological reaction as bereavement. Professor of social work Jerome Wakefield and colleagues argued that calling these people *depressed* resulted in "the classification of psychiatrically normal people as mentally disordered."[129] Instead, they posited that there were two categories of bereavement: complicated and uncomplicated. Uncomplicated bereavement was not pathological, because it lacked characteristics such as feeling worthless, suicidal thoughts, major impairment in functioning, and prolonged duration. In their opinion, people with complicated bereavement showed more severe pathology. Other researchers challenged this as an artificial distinction about the way people responded to loss.

The latest psychiatric manual continues to make a distinction between "responses to significant loss" and depression. It suggests that a person can suffer both grief and clinical depression at the same time and should be carefully evaluated for the latter. They offer no specific advice on how to do this other than to "exercise clinical judgment based on the individual's history and the cultural norms for the expression of distress in the context of loss."[130]

There is an additional problem when one tries to separate people responding to loss and depression. Psychiatrists Ronald Pies and Sidney Zisook point out that "fewer than 5 percent of all cases lacked an environmental trigger" for depression.[131] They cite studies showing there really are no differences in people diagnosed with major depression, stress-related depression, and depression with no known cause.

What can we conclude from this? Depression is the same as bereavement. It does not matter whether a clinician can identify a cause or not; bereavement is a normal human response to loss as perceived by the patient. It may be mild or severe, brief or prolonged, intermittent or sustained; all these variations exist on a continuous dimension. The box below tells the story of a woman who suffered from a terrible and debilitating mood state. Should we call it grief or call it depression?

An Unspeakable Tragedy

Over Christmas vacation in 2004, University of London economics professor Sonali Deraniyagala returned to her native Sri Lanka with her husband, Steve, and their two sons, aged seven and five. Joined by her parents, they went to a favorite hotel on the beach of Yala National Park. Suddenly, she saw a wave approaching. It was the Boxing Day tsunami.

Gathering up her family, but not even pausing to alert her parents, she raced to a waiting jeep. The jeep drove fast, but it was too late, and the jeep was overturned. Sonali found herself in the water, dragged and tossed and powerless against the massive waves. She eventually saved herself by grabbing a tree limb and was rescued, but she never saw any of her family alive again.

Initially, she was paralyzed by dread and despair and could not allow herself hope. Someone drove her back to her extended family in Colombo, the capital city. She later recalled thinking, "In a few hours it will be light. It will be tomorrow. I don't want it to be tomorrow. I was terrified that tomorrow the truth would start."[132] At her aunt's home, the next day, a doctor was called, because Sonali had a raging infection in her sinuses. Her only thought was, "A bit pointless ... I will kill myself soon." When she learned that the bodies of her parents and one son had been found, she barely reacted, thinking, "I'll wait until all the bodies are found.... Then I will kill myself."

She existed in a stupor and said she was horrified by anything in the world that her family would have enjoyed. "All [the things] that they were missing, I desperately shut out [of my own life]. I was terrified of everything because everything was from that [previous] life." Over the next six months, she could not even engage in the simplest activities like turning on a shower. She was so suicidal, her family never left her alone. She stabbed herself with a butter knife, smashed her head on a sharp corner, and stubbed cigarettes out on her hands. She would not willingly leave her bed except to go to the bathroom and brush her teeth every few hours. Months later, she searched the internet for ways to kill herself.

People attempted to get her to drink a glass of wine or a brandy to relax her. She refused, because, as she later wrote, "I had to be vigilant. What if, even for a single moment, I thought nothing has changed, that no one is dead?" Then, suddenly, she drank half a bottle of vodka and began drinking all the alcohol she could get her hands on. "Each night I hoped to die from my frenzied drinking. And it diluted my terror of getting to sleep." She began to hallucinate and "watched plump black worms crawl out from the air conditioner and slide down the wall." She told herself that she should be crazy: "My world gone in an instant, I need to be insane." She then began searching the internet "for images of the wave. Of scenes of destruction. Of dead bodies, mortuaries, mass graves. The more horrifying the better."

She existed in this state for six months or more. If we didn't know what had happened to her, we would say that Sonali was psychotically depressed. We would not have seen any difference in her state and the condition of people labeled with major depression. Would she have been psychiatrically hospitalized and given a cocktail of antidepressants and antipsychotics?

Sonali was not psychiatrically treated. Her only medications were alcohol and the sleeping pills, which were given to her and carefully rationed. Yet, slowly over the course of eight years and counting, Sonali made painful adjustments. Each time she allowed new exposures to remind herself of her lost family, it was a wrenching and terrifying experience. Gradually, she allowed the memories of each of her lost loved ones to return. Her misery and fear waxed and waned, but the pain gradually receded. She returned to academic life and traveled the world. It was seven years after the tragedy before she could even tell a kind stranger she met that she had been married and that her husband was dead.

There is one important reason for labeling the sense of loss as *depression* rather than *grief.* Depression pays and grief doesn't. As psychotherapist Gary Greenberg explains in describing one of his clients, "She could get the benefit of therapy without a diagnosis, but it is not clear that her psychiatrist and I could get our benefits that way."[133]

It does not matter if there is any scientific justification for the term. Nor does it matter that the label could refer to any presentation the clinician wishes to use it for. As long as it's acceptable to the patient and the insurance company—and the culture believes in it—depression will remain a psychiatric truth. It does not matter how hard DSM works to define *depression* as pathology. Just put a medical gloss on the term, and we will use it.

The Meaning of Loss

We all experience many losses throughout our lives. Some of those losses are obvious to the individual and to society in general. Many others are more subtle and go unrecognized or are discounted. As psychotherapists Carolyn Walter and Judith McCoyd point out, even the normal changes we all go through as we mature are forms of loss.[134] In a way, any forward movement in life entails loss, even when we don't recognize it as such. Walter and McCoyd suggest that these natural processes are "a unique form of loss in which one is expected to delight in the growth and ignore the loss aspect."

Any form of loss is destabilizing and uncomfortable, but, as Walter and McCoyd note, it "also promotes self-reflection and growth, particularly when the mourner's experience is validated and supported." Losses are beneficial to us when they give new meaning to our lives, which occurs when we are able to properly grieve them. Freud understood that grief could turn psychotic if the mourner turns away from reality and cannot accept it.[135] In his terms, the mourner needs time to withdraw from the lost object and reattach to new ones.

Clinical psychology professor Robert Neimeyer places grief in the context of our sense of self.[136] We order and make sense of our lives by the story we create about ourselves. "Significant loss—whether of cherished persons, places, projects or possessions—presents a challenge to one's sense of narrative coherence as well as sense of identity." Grieving people must tell and retell their stories of loss as they attempt to assimilate the meaning of the loss "into the overarching story of their lives." The same principle holds true for depression. Sufferers must make sense of their loss and find ways to make it meaningful, without letting depression define them.

When the full expression of loss is "policed," that is, it is not "recognized, validated and supported by the social world of the mourner," the result is what professor of gerontology Kenneth Doka describes as "disenfranchised grief."[137] Doka suggests that disenfranchised grief often occurs in five types of situations: (1) the loss occurs in a relationship that is not recognized as legitimate, such as a gay, lesbian, or extramarital relationship; (2) the loss is not recognized by social norms or is deemed unworthy of sympathy, such as abortion or the loss of a pet; (3) the mourner is not seen as able to grieve, such as a young child, the very old, or the developmentally disabled; (4) when a loss causes stigma or embarrassment, such as losses involving things that could be deemed to be moral failures, such as AIDS, alcoholism, or criminal activity; and (5) where the grief is not expressed in socially sanctioned ways, such as anger or acting out. These sorts of grievers are often excluded from social support and sympathy—sometimes their losses are not even recognized—and instead they often suffer in isolation or rejection. As a consequence, they may not be able to move through the grieving process in an adaptive way and, instead, be depressed.

Walker and McCoyd reviewed the types of maturational losses that frequently result in disenfranchised grief. Many of these losses are unrecognized or not seen as requiring any special support, but they are still experienced as loss. They are ignored or undervalued by significant others and society. Among such losses they mention are: (1) loss of the unconditional caregiving received in infancy to the increased expectations faced by the toddler; (2) the transition from home to the more judgmental school environment; (3) the change from dependence on the family for support in the juvenile to the self-reliance of an adult; (4) the loss of romantic relationships in young love; (5) the multiple losses involved when a couple has a child, especially the losses the couple's relationship endures; (6) the similarly unrecognized losses that occur with a miscarriage; (7) loss of employment, accompanied by feelings of shame and self-doubt; (8) midlife loss of the dreams of early adulthood, which is a blow to self-esteem; and (9) later life losses of a spouse or adult child. To these, I would add (10) retirement and the loss of a sense of purpose, along with the diminished capacities of later life. All of these may be seen as disenfranchised losses, which can lead to the kind of grief response we know as *depression.*

Psychiatrist Colin Murray Parkes summarizes the grieving process with an analogy.[138] "On the whole, grief resembles a physical injury more closely than any type of illness. The loss may be spoken of as a 'blow.' As in the case of a physical injury, the wound gradually heals, at least it usually does. But occasionally complications set in, healing is delayed, or a further injury reopens a healing wound. Sometimes, it seems, the outcome may be fatal."

Biology and Depression

The search for a biological cause for depression began with the development of a new class of drugs, which became known as antidepressants. The first such drug was iproniazid, which began life as a medication for tuberculosis in the 1950s, but patients who took it seemed to become unusually cheerful. The psychiatrist Nathan Kline studied the mental effect of iproniazid and called it a "psychic energizer."

In the language of psychoanalysis, Kline wrote, "the plethora of id energy would make large amounts of energy easily available to the ego so that there would be more than enough energy available for all tasks. Such a situation would result in a sense of joyousness and optimism."[139] For a brief time, iproniazid enjoyed a surge of popularity, but it was withdrawn from the market when frightening side effects were revealed. Besides, iproniazid had a stimulating effect on most people, not just people who were depressed. It wasn't a specific cure a disease called *depression*.

The next step was to find drug that would relieve depression that was not a general stimulant. Opium was thought to be such a drug, because it appeared to energize some depressed people. This led Swiss psychiatrist Ronald Kuhn to look for a drug that was better than opium in alleviating depression. He turned to antihistamines, which, like opium, were sedating.[140] The schizophrenia drug Thorazine was an antihistamine and also appeared to help depressed people. In 1957, Kuhn announced that he had found a similar drug, which he called *imipramine* (Tofranil). According to Kuhn: "We had achieved a specific treatment of depressive states, not ideal, but already going far in that direction." Imipramine was considered the first true antidepressant.

How did imipramine work? At the time imipramine was discovered, there was a theory that the brain's emotional systems were influenced by a kind of transmitter substance known as an *amine*. Two of these amines were norepinephrine and serotonin. Research determined that imipramine increased the availability of these amines in the brain. This connection led to the biogenic amine theory of depression, which, simply put, says that depression is caused by a deficiency of norepinephrine and serotonin in the brain—a chemical imbalance. This was a very attractive theory for psychiatry because, as Peter Kramer said it, "It made depression look like illnesses whose causes were well known."[141] Depression could now be said to be similar to diabetes (caused by a lack of insulin) or hypothyroidism (caused by low levels of thyroid hormones).

A major problem with this theory was that the effects of imipramine on the brain were wide-ranging. It affected not only amines but many other brain chemicals as well. It was nonspecific. And there were other problems. The drug reserpine, which lowers blood pressure, also depletes the brain of amines and should cause depression in people taking it. It rarely does. Furthermore, while imipramine acts to increase the action of amines very quickly, it takes weeks for a patient to report feeling less depressed. Depletion of amines could not be the whole story.

Many new antidepressants based on the imipramine model were developed over the next thirty years, in particular, a family of drugs called *tricyclic antidepressants*. Nothing really changed in the brain picture, though, until the development of Prozac. In the 1970s, researchers found that the chemical called *fluoxetine* (Prozac) specifically blocked the uptake of serotonin in the brain's synapses. This meant that when serotonin was released in the brain, it stayed around and could have a positive effect for a much longer time than it would naturally.

In 1987 Prozac was brought to market as an antidepressant by Eli Lilly. It was the first of a class of drugs called *selective serotonin reuptake inhibitors* (SSRIs). It did not seem to do much for people who were seriously depressed, but it did brighten the mood of people who were unhappy. The amine theory of depression could now be refined as the low serotonin theory.

The question of whether low serotonin is the cause of depression hinged on whether patients diagnosed with depression actually have less serotonin in their brains than other people. The early tests of this were not encouraging. These tests measured the metabolites that resulted from the breakdown of serotonin in the cerebrospinal fluid. Depressed people should have less of them. The results were ambiguous. Some had less, but some had more than normal.

A 1984 study tested the hypothesis that depressed people who had low levels of serotonin would respond best to antidepressants that block the reuptake of amines. No connection was found. The conclusion was that "elevations or decrements in the functioning of serotonergic systems per se are not likely to be associated with depression."[142] The introduction of Prozac brought a new round of similar studies with similar results. There has never been any convincing evidence that there is a deficiency of serotonin in the brain of depressed people. This led psychiatric maverick David Healy to opine, "The serotonin theory of depression is comparable to the masturbatory theory of insanity" (a once-common theory).[143]

Although serotonin is a significant transmitter substance in the regulation of the emotions, its role in what is typically called *depression* is far from clear. There have been recent genetic studies that connect a specific form of the serotonin transmitter system and depression. Research has shown that a genetic variation in a serotonin transmitter gene (called the *short allele*) was linked to depression and suicide in response to stress.[144] People with this variation were twice as likely to become depressed after stressful life events as others.

Further studies indicate that this genetic variation is associated with a hyper-reactivity in the emotional regions of the brain, including the amygdala. People with this short version of the gene showed more activity in the amygdala when exposed to viewing negative pictures, processing negative words, and matching emotional faces. The authors conclude that these people more rapidly acquire negative emotions, retain memories longer, and increase their vigilance.[145] These characteristics increase their physiological reactivity to depression.

My conclusion is that while there is no chemical imbalance accounting for depression, there probably is variation among people in parts of the serotonin system. We don't really know how it works, but this variation may leave some people more reactive to life's failures and losses than others. We are probably all biologically capable of the grief response; it is part of the human inheritance. But some people are likely to be more susceptible than others to the kind of prolonged or disproportionate grief reaction we call depression. This is the biological basis of depression. *Why* we become depressed is psychological.

Psychological Basis of Depression

There are several psychological theories of depression that focus on the cognitive aspects. Two of the pioneers were the psychologist Albert Ellis and the psychiatrist Aaron Beck. Both men focused on faulty or irrational thinking as a cause of depression and saw helping people change their thinking as the key to resolving it.

Ellis believed that, most often, depression is the product of what he called *irrational beliefs*—"absolutistic shoulds, musts, and other grandiose demands" on oneself, other people, and life circumstances.[146] He saw depression as a psychological choice rather than an affliction. He called it "self-drowning."

Ellis found two attitudes common among people who depressed themselves. The first is "I must perform important tasks well and be approved by people I find important or else I'm an *inadequate, worthless* person!" The other is "People and conditions I live with *absolutely must* treat me considerately and fairly, give me what I *really* want to, and rarely seriously frustrate me! Or else, I *can't* stand it, my life is *awful,* and I can't enjoy it at all!"

Worse yet, when people depress themselves, they also frequently create a "secondary" negative feeling. They tell themselves, "I must not have these depressed feelings! It's terrible to feel depressed." We double down on disturbance, Ellis wrote, when we "depress ourselves about depressing. This secondary disturbing ourselves comes from our refusal to merely observe and sorrowfully accept, instead of depressingly damn, our primary symptom."

The second father of cognitive-behavior therapy, if I may call him that, was Aaron Beck. Beck's theory of depression is similar to Ellis's, but it was more formal and research-based. His classic 1967 text of depression (now in its second edition) addresses the question "What has definitely been established regarding the nature, causes, and treatment of depression?"[147]

Beck coined the term *cognitive distortions* to characterize the kinds of thinking that resulted in depressed mood. His studies focused on "the verbalized thought content indicating distorted or unrealistic conceptualizations" and "the processes involved in the deviation from logical or realistic thinking" in depressed persons. The thinking of depressed people, he argued, demonstrates a *systematic error,* a bias against themselves. Beck categorizes five types of such errors.

The first he calls *arbitrary inference,* which is the "process of drawing a conclusion from a situation, event or experience when there is no evidence to support the conclusion or when the conclusion is contrary to the evidence." As an example, he describes a man in an elevator thinking, "He [the elevator operator] thinks I'm a nobody," and feeling sad.

A second error is *selective abstraction,* "focusing on a detail taken out of context, ignoring the more salient features of the situation and conceptualizing the whole experience on the basis of this element." He gives an example of a woman whose boss praised her work but asked her to stop making copies of her letters. Her immediate thought was, "He's dissatisfied with my work," and this idea negated all his positive statements.

The third error is *overgeneralization,* a "pattern of drawing a general conclusion about their ability, their performance or their worth based on a single incident." His example is a man whose wife was "upset because the children were slow in getting dressed." His thought was, "I am a poor father because the children are not better disciplined."

He called the fourth type of error *magnification and minimization,* referring to "errors in evaluation so gross as to constitute distortion." In other words, either exaggerating the magnitude of our problems or underestimating our abilities to handle them. Beck notes, "It was frequently observed that the patient's initial reaction to an unpleasant event was to regard it as a catastrophe."

The final error Beck calls *inexact labeling,* which contributes to the others. It is the use of dramatic and exaggerated language to describe events, followed by our emotional response to the words we used rather than to the event itself. For instance, a man was upset because he had been "clobbered" by his manager. What he really meant was that his boss corrected him. Once he used a more appropriate word for the event, he felt better.

The cognitive behaviorist Albert Bandura also made significant advances in our understanding of depression by casting the origin of depression in the light of his construct *behavioral efficacy,* the belief we develop over our lives that we are able to cope and obtain what we desire. Bandura writes, "the pattern in which people perceive themselves as ineffectual, but see others like them enjoying the benefit of successful effort is apt to give rise to self-disparagement and depression."[148]

Our belief in our ability to form satisfying social relationships is a factor in our vulnerability to depression. Social relationships "cushion the adverse effects of chronic stressors," but it takes a strong sense of social efficacy to form supportive and satisfying relationships with other people.

To sum up his argument, people whose positive life experiences lead to a solid sense of self-efficacy believe they can cope with life's adverse events and control their own negative thoughts. They do become depressed when they suffer losses, because that is the natural human response, but it is self-limiting. They have or are able to develop supportive relationships to help them through times of trouble. On the contrary, people with a weak sense of self-efficacy do not have the psychological and interpersonal resources needed to protect themselves from despondency over loss. Studies have shown that "the weaker the perceived efficacy to turn off ruminative thoughts, the higher the depression."

There is one additional cognitive theory of depression: *depressive realism,* the idea that people who are depressed may actually see the world more realistically—with its troubles and unpredictability—than most of us. The English psychiatrist Neil Burton has written about this extensively. "Most non-depressed people have an unduly rose-tinted perspective of their attributes, circumstances and possibilities. For instance, most people think they are better than average in what they do, overestimate the odds of success and underestimate the odds of failure."[149] Positive illusions form the basis of much of our self-esteem. Burton sees their advantages, as they allow us to "take risks, see through major undertakings and cope with traumatic events." Depressed people do not have such illusions.

The concept of depressive realism comes from studies that show people with mild to moderate depression can more accurately gauge the likelihood of "events that might or might not occur" and have "a more realistic perception of their role, abilities and limitations." At times, this may benefit a depressed person, making him or her more able to "shed the Pollyanna optimism and rose-tinted spectacles that shield us from reality, to see life more accurately and judge it accordingly." Burton turns depression upside down and redefines it as "the healthy suspicion that modern life has no meaning and that modern society is absurd and alienating."

On the other hand, taken too far, this tendency toward realism can become a debilitating depression. Burton recognizes the cognitive distortions that ensue, including "a focus on a single negative to the exclusion of more positive ones," "all-or-nothing thinking," and "exaggerating the possible consequences of an event or situation."

Ellis, Beck, Bandura, and Burton have given us a rich picture of the thinking processes that lead to the mood state we call *depression.* We may conclude that it requires a certain degree of positive illusions to be happy and resilient or even function effectively in this world. When positive illusions become too pronounced, however, they help create a mood that is the opposite of depression, one we call *mania,* which we'll turn to soon.

Social Aspects of Depression

Depression, like all other forms of psychological dysfunction, occurs in a social context, and the social response to it is usually sympathy and concern. This is usually warranted and helpful to the individual, but it is also a form of social reward for depressed behaviors. For a portion of the people labeled *depressed,* this extends the condition far beyond a mood state of grief and toward what I would describe as a lifestyle of suffering.

For people susceptible to these social rewards, there are distinct benefits. This is not meant as a moral judgment, but as an observation. Depressed people are relieved of many of the responsibilities and expectations of adult life. They may get disability payments and be excused from earning a living. Less may be expected of them at home and work. And they can get attention and medications from their providers. All this is very seductive to a segment of people who find it difficult to pursue a productive life.

I don't mean to imply that this is an intentional choice; it is an easy trap that people fall into unaware. Some depressed people will come to resent the dependency it represents and work hard to overcome it. This is a healthy development that good clinicians encourage; they will help the individual make depression a temporary phenomenon and not a way of life. We'll return to the therapist's role in easing or enabling a patient's dysfunction in chapter 14.

Mania

The characteristics of mania are polar opposites of those of depression, with which it is often paired (hence the term *bipolar disorder*). Two of the principal aspects of mania are grandiosity and overactivity (both mental and physical), whereas depression features retardation or slowing and self-devaluation. But if the primary mood of depression is sadness, that of mania should be joy. We do not, however, usually consider happy people manic. Mania is defined by an expansive or elevated mood, not joy. The only actual mood state mentioned in the psychiatric description of mania is irritability, which is a mood state related to anger.

There are similarities between mania and depression. Both are egocentric perspectives; the self is the focus, whether the appraisal is positive or negative.

A person's interest and attention is on one's self, not on the world and the people who populate it. With depression, this is expressed as low self-esteem, guilt, and withdrawal; in mania, a lack of restraint and an inflated sense of self that is at odds with the person's true accomplishments.

In both these mood states, a lack of realistic appraisal of the outside world may lead to a distortion of reality that we characterize as psychotic. The severely depressed person's delusions are about inadequacy and guilt; the manic person's, about great accomplishments and specialness. Severely manic people may believe that they should advise the president on how to run the country or that they are the apostles of God or that they are writing the great American novel.

Much of what we observe in mania is too much energy. Characteristically, a manic person's speech seems as though it was spewing from a fire hose (called *pressure of speech*), thoughts jump from subject to subject with minimal connection *(flight of ideas)*, attention is drawn to irrelevant or unimportant details *(distractibility)*, and the person has little need for sleep or food. We see an excess in all sorts of activities that is imprudent and unproductive.

Mania becomes increasingly dysfunctional when a person's judgment is impaired, and this overactivity becomes self-destructive. Manic people might go on spending sprees, buying things they can't afford or don't need or making foolish investments in businesses about which they have no knowledge. Similarly, they may engage in reckless sexual behavior or other dangerous activities. Manic people are exceedingly sociable, but in a way that becomes increasingly unwelcome. They intrude on other people's space and call people in the middle of the night. They are often domineering, demanding, and very difficult to interact with.

Unlike the case of depression, the manic individual does not complain about his or her condition and is not troubled by it. So *mania* is a judgment made by other people, who see a person as disordered. Moreover, the characteristics of hyperactivity and expansiveness may mark the personalities of people who are not considered mentally disordered (at least by society). They're often highly successful people with the social skills, influence, and connection to reality to make mania work for them.

I thought about this as I read a recent profile of John Sexton by Rachel Aviv in the *New Yorker.*[150] Dr. Sexton has been president of New York University since 2002 and has presided over an enormous expansion of the university, establishing satellite campuses in thirteen cities around the world. No one has officially declared him mentally disordered, but as I read about him, I thought that this man could be considered manic if he were psychiatrically evaluated.

Sexton can be intrusive. He indiscriminately hugs people. Aviv writes, "Hugging is essential to his managerial style and he estimates that he hugs about fifty people a day." He randomly recommends a book called Mr. Blue "to nearly all new students, as well as teenagers he happens to sit next to on the train." In conversation, "his primary method of relating to people is to tell long, folksy stories," and, according to a group of professors, "Sexton, whether at the keyboard or the lectern, prohibits conversation, paradoxically by going on at length about the need for it, and his own devotion to it." His speech can be so over-inclusive as to resemble *flight of ideas.* Aviv writes, "A conversation with alumni about overseas campuses turns into a tale about a puppy, his children, his decision to invest in his only suit … and a story about the Israeli ambassador, which becomes an account of how his brother-in-law told him, 'you reek of goyosity.'"

My point in relating this is not to diagnose Sexton or call him mentally ill. It is to show that mental disorders are not usually applied to successful and prominent people who don't desire them. This is part of the social context of mental-health diagnoses like mania. It makes them value judgments, not dispassionate science.

The Bipolar Conundrum

Now we turn to bipolar disorder, also called *manic depression. Manic depression* is a vivid and descriptive, if inaccurate, term. *Bipolar* is a nondescript and vague one. Perhaps that is the point. Who knows what it means to say a person has two poles.

The original idea was to describe a person who dramatically shifted from an extended period of low mood to one of elevated mood. The identification of such people stems back to the mid-nineteenth century and began with a fight over priority.

The protagonists were two French psychiatrists. According to David Healy, the first to make a public claim was Jules Bailanger in a presentation to the Academy of Medicine in Paris in 1854.[151] Bailanger observed, "There are no states which show more marked contrast from one to the other than melancholy and mania. It would therefore seem, in theory, that two states so opposed must be foreign one to the other, and that a great distance must separate them. This is not however that which is demonstrated by observation. Indeed we see, in many cases, melancholia succeed mania and vice-versa, as if a secret bond united these two diseases." Bailanger's name for this was *folie à double forme.*

The second, Jean-Pierre Falret, made his presentation to the French academy two weeks after Bailanger's. He said that he had been aware of this kind of insanity for more than ten years and that he had described similar cases to medical students many times. He called it *folie circulaire,* because the unfortunate patients afflicted with this illness live out their lives in a perpetual circle of depression and manic excitement.[152]

One thing both men agreed on was that it was a very rare condition. Between them, they could only point to a few cases in their two large asylums. Following Bailanger and Falret, several other French psychiatrists described patients with similar disorders and gave these disorders somewhat different names, but they made no impact in Germany, where the diagnosis of madness became an important issue.

Until the great classifier of madness in the asylum, Emil Kraepelin, proposed a second form of insanity he called *manic-depressive insanity.* These patients did not have the terrible downhill course of dementia praecox (schizophrenia), and they could get better. Initially, international psychiatry resisted the notion of a "manic-depressive" illness, but ultimately it became a name that worked. The classic form of manic-depression—alternating mania and depression—was not, however, what Kraepelin had in mind. He meant any kind of hospitalized psychiatric patient who could get better, including postpartum psychosis, simple mania, and various kinds of depression in people under fifty. He lumped depression in older patients, so-called involutional melancholia, with dementia praecox, because he did not believe they would recover.

It wasn't until 1966 that manic depression was renamed *bipolar disorder.* The impetus for making this distinction came from Joseph Schildkraut's 1965 hypothesis that depression was caused by a chemical imbalance.[153] In order to investigate this, psychiatry needed to specify what sort of depression they were talking about, and separating "unipolar" and bipolar forms fit the bill. In 1975, operational definitions for the two types were published,[154] which were later incorporated into DSM-III.

Having made this distinction, however, psychiatry faced a dilemma. They could categorize psychiatric patients who suffered from depression alone as *unipolar* and those with both depression and mania as *bipolar,* but what to do about patients who were hospitalized for depression, but who seemed also to have episodes of mild mania that didn't require hospitalization? Psychiatrist David Dunner suggested these patients had a type of bipolar disorder that he called *bipolar II* and said that their elevated moods were hypomanic.[155] People previously known as *depressed neurotics* were now *bipolar II disorder* patients.

When DSM-III was published in 1980, psychiatry adopted both bipolar I and bipolar II disorders and added two additional ones. The first was *cyclothymic disorder* or cycling moods, which were previously seen as a personality type. The other was *bipolar disorder, not otherwise specified,* or what David Healy characterized as "anyone with a touch of what their clinician felt might be bipolarity."[156] The categorization of a family of bipolar disorders was now complete.

Healy calculates that up to the 1960s, hospitalization for manic depression was so rare that there were fewer than ten new cases per million people (or less than 0.1 percent) throughout Europe. More recently, the loosening of criteria for bipolar disorder led to estimates of 1.3 percent of the population being diagnosed with the most serious form of the disorder, bipolar I, and as many as 5 percent with some form of bipolar disorder. Diagnostic inflation does not only involve bipolar disorders, but every kind of psychiatric diagnosis. As Paul McHugh, former chair of psychiatry at Johns Hopkins Medical School, scornfully pointed out, "Pretty soon, we'll have a syndrome for short, fat Irish guys with a Boston accent, and I'll be mentally ill."[157]

Even for true believers, psychiatry's diagnosis of bipolar disorders has a major credibility problem. Psychiatry's own studies have shown that using the DSM criteria to diagnose bipolar disorder is an extremely unreliable enterprise. Using a statistical analysis called *positive predictive value,* psychiatrist Mark Zimmerman and colleagues showed that bipolar disorder is both greatly overdiagnosed and, paradoxically, greatly underdiagnosed.[158] The problem turns on what psychiatry considers the gold standard of diagnoses, the Structured Clinical Interview for Diagnoses (SCID). Using SCID as a measuring stick, an independent psychiatrist can systematically ask all the relevant diagnostic questions. Using this tool as the standard of accuracy, Zimmerman proved that the bipolar diagnoses given to patients by their own psychiatrists were highly inaccurate in both directions. When something that purports to be a medical diagnosis is so unreliable, it loses any semblance of legitimacy.

Psychiatrist James Phelps countered Zimmerman by saying that accepting his results "is tacitly accepting that a clinician who does not know the patient, wielding an instrument that does not enhance the clinical relationship, is the authority. If SCID says bipolar disorder is absent while the clinician says it is present, the clinician is wrong." He challenges the assumption that "bipolar disorder is like bacterial sepsis or mononucleosis: the patient has it or he does not."[159] This is exactly the point. If the bacterial model does not and cannot work for mental-health categories, in what way are mental disorders objective medical diseases?

Ironically, Phelps goes on to report that when psychiatry first took up the revision of DSM in 2006, a spectrum approach was discussed, and "virtually everyone involved was in favor of incorporating a dimensional approach." Phelps's hope was that DSM-5 would "address this ... diagnostic dilemma.... Will it raise the value of a bipolar diagnosis beyond a coin toss?" We now know that DSM-5 did no such thing. Bipolar disorder and the other mood disturbances remain categorical.

Another blow to the idea that there is a discreet diagnostic category called *bipolar I disorder* is the fact that many psychiatric patients have symptoms of both bipolar disorder and schizophrenia. By the Kraepelinian medical model, patients should have either a mood disturbance or a reality disturbance, not a little of each. However, as early as 1924, Eugen Bleuler (the man who coined the name *schizophrenia*) recognized that there was no bright line separating manic depression from schizophrenia. People only varied in the proportion of each set of symptoms they displayed.

The name given for these intermediate forms of psychoses was *schizoaffective disorder*. Schizoaffective disorder is still part of the diagnostic scheme today, and it is my experience that its use is growing. The problem is that someone who is diagnosed with schizoaffective disorder on one psychiatric admission may be considered bipolar I on another and schizophrenic on a third. The point is that schizoaffective disorder is no discrete, separate condition. It is part of a continuum between a more definite mood dysregulation (depression or mania) at one end and a more definite reality distortion on the other.

The Grandmother

Mary was fifty-nine years old. She had attended college, had been married for forty years, and had six children and seven grandchildren. Much of that time, she seemed an ordinary person leading an ordinary life. However, she had been psychiatrically hospitalized twice, fifteen and thirteen years before, and for many years she had usually received psychiatric medications at a local clinic.

One day the police found her sitting in the middle of the road. She claimed that she had been raped by two men and also by her crisis worker and a nurse. At the hospital, she refused to cooperate and yelled, "You are all demons." Her speech was loud and pressured (what is called *pressure of speech,* as if her speech is spewing from a fire hose), and she couldn't stay on one subject. Her mood was all over the place. Sometimes she seemed depressed and fearful, sometimes hostile and belligerent, and sometimes elated and laughing. She also appeared to be responding to voices no one else heard.

On admission she was officially diagnosed with bipolar I disorder, currently manic with psychotic features, and with the consideration of schizoaffective disorder. She was involuntarily committed on the basis of grossly impaired judgment, paranoid delusions, and mania.

When I saw her a week later, she had calmed considerably. She talked to me pleasantly and tried to respond appropriately to my questions. Her thinking, however, remained roundabout, and she quickly got off the subject. Her mood seemed elevated and somewhat intense, and her speech was pressured and overproductive. When I asked her why she had been hospitalized, she responded, "I was doing fine before I came in. My husband wanted me to come in. He was upset that I said he'd stolen money, and he wanted to separate. He told me I was a fat, ugly old bitch, and he wasted his life." She then told me it was her who had called the police, and she said, "They told me I had to come to the hospital."

My assessment was that for some reason, perhaps conflict with her husband, Mary had suddenly "decompensated" (had a breakdown) after a long period of stability. Her mental condition had reached the crisis point of psychosis, and she was not able to live safely in the community at that point. Her dysfunction was not just about reality or mood, but a combination of both. She fit the schizoaffective disorder type.

Benefits of Mood Disturbance

Major depression and bipolar disorder are serious afflictions. No one could see any benefit in such major illnesses. Or could they?

Ordinarily, we might think that some people can succeed *despite* a mental disorder. They can adjust to it and work around their deficits, and we might even admire their grit and determination. But what if the seeming mental disorder is a major contributing factor to their success? Has there ever been a serious disease that was of direct benefit to a person?

In the mental-health field, there is a legitimate argument that there are people who would not have accomplished what they did without the madness they were or could have been diagnosed with. The prime exemplar is Abraham Lincoln, who has been frequently described as having been clinically depressed. According to Joshua Wolf Shenk, who has extensively researched Lincoln's life, Lincoln exhibited signs of depression most of his life.[160] As a young man, he frequently talked of suicide, and he wrote a poem about suicide when he was in his twenties. His law partner reported that "his frequent melancholy dripped from him as he walked." Even on a day of great success, when he was nominated for the presidency by his party, Lincoln was anything but joyful. One convention observer noted, "I then thought him one of the most diffident and worst plagued men I ever saw."

As his life went on, Lincoln had ample cause to be depressed, and bouts of depression often came after difficult life events. His first severe episode came after the death of a woman he loved when he was twenty-six. At age thirty-two, he had a second episode after he was rejected by a woman he had proposed to. His final and most severe depression came three years before his death, when Willie, his eleven-year-old son, died of typhoid fever.

Yet despite or because of these blows and what they did to him, Lincoln persevered and accomplished great things. Shenk writes, "with Lincoln we have a man whose depression spurred him, painfully, to examine the core of his soul; whose hard work to stay alive helped him develop crucial skills and capacities, even as his depression lingered hauntingly; and whose inimitable character took great strength from the piercing insights of depression." In other words, depression was the forge that created the steel of Lincoln's personality.

Psychiatrist Nassir Ghaemi described his interpretation of how depression made Lincoln great: "depression conferred on him, I believe, realism and empathy that helped make him a superb crisis leader."[161] Lincoln was arguably our nation's greatest president. He served at a time when the country needed him most. If it was his depression that somehow produced the qualities that helpd him save our nation, then his mental illness was no disorder at all.

As best we can know him, Lincoln was rarely, if ever, happy. We might describe him as having a depressed temperament, varying only with how unhappy he was. An emotional biography of Lincoln could be entitled *Fifty Shades of Blue*. A much more emotionally volatile figure than Lincoln was his Civil War general William Tecumseh Sherman. Ghaemi's biographical vignette of Sherman describes him as meeting the present-day criteria for bipolar disorder.

According to Ghaemi, Sherman had at least five episodes of serious depression, beginning at age twenty-seven. At other times, his behavior had manic qualities. He graduated from West Point in 1840 with top grades but left the Army thirteen years later to pursue a career in business. Much to his wife's exasperation, he moved around the country, borrowed a great deal of money, and generally failed at his endeavors. He started a bank in San Francisco that failed, leaving him bankrupt and despondent. Ghaemi reports that "his moods fluctuated with every attempt to settle into a stable, remunerative job." "I am doomed to be a vagabond," Sherman wrote to his wife, "and I shall no longer struggle against my faith."

Sherman had important political connections (his brother was a congressman and his wife was the daughter of a member of President Zachary Taylor's cabinet), so in 1859 he reentered the Army as superintendent of a new military college. He was antiwar and sympathetic to the South, but he opposed secession. When war came, he was appointed second-in-command of the Army in Kentucky, and then, after his superior was transferred, he assumed command.

He became anxious and paranoid. A reporter described him this way: "Sherman unceasingly talked, paced, smoked cigars.... He seemed to smoke not from pleasure but as if it was a duty to be finished in the shortest imaginable time.... Sherman simply never sat still.... And on and on he talked, nervously and obsessively.... He never hesitated at interrupting anyone, but he cannot bear to be interrupted himself.... He expressed himself entirely without reserve about men and matters ... and I could not help thinking that in doing so he said more than was wise and proper."[162]

Ghaemi sees "classic signs of mania" in this description, including "irritable mood, decreased need for sleep (sleeping little but being a bundle of energy), distractibility, rapid speech, increased talkativeness, hyperactivity, physical agitation, and inability to function at work." This period of mania was followed by two months of depression "with likely paranoid delusions." Sherman later wrote to his brother, "I should have committed suicide were it not for my children."

Despite—and perhaps because of—his recurrent extreme mood fluctuations, Sherman's "March to the Sea" was the turning point of the Civil War. He was the man who invented the scorched-earth strategy, including the destruction of Atlanta, though he also expressed sympathy for the plight of the Southerners. He led his campaign with extraordinary persistence and energy. Sherman was unapologetic about his actions: "if people raise a howl against my barbarity and cruelty, I will answer war is war.... War is cruelty and you cannot refine it."

As Ghaemi sees it, mania can enhance both creativity and the energy to pursue one's goals. Under the right circumstances, mania creates "the divergence of thought [that] allows one to identify new problems, and the intense energy keeps one going until the problems are solved." In Sherman's case, this meant that he succeeded where other Union generals failed. Rather than look for new ways to defeat Confederate armies, he posed the problem differently. His strategy, as Ghaemi concludes, was to "destroy cities and farms, attack the economy, target people and property, and you will win by undermining the Army's base of support."

In addition to Lincoln and Sherman, Ghaemi showed how mood dysfunction has been prominent in the lives of other great leaders. Along with Lincoln, he cited Winston Churchill as demonstrating the relationship between depression and realism. The lives of Mahatma Gandhi and Martin Luther King Jr. both show a link between depression and empathy. Both Franklin D. Roosevelt and John F. Kennedy were mildly manic (in Ghaemi's opinion), and this trait supported their resilience. Finally, the entrepreneur Ted Turner's mood swings enhanced his creativity in a manner similar to Sherman's. In Ghaemi's interpretation, these men contrasted with "well-known, mentally healthy contemporaries who failed in crises."

7

Anxiety and Its Consequences

The ancient Greek philosopher Epictetus once wrote, "Man is not worried by real problems so much as his imagined anxieties about real problems." Anxiety exists in our thoughts, not in threatening events themselves. Anxiety is to threat as depression is to loss. It is the feeling state associated with the emotional response fear.

Anxiety has been seen as the major cause of mental illness, at least of the neurotic variety, since Freud made it a household term. In 1917, Freud wrote that anxiety is "a riddle whose solution would be bound to throw a flood of light on our whole mental existence."[163] In this chapter, we will address that riddle and discuss what anxiety is and how it affects us.

Fear is a fundamental survival mechanism that kicks in when we react to a threatening situation. It is easy to visualize our early ancestors on the savannas of Africa—large but weak, slow, and without claws or large teeth to defend themselves. A hair-trigger fear response was vital. Make one mistake and you had no genes to pass on.

Fear, then, is an emergency-response system built on an "appraisal that there is actual or potential danger in a given situation."[164] When fear is activated, we respond in the same way our ancestors did, but this reaction may not be as useful in a complex Western world. Fighting, fleeing, or freezing do not necessarily work when most of the threats we face are social situations, not prehistoric carnivores.

Anxiety is the feeling evoked when we experience fear whether or not we perceive any actual danger. I suspect that anxiety became more dominant in the human condition as civilization became more complex. Immediate physical threat receded, at least much of the time, and was replaced by indirect and amorphous social threat, which was much harder to predict and avoid. Sustained anxiety is painful and requires either direct action to reduce it or psychological maneuvers to blunt it. It is this anxiety that troubles us and is the source of much of our dysfunction.

Anxiety functions to dramatize the fear response; the psychiatrist Aaron Beck called it an "attention-getter." Anxiety is not, in itself, a pathological process. In fact, it is an essential part of successful functioning. Appropriate social behavior is largely controlled by the fear of consequences. Anxiety alerts us when we are about to engage in imprudent actions; it is closely related to conscience. It constrains our expression of our desires and impulses. If a person feels angry enough to hurt others, greedy enough to cheat them, or sexually aroused enough to assault them, a form of anxiety called *guilt* ordinarily inhibits them. People who do not experience anxiety, such as psychopaths, do whatever their impulses dictate. For most of us, anxiety is usually a reliable guide to what we should and should not do.

Anxiety is also highly motivating. Anxiety over potential failure or losing our job prods many of us to go to work each day and do our best, even without immediate rewards. It helps us be sharper and faster. An athlete before a game, an actor before going on stage, and a surgeon before an operation—they all feel a surge of anxiety before they perform. I experience anxiety before I teach a class or evaluate a patient and did every day before I sat down to work on this book. It makes me more alert and energetic, and thus I perform better.

Most people cope reasonably well with anxiety and respond to it in productive ways, at least most of the time. Dysfunction results when people are overwhelmed by anxiety or develop maladaptive means of defending against it. It becomes increasingly dysfunctional when it is persistent and ineffective and based on "a misperception and exaggeration of the danger."[165]

Biology of Fear and Anxiety

Fear is the most carefully studied of the brain's emotional systems; we know quite a bit about its basic mechanisms. First, all emotional systems can be described as having three parts. They begin with input from what we perceive, information about changes in both the external and internal environment. Next, there is an evaluation of that input. Neuroscientist Joseph Le Doux characterizes this evaluation as "programmed by evolution to detect certain input or trigger stimuli that are relevant to the function of the network."[166] The third stage is output, which includes both automatic emotional behavior and information sent on to higher brain levels for further processing.

Emotional triggers can be either "natural" (innately programmed) or learned. For instance, in the fear system, stimuli associated with predators trigger the fear response in prey species like us. The fear system can also learn by association, so that we each develop our own triggers.

The emotional output is also both natural and learned. All mammals' respond to danger in remarkably similar ways. Le Doux describes a rat's behavior when exposed to a cat, even if it has never seen one before. It startles, stops anything else it is doing, and looks at the cat. Its emotional appraisal mechanism determines the scope of the danger, and it will either run away or freeze. If trapped, it will make fear noises and try to fight back. We humans do the same things.

Without getting overly technical, we can look at the fear system in a little more physiological detail.[167] Information from the senses first goes to a part of the midbrain called the *thalamus* for the first stage of perceptual processing. It sends its information on to the rest of the brain, but the amygdala gets it first. The amygdala is a major part of the emotional brain, often called the *limbic system*. The amygdala is the brain's early warning system. It attaches an emotional label to the new information, including if it poses any danger. It is interesting that the only sense that bypasses the thalamus and goes straight to the amygdala is olfaction. Smell is an extremely potent emotional trigger and vital to the survival of most mammals, because it quickly determines disgust or pleasure without any abstract thought. The amygdala not only relies on its innate triggers but also learns from emotional experience. After an intensely frightening or traumatic experience, the amygdala will be on high alert for signals that such an event is about to happen again.

Once activated, the amygdala starts a chain of events leading to a fear response pattern. When the hypothalamus receives the alarm, it initiates the stress response, stimulating the autonomic nervous system and the release of hormones, including adrenaline, which prepare the body for stress or action. Le Doux drew a picture of the standard bodily fear response: "nerves reaching the gut, heart, blood vessels, and sweat and salivary glands give rise to the taut stomach, racing heart, high blood pressure, clammy hands and feet, and a dry mouth that typify fear in humans."[168]

Adrenaline works wonders for responding in danger, war, and sports, but if we don't actually react with physical activity, it leaves us shaky and weak. Cortisol, another stress hormone, releases glucose to power the muscles, but if stress is prolonged or extreme, cortisol can damage brain neurons.

The amygdala's alarm also goes to the hippocampus, which is primarily responsible for turning experiences into long-term memory. The hippocampus helps provide the environmental context for the new threat. When the memory of a previously frightening experience is recalled, the hippocampus has the power to evoke a fear response even when no direct threat is present.

Continuing into the brain, we come to the functioning of a part of the upper brain called the *anterior cingulate gyrus*. This is an evolutionarily old part of our frontal cortex that acts as what John Ratey calls the executive secretary to the CEO of the frontal lobes.[169] The amygdala has already branded the incoming information, and the automatic emotional response has begun. Now the anterior cingulate rates the information. It decides whether to transfer the information to the frontal lobes and, if so, determines how much importance to place on it. The anterior cingulate also provides motivation to the prefrontal cortex and helps direct it toward useful solutions. If it is "too rigid or 'stuck' on a piece of incoming information from the limbic system, flexible thought and problem-solving is compromised and anxiety rises."[170]

The prefrontal cortex is the ultimate decision maker in the brain, because it gathers the information from almost everywhere else. It gets emotionally tagged data from the amygdala via the anterior cingulate, but it also gets more complete and accurate perceptual information from other cortical areas, putting the potential threat in a larger context. This allows a more considered response. It uses memory from the hippocampus to give it a historical context. It also receives feedback information about the results of the emotional response as it goes along. The result is that the emotional response becomes more attuned to reality and, hopefully, more effective, though that isn't always the case.

Like most of the brain, the prefrontal cortex has two hemispheres with somewhat different functions. It is the job of the left side to put emotional experiences into language. Language makes emotions conscious, and at that point we can make executive decisions about the experience and potentially control it. The prefrontal cortex can suppress a fear response by deciding there is no danger or by making an effective plan to deal with a threat. It can also increase the response with an incorrect assessment. Animals with damage to parts of the prefrontal cortex appear similar to people with anxiety disorders. They can't regulate their fear, even if there is no danger.[171]

The right side of the prefrontal cortex specializes in nonverbal functioning, including interpreting the emotions of others. It also specializes in assessing risk and generalizing the feeling of danger. It coordinates emotionally tagged perceptions with previous life experiences to make an appraisal of the current situation.

So far, we've been speaking about the emotional response of fear. Now let's bring in anxiety. Beck describes the feeling of anxiety as "a subjectively unpleasant emotional state characterized by unpleasant subjective feelings, such as tension and nervousness, and by physiological symptoms like heart palpitations, tremor, nausea, and dizziness."[172]

Psychological and Social Origins of Dysfunctional Anxiety

The anxiety problem is much more than a maladaptive fear response. The sensations of the fear are unpleasant and motivating, but not themselves the cause of major dysfunction. As a great psychological thinker once wrote (in *Hamlet*), "there is nothing good or bad, but thinking makes it so." It is our thoughts that create debilitating anxiety and dysfunctional behavior.

That is the position taken by Albert Ellis and his colleague Robert Harper.[173] They introduced the idea that anxiety results from a pattern of irrational thoughts, especially the thought "that if something is or may be dangerous or fearsome, one should be terribly occupied with and upset about it."

Destructive anxiety is a matter "of over-concern, of exaggerated or needless fear." It consists of thoughts about catastrophic consequences and frequently results in self-sabotaging behaviors. A simple example offered by Ellis and Harper is a professional who became anxious when he stood up to address a group. His first thought was, "I might make a mistake and fall on my face before this group of my peers." The second was of catastrophe: "wouldn't that be awful if I did make a mistake and fall on my face in public."

It was this second illogical statement that made him anxious. If, after the first thought, the man had thought, "So what? If I make a mistake and fall on my face, it won't be great, but it still won't be awful." That statement would not produce anxiety, because it would not predict harm.

Ellis and Harper described several ways that most anxiety-producing thoughts are illogical and should be challenged:

- If a situation is really potentially dangerous, you have two rational choices. You either do something effective to alleviate the situation, or you resign yourself to it. "The more you upset yourself about the existence of this dangerous situation, the less able you will be, in almost all instances, to assess it accurately and to cope with it."

- Let's say that something bad does happen to you. If you have taken reasonable precautions, it would be an unfortunate occurrence, but you couldn't have done anything more to prevent it. "Worry, believe it or not, has no magical quality of staving off bad luck."

- The catastrophic character of most adverse events is almost always extremely exaggerated. The worst thing that can happen in life is death, and that will come to all of us at some time. "Terrors, horrors and catastrophes are almost entirely figments of our worried imaginations."

- Worry itself is usually the "most dreadful" condition we can live with. If you can't avoid harmful consequences, "you would better frankly and fearlessly face up to your problems, and accept whatever penalties … may accrue from facing them, rather than continue to live a life of fear."

- Physical harms, not social consequences, are the only things we really need to fear. If you are disliked or disapproved of, or if people unfairly criticize you, it may make things tough, but not awful. "Why make the game of life so much more difficult by fretting and stewing about its existing inequities?"

- Young children may have no control over things that seem terrible and fearful, but adults "are not usually in this precarious position." We can take steps to change frightening circumstances or "philosophically learn to live under such conditions." The fears we suffered as children do not have to constantly control adult lives.

When we are anxious, we are mostly unaware of our illogical thoughts. Being human, we are all prey to these thoughts; "life is a ceaseless battle against irrational worries," Ellis and Harper assert. The least troubled of us have the ability to recognize and counter them with reason. People who are debilitated by anxiety have developed patterns of catastrophic thoughts that are automatic and unchallenged. Their attitudes and beliefs are colored by them and are the sources of their misery.

Dysfunctional Anxiety

The universe of anxiety disorders consists of a wide variety of fears and anxieties that interfere with our enjoyment of life. Here, in outline, are some of the most widely recognized forms of anxiety dysfunction, which I will discuss in more detail below.

- Some forms reflect the direct expression of chronic anxiety without a specific object of fear. These include generalized anxiety, panic, and agoraphobia.

- Some of them involve reacting with fear to objects or situations that are not objectively dangerous. These include phobias and social phobias.

- Some of them involve the aftereffects of being in traumatic situations. These include posttraumatic stress reactions and dissociative states.

- Some of them are the characteristic ways in which we block the feelings of anxiety through defensive maneuvers. These include obsessive-compulsive behaviors and psychosomatic ills.

I've made it sound as if these forms of anxiety exist in isolation from one another, that they are mutually exclusive categories. This is far from the truth. People with anxiety difficulties exhibit combinations of these characteristics in different proportions and at different times. Using labels such as *panic disorder* or *agoraphobia* is merely an attempt to name clusters of symptoms that generally appear together. In other words, they are general types of dysfunctional anxiety.

Chronic Anxiety

Panic

Most of us have experienced panic. If you have ever been badly startled, you know the feeling. Your heart beats faster, your breathing becomes rapid and shallow, and you might have felt light-headed or dizzy. You may have had a sensation of choking, chest pain, and nausea. You may have recognized a sense of dread, with accompanying feelings of unreality and perhaps even of being detached from your own body.

These unpleasant sensations are typically brief. As soon as you recognize the source of the fright, the symptoms start to subside and, at worst, are over in about twenty minutes. Afterward, you might have said, "you almost gave me a heart attack," but you don't really believe you are seriously ill. You realize the cause of your arousal and bring the feelings under control.

If you have ever been in any kind of competition, you've had similar sensations before a big event. You had all the physiological arousal symptoms as you prepared, but when the competition starts, you discharge all that anxiety and tension in action. You might have even come to expect and relish these sensations, because you feel they get you ready for the game.

Psychology has known for decades that there is an inverted *U*-shaped relationship between stress response and performance. Too little stress, and you are unprepared for a challenge, either physical or mental. Most of us have experienced times when we took on something and failed miserably, because we were not anxious enough. On the other hand, if we become too stressed, the challenge feels like a threat, and our attention is diverted to escape rather than to the task at hand. The balance we seek is to be just stressed and anxious enough to do our best, but not so much that we are overwhelmed.

Under certain circumstances, the stress response can escalate into a full-blown panic episode. Aaron Beck and his coauthor, Gary Emery, described one such circumstance.[174] A forty-year-old man was skiing in Colorado. His brother had died of heart attack a few weeks before, but he wasn't thinking about that. He was enjoying skiing when he suddenly felt cold, started to perspire profusely, and felt weak and faint. He began to have trouble focusing, and then waves of anxiety and a sense of unreality began. He had been skiing at that altitude many times in the past and had experienced rather similar symptoms before, but this time was different. His condition reached such a point of desperation that he had to be taken off the slopes and to the hospital by ambulance. There was nothing wrong with him, and he was told it was an acute anxiety attack.

In retrospect, he recalled that prior to his experience, it had occurred to him that if he had a heart attack on the mountain, it would be hard to rescue him. When he began to experience his symptoms, he did not think logically but thought he was having a heart attack, like his brother. In a "flash," he imagined himself in a hospital bed with tubes running out of him and doctors around him. He did not intentionally construct this scene; it was an automatic picture. His thoughts and images escalated and prolonged his panic, and he could not think clearly about the event until he was at the hospital and had been reassured that he was fine.

One panic episode does not a disorder make, but when these episodes recur, and the person comes to dread them, panic becomes increasingly dysfunctional. Often the person has no awareness of the thoughts and images that lead up to an attack. People who experience such startling and seemingly inexplicable events are often terrorized, thinking, *I am going to die! I am going crazy!* or *I am losing control!*[175] The fear of having another attack feeds on itself. Fear makes a person hypervigilant to any sign of physiological arousal that might indicate another one. Worry evokes and escalates the arousal, and full panic attacks arise.

The major source of dysfunction in panic attacks is the behaviors that people engage in to avoid anything they believe may cause one. Psychologist Margaret Wehenberg and psychiatrist Steven Prinz characterize three sorts of panic-avoidance strategies.[176] The first is mental avoidance. People try to negotiate their mental world so as to avoid thinking about anything that might arouse them to panic. This means eternal vigilance over one's own thoughts. It severely limits people's imagination and emotional life.

A second strategy is to avoid activities that might trigger panic. But since it is not the activities themselves that cause people to panic, it does not work very well. What then happens is that avoidance begins to encompass routine activities that they might have once done quite readily, including, often, driving on the highway, returning telephone calls, and eating out.

The third strategy is to try to avoid ever feeling the least bit of fear. Panicky people can become so wary of fear that their whole life revolves around controlling arousal. They give up opportunities to feel joy or accomplishment and instead just focus on avoiding fear.

There are many reasons why panic disorder might develop in some people but not in others. Some people are likely born with an increased sensitivity to stressors. There is evidence that people who are overresponsive to anxiety-producing situations as children are likely to exhibit panic-disorder conditions as adults.[177]

Biology, though, is not likely to be a sufficient explanation for panic attacks. Although some infants may be predisposed to developing an overactive stress system, it is the parents' response that matters more. According to Wehrenberg and Prinz, caregivers train a baby about when and how much it should react to different situations, which they explain with an analogy: "a newborn baby is a little like a furnace whose thermostat has not yet been programmed. The furnace can kick in and heat up, but it does not know how hot to get or how long to run. The caregiver's response to the infant programs the thermostat."

Much of this training comes from the modeling and reinforcing responses of the parents. Some caregivers are calm and some are easily agitated, and children tend to imitate their parents' manner of response. Even more significant is the parents' response to a child's agitation. Some parents calm down, which puts the source of stress in perspective for the child. Others react negatively or in an overly alarmed way to a child's distress, only escalating the child's stress response.

Wehrenberg and Prinz ask us to imagine what happens when a temperamentally high-stress child meets overly fearful or angrily responsive parents. When the parents overreact to the child's excessive display of distress, the child has learned a dysfunctional anxiety response. Such a child "does not learn how to calm herself. Rather, she feels intolerable degrees of upset over what might otherwise be normal degrees of stress."

Even an overactive stress system and poor parental training may create a susceptibility to panic or to other types of anxiety dysfunction. Traumatic life events and unresolved psychological conflicts may be what tip the scales. A panicky person might be able to recognize these causes or might have no awareness of them at all. The result, however, is a perception of vulnerability, that the person is "subject to internal and external dangers over which his control is lacking or is insufficient to afford him a sense of safety."[178] The common stressors that we all face start such a person on the road to habitual panic.

Generalized Anxiety

The difference between the panic-disorder type and the generalized-anxiety type is a matter of degree, not kind. Generalized anxiety is more continuous and less dramatic. In place of terror and dread, there is constant worry; people with generalized anxiety problems "become experts at worrying about things that may never happen and over which they have no control."[179]

Anxiety-generating thoughts and images become automatic and persistent. They can occur in almost any situation; the individual does not necessarily have to have any sense of threat. A study led by Beck describes the major categories of anxiety ideation.[180] Thoughts and images revolve around fears of (1) physical injury, illness, or death; (2) having mental illness; (3) loss of control; (4) failure or not being able to cope; and (5) being rejected, depreciated, or dominated. Most of the anxiety patients studied had fears in at least three of these categories.

There is also a difference between generalized-anxiety patients who tend to have panic attacks and those who don't. The thoughts of those who have episodes of panic tend to run toward physical disaster. Those who don't panic usually have more thoughts about not being able to cope with other people.[181]

Agoraphobia

Agoraphobia literally means "fear of the marketplace" and describes people who are afraid of being in public places, where they might not be able to get help or from which they might not be able escape if they become incapacitated. The thing that distinguishes agoraphobia from panic and generalized anxiety is that the agoraphobic usually feels relatively safe at home. The zone of safety may be narrow or broad. The most incapacitated are those who feel intense anxiety or even panic if they are not at home with a trusted person nearby. Others might feel okay as long as they are home—even if alone—or may feel able to handle the outside world in the company of a loved one.

The least dysfunctional agoraphobics have more specific danger areas. At that end of the spectrum, agoraphobia begins to merge with specific phobias that we will talk about in the next section—fear of being in crowds, open spaces, enclosed spaces, on public transportation, or some combination of these.

What makes agoraphobia extremely dysfunctional is the degree of avoidance the feelings of fear can generate. People who panic or suffer continuous anxiety can at least take care of their own basic needs. They are usually able to work, shop, and socialize. Agoraphobics may be wholly dependent on others for their survival. Unless you are nobility, it isn't easy to live confined to your own home or to have someone who can accompany you if you do go out. People who are this demanding wear out their welcome with most others and cannot have healthy, mutual relationships, because others generally feel they must serve them.

Agoraphobia embodies an extreme form of magical thinking, making irrational connections between unrelated things. The normal world is divided into safe areas (home) and dangerous ones (away from home). The people in it are either threatening or necessary for your safety. The unstated belief of agoraphobic persons is that they are particularly vulnerable in this dangerous world and that unless certain people are there to take care of them, disaster will strike.

Raeann Dumont is a therapist who works with people in their home environment. She could observe and learn far more about the person in this real-life setting than any patient could or would explain in a therapist's office. In her book, she describes an agoraphobic woman, Nora, whose case demonstrates many of the common features of how the condition develops.[182]

Nora was a thirty-three-year-old mother of two young children when her symptoms first developed. It is usual for agoraphobia to materialize past the age of twenty. Nora had a stressful life, especially since her husband was a heavy drinker who could become abusive, and he had been unemployed for several months. His drinking was getting worse. Her nine-year-old son had been caught stealing in school, and her daughter, age six, seemed to be having difficulty learning. Nora leaned on her mother as her only real source of support.

Her anxiety problem began with what we recognize as the symptoms of panic. Her mother was in the hospital, and Nora was going to visit her one cold evening. Walking up the hill, Nora felt a sense of unreality; it seemed her head wasn't connected to her body. Her heart pounded, and she couldn't breathe. She immediately took a taxi home and went to bed. The next morning, she felt better and went to work as usual. Her mother came home before Nora could visit her in the hospital.

Two weeks later, she was in the supermarket with her two kids. She was trying to keep an eye on her son to make sure he didn't steal anything while at the same time dealing with her daughter, who was begging her to buy candy. She again felt the feelings of panic and thought she was going to die. She grabbed her children, rushed from the store, and when she got home, she called her mother to take her to the doctor. The doctor told her that he could find nothing wrong, but this only upset her more, because she knew she had something terrible and that it was incurable.

She began to go about her life with the dread that another attack would happen—and it did. Again, she was in the grocery store, this time in line by herself. She felt self-conscious and embarrassed, and when the feeling became unbearable, she left her groceries and ran out. She saw another doctor, who prescribed a tranquilizer. This helped for a time, but a few weeks later, on the way home from work, she had another attack.

At this point, she was sure she had a terrible disease or was going insane. Either way, this would be the end of her. She continued to go to work but would have attacks on the way home. Exhausted by them, she would go right to bed. Her husband was still unemployed, and they needed her income, so he agreed to take over her household duties and to drive her to and from work.

This arrangement worked well until her husband finally got a job. She then had to drive again, and her attacks worsened. She took a leave of absence from work, and for a few weeks, she rested at home and felt comfortable. She accomplished a lot around the house and spent a lot of time with her children. The thought of going to the supermarket made her anxious, so she had her husband do it. When her mother invited her out, she declined, with various excuses. When the school called for her to come in to discuss her children, she didn't show up for the meetings. A year went by, and she was housebound.

Meanwhile, life around her was in crisis. Her husband was intensely angry because he had to do all the shopping and they had no social life. Her mother was upset because Nora would no longer go out with her. The school thought she didn't care about her children. The only social contacts she had were her husband, her children, and her mother. Whenever she thought of leaving the house, she felt terrible. She read that people like her had a chemical imbalance, but she could not understand how she could feel fine one minute and have an imbalance the next.

From the outside, it is rather easy to see what was wrong with Nora. She was a person with limited ability to cope with life's difficulties and a vulnerability to anxiety. She muddled along as best she could in a miserable marriage with a husband who was often intoxicated and who would sometimes fly into drunken rages and hit her and the children. Her children were increasingly a source of concern and conflict rather than solace. She felt responsible that she could not protect them from her husband. Her only source of emotional support was her mother.

Two precipitating factors led to her descent into agoraphobia. The first was her husband's unemployment. This not only worsened his behavior toward her and the children but also left her responsible for the financial support of the family. The second was her mother's illness, which aroused the fear that her mother might die or that Nora might have to care for her mother rather than the reverse. Although she could not speak about her fears, they generated panic, and agoraphobia was the solution. Staying home magically protected her and bound her family to her. Although she was unaware of it, her illness relieved her of responsibility and forced her significant others to take care of her.

Phobia

The term *phobia* is derived from the name of the Greek god Phobos, who could strike fear and panic in his enemies. It came to mean what Sigmund Freud called *morbid anxiety*, evoked by relatively specific and benign objects or situations. In Freud's time, almost every possible phobia had its own Greek-derived name, some of which we still use. For instance, arachnophobia is fear of spiders, claustrophobia is fear of enclosed spaces, and aquaphobia is fear of water. The current DSM describes five areas of specific phobias: animal (e.g., spiders or dogs); the natural environment (e.g., storms or heights); blood, injection, or injury (e.g., needles); situational (e.g., elevators or airplanes); and other (e.g., loud sounds or choking). There is a separate category for social phobias, which we will discuss later.

According to Beck and Emery, "the main quality of a phobia is that it involves the appraisal of high risk in a situation that is relatively safe."[183] It is likely that phobias come with the genetic inheritance of being human. Early hominids who didn't respond with arousal and fear to the proximity of snakes or large animals or other potential dangers wouldn't have survived long. But this reaction can be superseded by more deliberate appraisal. The panic we would experience if we suddenly met a lion on the street would not be aroused if we saw the same lion caged in a zoo. People who learn to bungee jump or handle poisonous snakes feel a controllable degree of stress, but not panic.

The difference between a phobic and non-phobic person is that the phobic seems unable to learn how to put the dangerousness of an object into perspective. What most of us come to see as innocuous or only mildly arousing continues to evoke a threat response and a vicious cycle in the phobic person. The closer he comes to the feared object or situation, the more intense the physical and emotional distress and the more powerful the desire to escape or avoid it. He never learns to overcome the fear, because he never allows himself to come close enough for a realistic appraisal.

Many of us have circumscribed phobias that do not matter very much. We may be terribly afraid of snakes, but if we live in a northern climate, we don't encounter them. We may avoid taking vacations to places with lots of snakes or even avoid zoos, but that doesn't limit us very much. However, if the phobia becomes severe enough, it can be extremely dysfunctional. Even a snake phobic who lives in Alaska might have such an exaggerated appraisal of the danger that she can't venture beyond what she sees as snake-free boundaries. In some environments, common phobias can be so profoundly limiting that a person can barely exist. How could one survive in New York City if one was morbidly afraid of enclosed spaces?

Raeann Dumont offers an example of the consequences the fear of crossing a bridge had on one particular man.[184] Her patient, Norm, was thirty-four when his phobia struck, seemingly out of the blue. At that time, he appeared to be a well-functioning man with a good job in business and a wife and three young kids. When Dumont began working with him, he had not driven across a bridge in many years and was dependent on alcohol to calm himself down.

When Dumont met him, Norm had no idea why he had been suddenly stricken by a bridge phobia, but she was able to piece together his story. At the time of onset, his father was dying, and when the family gathered at his parents' home for dinner each Sunday, nobody talked about it. Denial was the family's and Norm's way of handling unpleasant facts. As his father's health deteriorated, Norm said, "The Sunday dinners and the charade had gotten increasingly stressful."

One Sunday near the end, Norm was extremely upset, and as his family got into the car to return home, the three children started fighting. At the end of his rope, Norm left his wife in the car with the children and went to get a drink. He soon returned and began the thirty-minute drive home, but when he was approaching the bridge from Philadelphia to New Jersey, he began to have the symptoms of panic. He pulled over and slumped over the wheel, shaking and gasping for air. His wife was terrified that he was having a heart attack. After ten or fifteen minutes, however, his symptoms had receded, and his wife drove the rest of the way home.

Norm's father died a few days later, and during the mourning period, his wife drove them back and forth over the bridge. About a month later, he made his first attempt to drive across the bridge alone to get to a business meeting. As he got on the bridge, his heart raced and his hands shook, and he feared he would lose control of his car. He inched along, sweating and gripping the steering wheel, but as he got over the top of the bridge he felt a little better.

All that day, his attention was focused on his business, but as he approached the bridge on his way home, he worried about the terrible experience happening again. With that thought, all the sensations of panic returned, and he called his wife to come get him.

For a while, he had his wife drive him to all appointments, but he gradually began to panic when they went over a bridge even with her driving. His doctor prescribed tranquilizers, which he took on days when he had to be driven over the bridge, but he still felt a sense of dread. He found that drinking some vodka with his orange juice in the morning helped. He began coming to work drunk, and his job performance deteriorated.

After several months of this, he was fired. At first he was relieved, because he would no longer have to drive over bridges. His wife, though, angrily reminded him of his responsibilities, and as money troubles mounted, he drowned his guilt and shame in more vodka.

A year later, he had made some adjustments, and he and his wife were able to start a home business. He still could not drive over bridges, and he had to abort a planned trip to San Francisco with his wife due to his anxiety, but he didn't recognize that he had a major problem. But when he began working with Dumont, more than a decade later, a crisis was finally reached—two of his children were in college, and he would not be able to attend their graduation, because he could not cross bridges.

At this point, Norm had made no connection between his first panic attack and his father's impending death. Dumont theorized that he would not have become phobic if he had associated his panic sensations with his father's illness rather than with crossing a bridge. Norm considered his bridge phobia an isolated problem, but he soon realized that it ruled his life. He was continuously calculating driving routes that didn't involve bridges, and he would not drive anywhere without his wife in the car with him.

Norm depicted his wife as supportive, understanding, and loving. In reality, she was angry and extremely unhappy. She felt used and manipulated, and Norm was afraid she would leave him. She told Dumont, "I've been mad at him since he screwed up our trip to California. That was five years ago. Since then he hasn't even tried to go anywhere." Her life was as limited as his, because the only places they ever went were to her parents or his doctors. She was his caretaker.

Norm's fears were all phrased in the future tense. What if he went crazy? What if he had a stroke or a heart attack and died? What if he lost control and drove his car off a bridge? The fact that all these "what ifs" were unrealistic did not stem his irrational catastrophizing. His biggest worry was that he would never get better. He was disgusted with his panic and anguished about his future.

Over the course of time and with the assistance of Norm's wife, Dumont gradually helped Norm conquer his fear bridges. He began to understand his self-defeating fears and to learn to deal with the present without worrying about the future. He developed rational responses to his irrational thoughts. As he progressed, his wife's anger diminished. She once told Dumont, "I'm so pleased with the way things are going. I can't even remember the last time Norm got drunk." There are several points we can make about Norm and his phobia:

- Even if there is an innate fear response to some objects or situations, such as heights, the fear is usually overcome by life experiences that allow us to realistically appraise the danger.
- Fears only become debilitating phobias when they are accompanied by catastrophic thoughts about improbable disasters that might happen.
- Although the individual may be totally unaware of the origin of these irrational beliefs, they typically arise from a chance connection between some anxiety-producing life event and the phobic object.
- The real dysfunction of the phobia does not lie in the fear the object elicits. The symptoms of panic dissipate rather quickly. The true dysfunction lies in the need for a person to avoid contact with or

even think about contact with the object or situation. It is fear of panic, not panic itself, that controls the person's life.

Social Anxiety

One particular form of phobia, which is differentiated from others, is based in social anxiety. Since so much in life hinges on our ability to interact with others, especially with people who are not close to us, social phobias can be particularly debilitating. The anxiety generated by social situations can range from narrow to broad situations and from mild to intense.

The degree of dysfunction created by social anxiety depends on how often people find themselves in that frightening situation. One common and fairly narrow one is public speaking or performing. People report that their minds go blank, that they can't think or concentrate in front of other people. This phenomenon has little effect on the lives of most people, unless they happen to be in a profession that requires them to talk in front of others.

I had an experience of social anxiety early in my career that I still vividly remember. I was teaching a college course in physiological psychology in front of about sixty students. This was rather technical material and not the sort of thing that I could just gab about. My notes were prepared, but my mind must've been elsewhere. I began to realize that I didn't know what I was trying to say, and my attention quickly diverted to my own discomfort. I thought, *How am I ever going to get through this?* I continued reading from my notes, but they made no sense to me. My anxiety mounted, and I was about to walk out, when I looked up at my students. I saw that half of them looked puzzled and the other half was asleep. I almost laughed, as I realized none of them really recognized my anxiety. That broke the panic, because I could no longer catastrophize about my situation. My focus regained, I simply joked about it and started over.

What often happens with social phobias is that they may begin as confined and specific phobias and then grow to encompass more social situations. These may include talking to strangers or meeting new people or even interacting with bosses or coworkers. They may expand to ordinary activities, such as eating or drinking or even walking in public.

157

What all these social situations have in common is that they involve scrutiny by others, with the possibility of being judged. The typical scenario for a social phobia is a vicious cycle. It begins with a temperamentally shy person or one who otherwise lacks self-confidence. Put such a person in front of people who might be evaluating him, and he imagines humiliation or rejection. These thoughts arouse the physiological manifestations of anxiety. This is compounded by the fact that the person expects that others will notice his fear and subject him to humiliation, which increases his embarrassment.

When confronted with a difficult social situation, the socially anxious person freezes, much like a rat facing a cat, unable to properly appraise the true threat, if any, of the situation. The limbic system sounds the alert, and the person is prepared to flee, not think. When this occurs on multiple occasions, the person learns to avoid the apparent source of the anxiety. Such people often become generally avoidant. They try to stay in the background and avoid being noticed. This inhibits their ability to make friends or engage in rewarding social activities. If they are in the workforce, they may avoid job interviews or promotions.

Beck and Emery point out the paradox of social phobias.[185] The fear of a bad outcome in social situations—such as not being able to carry on a conversation on a date or going blank during a job interview or when speaking in front of others—causes just the consequences the person most fears. On the other hand, the person who does not experience the fear of inept performance in a particular situation is substantially less likely to respond ineptly.

Anxiety Defenses

People often don't recognize their feelings of anxiety or don't express them directly. Instead, they defend against them by developing patterns of dysfunctional behavior in an attempt to deflect such feelings. There are three sorts of defensive strategies that we can identify. The first involves developing a pattern of repetitive, ritualistic behaviors called *compulsions*. The second focuses on dissociation, which is a kind of mental partitioning or splitting of mental processes that are usually interrelated. The third influences perceptions of ill health and physical symptoms, which will be discussed in a later chapter.

Obsessions and Compulsions

The humorist Alexander King used to joke that before he entered his home, he would always say, "May this house be safe from tigers." You might laugh at him, but it always worked. Probably all of us have engaged in magical thinking of this sort from time to time. Our worlds can be threatening and unpredictable, and we look for ways we can control those dangers. Superstitions and little rituals can make us feel safer.

Most of our superstitious behaviors are benign and culturally reinforced. We avoid walking under ladders or breaking mirrors, or we knock on wood to prevent bad luck. We know these rituals are silly and that there is no causal connection, but we do them anyway, just to be sure.

At root, we have made a false assumption about cause and effect, even if it is a transient one. We believe that some arbitrary action can control our destiny in some way. But what happens if the danger seems more real to us—even though it exists in our own imagining? Our rituals may then become more serious and intrusive.

The therapist Raeann Dumont gave a striking example of how such a ritual came about in her own life.[186] As a young child, she developed impetigo, a serious facial rash, on the lower part of her face. The doctor told her mother that it was probably caused by putting dirty things in her mouth. Her mother began compulsively washing her and everything that she could come in contact with. Dumont recalled, "The cause and effect were etched indelibly in my mind. Something dirty in my mouth equals the pain and suffering of impetigo."

A few years later, a terrible polio epidemic began. Dumont became a compulsive hand washer, because "outside were unseen germs ready to wreak havoc on my person, and my defense was to wash." She continued this ritual despite social embarrassment and the knowledge that some children ate with the dirtiest hands and nothing bad happened to them.

When she felt her hands were dirty, "they felt huge and as if they were vibrating." The sensation soon spread to her stomach. She began to have obsessive thoughts: "I can't feel right until I wash my hands. I must feel right immediately or something bad will happen."

When the compulsive hand washing continued into her teens, her mother unwittingly contributed to it when she teased Dumont about having a "Lady Macbeth syndrome," saying, "you must feel guilty about something." Being a typical teen, Dumont did indeed believe she had plenty to feel guilty about. She was even more self-conscious about her hand washing and felt she was a "defective person" to boot.

Dumont did grow up and overcome her compulsion, at least to the extent that the need to wash her hands no longer dominated her life. For less fortunate people, ritualistic behavior cannot be so easily conquered. For some people, their own thoughts seem so unacceptable and dangerous that they must forever be on guard against them. They must continually counter the threatening thoughts with magical rituals. But these rituals are only so effective and thus must be repeated over and over.

We have, of course, been speaking of what is commonly known as *obsessive-compulsive disorder.* At its most severe, obsessive-compulsive behavior is vicious cycle. It starts with unacceptable imaginings of dreadful consequences. When a person can reveal these thoughts, they often have something to do with sex or aggression. They may be expressed as illogical fears of punishment or contamination.

Whatever the source, these thoughts arouse threatening sensations of anxiety and must be neutralized. Rituals temporarily accomplish this, but must be done correctly. The obsessive-compulsive person can never be sure she has done it perfectly, so she keeps repeating it.

One patient of mine had a persistent fear that he had accidentally hit someone driving to work. He would circle back and retrace his drive to see if he had done this, but he could never be certain, so he felt compelled to circle back over and over. Like many obsessive-compulsives, he knew that this was illogical behavior, and each repetition made him increasingly frustrated and upset with himself. Since his lateness did not please his employers, he became even more anxious about possibly losing his job. The ritualistic behavior that initially relieved his distress now became the source of even greater distress as it took over his life.

Lately, there has been growing recognition among those who would categorize mental disorders that there is no single type of obsessive-compulsive disorder. A worldwide survey of OCD experts found wide agreement that there are several varieties of "overlapping symptoms and dimensions" within the OCD umbrella.[187] Not only that, but more than one symptom dimension can exist within a single individual, and there is continuity between "normal" obsessions and compulsions and what should be defined as a disorder.[188]

There are several interesting questions about OCD. What different types can we distinguish? Are they stable and consistent? Where do they come from? And are they marked by any kind of brain differences?

Michael Bloch and his colleagues from the Yale University OCD clinic, doing a statistical analysis of a large number of studies, found that there were four distinct and consistent OCD factors.[189] Each of these factors had typical obsessive thoughts (defined as "repetitive, intrusive thoughts and images") accompanied by characteristic compulsive behaviors ("repetitive ritualistic physical or mental acts perform to reduce anxiety"). The four factors are:

- *A symmetry factor.* Obsessions about maintaining symmetry and order, with the compulsion to put objects just so and to repeat and to count.

- *A forbidden-thoughts factor.* Disturbing obsessions having an aggressive, sexual, or religious content. The related compulsions usually involve checking.

- *A cleaning factor.* Obsessive thoughts about contamination. Related compulsions include things like hand washing or avoiding touching objects.

- *A hoarding factor.* Obsessions about the need to save things, with the resulting compulsive hoarding.

On the subject of how these obsessive-compulsive features might be generated, the answer seems to be they are part of normal human development. The same researchers who did the four-factor study observed in another study that, "typically, developing children engage in a significant amount of ritualistic, repetitive, and compulsive-like activity."[190] This behavior seems to peak about age two and closely resembles the OCD symptom dimensions. Parents reported that beginning about age two, their children arranged objects or repeated behaviors until they were "just right," "seemed very concerned with dirt or cleanliness" and began to "collect or store objects." The researchers noted that "these ritualistic and compulsive-like behaviors are correlated with the children's fears and phobias." Although no direct relationship has been established, they suggest the possibility that these are the precursors of later problematic obsessive-compulsive behavior.

There is a surprising connection between people, especially children, labeled OCD and tic disorders, especially Tourette's syndrome. Tics are "sudden, rapid, recurrent, non-rhythmic motor movement or vocalization," and Tourette's is defined by multiple tics of both kinds.[191] The combination of OCD and tics has been found in 10 percent to 40 percent of children with OCD. The Yale group noted that children who exhibited both also had higher rates of disruptive behaviors and developmental disorders.

The Yale group looked for a possible biological connection for this constellation of problems and reported another surprising connection. There is some evidence that there might be a link to an infection by streptococcal bacteria (a condition called *PANDAS,* an acronym for *pediatric autoimmune neuropsychiatric disorders associated with streptococcal infection*), though further research is needed.

Dissociative Experiences

Dissociation refers to the disruption or fragmentation of conscious experience. Dissociation disorders are conceptualized as a breakdown in one's sense of self and in the continuity of a person's memory or identity. We have already briefly encountered two varieties of this discontinuity when we discussed the symptoms of panic, *depersonalization* and *derealization.* There are also two other forms of dissociation, which are more dramatic, known as *dissociative amnesia* and *dissociative identity* (previously known as *multiple personality*).

We will discuss each of these, but first we must consider why we should sense our conscious selves as continuous at all. Consciousness is not really continuous. Our minds wander here and there; sometimes we are sleep, sometimes awake. Sometimes we are focused on a task and have no sense of self and sometimes we fantasize about alternative selves. We create the illusion of continuity of consciousness by narrating a story of self that brings all these disparate pieces together.

The psychological theorist Julian Jaynes contends that consciousness plays only a limited role in our existence and that much of the time we are not consciously aware at all.[192] Jaynes offers an analogy of a flashlight endowed with consciousness. The flashlight can only be conscious of being on when it is on, not when it's off. If what it sees whenever it comes on is pretty much the same, the flashlight will have the illusion that it is continuously on. Similarly, we can't be conscious of times when we are not conscious.

The idea of continuous consciousness is important for our psychological well-being. We work hard to construct a coherent narrative that links our remembered life experiences and changing mental states into one continuous whole, which we call our "self" or our "personality." Dissociation is the breakdown of this narrative and can cause us great discomfort.

Depersonalization and derealization are the two simpler forms of this disruption. Depersonalization is a feeling of being disconnected from oneself. People describe it as feeling as though they were observing themselves from outside or watching themselves from a distance. Depersonalization has been a frequent report of people who have had a near-death experience. Actually, it is a common experience; an estimated 50 percent of the population has experienced depersonalization.[193] Derealization is the feeling of being disconnected from reality. People say they feel like they are in a dream, and the world seems to move in slow motion. Derealization is depicted in the 1998 film *Saving Private Ryan,* when Captain John Miller (Tom Hanks) has been shot and watches what is happening as if it is a slow-motion, silent movie.

Depersonalization and derealization usually go together and are now seen as two aspects of depersonalization disorder. Minor disruptions of consciousness may startle us, but are of little concern. If they are persistent and seem frightening to us, they become more dysfunctional.

The source of the dysfunction is not the symptoms themselves—those are just the consequences of stress interrupting the flow of consciousness. The real dysfunction is the catastrophic meaning people put on the symptoms and the efforts they make to avoid the feelings. They then become just like a phobia.

The more dramatic and usually more impairing forms of dissociative behaviors involve the loss of memory and the creation of alternative personalities. Dissociative amnesia may involve the simple forgetting of certain life events. People who had problematic childhoods or experienced traumatic events often say they can't remember that period of time. Far more puzzling, however, is dissociative fugue. The term *fugue* comes from the same root as *fugitive*. It applies to people who seem to suddenly forget their entire past. The typical fugue story that makes the news tells of a person who arrives in a strange city with no name or past. That person may adopt a new identity and a new life until one day he suddenly realizes who he is and where he came from.

In dissociative identity disorder, the person displays one or more alternative personalities, or "alters," in addition to the primary one. These alters appear in control of the physical person at different times. They may have entirely different ways of interacting with the world and may be different ages and even different sexes. The alters may know about the primary person, but the primary usually acts as if he or she has no clue about the existence of the alters.

The common way of understanding dissociative phenomena is as a defense reaction to intense stress or trauma. This is particularly true for dissociative identity disorder, believed to be caused by trauma early in life. The modern psychoanalytic view is that we form our sense of identity from our interactions with the most significant people in our lives and from the culture around us. When we experienced trauma in these relationships, memories and feelings associated with these events must be walled off to maintain our attachments to these important people.[194]

Dissociation is conceptualized as a "posttraumatic condition, resulting from overwhelming childhood experiences, usually severe child abuse."[195] Psychologist David Gleaves describes the creation of alters as a creative survival strategy that helps a person cope with such trauma. In support of this theory, he cites seven large studies of dissociative identity disorder patients who reported a history of childhood sexual or physical abuse in upward of 90 percent of the cases. In most cases, the reported abuse was "severe, extensive and sadistic." Further, he concluded that the occurrence of the disorder is much higher than had been thought and "approximately as common as anorexia nervosa or schizophrenia."

As reasonable as this may seem to us, the posttraumatic theory—and even the existence of dissociative identity disorder—is hotly disputed. No one would dispute the terrible effects that severe childhood abuse can have on a person, but is it the cause of fractured identities? More significantly, are the reports even true? Is the splitting of a person's identity into alters a real phenomenon or something akin to demonic possession or hypnosis?

There are reasons to be skeptical about the details of horrific abuse reported by dissociative identity disorder patients. Almost all studies of it depend on the recollections of the patients, without any objective corroboration.[196] Studies of abused children have mostly found no connection between childhood abuse and adult dissociation.[197] Also, a high proportion of people who seek psychiatric help report childhood abuse, so that abuse may relate generally to psychological distress rather than specifically to dissociation.

The history of what we now call *dissociative identity disorder* is an intriguing story. According to psychologist Nicholas Spanos, there were only sporadic reports of multiple personalities throughout most of the nineteenth century.[198] There was a big rise in cases toward the end of the nineteenth century and into the first two decades of the twentieth century, which coincided with the height of the Freudian era. From the 1920s to 1970, however, there were almost no cases reported. And then, after 1970, there was an "astronomic" increase in reported cases.

The great expansion was not universal. It was mostly restricted to North America, with only rare cases in France, Great Britain, Russia, and India. And beyond that, Spanos calculated that 66 percent of these diagnoses were made by .09 percent of American psychiatrists; the vast majority of psychiatrists had never seen a case. Perhaps they were not asking the right questions (as suggested by Gleaves) or perhaps the ones doing the diagnosing were helping their patients create the condition (as suggested by Spanos).

The significant event that coincided with the great increase in diagnosed cases of dissociative identity disorder was the publication of the bestseller *Sibyl* in 1973,[199] followed by a 1976 television drama based on it. The case of Sibyl and her sixteen personalities captured the imagination of the public and attracted a core of dedicated psychiatrists and therapists. Largely due to the efforts of these psychiatrists, DSM officially adopted multiple personality disorder in the 1980 edition.

The True Story of Sibyl

The truth of the case of Sibyl was uncovered largely through the efforts of investigative reporter Debbie Nathan after the parties were all deceased and voluminous records were uncovered in the archives of John Jay College.[200] It was a fraud perpetrated by three women: a vulnerable patient, whose real name was Shirley Mason; a deluded psychiatrist named Dr. Cornelia Wilbur; and an ambitious author, Flora Rheta Schreiber, who was willing to make up "facts." The publication of *Sibyl*, and the television drama that followed, precipitated a kind of mass hysteria. A multitude of susceptible young people, mostly women, learned, with the aid of their therapists, that they had been horribly sexually abused by their parents and then, as a result, had developed multiple personalities. As each new case was unveiled, a rash of new cases was produced, until there was an epidemic of thousands of diagnoses.

The true story of Shirley Mason begins with a lonely, highly imaginative girl growing up in a fundamentalist Seventh Day Adventist family. Her parents taught her that her imaginative world and her artwork were sinful. She became conflicted, anxious, and secretive. She developed obsessive fears of illness and compulsive rituals. She prayed and asked God to cure her and when he didn't, she became angry. When she was a high school senior, her mother caught her masturbating with a hairbrush, but there was never any indication that she was abused by her mother.

Fast-forward to 1956, when Mason came to see Dr. Wilbur and recounted that she had been standing outside her classroom at Columbia University, and the next thing she knew, she was in a strange city, Philadelphia, and five days had elapsed. She told Dr. Wilbur that she had "lost time" on many previous occasions. She had found herself in places with no idea how she had gotten there, and she had discovered clothing in her closet with no recollection of buying them. At that time, she had no awareness of alternative personalities.

Dr. Wilbur decided that Mason had suffered terrible traumas as a young child and that she had created other personalities to cope with her pain. Dr. Wilbur's interpretation was that Ms. Mason's had "alters" that were responsible for her odd behaviors, but that Mason was unaware of them. Wilbur began a course of therapy designed to integrate the alters, the number of which grew, over time, to sixteen.

Wilbur's treatment involved drug-induced hypnotic trances to help Mason get in touch with her past abuse and learn about her many alters. Wilbur was a persuasive therapist, and Mason a highly cooperative patient. Under Wilbur's tutelage, Mason came to recall that her mother had done many bizarre and awful things to her. On numerous occasions, her mother had raped her with household utensils, tried to suffocate her, and gave her ice-water enemas. Her mother also made Mason watch as she defecated on a neighbor's lawn, held lesbian orgies in the woods, and fondled babies' genitals.

Therapy lasted eleven years and, during it, Mason moved in with Dr. Wilbur; they formed a symbiotic relationship in which Wilbur was the nurturing mother and Mason was the dependent, good child. In the 1990s, a psychiatrist who had occasionally seen Mason during this period—when Wilbur was away—revealed that Wilbur "wanted her to act as though she had different selves inside her." He also recalled that Wilbur told him she wanted to write a book on multiple personality.

After Dr. Wilbur felt that Mason was sufficiently integrated, she brought in Flora Rheta Schreiber to write a book about the case. The three formed a company called Sibyl Incorporated and agreed to split the profits. They made a great deal of money and spawned the official multiple personality diagnosis.

By the 1980s, multiple personality disorder had become a social movement with advocacy groups, self-help groups, and some patients asserting their right to keep their alters. There were therapists employing their multiple personality disorder patients "as co-therapists to help convince skeptical new patients that the multiple personality disorder diagnosis is accurate," and as many as 17 percent of therapists treating it were dissociative disorder patients themselves.[201] Spanos concluded, "these therapists, who help socialize new patient recruits into the [multiple personality disorder] role are reminiscent of those in traditional cultures who, after their own possession, join and sometimes become leaders of possession cults that shape and legitimate the spirit possession enactments of new members."

Spanos's theory—and that of others who don't believe the model of early trauma leading to dissociative disorders—is called the *sociocognitive model*. According to this theory, the roots of purported multiple identities, dissociative fugue, and similar presentations lie in social learning and expectancies. It starts with distressed persons who are suggestible and fantasy-prone and searching for an understanding of why they are the way they are. They have probably heard about multiple personalities and its association with childhood trauma but may never have thought it applied to them. Then they see a therapist who is a believer, who helps them see the truth about themselves. The therapist asks suggestive questions such as "Are there other parts of you we haven't talked to?"[202] The therapist may use hypnosis or drugs to assist the patient's memory, as Sibyl's psychiatrist did. If patients tentatively talk about alternative personalities, their therapists encourage them to give their alters specific identities and to establish contact with them.

Dissociative phenomena like fugue and multiple identities may seem peculiar and alien to us, but they are related to commonplace and even desirable activities. Consider an actor who gives a great performance. For a time, the actor becomes his character. To convince his audience, the actor first convinces himself. For the actor, there remains a kind of cognitive duality. He maintains an awareness of who he is, and he can leave the role, but I've heard actors speak of staying in character for weeks at a time while they shoot a movie. Playing a role is not a self-conscious attempt to deceive, but the art lies in deception.

More mundanely, we all adopt poses and present ourselves to the world to the best advantage we can. If you met me, I would try to exhibit a personality that best fits the situation and that is somewhat different from the one that my wife sees. In fact, we expect people to adjust their personalities to the social circumstances they encounter. We are not trying to be deceptive, yet we too are playing a role. Similarly, when we read fiction or watch a movie, we may identify with the characters and lose our own identities for a time. We consider this entertainment, not a dissociative disorder.

I also have a certain kind of amnesia—and I suppose you do as well. I try to forget the painful episodes of my life, such as the failures and humiliations—those things that we all endure. It's not that I can't remember them, but if possible, I choose to be the hero of my own life and forget the bad things. I prefer to fantasize about success, rather than remember pain. I consider this adaptive.

It seems likely that people diagnosed with dissociative identity or fugue are also displaying a form of this role-playing. What separates their behaviors from ordinary social behavior is the dramatic intensity and apparent lack of awareness they display. If we stand back a pace and look with a skeptical eye, however, we can usually see what benefit a person is getting from playing this role.

I don't know to what extent the person intentionally creates dissociative behaviors, nor can I. I don't think it is usually planned or purposeful, as the fraudulent behavior of a con artist might be. The rewards for the dissociative person are not tangible; they are psychological and social, such as gaining sympathy, being cared for, or having a special place in the world.

Posttraumatic Stress

When we are faced with a sudden stressful event, our stress-response systems kick in to deal with the emergency. Ordinarily, we are successful, and afterward, we calm down and go about our business. Extraordinarily dangerous or harmful events, however, can overwhelm our ability to cope. The after effects of a traumatic event is a typical pattern of experience we call an *acute stress response*.

Acute stress has features in common with dissociative responses. In fact, dissociation may be the model for how humans usually experience traumatic events, including grief. Read down the list of symptoms of acute stress in DSM-5, and you will find two explicitly involving dissociation: an altered sense of reality and an inability to recall some or all of the traumatic event. There may also be flashbacks, in which a person feels or even acts as if the terrible event is reoccurring. Other kinds of cognitive effects include having involuntary memories and recurrent dreams about what happened.

There are also emotional and arousal symptoms that are reminiscent of what we recognize as depression. These include not being able to experience positive emotions, being irritable, and even having angry outbursts. Sleep disturbance and problems with concentration are common. Other symptoms are much like those we see in people displaying agoraphobia and other severe phobic responses, including sudden psychological distress and a physical reaction to reminders of the event. Hypervigilance and exaggerated startle response are also part of a posttraumatic package.

Acute stress reactions are also the model for how we generally cope with intense fear—we avoid. People who have recently experienced a traumatic event make efforts to avoid remembering, thinking about, or experiencing the feelings of the trauma or anything like it. Part of that effort is to avoid coming in contact with anything that might remind them of it.

An acute stress response, like grief, usually dissipates over time. The memories and feelings remain, but most people adjust and no longer exhibit the emotional intensity or disturbed behavior they did previously. If the acute pattern of symptoms continues over an extended period of time (measuring many months or years), it becomes labeled *posttraumatic stress disorder* (PTSD). The relationship between acute and posttraumatic stress parallels the one between grief and depression. There is no dividing line, but continuity in both dimensions. The paradox is that what starts out as a protective response—a time-out, during with one can readjust one's life—becomes increasingly dysfunctional as time goes by and the person does not regain a productive and satisfying life.

The factor that separates acute and posttraumatic stress from other forms of psychological distress is the nature of the trauma. The DSM-5 definition begins with "exposure to actual or threatened death, serious injury or sexual violence."[203] This definition seems to clearly distinguish what are considered traumatic stressors from the many other kinds of adverse things that can happen in a person's life. DSM muddies the waters, however, by adding progressively less direct forms of trauma. According to the latest DSM, stress disorders can also be caused by witnessing traumatic events occurring to others, learning of traumatic things that happened to family members or friends, or being repeatedly exposed to traumatic events, as in the case of "first responders collecting human remains" or "police officers repeatedly exposed to details of child abuse."

When the term *posttraumatic stress disorder* first entered the official psychiatric lexicon in 1980, trauma "was conceptualized as a catastrophic stressor that was outside the range of usual human experiences."[204] The problematic consequences of the wide variety of ordinary but painful stressors that might occur in a person's life were classified as adjustment disorders. The reasoning was that generally resilient people had the ability to adjust to ordinary stress. Catastrophic events, on the other hand, could overwhelm just about anyone's coping resources.

The rationale for the current change in the definition of *trauma* appears to be that people's perception of traumatic stress is variable. "Like pain, the traumatic experience is filtered through cognitive and emotional processes before it can be appraised as an external threat."[205] This logic blurs the lines, however, and PTSD loses any sense of distinctness. The classification becomes generic and expandable, so that almost any type of dysfunction, from depression and agoraphobia to schizophrenia could be labeled PTSD. DSM-5 seems to have partially recognized this problem of expansive pathologizing. Psychiatry did exclude "exposure through electronic media, television, movies, or pictures, unless this exposure is work-related" from traumatic stressors.

What Is the Real PTSD?

The diagnosis of PTSD has become increasingly controversial over recent years, and with the DSM-5, the new definitions have come under outright attack. PTSD was considered the one psychiatric disorder that had a specific cause (trauma) and a particular clinical syndrome that distinguished it from all others.[206] If true, PTSD should provide a unique opportunity to find medical markers and specific mechanisms that would align it with medical diseases. Despite a great deal of research, attempts to show that PTSD is different from other disorders have failed.

The first part of the problem is defining what constitutes a trauma. There must be a definition, because "without exposure to trauma, what is posttraumatic about the ensuing syndrome?"[207] But what makes a particular event traumatic? Is it the nature of the event itself, the degree of a person's exposure to it, or the individual's reaction to an event?

What constitutes a "qualifying" traumatic event? There are all kinds of devastating life events that can create many of the symptoms of PTSD. Psychiatrists Gerald Rosen, Robert Spitzer, and Paul McHugh propose a number of diagnostic categories that could be based on the PTSD model, including "prolonged duress stress disorder, post-traumatic relationship syndrome, post-traumatic dental care anxiety and post-traumatic abortion syndrome."[208] They see this sort of trauma ambiguity as "criteria creep." One suggested solution to this problem has been to eliminate the requirement of a stressful event from the definition of PTSD.[209]

Even if PTSD-qualifying events are limited to exposure to physically catastrophic events, as DSM-5 attempts to do, how intimate does that exposure have to be? Many people witnessed the terrorist attacks of 9/11 with horror. Some, like a close friend of mine, was in one of the World Trade Center towers when it was hit and escaped by running down some eighty flights of stairs. Some of her coworkers stayed behind and died. Other people saw the towers collapse from miles away and feared that they, too, were in danger. Post-9/11 studies found PTSD symptoms in people as far away as Houston and Los Angeles. Psychiatrist Carol North and her colleagues raise the question as to whether these reactions to such an extreme event should be considered psychopathology at all. Should it be considered a normal human response? As Rosen, Spitzer, and McHugh write, "Labeling situation-based emotions and upsetting thoughts as symptoms is akin to saying that someone's cough in a smoky tavern is a symptom of respiratory disease."

Another problem with the conception of PTSD is whether there is a unique connection between a traumatic event and a specific syndrome. The same set of clinical symptoms might just as readily be labeled major depression, anxiety disorder, phobia, dissociation, or substance abuse. Gerald Rosen and his coauthors offer a hypothetical example of a boat captain whose vessel goes down at sea. Several members of his crew die, but he is uninjured. He becomes tense, sleeps poorly, and withdraws from things he usually enjoyed. He is anxious about returning to sea, so he turns down job offers and has no income. As a result of all these factors, he becomes increasingly anxious and depressed. As the authors report, the captain's condition could be seen as normal bereavement complicated by a phobia about returning to sea and a situational adjustment issue causing him anxiety and depression.

Rosen summed up his thoughts about the overextended PTSD diagnosis this way: "the overlap issue worries me tremendously. We have to ask how we got here. We have to ask ourselves, 'what do we gain by having this diagnosis?'"[210]

The prototypical cause of PTSD is exposure to trauma on the battlefield. The acute response to battlefield stress has been written about since ancient times. Three thousand years ago, an Egyptian soldier wrote, "You determine to go forward.... Shuddering seizes you, the hair on your head stands on end, your soul lies in your hand."[211] The first known label for an acute combat syndrome was used by seventeenth-century Swiss military physicians. The term used was *nostalgia,* which was described as "melancholy, incessant thinking of home, disturbed sleep or insomnia, weakness, loss of appetite, anxiety, cardiac palpitations, stupor and fever." German doctors of the same era called it *homesickness.*

During the American Civil War, many soldiers succumbed to what was called *soldier's heart.* Those suffering from extreme cases were simply discharged. The name of their hometown was pinned to their clothing, and they were either put on a train or left to wander about until they starved. These soldiers were considered insane, and their large numbers led to the establishment of the first military mental hospital, in 1863. What perplexed military physicians more than these cases of what they saw as battlefield insanity was something more difficult to understand. There were large numbers of soldiers who showed no sign of emotional distress during the fighting but who broke down when they went home on leave.

The terrible fighting in World War I created huge numbers of psychiatric casualties, but the military had a short memory and believed this was a new condition. It was decided that the problem was a neurological one—a brain concussion caused by exploding artillery shells: *shell shock*. Sigmund Freud contributed his part by calling it *war neurosis* and said it was caused by a conflict between a soldier's "war ego" and his "peace ego."

After World War I, it was calculated that of the two million Americans soldiers who fought, about 204,000 were wounded, while 159,000 were put out of action for psychiatric reasons, 70,000 of whom were permanently discharged. In World War II, the statistics were even worse. Of the approximately 800,000 soldiers who saw direct combat, more than a third became psychiatric casualties. The recognition that it was the stress of battle that was causing men to break down led to the new terms *combat exhaustion* and *battle fatigue.*

By the time of the Vietnam War, the recognition that something more than battlefield fatigue was going on was beginning to dawn on some. War is fought by boys who go in naïve, optimistic, and committed and quickly become cynical, detached, and heartless. This attitude is "all-consuming and pervades the soul. You carry it with you when you leave the battlefield. You carry it home, where you live with it. You share it with your family and your friends and ultimately with your society. And it is poisonous, exceedingly poisonous."

The new conception of PTSD in soldiers is that it is not merely a continuation of acute stress response in vulnerable individuals. It is not just memories of intense fear that is so psychologically debilitating. A major part of the cause of PTSD is the moral revulsion or "moral injury" suffered by the men and women engaged in war. According to psychologist Brett Litz and his colleagues, soldiers, "may act in ways that transgress deeply held moral beliefs or they may experience the unethical behaviors of others. Warriors may also bear witness to intense human suffering and cruelty that shakes their core beliefs about humanity."[212] Describing the aftereffects of such devastating moral conflict as a mental disorder does not do justice to the shame and guilt experienced by these young people who come back to be treated as heroes and expected to resume normal lives.

Summing Up

Fear, along with its companion, anxiety, is one of the basic emotions hard-wired into us, what neuroscientist Jaak Panksepp calls *evolutionary emotions.*[213] Anxiety itself is not dysfunctional. It is necessary for safe and effective functioning in this world. People who do not experience sufficient anxiety get into trouble, because they do not automatically inhibit their rash actions, as most of us would.

Anxiety causes us misery and dysfunction when we treat it as pathological or develop life-constricting symptoms to control it. People who learn to accept their anxiety as only a feeling—and one they can use as a guide, if they can understand its message—lead much happier lives.

8

Cognitive Competence

Our cognitive abilities are the hallmark of our species. We do not have fangs or claws to protect ourselves, and we are not very strong or swift. The secret to our evolutionary success lies in our ability to form complex groups and work together, to creatively solve problems, and to pass these solutions onto others. Although we are no longer easy prey to nonhuman predators, intelligence plays an ever-increasing role in our ability to thrive in the modern world. Intellectual ability probably has more impact on the quality of our lives than at any prior point in human history.

Human beings vary in their intellectual abilities, and lower intelligence impedes our ability to succeed, particularly in advanced societies. We long recognized this fact with the term *mental retardation,* which has now been supplanted by *intellectual disability.*[214] DSM describes four severity levels of intellectual disability: mild, moderate, severe, and profound. Previously, these levels were defined by IQ ranges, but the current DSM has replaced numbers with descriptions, which we will return to later in the chapter. But in reality, there are no breaks along the intelligence dimension. Intelligence is a continuous quality from lowest to highest.

Intellectual disability is also called *intellectual developmental disorder,* because it is presumed to be a product of the early developmental period. Although this may not always be so, it does reflect early difficulties in acquiring intellectual skills. At the other end of life, as we age, we all have diminished abilities in some areas, though (hopefully) we acquire wisdom. Some people, however, decline much faster and in more ways than others, due to many different causes. We lump this decline under the term *dementia,* whatever its specific origin. This chapter includes both intellectual disability and dementia along one dimension that I called *cognitive competence*.

In writing this chapter, I cast about for a good general definition of *intelligence*. One promising candidate was, "an intrinsic ability to process information from abiotic and biotic stimuli that allows optimal decisions about future activities in a given environment."[215] Good, perhaps, but it applies to plants. A human-oriented definition was offered many years ago by David Wechsler, one of the pioneers of IQ testing. He defined intelligence as the "capacity of the individual to act purposefully, to think rationally and to deal effectively with his environment."[216]

Some neuropsychologists consider *intelligence* an outmoded term and would dispense with it altogether. "General intelligence is as valid as the 'strength of soil' is for plant growers. It is not wrong, but archaic."[217] There is only a collection of discrete cognitive functions "that work together so smoothly when the human brain is intact that cognition is experienced as a single seamless attribute."[218] For neuropsychologist Muriel Lezak, this suite of cognitive functions includes receptive functions, memory and learning, thinking and expressive functions. To these, I would add executive functions, those functions that the neuropsychologist Elkhonon Goldberg described as *s* the smart or shrewd factor. *S* is "our ability to form insight into other people and to anticipate their behavior, motives and intentions.... Whether you want to cooperate with someone's intentions or thwart them (and particularly in the latter case) you must first understand and anticipate the other person's intentions."[219]

It is true that these cognitive functions can be measured separately and separately impaired. It is also true that the totality of cognitive abilities is more than the sum of its parts. As Wechsler phrased it, "the attributes and factors of intelligence, like elementary particles in physics, have at once collective and individual properties, that is, they appear to behave differently when alone from what they do when operating in concert."[220] The factors measured by intelligence tests do correlate with one another. Large statistical studies of intelligence have concluded that there is a general factor of intelligence that varies among people.[221]

Intellectual Disability

A History of Intelligence

Darwin's publication of *On the Origin of Species* and his speculations on how human traits like emotion and intelligence arose sparked a great deal of interest in studying these issues scientifically.[222] Darwin's cousin, Francis Galton, founded the "Anthropometric Laboratory" in 1884 with the idea of finding empirical evidence of intellectual differences.[223] He believed that measurements of physical abilities, such as energy, reaction times, and sensory acuity, was the best way to ascertain who had the most "natural ability." Darwin did not agree with his cousin; he wrote, "I have always maintained that, except for fools, men do not differ much in intelligence, only in zeal and hard work." Galton was entirely on the wrong track about how to measure intelligence, but he introduced the idea that there was something to measure and developed the statistical methods to do it.

At the dawn of the twentieth century, the Englishman Charles Spearman refined the concept of intelligence. Experimenting with schoolchildren, he determined that while sensory abilities were related to school performance, thinking was more important. To capture this factor, he formulated the idea of a general intelligence, which he referred to by the letter g.[224] G was the factor involved whenever thinking was important.

Working at the same time as Spearman, the French psychologist Alfred Binet came up with the first reasonable idea for measuring intelligence. At the end of the nineteenth century, the French government enacted universal education laws, which required all children to receive schooling. This meant that even children who were intellectually deficient or "subnormal" had to attend special classes. Binet was appointed a commissioner on a panel to investigate how to do this.[225]

Binet realized that the first step was to find a reliable method of identifying these children. He started with two groups of children, one of children identified as "mentally deficient" by teachers and doctors, and the other of kids considered "normal." He and his colleague, Théodore Simon, explored a wide variety of tests to try to distinguish between the two groups. He wanted tasks that were not too dependent on school learning and ones that incorporated real-life functions. His problem was that he couldn't create tasks that all the "normal" children could do but the "mentally deficient" could not.

Then Binet hit on his big idea. He factored in age. He recognized that his subnormal group could pass the same tests as the normals, but at an older age. He wrote, "What especially strikes us are the resemblances between very young normal children and subnormals considerably older."[226] Based on this insight, he and Simon created a series of thirty tasks of increasing difficulty to administer to both groups.

The simplest task was to have the children follow a lighted match with their eyes, which Binet and Simon saw as a test of the capacity for attention. Other tasks followed, such as unwrapping and eating a piece of candy. Normal children could complete all the simple tasks by age two. The most profoundly impaired failed some or all these tests no matter what their age. Older children whose maximal capacity was that of a normal two-year-old were classified as "idiots." Functionally, this group could not interact socially or use language with others.

Intermediate tasks were those that were passed by a normal five-year-old. They included pointing to body parts by name, repeating three-digit numbers, and determining which of two boxes was heavier. They also included basic vocabulary and ability to comply with simple requests. Older children who maxed out between the two- and five-year level were characterized as "imbeciles."

The highest-level tasks were passed by normal children between the ages of five and eleven. These included conceptualizing, similarities, rhyming, sentence construction, and social comprehension. The children who couldn't pass most of these tests were described as the "weak-minded" or the "moron" group.

Over the next several years, Binet refined and extended his test. He created a pool of tasks that the average normal child first passed at any specific age from three to thirteen. He later extended the scale to include fifteen-year-olds and adults. He then calculated a way to determine the intellectual level of any child taking the test, based on the norms he had obtained. Thus, a twelve-year-old who could only pass the ten-year-old test had an intellectual level of ten.

Binet found that his scale provided useful information for educating intellectually deficient children. Those at an intellectual level one year behind their chronological age could usually cope with standard school programs. Those that were two or more years behind, on the other hand—only about 7 percent of children—could not handle an ordinary school. Nevertheless, Binet did not take intellectual level too seriously. He realized that there were both errors of measurement and room for change. He cautiously noted that, "one who is an imbecile today, may perhaps by progress of age be able to reach the level of [moron] or on the contrary, remain an imbecile all his life."[227]

In 1912, the German psychologist William Stern renamed *intellectual level* as *intellectual age* because he thought this was a more precise term (his American translator called it *mental age*). He then made the intelligence concept a scalable dimension by making a ratio by dividing mental age by chronological age and calling it the *intelligence quotient*.[228] The final step was taken by Lewis Terman, a Stanford University psychologist, who suggested multiplying it by one hundred to remove the fractions and shortening the term to *IQ*.[229]

In 1916, Terman brought a revised and sophisticated version of Binet's tests to America under the name Stanford-Binet, which became the gold standard for IQ tests. When the United States entered World War I in 1917, the American Psychological Association lobbied to have all new recruits tested, so they could be correctly assigned military duties. Terman proposed a version of his test that could be administered to a group. It was probably the first published multiple-choice test.[230] It became known as the Army Alpha Test.

As many recruits were illiterate or were not native English speakers, a nonverbal intelligence test was also required. A picture-based performance test was created and called Army Beta. By the end of the war, 1,750,000 men had been given one or the other of these tests. Intelligence testing was launched and soon became a ubiquitous feature in the American landscape.[231]

The next major figure in intelligence testing was David Wechsler. He was a veteran of the Army's testing program, having been assigned the task of administering the Stanford-Binet to selected recruits. After he completed his PhD, in 1925, he continued to study intelligence tests. In one study, he found that the variability of mental age decreased as children got older.[232] He interpreted this as demonstrating the homogenizing effect of education. It also meant that intelligence was not a fixed quantity but could be modified by environmental influences. Some years later, he reported that the Alpha Test was better at identifying special abilities and disabilities than the Stanford-Binet.

When, in 1932, he was appointed chief psychologist of New York's Bellevue Hospital, Wechsler had the opportunity to develop an intelligence test of his own. What he wanted was a test tailored to adults and one that would describe a pattern of intelligence attributes—not just give a single number. He also realized that the concept of a "mental age" did not apply past the teenage years, because intelligence did not continue to grow. In fact, absolute scores declined after the early twenties.

Wechsler's resolution of the first problem was to combine the Alpha and Beta Tests, so that he could measure both verbal and performance abilities. By testing a wide variety of abilities, he could get not only a single IQ number but also a pattern of each person's strengths and weaknesses. Wechsler was not convinced that there was any such thing as *g*—a general intelligence—but since scores on the subtests were related to one another, a single number did indicate a person's general ability to do intellectual work.[233]

To address the mental-age problem, he derived something called *deviation IQ*. The age of adults didn't matter, but the number of correct answers relative to the results of other people of the same age did. Give enough people a series of tasks of graded difficulty and the number of correct answers will form a bell curve. That is, most scores will cluster in the middle—the average—with relatively few at either extreme. To get an IQ score, all you had to do is calculate how far a person's raw score is from the mean for his or her age.

In order to standardize the IQ dimension, Wechsler arbitrarily assigned the number 100 to the mean score for any given age group. He then set a measure of variability called *standard deviation* to 15 IQ points.[234] Bell curves have certain statistical properties. Approximately 68 percent of the scores fall between -1 and +1 standard deviations from the mean. This means that about two-thirds of the population has an IQ between 85 and 115 and that about 16 percent has an IQ below 85 or above 115. Only 2.3 percent has an

IQ below 70, which is considered the top of the "intellectually impaired" range, and a similar 2.3 percent has IQs above 130. The IQ numbers have come to be considered representative of where a person stands on the scale of general intelligence.

More recently, there has been a lively debate about whether there is really only one intelligence factor, which can be broken into component parts, or whether there are several independent intelligences. One theory posits that there are two types, *fluid* and *crystallized intelligence*.[235] Psychologists John Horn and Raymond Cattell defined *fluid intelligence* as "the ability to perceive relationships independent of previous specific practice or instruction concerning those relationships." *Crystallized intelligence* is the ability to acquire knowledge through prior learning and experience. In this theory, both forms of intelligence increase throughout childhood, but fluid intelligence peaks at the end of adolescence and begins to decline at about age thirty. Crystallized intelligence continues to increase throughout adulthood. These two kinds of intelligence, however, work together in solving most problems in life, and people who have more of one at any given age, tend to also have more of the other.

Developmental psychologist Howard Gardner has advanced a theory of multiple intelligences, rejecting the idea of a single intelligence factor and the notion that intelligence can be measured by a single test.[236] In his view, these intelligences are independent and follow different developmental courses and depend on different brain processes. These intelligences can be assessed only by observing an individual's interactions with the everyday environment, not by isolated tests.

Gardner's strategy was to search the scientific literature for significant human attributes—what he called "candidate intelligences"—and then to apply eight criteria to determine which should be called a human intelligence. He came up with seven attributes that he considered independent of one another, which he characterized as linguistic, logical-mathematical, musical, body-kinesthetic, spatial, interpersonal, and intrapersonal. Later he added two additional intelligences: naturalistic and existential.[237]

Gardner's theory has been heavily criticized on a number of grounds. A major complaint is that he has not defined *intelligence* in a way that it is usually understood. He has broadened it to include attributes more typically considered abilities or aptitudes, without a coherent rationale. His criteria for considering something an "intelligence" is seen as subjective and as arbitrary. Different researchers could come up with completely different criteria.[238] Even Gardner admitted this: "the selection (or rejection) of eight candidate intelligences is reminiscent more of artistic judgment than of a scientific assessment."[239]

Another major criticism is that multiple-intelligence theory lacks any empirical studies validating it.[240] Harvard professors Richard Herrnstein and Charles Murray in *The Bell Curve* described it as "uniquely devoid of psychometric or other quantitative properties."[241] Even Gardner had to admit that he would be "delighted were such evidence to accrue." By contrast, there have been thousands of studies that have demonstrated that IQ does predict school and job performance (I will discuss this in more detail later).

What Intelligence Tests Consist Of

There are a wide variety of psychological tests that purport to measure intelligence in one way or another. Some, like Raven's Progressive Matrices (discussed below), try to minimize cultural bias by employing a novel kind of problem solving that avoids language and contains no recognizable symbols. This is meant to be a test of fluid intelligence.

Other intelligence tests are also specifically designed as nonverbal, but cover a broader range of intellectual abilities, and are meant to overcome deficits in language or education, as well as cultural barriers. The General Ability Measure for Adults (GAMA) uses abstract designs, shapes, and colors in tasks involving matching, analogies, sequences, and construction. Another is the Comprehensive Test of Nonverbal Intelligence (CTONI2), which uses both familiar objects and geometric forms. It assesses pictorial and semantic analogies, pictorial and geometric categories, and pictorial and geometric sequences.

Other tests, like the SAT and the ACT, go in the opposite direction. They are culture-bound intelligence tests that measure crystallized intelligence or acquired knowledge. They have the specific purpose of predicting college success, but they, too, are attempts to measure general intelligence.

There are many other intelligence tests, each with its specific purposes, but the two most well known and most comprehensive are the Stanford-Binet and the Wechsler Scales. The Wechsler tests are the most commonly used. Three of them cover a wide range of ages, and each is now in its fourth edition. The Wechsler Preschool and Primary Scale of Intelligence (WPPSI-IV) assesses the children from age two and a half to seven and a half. It is kid-friendly, assesses intellectual potential and cognitive delays, and is often used for admittance to private schools. The next age range, from six to sixteen, is assessed by the Wechsler Intelligence Scale for Children (WISC-IV). The adult version, the Wechsler Adult Intelligence Scale (WAIS-IV) covers people from age sixteen to ninety. This is the test I know best, so I will focus on it.

The WAIS-IV tries to sample a wide range of cognitive abilities—some fluid and some crystallized, some verbal and some nonverbal, and some more social and some more abstract. There are ten core subtests, along with five supplemental ones that may be administered if desired. Each subtest has questions or tasks that are graded from easy to complex. They are arranged into four "domains" of intelligence, so in addition to an overall IQ score, each domain also has its own score.[242]

The Verbal Comprehension domain consists of three subtests: Vocabulary, Information, and Similarities. In Vocabulary, the examinee is given a word, both visually and orally, and is asked to define it. It is designed to measure crystallized intelligence involving "verbal concept formation and reasoning." The second subtest, Information, another crystallized intelligence test, asks for facts of general knowledge ("what is the capital of Russia?"). In the Similarities subtest, the examinee is given two words and asked what they have in common. It is also a test involving both reasoning and verbal concepts, but on a more abstract level.

The Perceptual Reasoning domain assesses nonverbal problem solving in various ways. The core subtests are Block Design, Matrix Reasoning, and Visual Puzzles. In Block Design, the examinee is shown a geometric design and asked to reproduce it using blocks that have red surfaces, white surfaces, and half-red, half-white surfaces. This is a fluid intelligence task involving the ability to "analyze and synthesize abstract visual stimuli" and then quickly make a motor response. The Matrix Reasoning subtest also requires a person to analyze geometric figures, but no motor responses are needed. The examinee looks at a series of figures and has to choose which design comes next. The Visual Puzzles subtest is a less abstract nonverbal task. The examinee is shown a completed object and puzzle pieces to choose from. The person has to select which three pieces go together to form the object.

The Working Memory domain has core subtests of Digit Span and Arithmetic. What these tasks have in common is they require the ability to hold information in memory and to do something with it. In Digit Span, the examiner reads number series of increasing length. In the first part, the examinee is asked to simply repeat the numbers as presented. Then another set of number series is presented and the examinee is required to say them backward. The Arithmetic subtest is a more practical task, in which the examinee must mentally solve arithmetic problems. It involves both crystallized knowledge and fluid problem solving, along with concentration and mental manipulation.

The last domain is Processing Speed, which measures "mental and graphical motor" speed. There are two core subtests, Symbol Search and Coding. In Symbol Search, the examinee looks at a series of symbols and then tries to pick the target symbol that matches one of them or to determine that none do. In Coding, the examinee first sees a sequence of numbers, each matched by an arbitrary symbol. Below this is a page full of numbers with an empty box below each. The examinee's job is to put the correct symbol in as many boxes as possible in a designated period of time.

The scores on these core subtests are used to complete four composite scores. The supplemental subtests can be substituted for core ones, if necessary, or to provide further information. The reasoning behind these composites is that statistical analysis shows that general intelligence can best be described as a combination of these four factors. Each individual will have a somewhat different mix of abilities, but the scores are all related to one another, and an overall IQ can be obtained from them.

The Dark Side of Intelligence

Any attempt to connect intelligence and dysfunction must deal with the dark history of the concept. For the past half-century, the measurement of intelligence "has been a pariah in the world of ideas,"[243] and for good reason. It has been used to discriminate between groups of people on the basis of race and ethnic origin and to eliminate the "feebleminded" from the population. Along the way, there have been scientific scandals concerning the inheritance of intelligence.

In the beginning, Francis Galton's impetus for defining intelligence was set in the classist and racist assumptions of his age. In Hereditary Genius, he attempted to demonstrate statistically that high intellectual ability ran in eminent families, such as his own.[244] "I began thinking over the dispositions and achievements of my contemporaries at school, at college, and after in life and was surprised to find how frequently abilities seem to go by descent." He also expressed the firm belief in the inferiority of African peoples. "The number among Negroes of those we should call half-witted is very large," he wrote. "I was myself much impressed by this fact during my travels in Africa."

More significantly, Galton recommended eugenics as a way of increasing the intelligence of the human species. Based on his cousin's theory of evolution, he posited that we could speed up the process of natural selection by selective breeding, as has been done with dogs. He called eugenics "the science of improving the [human] stock."[245]

The makers of IQ tests, like Binet, may have been well intentioned in their attempt to use intelligence testing to improve education, but their ideas were quickly co-opted by the growing eugenics movement. Between 1907 and 1917, sixteen U.S. states passed sterilization laws, mostly aimed at trying to eliminate "mental retardation."[246] An influential American psychologist by the name of Henry Goddard spurred this movement with his study of the Kallikak Family.[247] He claimed that he could prove that Deborah Kallikak was the product of six generations of mostly feebleminded parentage and opined that they should have been stopped from passing on this gene to poor Deborah.

In 1923, a young American psychology professor used data from the U.S. Army's intelligence-testing program to argue that immigrants from southern and eastern Europe had lower IQs than those of more northerly stock. He argued that immigration should be restricted to Nordic peoples.[248] Just a year later, Congress passed the Immigration Restriction Act to accomplish that very thing. Even the great Supreme Court justice Oliver Wendell Holmes jumped on the eugenics bandwagon. In the 1927 *Buck v. Bell* decision, upholding sterilization laws, he stated, "three generations of imbecility are enough."[249]

There was pushback against the eugenics movement. As part of an exchange with psychologist Lewis Terman in the *New Republic,* the columnist Walter Lippmann wrote, "I hate the impudence of a claim that in 50 minutes you can judge and classify a human being's pre-destined fitness in life. I hate the pretentiousness of this claim. I hate the abuse of the scientific method which it involves. I hate the sense of superiority which it creates, and the sense of inferiority which it imposes."[250]

The eugenics movement reached its horrible apogee in Germany during the Nazi era. By the end of World War II, the Nazi regime had sterilized an estimated four hundred thousand people within the Reich and exterminated over two hundred thousand disabled people, many on the basis of "feeblemindedness." After the war, the zeal to stamp out feeblemindedness died down in America and Western Europe. The focus turned to the other end of the IQ spectrum, and few attempted to use IQ to promote eugenics. The controversy erupted again, however, in the 1960s and 1970s.

The civil-rights movement and the war on poverty discouraged any discussion of a genetic basis for intelligence. At the same time, there was a rise in the behaviorist movement in psychology, led by experimenters such as B. F. Skinner.[251] Research on rats and pigeons seem to imply that learning was independent of species, let alone human genetic variation. According to Herrnstein and Murray, "to those who held the behaviorist view, human potential was almost perfectly malleable, shaped by the environment."[252] If the right public policies were put in place, it was believed, any intellectual deficiencies would soon be ameliorated.

A firestorm of controversy was lit by Arthur Jensen's 1969 study, published in the *Harvard Educational Review,* exploring why the remedial programs initiated by the war on poverty had yielded such poor results.[253] Despite those efforts, blacks still lagged behind whites in educational achievement. After reviewing the evidence, Jensen concluded that it was "a not unreasonable hypothesis that genetic factors are strongly implicated in the average Negro-white intelligence difference." The reason remedial efforts were failing was that they were aimed at generally low IQ children and that inherited low intelligence precluded school success.

The furor was exacerbated by William Shockley, a scientific crank who had won a Nobel Prize in physics and then turned his attention to intel-, ligence.[254] He supported a sperm bank for geniuses and proposed—as a "thought experiment"—paying people with low IQs to be sterilized.

The outcome of Jensen's and Shockley's articles was that any mention of an inheritance factor in intelligence—and IQ testing in general—became socially unacceptable. The movement against intelligence testing reached a peak in 1978, when a U.S. District Court ruled it was unconstitutional to use IQ tests "for placement of children in classes for the educable mentally retarded if the use of those tests resulted in the placement of 'grossly dispro-portionate' numbers of black children."[255]

Herrnstein and Murray added fuel to the fire when they cited evidence that there was an IQ hierarchy among various American ethnic groups. Jew-ish Americans led the way, with an average IQ of 113, followed by Asian Americans, with an average of 106. White IQ averaged 103, while Latinos and African Americans lagged behind with average IQs of 89 and 85, respectively.

The IQ Puzzle

In the early 1980s, James Flynn observed and documented a peculiar phe-nomenon. Since modern intelligence testing was first developed, IQ test scores had been steadily rising. This was occurring throughout the devel-oped world. It was such a significant finding that Herrnstein and Murray christened it the Flynn Effect, and the name has stuck.

Flynn first noted data indicating that there had been huge gains in scores of the intelligence test called Raven's Progressive Matrices, to the tune of about 25 or more IQ points between 1947 and 2002 in countries as diverse as Norway, Britain, Israel, and Argentina.[256] What is special about Raven's Progressive Matrices is that they seem to test pure abstract reasoning, or what Flynn described as "solving problems on-the-spot." The task involves examining a series of designs and determining which of several choices logi-cally comes next. It is not a task familiar to most people and should have no cultural biases.

Similar data came from the much broader Wechsler Intelligence Scale for Children. Here again, there were significant gains in IQ over the same time span, although they were smaller than on the Raven's, about 18 IQ points. The difference between the Raven's and the WISC data is that the WISC has 10 subtests, three of which had shown little gain: Arithmetic, Information, and Vocabulary. On the other hand, there had been a huge gain in the Similarities subtest, as well as large gains on the five Performance subtests.

The WISC Similarities subtest is much like Raven's in that it is an abstract concept task. People are given questions in the form of "how are a dog and a cat alike?" For full credit, they must say both belong to a general category, like "animal." A more concrete answer, like "they both have four legs," gets reduced credit. A functional answer, like "dogs chase cats," gets no credit. In Flynn's analysis, Similarities shares the on-the-spot, nonpractical problem-solving quality of the Raven's. The Arithmetic, Information, and Vocabulary tests share very little of it. They are more associated with school learning and skills needed in everyday life.

Flynn asked the obvious question. Why should this rise have occurred and only in some parts of intelligence? Are we really more intelligent than our grandparents? Did evolution take a great leap forward? That is absurd. Our children do not appear to be so brilliant, nor do our forebears appear to have been dull. Yet there must be some explanation. The increases are real, not some sort of testing artifact.

Flynn points to cultural changes that have occurred in the developed world. Advancing science and technology has made us much more comfortable with abstractions and with scientific categories. We are not as tied to the concrete world. "If the everyday world is your cognitive home," Flynn writes, "it is not natural to detach abstractions and logic and the hypothetical from their concrete reference."

To describe the impact of such social change on patterns of thought, Flynn cites interviews that the Russian neuropsychologist Alexander Luria had with remote peasants.[257] Luria asked one man to consider the logical proposition, "All bears are white where there is always snow. In Novaya Zemlya, there is always snow; what color are the bears there?" The reply was, "I have seen only black bears, and I do not talk of what I have not seen." This peasant was no less intelligent than the average city dweller. It was just that abstract formulations had no place in his very practical world.

The consistency of scores on the three school-related tests demonstrates that general intelligence is not increasing. In the United States, broad educational testing has shown no gains for high school seniors year by year. There have been gains in early school years, due, perhaps, to better education, but these gains have evened out by the twelfth grade. There is one exception. According to Flynn, "today's youth are much better at on-the-spot problem-solving without a previously learned method."

In a sense, intelligence has shifted from an intensely practical understanding of the world to one of abstraction and logical thinking. This fits Western societies shift from a world of labor and role-based routine occupations to one where managerial, professional, and technical skills are necessary to find success. This shift puts an increasing premium on general intelligence.

Even though what "general intelligence" looks like changes over time, due to cultural influences, its impact on the components of intelligence remains consistent. This can be demonstrated by the interrelationships between the Wechsler subtests. People who have a higher IQ score tend to have higher scores on each of the areas measured than people with substantially lower IQs, but the impact is not the same on all subtests. As Flynn notes, "good performers consistently open up a larger gap on the average person at some cognitive tasks than others." These tasks are generally the more cognitively complex ones.

Flynn comments that we should not be particularly surprised that there is a general factor for intelligence. He gives a sport analogy. The decathlon consists of a series of ten track-and-field events. In any given competition, stronger decathletes are likelier to be better at the shotput, while swifter ones will be better at sprinting. However, an Olympic decathlete is most likely better at all ten events than an average decathlete. We could calculate a general decathlon ability and predict that when two people compete, the one with the higher ability will win.

Ethnic Differences

One of the less controversial topics concerning ethnicity is the intellectual success of Chinese Americans. Even fifty years ago, they occupied a highly disproportionate share in the ranks at the highest levels of the professions. Economist Nathaniel Weyl described them as "the American natural aristocracy."[258] Despite being little more than 2 percent of the population, Asian Americans (a large proportion of them Chinese) represented 25 percent of the class at Berkeley, 20 percent at MIT and 14 percent at Harvard in 1987[259]

To understand the relationship between IQ and success, Flynn examined two groups of Chinese American children. One group turned eighteen years old around 1966 and the second group around 1990. He compared them to white children of similar age. In grade school, the Chinese American class of 1966 had slightly lower IQs than their white counterparts, but they had slightly higher achievement test scores when matched by IQ. They were also less likely than whites to lag a grade or more behind in school.

In high school, the achievement gap widened, so that the Chinese Americans were academically outperforming their white counterparts, despite having no higher intelligence. This was particularly true for advanced mathematics, where they outperformed their IQs by 15 points. During their senior year, the Chinese American students had an IQ of 97 in verbal subtests and 100 on performance subtests, about 4.5 IQ points lower than comparison white students. Yet 50 percent of the Chinese American students took the SAT exam, compared to just 30 percent of whites, even though the average scores of the two groups were similar.

What these statistics meant was that more Chinese American students with lower IQ scores gained admission to elite schools like Berkeley. Once there, they did just as well as whites. Then, at the end of college, a larger percentage of them took graduate exams and went on to graduate school. In 1980, 55 percent of the Chinese-American cohort was in managerial, professional, or technical occupations, compared to 34 percent of whites, and their incomes were 20 percent greater.

This achievement difference was not due to intelligence as measured by IQ tests, but to culture. The ethnic Chinese parents, Flynn said, "surround them with a childhood environment more cognitively demanding than that enjoyed by white Americans." Their children responded with "a desire for cognitive challenge" and "a passion for educational achievement."

Forward to the class of 1990. These Chinese American students were raised in more economically advantaged homes than their parents were. They had an even more greatly enriched cognitive environment from a young age. The result was that their measured preschool IQs were almost ten points higher than their parents' had had and nine points higher than those of white children. Interestingly, this gap diminished as the children grew older and their parents' influence waned. Chinese American IQs, however, still averaged three points higher than whites as they entered adulthood.

This exercise shows that the Chinese American IQ increase was not related to genetics. "Chinese-Americans are an ethnic group for whom high achievement preceded high IQ rather than the reverse," notes Flynn. The ethnic Chinese intelligence increase was real, but the reasons for it are cultural, not intrinsic to Chinese inheritance.

Why G Matters

All controversy and theoretical difficulties aside, there is an extraordinarily large body of evidence indicating that g (as measured by intelligence tests) really does matter. The most extensive review of the data can be found in a review article by professor of educational psychology Linda Gottfredson in 1997.[260] And the importance of g for success in the real world has probably increased in the almost twenty years since she wrote it.

At the outset, I must state that high intelligence does not ensure success in life, nor does low intelligence rule out a satisfactory life. It is a matter of probabilities, and as Gottfredson writes, "higher intelligence improves the odds of success in school and work. It is an advantage, not a guarantee." There are many other traits (such as persistence, conscientiousness, and affability) that are significant contributors. Similarly, environmental advantages (such as family resources, having a mentor, and receiving supportive social services) help. As Gottfredson summarizes, "such compensatory advantages may frequently soften, but probably never eliminates the cumulative impact of low IQ. Conversely, high IQ acts like a cushion against some of life's adverse circumstances, perhaps accounting for why some children are more resilient than others in the face of deprivation and abuse."

A great deal of data shows that IQ can predict performance in almost any kind of job. The more complex the job, the more accurate that prediction becomes. In fact, Gottfredson reported that IQ is a better predictor of job performance than any other single measure, including education, experience, specific aptitudes, or personality factors. The best data demonstrating this comes from the armed forces, which, for many years, measured the intelligence of all recruits before induction. The armed forces have also expended a great deal of resources attempting to train men (and now women) of low ability. According to Gottfredson, multiple studies have shown that "such training fails to improve general skills and, at most, increases the number of low-aptitude men who perform at minimally acceptable levels."

These studies suggest that there are minimum IQ floors for jobs of different levels of complexity. There are very few jobs available for people with an IQ below around 80. It requires an IQ of about 90 or more for jobs like custodian or materials handler. Jobs such as bank teller, cashier, or meter reader generally require an IQ of 100 or more to be successful. Accountants and teachers typically have IQs above 112. The highest-level jobs in our society usually require an IQ above about 120 to be competitive. Put another way, "virtually all occupations accommodate individuals down to IQ 110, but virtually none routinely accommodates individuals below IQ 80."

Although most studies of IQ concern job performance, the same abilities also apply to the tasks of daily life. Parenting is a good example. While some parenting tasks are of low complexity, many are of moderate to high complexity, equivalent to "teacher, counselor, dispatcher, police officer, and accountant."

For adults at the low end of the IQ spectrum (below about 75) independent living is difficult without substantial support. They "tend to live volatile, unpredictable lives, because they lack the stabilizing resources that greater competence brings." For people with between 76 and 90, life tends to be somewhat easier, but "socioeconomic progress and stability remain tenuous." At the other end of the intelligence continuum, adults who fall in the IQ range 111 to 125 generally do well in life, with few suffering from poverty. Those above IQ 125 have their share of life's problems, but they have the best odds of success. "Their prospects of living comfortable lives are comparatively rosy."

The IQ gains in the last century reported by Flynn "are significant even though they have little to do with improved competence to cope with the concrete world of everyday life."[261] Tests of competence in ordinary life tasks, such as the Vineland Adaptive Behavior Scales, show essentially no change over the same time period. The same "small minority" of the population (about 2 percent) is unable to manage the tasks of ordinary life (on the basis of lack of intellect) despite the increased complexities of the modern world.

What makes the IQ gain significant is it represents something beyond what Flynn calls "adaptive behavior in the context of concrete reality." Contemporary people are more able to exhibit "innovative thinking in professional work roles, being comfortable with the hypothetical when it is used to pose abstract or moral problems and so forth." Formal education and exposure to abstractions and generalities has lifted all boats.

A Typology of Intellectual Disability

The most recent DSM offers a typology of intellectual disability, with extensive descriptions of each level. Previous DSM editions assigned IQ ranges for each type with a range of 50 or 55 to about 70 for *mild impairment*, 35 or 42 to 50 or 55 for *moderate*, 20 or 25 to 35 or 40 for *severe*, and below 20 or 25 for *profound*. The current DSM omits the numbers.

DSM-5 describes three domains of impairment—of conceptual, social, and practical abilities.[262] For mild intellectual disability, conceptual difficulties are first noticed in school-aged children. They lag behind other children in learning academic skills but can meet age-related expectations with some support. For adults, there are notable deficiencies in abstract thinking, executive functioning, and short-term memory. They also show difficulties in using academic skills in daily functioning, such as managing money and reading. Problem solving tends to be more concrete or bound by actual objects with an absence of concepts and generalities.

In the domain of social functioning, people with a mild intellectual disability are more socially immature. They have more difficulty interpreting social cues and communicating with others. They tend to have more problems regulating their emotions and behavior, and they also have more difficulty understanding social risk and are more easily manipulated.

In the practical domain, they usually have the ability to take care of themselves appropriately, but may need some help in complex life tasks, possibly including child care, wise food preparation, and money management. They typically can engage in recreational activities, but judgment about how to take care of themselves may be inadequate. They need help with decisions about health care and legal matters, as well as how to effectively raise a family. Vocationally, they have problems learning job skills but can work at jobs that don't require conceptual competence.

For people with moderate intellectual disability, deficiencies are more pronounced in all domains. In the conceptual domain, they progress very slowly in learning basic academic skills and have a low ceiling. For adults, skills such as reading, writing, math, and understanding time and money remain at a rudimentary level. They need continuous support from others to accomplish the conceptual tasks of everyday life and may need others to take over these responsibilities.

In the social domain, they can use spoken language at a simple level. They can maintain relationships with family and friends and often engage in romantic relationships. But they are very limited in social judgments and decision making. They need caretakers to assist with interpersonal decisions.

In the practical realm, they can learn basic self-care but require extensive time and effort before they are independent in these areas. They can help with simple household tasks with a great deal of teaching and support. They may be able to work in some simple capacity, if given a lot of support and guidance, but others must take responsibility for such things as scheduling, transportation, and money-management.

At the severe level of intellectual disability, people have little ability to attain cognitive skills. Communication is limited to simple words or phrases, and understanding written language is almost impossible to achieve. People are generally unable to understand money, time, or number. Caretakers must take control of basic problem-solving throughout the individual's life.

In the social domain, language is used for basic social communication rather than for explanation, and it focuses on what is happening right now. They have some ability to understand simple speech and gestures, and they can form relationships with family and other familiar people and look to them for pleasure and help.

In the practical domain, severely impaired people need support in the basic activities of daily living, including dressing, eating, grooming, and toileting. They cannot make independent decisions regarding their own well-being or that of others. They may have some ability to engage in recreational or home tasks with a great deal of assistance. Some of them engage in self-injurious and other maladaptive behaviors.

At the profound level of impairment, only the most concrete conceptual abilities can be observed, those involving the immediate physical world. People may be able to use objects in a goal-directed manner, but this is often limited by sensory or motor impairments. At best, they may achieve visuospatial skills involving matching or sorting objects by their physical characteristics.

Socially, there usually remains some ability to communicate desires and feelings in nonverbal ways. Understanding symbolic language or gestures is minimal, if it exists at all. Quite often, profoundly impaired people can enjoy social interactions with people they know well, though in some cases, severe sensory and motor impairment may make social interactions and most activities impossible.

In the practical realm, people are totally dependent on caretakers to provide for all their needs, although they may participate in some of these activities. For instance, they may be able to help with simple things like carrying dishes or grooming. Often they can enjoy some recreational activities, such as taking walks or listening to music.

A Biopsychosocial Perspective

I've used IQ to represent cognitive competence, because it provides a useful dimensional number. I do, however, recognize its limitations. Intelligence tests can measure only those aspects of behavior that can be assessed in a formal testing setting. While all the educational testing in our schools has made us more comfortable with these procedures, there are some people who are better test takers than others, without necessarily being more intelligent. Howard Gardner is correct in his belief that testing cannot capture all that we mean by *intelligence.*

Yet IQ is the only objective measure we have to characterize the general dimension of cognitive competence. It is better to have a reasonably objective number, validated by numerous studies, than to simply make subjective judgments about individual people's capacities. While we can recognize that success in this world demands many other personal characteristics—self-motivation, persistence, sustaining hope and many other personality or situational factors—nevertheless, our intellectual capacity, as measured by IQ, does place limits on our ability to succeed and can determine dysfunction.

Much of the controversy concerning IQ may be reduced when intelligence is seen as a complex biopsychosocial phenomenon. Inheritance plays a role, but it is not baked in the genes and unchanging. To understand this, we will begin with what the hereditary construct really means.

Heredity is a statistical measure of degree of relatedness or correlation, not a genetic truth. That is, it tells us how much of the variance or spread of IQ scores can be accounted for by genetics. It explains how the closeness of the genetic relationship between two people affects the gap between their IQ scores. The correlation is a number between zero and one, one meaning that there is a perfect one-to-one relationship and zero indicating there is none at all.

For example, the measured heritability of height within families is estimated to be 0.80,[263] which is quite high. In comparison, the estimated heritability of IQ across many studies is a more moderate 0.50.[264] As we will see in a moment, however, this number varies widely, depending on the sample studied.

First, let's look at some typical IQ correlations for people of different degrees of relationship.[265] When the same person takes the test twice, the correlation is 0.95. For identical twins (who have the same genes) who are reared in the same family, the correlation drop slightly to 0.86, and if reared apart, it drops farther, to 0.76. Fraternal twins (who have the genes of siblings) correlate at 0.55 if reared together and only 0.35 if reared apart. Unrelated children reared together correlate at 0.28, but this is still higher than cousins (who are related, but reared separately) at 0.15. Finally, a parent and a child living together show a moderately correlated IQ of 0.42, but if apart, the correlation is a low 0.22.

What this pattern of results suggests is that there is a strong genetic component to intelligence, though psychosocial influences also play a significant role. Besides, just what is inherited is a mystery, although one intriguing study suggested faster brain-processing speed was involved.[266]

The genetic picture gets a lot cloudier when we look at some anomalous data. One of the oddest findings, which is seen in many studies, is that the hereditability quotient increases the older we get. It starts at about 0.2 in infancy, increases to 0.45 in middle childhood, and reaches a high of 0.70 to 0.80 in adulthood.[267] This would seem to make little sense. Genetics should have the strongest influence early in life, before environmental factors have much chance to act. One explanation is that genes and environmental influences interact throughout life. Psychologist Robert Plomin conjectures that "relatively small genetic effects early in life snowball during development, creating larger and larger phenotypic effects as individuals select or create environments that foster their genetic propensities."[268] This points to a model of intelligence that posits that "those who have an advantage for a particular trait will become matched with superior environments for that trait."[269] Simply put, we seek what we are naturally good at.

A second anomaly is that the heritability of IQ is related to socioeconomic status. One study of twins showed that for children reared in impoverished families, most of the IQ variance between them could be accounted for by the family environment and the genetic contribution was almost 0. For affluent families, the proportions were the reverse.[270]

Another study evaluated French children who were adopted between ages four and six.[271] Prior to adoption, most of these children had been abused or neglected or had been shuttled between foster homes. At the time of adoption, their average IQ was 77, but nine years later, their IQs diverged. Those reared in homes of low socioeconomic status achieved an IQ boost to 85.5, while those placed in middle-class homes averaged 92. The children put in affluent homes achieved average IQs of 98.

These and other studies demonstrate how much the socioeconomic status of the home matters if a child is to reach his or her intellectual potential. But affluence itself is not the determining factor. It is the cognitive demands of the child's environment that matters most. This principle was demonstrated in an interesting study by biological psychologist Kees-Jan Kan and his colleagues.[272]

First, Kan assessed the "cultural load" of the various subtests on the Wechsler Intelligence Scales. As might be expected, the Vocabulary, Information, and Comprehension subtests were the most culturally loaded, while Coding, Digit Span, and Object Assembly were the least. He then examined the IQ results of twenty-three twin studies. What he determined was that the greater the cultural load, the larger the correlation between IQ scores. Twins tended to learn the same things. What that meant was that "the extent to which a cognitive test correlates with IQ is the extent to which it reflects societal demands."[273]

The second, even more significant discovery Kan made was that the heritability of the subtests varied. Kan concluded, "The higher the heritability of the cognitive test, the more the test depended on culture."[274] Psychologist Scott Kaufman interpreted this to mean that "cognitive abilities and knowledge feed off each other. Those with a proclivity to engage in cognitive complexity will tend to seek out intellectually demanding environments."[275]

With these findings, we can return to the issue of racial and ethnic differences in IQ and cultural influences. Heredity of intelligence is relevant to individuals, not groups. The Flynn Effect shows that IQ in general is increasing all the time. To compare the IQ of one group fifty years ago to another group today would be invalid, because the societal cognitive demands have changed so drastically. Similarly, different cultures make different demands. To compare IQs across markedly different cultures is meaningless.

The disparity in IQs between whites and blacks in America is best seen as a cultural phenomenon, not a hereditary one. Up to the present time, African Americans usually grew up in a very different intellectual environment than whites. As the intellectual demands of black culture began to look more like those of white culture, the IQs of blacks began to resemble that of whites.[276] Between 1972 and 2002, black Americans gained an average of 5.5 IQ points on white Americans. By 2002, the average gap was 5.3 points, and it has probably closed further in the past decade. Further, as Kaufman concludes, "The bigger the difference in cognitive ability between Blacks and Whites, the more the difference is determined by cultural influences."[277]

Dementia

We used to call it *senility* and thought it was simply the inevitable decline of old age. We have learned in recent decades, however, that there are several different processes of brain degeneration that lead to cognitive decline. Dementia of all sorts is the product of an aging brain, and with each decade of life after fifty, an increasing proportion of us will suffer from dementia.

It is estimated that the percentage of people exhibiting the most common form of dementia, Alzheimer's disease, doubles for each five-year interval past age sixty-five, rising to as many as 50 percent of people aged eighty-five or older. In 2014, an estimated 5.2 million people in the United States had Alzheimer's; about 200,000 of them were below age sixty-five. By 2050, the number of Alzheimer's victims is expected to more than triple, to 16 million. The direct cost to American society today is about $214 billion; one of every five dollars Medicare spends is for people with dementia. As noted by the Alzheimer's Association, Alzheimer's is the sixth leading cause of death in the United States, and death attributable to it increased by 68 percent between 2000 and 2010.[278]

Right now, there is no way to prevent or reverse most dementias. The major mental-health problem is to find ways that we can help people with dementia live as satisfying and independent lives as possible for as long as possible.

Alzheimer's Disease

There is no one disease called *dementia*. It is a collective term describing a deterioration of cognitive and social abilities that is severe enough to interfere with daily functioning. The National Institute of Health defines *dementia* as the impairment of two or more mental functions, including "memory, language skills, visual perception, and the ability to focus and pay attention." Other characteristics of some dementias are the loss of control of emotions, personality changes, delusions, and hallucinations.[279]

Alzheimer's disease (AD) and its variants are the most common form of dementia, affecting between 60 percent and 80 percent of dementia sufferers. AD, like most dementias, is a clinical diagnosis—the only way to know for sure that a patient has it is by autopsy. It is named after Alois Alzheimer, who discovered the condition in 1906. He cared for a middle-aged woman whose cognitive capacities declined over several years. After she died, he examined her brain under a microscope and found that it contained plaque deposits and "tangled" nerve cells. He concluded that the plaques and tangles had disrupted the normal functioning of her brain.

Medical science today has discovered that the plaques are clumps of a protein called *beta-amyloid,* which gathers in the spaces between brain cells. The tangles are caused by another protein, called *tau,* which becomes twisted and clumps inside brain neurons. These neurofibrillary tangles are thought to cause neurons to die. No one knows yet if the plaques and tangles are the actual cause of AD or if they are the result of some other process causing neuronal death.

AD progresses slowly; seven to ten years may pass between when it is first suspected and eventual death. It is now believed that neuronal death may begin many years before cognitive decline is observed. The uncertainty as to whether early complaints of memory loss or other cognitive concerns represents AD has led to a characterization called *mild cognitive impairment* (MCI). MCI is often the expression of other psychological dysfunctions, such as anxiety, depression, or even schizophrenia, but a certain percentage of these patients "convert" to AD each year. At this time, we have no accurate way of detecting who is in the beginning stages of dementia and who is not.

The Retired Doctor

When I first came to town, Sven was a prominent physician in our community. With the retirement of older docs, Sven had become the leader of his specialty group at our hospital. He was known for his medical skills, his good patient relations, and above all, his excellent judgment. He was one of those rugged Nordic types who could cross-country ski or ride his bike for many miles. Sven was also sharp and witty, and I enjoyed conversing with him.

Fast-forward twenty-five years. Sven was referred to me for evaluation by his internist. At that time, he was seventy-seven years old and had been retired for five years, but he still looked young and fit. His wife reported that her concerns became acute when she found him standing in the middle of their garage, staring into space and not knowing what he was doing there. She had also been noticing changes in his personality. She told me that he had gone from being a "gentle man to being paranoid and hostile." She had spent the summer living in their camp, away from him. She said, "It was dangerous for me to live at home." In retrospect, she realized she had been noticing that he had had memory problems and confusion for about the previous three years.

Sven did not see himself as having any major problems. He did recall that he had been seen by an internist and a neurologist, who both believed he had cognitive deficits, but he told me, "They used it as a weapon. For some reason, they had a problem with me." He blamed his wife and believed that she was the only one who really believed he had memory problems.

For Sven, the only real issue was that his driver's license had been suspended. His doctor had reported his condition to the Motor Vehicle Bureau, and Sven failed the written driver's test. He did get a provisional license, but his wife told me of an incident that occurred just three weeks previously. He had passed a pick-up truck at a dangerously high rate of speed. The other driver had reported his license plate number. "When [Sven] got home, the police were waiting in the driveway." His license was again suspended. Sven wanted me to get him his license back, although he actually told me, "I have a perfectly good license."

My job was to do a neuropsychological evaluation to help determine whether he was suffering from a dementia, and if so, what type. It was also possible that he was depressed or had some other form of psychological condition that was causing his impairment. Neuropsychological assessment consists of a battery of cognitive tests designed to determine whether there are significant deficits in any area of cognitive functioning. Since there usually aren't any previous test results for comparison, inferences have to be made about how a patient would have performed earlier in life. In Sven's case, this wasn't difficult, because his life history predicted that he should have cognitive skills well above average.

The first thing I noticed was that Sven had a great deal of difficulty understanding and completing the initial paperwork. In the interview, he was focused on his driver's license and said, "I have never been more surprised in my life when I heard someone say I couldn't get my license." On testing, he had an IQ of 101—not bad, but much lower than expected for a physician. His memory and expressive-language results were lower still, well below the normal range. On a task designed to test abstract concept formation and mental flexibility, he did very poorly. There were no indications of depression or psychosis. I concluded that he did indeed have severe deficits in memory and other areas of cognitive functioning and that he had a degenerative dementia, probably Alzheimer's disease. I was concerned about his ability to live independently, let alone drive.

Sven requested a follow-up appointment with me. His sole purpose was to try to convince me that he should get his driver's license back. I tried to convince him that he was too cognitively impaired, but he kept arguing with me about the test results. I tried to suggest he should make realistic plans about his future and perhaps move into retirement community. He would not consider this solution.

The first signs of AD are subtle. It may begin with minor lapses in short-term memory and slight personality changes. To try to detect changes that will eventually lead to an Alzheimer's diagnosis, one prospective study gave a group of elderly people a battery of cognitive tests and followed them for several years.[280] Of the 551 people tested, 68 were later determined to have developed AD. The subjects who developed AD had had lower scores in two cognitive areas, memory functioning and executive functioning. Documenting early cognitive deficit may be helpful, but it is statistical and no sure predictor of AD.

Another approach to detecting the onset of AD while it may still be possible to do something about it is the search for biomarkers. Neuroimaging is one promising approach. There are several molecules (such as Amyvid and Vizamyl) that bind to beta-amyloid in the brain and can be detected by positron emission tomography (PET) scans. These scans may reveal which people have beta-amyloid, but many people have beta-amyloid plaques and don't develop cognitive decline, so the scans can't absolutely predict AD.[281]

A second kind of test uses magnetic resonance imaging (MRI) or computerized tomography (CT) to measure brain shrinkage. Early AD is characterized by shrinkage, particularly in some areas of the brain, such as the hippocampus (which is necessary to form new memories). Unfortunately, there is not sufficient data for normal brain volumes to authoritatively determine the amount of shrinkage characteristic of presymptomatic AD.

The same problem exists for what is called *functional brain imaging.* People with AD show reduced brain activity in the hippocampus and other brain areas, but again, there is such a wide range of brain activity among normal adults that these tests cannot be used to determine which individuals have incipient AD.

Some studies are attempting to find biomarkers of AD in the cerebrospinal fluid and blood, including traces of proteins such as beta-amyloid and tau. Other studies are searching for genetic markers. So far, three very rare gene variations have been found that predict a small number of people will develop AD. And other studies are looking for genes that appear to increase the risk for developing AD, including a gene called APOE-e4. As yet, this is only a research tool and not an accurate predictor.

AD and other dementias are progressive, but people do not deteriorate at the same rate or in the same ways. But efforts have been made to characterize the common progression into stages or levels of dysfunction. Because this is a clinical dimension, these stages are qualitative. They represent descriptive types, just as do all mental disorders.

The descriptive scale endorsed by the Alzheimer's Association (and one I have used for thirty years) is based on the Global Deterioration Scale for Age-Associated Cognitive Decline and Alzheimer's Disease (GDS).[282] It is a seven-level scale and starts with presumed normal functioning or at least no detectable memory problems. This is stage 1.

Stage 2 is called *very mild cognitive decline,* which is essentially equivalent to MCI. Memory complaints are subjective and don't interfere with life. They may consist of occasionally forgetting familiar words or where you put something. There is a small chance that it represents the beginning of AD.

At stage 3, cognitive decline becomes noticeable to others. It is called *mild cognitive decline* and may represent incipient AD. At this stage, people are showing difficulty performing in more demanding work or social settings. Problems with planning and organizing is more apparent. People lose things, can't remember the names of people they just met, and can't recall words. At this level, there is still uncertainty about whether there is really a dementia, so MCI may still be the appropriate label.

Stage 4 deterioration goes beyond any "maybe" and is generally obvious to everyone, except the person suffering from it. It is called *moderate cognitive decline* or *early-stage AD.* People can no longer accomplish complex tasks or recall many recent events. Even personal history facts are forgotten or made-up. People do very poorly on challenging cognitive tasks involving executive functioning and forming new memories. They tend to withdraw socially and appear depressed, because they become emotionally flat or moody.

By stage 5, people can no longer survive on their own. They can still do basic things like eating and using the toilet, but they need help choosing appropriate clothing. They become confused about where they are or what day it is and forget their home addresses and telephone numbers. They can still recall major facts about themselves and recognize those close to them.

This stage is considered the *moderately severe decline* of mid-stage AD.

Stage 6 represents *severe cognitive decline* and is a continuation of mid-stage AD. At this stage, people lose awareness of their surroundings and do not recall recent experiences in their lives. They are totally dependent on the care of others. They can distinguish familiar and unfamiliar faces, but often don't know the names of their spouse or caregivers. They may wander and get lost. They may be increasingly incontinent and have trouble with the details of toileting. At this point, there are often major changes in personality and behavior, making the person difficult to manage. These can include paranoia and other delusions, compulsive rituals, and expressions of anger and aggressiveness.

The end is stage 7 or *very severe cognitive decline*. People in this final stage lose the ability to interact with their environment. They may still say words or phrases, but they can't converse. They need total care. Eventually, basic motor functioning deteriorates. They may lose the ability to smile or even hold their heads up. Their muscles grow rigid and reflexes abnormal, and even swallowing becomes impaired.

Other Dementias

There are multiple other forms of dementia of unknown cause that can be distinguished from AD. We should keep in mind, however, that there is a great deal of uncertainty as to which are truly distinct and which are variants of the same process.

Lewy-body dementia is marked by balloon-like protein structures, called *Lewy bodies,* that form inside neurons. This can only be detected on autopsy. This dementia has some clinical differences from AD, at least in its early course. The first signs of this dementia usually include sleep problems, loss of smell, and visual hallucinations. Later, memory loss, poor judgment, and confusion develop, which are similar to AD. One big difference is that in Lewy-body dementia, cognitive symptoms fluctuate greatly during the course of the day, while they are more constant in AD.

There is a great deal of overlap between Lewy-body dementia and Parkinson's disease dementia—so much so that the two are often lumped together. Both varieties exhibit movement disorders, such as changes in posture and a shuffling walk. They also both exhibit pronounced changes in alertness and attention and in executive functions.

There are other assaults to the brain that are well-known causes of dementia. One of these is the group of vascular dementias. The most common is *multi-infarct dementia,* in which people have multiple small strokes that kill off brain cells a little at a time. These strokes are much harder to detect than a major stroke, and the cognitive functions lost depend on what parts of the brain are damaged. Unlike other dementias, there is a pattern of some functions lost and some preserved. Since our brains have redundancies and plasticity, multi-infarct dementia can be undetectable for a long time after it begins.

We might mention another form of brain injury that is much in the news lately. *Chronic traumatic encephalopathy,* or *dementia pugilistica,* occurs when the brain is subjected to multiple concussions. Boxers often develop this form of dementia (as in the case of Mohammed Ali), along with football players and some soccer players (from heading the ball). Sufferers often develop symptoms of poor coordination, slurred speech, and other Parkinsonian features. One suggestive finding is a similarity to AD. Both groups exhibit brain atrophy and deposits of the protein tau.

There are also a number of genetic and prion brain diseases that cause dementia. The most famous is Huntington's Disease. This is caused by a genetic abnormality for the protein *huntingtin.* It appears at about age thirty or forty, when the person develops abnormal, uncontrollable movements called *chorea.* In time, there is also a decline in cognitive functions, such as memory and judgment, until the person completely loses the ability for self-care.

Creutzfeldt-Jakob Disease, which we also know as "mad cow disease," is believed to be caused by infectious proteins called *prions.* It is a spongiform encephalopathy; the brain forms microscopic swellings that make it look like a sponge. Most of the time, there are no known risk factors for this disease, and some cases appear genetic. One form of this disease, called *fatal familial insomnia,* begins with altered sleep patterns, when the part of the brain that regulates sleep deteriorates. Prior to death, people with fatal familial insomnia show poor reflexes and hallucinations.

It must be stressed that none of these dementias can be cured or reversed. There are some medications that can help delay the progress of memory decline and confusion for a time, which allows the individual to live more independently for up to a year or so longer. The best-known ones (such as Aricept, Exelon, and Cognex) act by keeping the messenger chemical *acetylcholine* in the synapse longer, thus increasing the efficiency of communication within the brain. The underlying process of slow nerve cell death, however, goes on unabated. The search continues, of course, for some chemical that will effectively halt or slow the process of deterioration, especially at the MCI stage.

Final Thoughts on Cognitive Competence

Advancing technology presents both an opportunity and a challenge for people with low or declining cognitive abilities. Automation helps people live independently. Smart homes equipped with alerting and monitoring devices can help such people live safely outside of institutions. I'm hoping that the new self-driving cars make it to market by the time I need one. Progress should make technology increasingly available to people who require a simpler world in which to live.

On the other hand, automation is taking away the livelihoods of many people, particularly at lower cognitive levels. People with above-average intellects who lose their jobs can usually be reeducated and can find new careers. People with below-average intellects, however, have fewer opportunities.

The point was brought home to me by economists. A recent study has shown that 47 percent of American jobs are in danger of being automated out of existence in coming years.[283] Corporate earnings since 2000 have doubled, while household incomes have declined from $55,986 to $51,017. Total employee compensation has dropped from 47 percent to 43 percent of the gross national product. Corporations are making more money, while employing fewer people.

In their recent book *The Second Machine Age*, MIT professors of information technology Eric Brynjolfsson and Andrew McAfee note that in the past, increasing productivity always led to more jobs and higher incomes.[284]

This began to change about 1980. Technological advances started destroying more jobs, particularly low-skills ones, than they were creating. There was about an 11 percent decline in routine jobs, such as bank tellers and machine operators, between 2001 and 2011, and the trend is accelerating.

It is easy to predict what is going to happen, because it is happening now. More and more people will despair and drop out of the productive workforce. If we do not find the societal solutions that offer all people a dignified and pro-social way to make a living, dysfunction associated with low cognitive capacity will increase. Larger numbers of people will appeal for disability payments or public assistance, will live on the streets, or will do antisocial things to get by. This is destructive not only to individuals but also to the fabric of society.

The problem of cognitive dysfunction is somewhat similar at the dementia end. As advanced societies age, the number of elderly people with increasing cognitive impairment is growing. Placing all these people in nursing homes or other institutions is economically infeasible and individually undesirable. Again, the solutions must be societal. We must use our advancing technology to help people live relatively independent lives for as long as possible.

9

Social Competence

We humans are intensely social animals. Sociality is probably the key to our survival as a species. Advanced social skills are certainly necessary to successfully negotiate the complexities of modern society. To fit in and prosper, we need to read the minds of our fellow humans and learn to understand and predict their reactions, intentions, and emotions. We need to recognize the degree of our relationships with many people and where we belong in the many social hierarchies we encounter. We must also learn how to control and conform our behavior in the different social environments we meet, both inside and outside the family.

Our ability to do this is what I will call the *social competence dimension.* People's social skills vary widely, and like all other dimensions, there is no dividing line between the competent and the socially dysfunctional. There are, however, two commonly recognized types of social incompetence that make life particularly difficult, especially for children: autism (or *autistic spectrum disorder,* as it is now called) and attention deficit hyperactivity disorder.

The Autism Spectrum

Just what should be included under the term *autism* and how it should be diagnosed has been controversial almost since Leo Kanner and Hans Asperger independently and almost simultaneously described two versions of the syndrome. Kanner was first; in 1943 he described a pattern of behavior he called *infantile autism.*[285] *Autism* was a term first used by Eugen Bleuler to describe the social withdrawal that characterized people he labeled *schizophrenic.*

Kanner distilled the major traits that characterized the children who fit this new diagnosis. The first he called *autistic aloneness,* which referred to their extreme social withdrawal. He concluded, "we must, thus, assume that these children have come into the world with innate inability to form the usual, biologically provided affective contact with people, just as other children come into the world with innate physical or intellectual handicaps."

The second feature involved peculiarities of language. Speech, if it developed at all, was largely noncommunicative. Half of the children he evaluated never acquired functional speech. Even nonverbal communication such as pointing to an object or blowing a kiss was seldom seen. Autistic children who did speak did so in a repetitive and peculiar way. Kanner gave the example of Donald, whose "conversation consisted of questions of a repetitive nature. He was inexhaustible in bringing up variations: 'how many days in a week, years in a century, hours in half a day, weeks in a century, centuries in a millennium', etc., etc."

The third Kanner feature was a pattern of repetitive and stereotyped behavior, interests, and activities. Autistic children had an obsessive need for sameness. Their playing seemed to lack imagination and consisted of doing the same activity over and over—a child might spin a plate for hours at a time. These activities were seen as pointless, as can be seen in Kanner's description of Donald: "another of his recent hobbies is with old issues of *Time* magazine. He found a copy of the first issue of March 3, 1923, and has attempted to make a list of the dates of publication of each issue since that time."

Kanner summarized his impression of the autistic child this way: "The most impressive thing is his detachment and inaccessibility. He walks in a world of his own where he cannot be reached."

At the same time Kanner was describing infantile autism, an Austrian physician, Hans Asperger, was describing a similar syndrome he called *autistic psychopathy.* Because this was during World War II, the two men did not know of each other's work. In fact, Asperger's work was not generally known to the English-speaking world until Lorna Wing introduced it in 1981.[286]

Most of Asperger's description of these children was similar to Kanner's, except that the children he evaluated had no cognitive impairments or language delays. They also had fewer social impairments. While

Kanner's kids could not engage in social situations, Asperger's were only socially clueless.

Oliver Sacks has described the essential distinction between Kanner's autistic syndrome and what came to be called *Asperger's syndrome*.[287] He suggests that the children Kanner saw were an "unmitigated disaster," often with mental retardation, neurological signs and symptoms, and abnormal sensory responses. Asperger saw a more benign picture, which included "particular originality of thought and experience, which may well lead to exceptional achievements in later life." *Autism* became a term for extremely impaired children who were destined to become severely disabled adults. Asperger's children, on the other hand, could "develop into autonomous human beings that may appear full and normal" even when the picture at age three is bleak.

Kanner's autism proved difficult to define with any precision, and over the years, there were many debates about the diagnostic criteria.[288] Particularly, which features were specific to autism and not generally found in other disorders, and which of them were developmentally inappropriate. Many of Kanner's characteristics could be found in the normal development of young children, but they did not persist. Where could one draw the line?

The first official attempt to form diagnostic criteria for autism came in the DSM-III in 1980. Autism was listed as a "pervasive developmental disorder," and six criteria were used to diagnose it, though they were hardly precise.

A second attempt was made with the 1987 revision of it (DSM-III-R). Now there were sixteen criteria divided into three categories, and children needed to exhibit at least eight of them to be labeled autistic. This led to a large increase in autism diagnoses. One study looked at a sample of preschoolers deemed to have "salient social impairment."[289] When the DSM-III criteria were applied to this group, 51 percent were diagnosed autistic, but when the DSM-III-R criteria were used, 91 percent were. DSM-III-R also changed and expanded the earlier diagnosis of *atypical pervasive developmental disorder* into *pervasive developmental disorder not otherwise specified*.

Psychiatry made another attempt to define the pervasive developmental disorder category in the DSM-IV in 1994. There were now five specific disorders that were considered distinct from childhood schizophrenia. Autistic disorder and pervasive developmental disorder not otherwise specified were joined by Asperger's disorder and two rare disorders called *Rett's disorder* and *childhood disintegrative disorder*. The result was that autism became "epidemic," and in 2005, professor of psychology Laura Schreibman estimated there were as many as 1,500,000 people diagnosed with autism in the United States, and this number was growing at a rate of 10 to 17 percent a year. She concluded, "Not surprisingly, the efforts to identify subgroups in this population have so far been controversial and have met with limited success."[290]

With the publication of DSM-V in 2013, psychiatry came to the same conclusion. "Researchers found that these separate diagnoses were not consistently applied across different clinics and treatment centers."[291] The Neurodevelopmental Work Group decided that "a single umbrella disorder will improve the diagnosis of ASD [autism spectrum disorder] without limiting the sensitivity of the criteria, or substantially changing the number of children being diagnosed." DSM-5 eliminated all the specific pervasive developmental disorders in favor of a single diagnosis of autistic spectrum disorder.

This caused an uproar about the social and political effects of these changes. Some psychiatrists and many parents thought the proposed criteria were too strict and that too many children who had previously been diagnosed with Asperger's or pervasive developmental disorder not otherwise specified would be excluded from the autism spectrum. The consequence would be that these children would be denied special services, because, "in many cases the type and number of symptoms looked for when diagnosing autism determines how easy or difficult it is for autistic people to access medical, social and educational services."[292]

The Yale university psychiatrist and autism researcher Fred Volkmar quit the diagnostic revision panel, saying, "I want to be sure we're not going to leave some kids out in the cold."[293] He suggested the revision would exclude 40 percent of children now diagnosed with autism. And studies indeed showed that the proposed criteria did eliminate a substantial number of people. One study found that if the APA decreased the number of necessary symptoms from five out of seven to four out of seven, it would bring 12 percent of the excluded children back into the fold.[294]

People who had previously been diagnosed with Asperger's expressed a different set of concerns. Either they would have to be lumped into a category with severely autistic people or they would possibly be shunted off into a newly created "non-autistic social communication disorder" category. As one concerned person commented, "I personally am probably going to have a very hard time calling myself autistic."[295]

What was finally determined to be the diagnostic criteria for autism spectrum disorder (ASD) is a typical American Psychiatric Association political compromise. Instead of clarifying matters and making the description of autism more precise, it does a good job of muddying already turbulent waters. First, DSM-5 separates the criteria for diagnosing ASD into two domains: (1) "deficits in social communication and social interaction across multiple contexts" and (2) "restricted repetitive patterns of behavior, interests or activities." The social part has three prongs, which are called "illustrative, not exhaustive." These are (1) "deficits in social-emotional reciprocity"; (2) "deficits in nonverbal communicative behaviors"; and (3) "deficits in developing, maintaining and understanding relationships." DSM-5 does not indicate whether a patient must meet just one or two or all three of these requirements.

The patterns of behavior domain has four possibilities, and DSM-5 explicitly states that a patient has to meet at least two of them. They are also "illustrative, not exhaustive" and include (1) "stereotyped or repetitive motor movements, use of objects or speech"; (2) "insistence on sameness, inflexible adherence to routines, or ritualized patterns of verbal or nonverbal behavior"; (3) "highly restricted, fixated interests that are abnormal in intensity or focus"; and (4) "hyper or hyporeactivity to sensory input or unusual interest in sensory aspects of the environment."

And here's the mud! First, none of these attributes have to be directly observed by the clinician—they can be determined "by history." Next, anyone who already has a diagnosis of autism, Asperger's, or pervasive developmental disorder not otherwise specified is automatically grandfathered into ASD. Finally, there are three levels of severity for ASD, labeled "requiring very substantial support," "requiring substantial support," and "requiring support." There is no indication as to how they are to be assessed. Additionally, to further complicate the characterization of ASD, the clinician must determine whether there is intellectual impairment, language impairment, or "a known medical, genetic or environmental factor."

My major criticism of ASD is not about its political or social implications or its complexity. It is about its scientific validity. It appears to be a step toward describing a dimension, but that is deceptive. What it does is define a whole range of human characteristics as abnormal. By eliminating even a suggestion that these are types of social dysfunction that may affect a person's ability to cope with society's demands, it calls a wide and varied swath of humanity as simply *disordered.*

The Temple Grandin Story

Temple Grandin is the world's most famous autistic person. She is more than remarkable. She has a PhD with research in animal psychophysiology and is currently a professor of animal science. She is also an engineer who invented animal chutes and squeeze boxes. She is the author of dozens of books and articles ranging from "Observations of Cattle Behavior Applied to the Design of Cattle Handling Facilities"[296] to her most recent book, *The Autistic Brain.*[297] What makes her so special are not so much her accomplishments but what she overcame to get there and the limitations she still has.

Grandin was diagnosed as autistic at the age of three by a neurologist. She had almost no speech, and her only method of expressing her feelings was by screaming. She could understand most of what was said to her, but as hard as she tried to speak, words wouldn't come out. She couldn't tolerate being touched, and when her mother tried to cuddle her, Grandin "clawed at her like a trapped animal."[298]

From the point of view of others, Grandin was a destructive child. She repeatedly scribbled on the walls with any pencil or crayon she could find. Describing her childhood, she later wrote, "Normal children use clay for modeling; I used my feces and then spread my creations all over the room. I chewed up puzzles and spit the cardboard mush out on the floor. I had a violent temper, and when thwarted, I'd throw anything handy—a museum quality vase or leftover feces. I screamed and continually responded violently to noise and yet appeared deaf on some occasions."

Much of her time was spent in compulsively repetitive activities. Spinning was her favorite; she spun objects and herself. It was self-stimulating and made her feel powerful. She later interpreted this autistic behavior: "it is as

216

if their bodies were demanding more spinning as a kind of corrective factor in an immature nervous system."

The prognosis for a child like Grandin was bleak. Many would have said her destiny would be a lifetime of institutionalization. Grandin believes that this would have been her fate if she had been born ten years later, when her mother would have been told that she had "a psychological problem—it's all in her mind." As it happened, she was born only four years after the pattern called *autism* was discovered, and it was considered a biological disorder. Her neurologist concluded she had suffered brain damage and recommended speech therapy. Some years later, she would've been considered the irreversible product of a "refrigerator mother" (ice cold).

Grandin considers her mother the hero of her story. She was a first child, and her mother was only nineteen when she was born. At first, her mother was worried that she was at fault; the neurological diagnosis relieved her anxiety about that. Although her mother was troubled by Temple's strange behavior, she never rejected Temple. In her diary, her mother wrote, "I must say, though, that even on her worst days, she is intelligent and exciting. Temple is fun to be with and a dear companion." What her mother did was love her. Oliver Sacks paints a vivid and sensitive picture of her in *An Anthropologist on Mars*.[299] He presents her social deficiencies and her genius as two sides of the same coin. It is also a story of how her environment and her own perseverance permitted her to overcome the obstacles presented by her lack of intuitive social perceptions, her rigidities, and her misaligned reactions to sensory stimuli.

The title of Sacks's book comes from a comment that Grandin made: "much of the time, I feel like an anthropologist on Mars." She told Sacks she could understand the "simple, strong, universal emotions" displayed by other people, but when she saw the back-and-forth subtleties of human interactions, she was left feeling like she was watching an alien species. She could not react to these things and needed to puzzle out the rules from what patterns she could see. Sacks observed that she had learned a great deal about how to proceed in social situations, but unless she was talking about one of her interests, her responses were oddly stilted and slightly inappropriate.

The story that Temple Grandin tells in her autobiography, *Emergence,* is a coming-of-age tale of a young woman.[300] This young woman, however, would never have made it without the financial resources of her family, the compassion and guidance she received from significant people in her life, and a good deal of luck. It is also a tale of a person with severe deficits who not only overcame these liabilities but also used them to make major contributions to our world.

Grandin's mother hired a governess to look after her and her sister when they were children. This governess was, in Grandin's words, "an old maid" who "didn't believe in frivolous hugging." The governess was also attentive, organized, and constant. She was exactly what Grandin needed.

When it came time for her to go to school, her family had the means to send her to a small private school. She was often frustrated, naughty, and had a great deal of difficulty with schoolwork and social activities. She was frequently agitated and overstimulated and had many fixations. "Constantly asking questions was another of my fixations," she writes, "and I'd ask the same questions and wait for the same answers—over and over again. My fixations reduced arousal and calmed me."

When she was in second grade, she "began dreaming about a magical device that would provide intense pleasant pressure stimulation on [her] body." She craved the simulation of touch, but it needed to be impersonal and under her control. By third grade, she began to imagine designs for such a machine. The idea did not come to fruition until late in high school.

Elementary school was a relatively positive experience, although she reports, "my reputation … was shaded with the impulsive, erratic behavior, temper tantrums, and the worst report card possible, but I also was known for unique and creative abilities." The change from a small, accepting school to a large private junior high school filled with affluent girls was a disaster. Grandin faced noise, large classes, changing teachers, peer rejection, and the negative attitudes of teachers. She was unable to deal with subjects that were abstract and conceptual rather than precise and visual. "When I didn't understand the subject, I became bored and when I was bored, I was naughty," she writes. She had temper tantrums and was expelled after two and a half years when she physically assaulted a girl who had insulted her.

Luckily, her mother then brought her to a small private boarding school in New Hampshire, where she was treated as an individual, not as a problem.

It was a school for gifted but emotionally troubled youth. It had farm animals for interested students to help care for, and Grandin liked animals. She particularly loved galloping horses.

The rest of puberty was extremely difficult. She suffered debilitating "nerve attacks," her behavior became increasingly erratic, and her fixations increased. She was desperate. At age sixteen, she chanced to learn that a spinning ride called the Rotor gave her "the sensation of comfort and relaxation" that calmed her anxiety. She became fixated on having the school build her a Rotor, but they wouldn't. Then she found a small room, the Crow's Nest, that was being constructed at the top of a dorm, where she could find the same relief. For her, "beyond the door was me, life, God, and freedom of choice."

Although she failed her subjects, there were a couple of teachers who accepted and challenged her. She learned about animal behavior and philosophy from them. Mr. Carlock, in particular, became her friend, confidant, and guide. For the first time, she wanted to succeed in school and to learn.

In the summer after her junior year, she went to her aunt's ranch in Arizona. This was a life-changing experience. Her aunt was a kind, patient, and understanding woman. She directed Grandin's fixations into creative physical work and riding horses at a gallop. Above all, there were cattle and a squeeze chute to hold them for procedures. Grandin spent hours observing agitated cattle calming down when they were gently squeezed in the cattle chute. She begged her aunt to let her try it. It worked; "the squeeze chute provided relief for my nerve attacks. True to form, I became fixated on it."

Back at school, Mr. Carlock helped her build a human version of the squeeze chute for herself. Of course, the psychologists and psychiatrists interpreted her project as a problem occurring in her own mind. Her psychologist told her, "[I cannot decide] whether this contraption of yours is a prototype of a womb or a casket." The psychiatrists took it away from her. This reaction only made her think more about why the mechanical pressure of the chute might soothe cattle and her and whether it might help other people.

She did build her chute and kept it and invented a way to operate it without needing another person to release her. Using it was a breakthrough for her. Not only did it relieve her panic attacks, but it released positive emotions and allowed her to feel the love and concern of others. She said, "the squeeze chute not only allowed me to express my feelings, but since I wouldn't allow myself the relaxation/stimulation of the chute until my homework was completed, the squeeze chute served as an incentive."

The next year, Grandin finished high school and was chosen to give one of the speeches at graduation. She talked about the time on her aunt's ranch, the cattle chute, and the door in the Crow's Nest. "To be able to walk through the little door, one must be mature enough to handle the challenges and responsibilities that have to be faced. One must have faith in oneself and faith in others. There are many times one must trust other people. One must go to these situations without fearful apprehension, because faith will conquer fear," she said.

Years later, when Oliver Sacks met her at the university where she taught animal sciences, he was struck by her lack of what might be called intuitive empathy. There was no small talk or social niceties; she immediately began talking about her work. Sacks had had a long trip and was exhausted and hungry. He writes, "after an hour, almost fainting under the barrage of her over-explicit and relentless sentences, and the need to attend to several things at once,... I finally asked for some coffee." It was not that Grandin was unkind or unconcerned; she was just insensitive to his needs—she literally could not sense them—but as soon as he made his request, she immediately took him to get coffee.

Grandin was willing to talk about her deficiencies, and without pretense or defensiveness. She told Sacks that she had learned how to understand the social responses of other people by building up a catalog of experiences and studying them as if they were videos. She told him that she had to learn to be suspicious by using her analytical skills. She was entirely unselfconscious and had no sense of embarrassment.

It was her analytical skills, which were the flip side of her autism, combined with her high intelligence, which made her so successful. Sacks came to this conclusion: "I had earlier thought that there might be a separation, even a gulf, between the personal—and, so to speak, private—realm of her autism and the public realm of her professional expertise. But it was becoming increasingly clear to me that they were hardly separated at all; for her, the personal and the professional were completely fused."

It was also clear to Sacks that Grandin did not lack for sympathy or strong feeling, particularly toward animals. She reacted viscerally and passionately to an animal's pain and terror; she had the same reaction to humans, too, if their emotions were overt and not subtle. Her understanding of animal feelings and her compassion for them motivated her in her career work of developing humane methods of slaughtering animals. Her ability to think in a concrete, pictorial, and logical fashion allowed her to accurately design and create the devices for doing this.

Brain Biology and Autism

The whole autism spectrum is referred to as a *neurodevelopmental disorder.* This designation implies that something went wrong in early brain development, and these errors account for the observed features of autism. To even begin to search for any deviations in the ultra-complex processes of brain maturation, we would need to specify the core deficits in autism that we wish to explain. This has been an elusive goal. To help you understand why, let me begin with a brief description of normal brain development.

The human brain consists of an immense number of its basic component, neurons. The brain follows a principle often seen in nature: the achievement of great complexity through many permutations of simple elements. Neurons start to develop in the fetus about two weeks after conception. Over the first few months, primitive neuronal cells (called *neuroblasts*) are created at a furious pace, up to 250,000 a minute.

The developing neurons migrate to specific locations following a scaffolding of another kind of brain cell, called *glia.* On their journey, neurons extend a hand to neighboring neurons, making connections with others and traveling with them. They reach their destinations as little social colonies and become functional regions of the brain.

The Nobel laureate Gerald Edelman observed that "one of the most striking features of the brain is its individuality and variability."[301] Edelman's genius was to explain this fact by invoking a selection process during brain maturation he called *neural Darwinism.* Genetic inheritance sets the early development of the brain in accordance with the limitations of our species. Constraints are set by natural selection, but within those constraints, each individual's brain develops uniquely. Genetic selection, however, is only the beginning, and what Edelman calls *somatic selection* is more significant in determining human traits. Edelman explains that in their migration through the brain, neurons branch in many directions and create a huge variety of neural circuits. Some of these work well and are activated frequently, while others are not used at all. The commonly used circuits strengthen, while others weaken. As Edelman puts it, "Neurons that fire together, wire together"—essentially, "use it or lose it."

Somatic selection is a pruning process. The developing brain is estimated to have twice the number of neural connections that we will need as adults. This pruning is necessary and normal in order to eliminate wrong or weak connections. Although much of the pruning occurs prenatally, even after birth, connections that aren't used enough die away, while strong, efficient ones increase and strengthen. This helps explain the phenomenon of brain plasticity—after someone experiences brain damage, healthy brain areas will take over functions lost by damaged brain circuits.

Our current view is that the brain is more like an ecosystem than a machine. Many brain systems are in constant competition with one another throughout life. Each neural network strives against others to gain feedback from the world outside the brain. Life experiences strengthen some brain functions and weaken others. At the same time, there is a degree of coordination—or synchronization—among brain areas, just as there is among species. Edelman describes a brain process that integrates different brain systems such that they are bound "into circuits capable of temporarily coherent output."

It is generally assumed that the characteristics of autism are caused by anomalies of brain development.[302] In a system as complex as the one I have described above, there are many places that development can go wrong. Something could go wrong with the glial scaffolding or the genetic program guiding neurons to their destinations. If neurons don't migrate to the right spots, brain functioning is impeded. There are some who think migration problems are the source of a host of disorders, including autism, dyslexia, schizophrenia, and epilepsy.[303] But without a wiring diagram of the normal brain, no one knows if this is true.

A second possible brain issue involves the pruning and strengthening process of neuronal selection. Perhaps the sensory inputs and experiences—even in the prenatal environment—eliminate valuable circuits and strengthen ones that are not going to work well in the child's world. This might help explain how people like Temple Grandin can look so hopelessly dysfunctional at an early age, yet become productive and functional adults, if still a little odd. They may start out with the wrong neuronal connections, but as life goes on, the brain's plasticity allows for adjustments and the best circuits take over and win out.

At a higher level, deficiencies in the brain's reentry system may cause problems in synchronization between brain systems. For instance, in many persons with autistic features, there seems to be a disconnect between sensory and emotional systems. Temple Grandin, for instance, describes her sensitivity to some stimuli and under-reaction to others. She writes, "The autistic child often withdraws from her environment and the people in it to block out an onslaught of incoming stimulation."[304] It could be that the integration of information entering through the sensory systems with the emotional reactivity systems is misaligned. Though this, again, is theory with no concrete evidence.

Before we can even begin to look for specific brain problems in autism, however, we must identify a clearly defined core deficit. As we have seen with descriptive psychiatric disorders such as schizophrenia, this is difficult to do. I have not directly discussed this issue previously; I will do so now with reference to autism.

According to Schreibman, there are four requirements for defining a core deficit in autism.[305] The deficit must be specific to autism and not characteristic of people labeled with other kinds of disorders. It must be universal; it must be seen in all persons with autism. It must be persistent; it affects the person over the course of development. And it must show precedence; it must begin early in development and lead to "a cascade of further, but related deficits down the line."

There is no single candidate for a core deficit that uniquely defines autism (as is the case with every other psychiatric disorder). It could be that one has yet to be found, or it could be that none exists. Schreibman writes, "because of the complex nature of autism, it is unlikely that a single core deficit will be found that explains all the features of the disorder." Her opinion accords with my belief that the entire autism spectrum is a heterogeneous group of types on a dimension of social incompetence.

There are, however, theories about what kinds of brain anomalies might generally be involved in persons with autistic features. These are usually presented as defects, but I would rather cast them as differences that may be disadvantageous or advantageous, depending on the circumstances. Schreibman summarizes the research on these differences into several major areas.

The first area is deficiency in what is referred to as *theory of mind.*[306] Children as young as age eighteen months begin to develop the ability to understand that other people's perspective is different from their own. Over time, they learn to recognize not only another person's beliefs and knowledge but also his or her intentions and desires. Schreibman suggests a defective theory of mind "may explain why [children labeled autistic] seem to understand so little of their social environment."

Theorists point to some specific skills that they see as necessary to create an adequate theory of mind and that seem lacking in many autistic people. One is the ability to formulate an alternative reality and hold it in mind along with perceptual reality. This ability is necessary for pretend play, such as pretending a stick is a gun. It is also necessary for a child to know both where a hidden object is and where someone else thinks it is. Children deemed autistic often seem to lack ingredients needed for theory of mind.

A defective theory of mind seems to be a useful construct for describing at least part of the social incompetence dimension, but it fails most of Schreibman's tests for an autistic smoking gun. First, theory of mind must be defined by a series of tasks, such as false-belief scenarios, which measure a child's ability to see the difference between what the child knows is true and what another child falsely believes is true.[307] The classic illustration of one of these tasks is for a child to watch a little play performed by two dolls. Doll A (Sally) plays with a marble, then puts it in a basket and leaves the room. Doll B (Ann) enters the room, plays with the marble, and then puts it in a box. The child is then asked where Sally will look for the marble when she comes back. Children with a developed theory of mind, who might be as young as four, will say Sally will look in the basket, because that is all Sally knows. Children described as autistic usually can't recognize that Sally doesn't know what they themselves know.

Autistic children, however, are not the only ones who fail some or all of the theory of mind tasks. Some children with intellectual disabilities, some with specific language disorders, some labeled with schizophrenia, and even some blind or deaf kids also do poorly on these tasks. Theory of mind does not seem to be a specific identifier of autism. Nor is it universal, since some children called autistic, especially higher-functioning ones, are able to pass the tests. Even whether a theory of mind deficit is a core deficit for autism is under dispute, because autistic features are often apparent long before theory of mind develops. A theory of mind hypothesis can't be used to explain observations that occur before it develops. Theory of mind deficiencies do seem persistent. Children with autistic features do continue to have difficulties seeing through pretense. There are a number of such people, however, including Temple Grandin, who have been able to overcome theory of mind deficits to a large extent.

There are a few other theories about what is the core deficit in autism that I will mention briefly. One is the development of *joint attention,* which is often seen as a precursor to forming a theory of mind. This is "the capacity of individuals to coordinate attention with a social partner in relation to some object or event."[308] This ability emerges at six to nine months and is considered the first form of intentional communication for a child. It begins when a parent makes eye contact with the baby, then looks at a nearby object, and the baby follows the parent's gaze and also looks at that object. The next step is for the baby to direct the parent's attention by making eye contact, then looking at an object, such as a cookie, and then back at the parent.

Research has shown the children later diagnosed as autistic were less apt to initiate joint-attention activities at an early age than other children. Joint-attention deficits reliably predict language delays.[309] Such a deficit may cause children to shift attention from social to nonsocial stimuli, leading to many other features described as autistic. Whether it can be considered a specific or universal deficit in autism, however, is highly debatable.

Another, perhaps even earlier, form of social communication for a child is called affective reciprocity.[310] Even an infant less than six months old begins to make eye contact and to display that they are, in Schreibman's phrase, "emotionally tuned in to the world about them." According to Peter Hobson, professor of developmental psychopathology, autistic children innately lack the ability to perceive and appropriately respond to emotional information.[311] One of his studies showed that while non-autistic children and even intellectually impaired children sorted pictures by emotional facial expression, autistic children sorted them on the basis of hats. Whether this deficiency can be described as specific to autism or universal to the entire spectrum is not so clear.

There is an intriguing neuropsychological finding that might be capable of explaining at least the social dysfunction of people on the autism spectrum—the discovery of mirror-neuron systems in the brain. In the early 1990s, an Italian neuroscientist, Giacomo Rizzolatti, made a serendipitous discovery while he and his team were studying the motor cortex in the brains of macaque monkeys. They were recording the pattern of activity in single neurons while the monkeys preformed a specific action, such as reaching for a piece of food.[312] Rizzolatti noticed a strange phenomenon. When he reached for a raisin, the monkey's neuron responded in exactly the same way as if it had reached for the raisin itself. He was able to rule out trivial explanations, such as the monkey moving its arm in imitation of the investigator, and concluded that the response was "a true representation in the brain of the act itself, regardless of who was performing it." Rizzolatti named these *mirror neurons.*

Rizzolatti's next series of experiments established that a monkey's mirror-neuron circuits fired not only if the monkey saw an action but also if it had "sufficient clues to create a mental representation of it." The final step in Rizzolatti's research was to show that mirror neurons also respond to intention. To do this, he looked at mirror-neuron responses when a monkey watched the experimenter bring food to his mouth compared with when he put it in a container. Indeed, the mirror neurons responded more strongly when observing this "grasping-to-eat" motion, and this was the same as when the monkey did the action itself.

The mirror-neuron findings were extended to human volunteers in a series of functional MRI studies. People's brains responded to the intention of the act in the same way the monkeys' brains did. There was more: human mirror neurons also responded to emotion observed in another person as if they had experienced it themselves. For instance, mirror neurons in the insula reacted to watching someone smell a disgusting odor as if the test subjects themselves had smelled it.

It is reasonable to speculate that since mirror neurons seem to play a prominent role in human social interaction, deficiencies in the system might be implicated in autism. Specifically, could a functioning mirror-neuron system be necessary in order to form a theory of mind, and could the lack of it lead to social isolation and diminished empathy?

Neurologists Vilaynur Ramachandran and Lindsey Oberman formulated such a theory.[313] They began with the hypothesis that "if the mirror neuron system is indeed involved in the integration of complex intentions, then a breakdown of the neural circuitry could explain the most striking deficit in people with autism, their lack of social skills." They set out to investigate this by studying a type of brain wave called the *mu wave*, which is known to become blocked when a person makes a voluntary muscle movement or watches someone else make one.

They started with high-functioning autistic children and found that the mu wave was indeed blocked when the children made a voluntary movement, as is normal. However, the mu wave was not blocked when the children watched another person make that movement.

Next they considered whether there was a connection between this deficit and the difficulty autistic children have in interpreting proverbs and metaphors. Perhaps the same mirror-neuron system was necessary to extract information required to understand intention and to understand metaphors. They focused on a part of the brain called the *angular gyrus* both because it was known to have mirror-neuron cells and because it "sits at the crossroads of the brain's vision, hearing and touch centers." They found that people who had sustained damage to the angular gyrus had difficulties understanding metaphors similar to those of autistic people.

Finally, they conjectured that there might be a connection between the mirror-neuron system and the emotional brain. They theorized that the mirror neurons feed information to a part of the emotional brain called the *amygdala* about the "salience" of environmental events, so that the individual can prepare for action. They concluded that "over time, the amygdala creates a salience landscape, a map that details the emotional significance of everything in the individual's environment." They thought that in some way, a "scrambled connection" between mirror neurons and the emotional brain might account for many of the symptoms that characterize the autistic condition.

More generally, Ramachandran believes that the discovery of mirror neurons "will do for psychology what DNA did for biology: they will provide a unifying framework and help explain a host of mental abilities that hitherto remained mysterious and inaccessible to experiments."[314] He thinks that the evolution of the mirror-neuron system some fifty thousand years ago allowed humans to take "a great leap forward" and made human culture possible, including language, social organization, and tool use. One implication of mirror neurons is that we mentally rehearse or imitate every action we witness. Not only does this help us learn complex actions, but it may also be the basis of empathy and understanding what other people are thinking and feeling.

Psychological and Social Context

Is autism a disability visited on us by faulty genes, a paucity of mirror neurons, or some other brain abnormality? Or does it describe one variation in the way people perceive and feel—a "different mind" as Penny Spikins calls autism. Is it possible that the traits of autism have existed in society for many millennia and continue to exist today because they bring important assets to our species? Despite any social disadvantages autism may create, individuals with these traits can and do make significant contributions to society.

Spikins, an archaeologist from Cambridge University, has theorized that autistic traits have been part of the human genome for as long as 160,000 years.[315] The emergence of modern human behavior brought with it the human trait of compassion for others, which allowed the acceptance of these different minds. She believes that it is precisely these autistic minds that made many of the technical and cultural advances that mark our species and gave us an evolutionary advantage over other hominids.

She has written, "Individuals with autism may have brought into our societies extraordinary focus, talents in analytical thought and skills in innovation."[316] It may have been what DSM-5 calls autism's "restricted repetitive patterns of behavior, interests or activities" that led to innovations from making tiny stone tools to recording and understanding astronomical systems. Spikins writes, "part of the reasons *Homo sapiens* were so successful is because they were willing to include people with different minds in their society."

Even in our modern world, there is a good deal of evidence that people with autistic traits can have unique capabilities. If the social circumstances are right, such people can be highly successful because of—not despite—their autism. This is not to say that there aren't autistic children who are very impaired and extremely difficult to rear. But even some of these children can learn to overcome their serious social limitations and allow their extraordinary talents to shine through. The real challenge for our society is creating a tolerant and effective environment that allows such people to thrive. As professor of psychiatry and autism researcher Laurent Mottron states, "most (autistics) face the harsh consequences of living in a world that has not been constructed around their priorities and interests."[317]

Mottron has offered a very different environment for autistic people. He has welcomed eight of them into his research group and has seen them do extremely well. He knows that they can contribute a great deal in settings such as scientific research. His long-time collaborator is an autistic woman named Michelle Dawson. He met her while filming a television documentary on autism and hired her as a research assistant. He writes, "when she edited some of my papers, she gave exceptional feedback and it was clear that she had read the entire bibliography."

Dawson helped Mottron challenge the assumptions and negative bias that even people studying autism tended to have. He has pointed out that the diagnostic criteria for autism omit any positives. Even when autistic people outperform others on tasks, it is usually considered compensatory for deficits. The data, though, tell a different story. For instance, autistic people outperform others on a range of perceptual tasks, including spotting a visual pattern within a distracting environment, discriminating sound pitches, and "mentally manipulating complex three-dimensional shapes."

Studies of functional brain scans also tell a different story about autistic people Mottron reported. When non-autistic people look at a picture, both visual processing and speech areas of the brain are activated. When autistic people look at the same picture, there is much more activity in the visual networks than in the speech networks. While this neurological difference may create a speech disadvantage, it enhances perceptual receptivity.

Mottron and colleagues did a study to determine whether autistic people have an intellectual disability.[318] Using the typical verbally based intelligence tests, such as the Wechsler scales, they do. But given a nonverbal intelligence test, such as Raven's Matrices, there is no difference between autistic and non-autistic adults. Mottron concluded that there is no intrinsic intellectual deficit in autism.

Mottron learned to capitalize on Dawson's strengths, which she shares with many other autistic people. She has a phenomenal memory. She easily remembers what she reads and rarely misremembers data. She is "good at spotting recurrent patterns in large amounts of data and instances when these patterns have been broken." Above all, she remains focused on the data and generates ideas based only on facts. She incorporates a great deal of data in her models, which are "almost infallibly accurate." Mottron, on the other hand, is a top-down thinker who starts with a general idea, then looks for facts. With Mottron and Dawson, "combining the two types of brains in the same research group is amazingly productive."

Simon Baron-Cohen, a University of Cambridge psychologist, is a leading theorist on the upside of autism. In the 1990s, when most researchers were focused on the social deficits, Baron-Cohen became interested in "the obsessive, narrow interests and repetitive behaviors" that mark the autistic person.[319] These behaviors were usually seen as pointless, but Baron-Cohen disagreed: "The child is doing it to understand the system." He theorized that the strength of autism is an "aptitude for understanding and analyzing predictable rule-based systems" with a corollary inability to understand the intentions and feelings of other people. He speculated that many scientists and engineers, including all-time greats such as Isaac Newton and Albert Einstein, had the traits of Asperger's syndrome.

Where Do We Stand with Autism?

Temple Grandin and many others may have different minds and a pattern of behavior that we describe as autism. As of this time, no one can be certain what brain mechanisms lie behind these differences. It is likely, however, that they are differences in degree, not kind. There are no diseases here.

Whether we should consider autistic features a disorder depends on whether they are truly the cause of impairment. There is no doubt that Grandin had a very difficult childhood, due to the social dysfunction her autism created, but what are we to make of the assets it conferred upon her? Are they a disorder, too?

Grandin overcame the difficulties her autism created for her and became very successful. She is still socially different from most of us, but she recognizes her deficits and social limitations and has consciously worked to overcome them. Does she still have a disorder?

In my view, to say that Temple Grandin has an autistic disorder is demeaning and unhelpful. No matter how we try to pretty it up, we are separating her from us and calling her less than an adequate human. It is much more desirable to describe her as exhibiting a type of personality or mind that we label *autistic* and that is socially limiting. Then it is up to us to create the social environments that help these people grow up with the minimum social dysfunction possible.

Attention Deficit and Hyperactivity

The attention deficit hyperactivity label agitates me more than any other psychiatric diagnosis. It is a designation imposed on children, who have no say in the matter, and it seems to be applied to almost any child that teachers, doctors, or parents find disruptive or difficult to manage. The most troubling fact is the large number of children being put on stimulant drugs with unknown consequences for their futures.

The ambiguity of the disorder is complemented by the enormous increase in its popularity. A study authored by pediatrician Craig Garfield reports that the number of American children diagnosed with ADHD in doctor's offices grew from 6.2 million in 2000 to 10.4 million in 2010.[320] It is increasingly diagnosed in children as young as six. Rates of drug treatment with Ritalin, Adderall, and similar medications are also on the rise.

History of ADHD

The idea behind the ADHD concept has probably been around as long as there have been parents disciplining children. There was a popular children's book written by a German physician in 1845, who probably gave the condition its first name—Fidgety Phil.

> The Papa bade Phil behave;
> And Mama looked very grave.
> But fidgety Phil,
> He won't sit still;
> He wriggles,
> And giggles,
> And then, I declare,
> Swings backwards and forwards,
> And tilts up his chair.[321]

In the nineteenth century, Fidgety Phil was not considered a medical disorder, merely a matter of temperament or character. In 1890, William James's *Principles of Psychology* described his conception of Fidgety Phil: "there is a normal type of character, for example, in which impulses seem to discharge so promptly into movements that inhibitions get no time to arise. These are the 'Dare-devil' and mercurial temperaments, overflowing with animation and fizzling with talk."[322]

Then, in the early twentieth century, an English physician named George Still described a group of children whom he saw as having deficits in *volitional inhibition* and *moral control*.[323] His description is seen as an early precursor to the ADHD diagnosis. Some years later, the concept shifted from morality to a physiological problem. In the 1920s, it was observed that some incidents of hyperactivity and impulsive behavior were to be found in children who had suffered some form of brain damage, such as a brain infection.

The idea that all such behavior was the result of mild brain damage became common, although there was no evidence for damage in almost all such cases.

In the 1950s, the term for a child who displayed hyperactive behavior and poor impulse control became *hyperkinetic impulse disorder,* thought to be caused by cortical overstimulation.[324] This designation soon changed to the more descriptive *hyperactive child syndrome* with an emphasis on excessive motor movement.[325] In 1968, DSM-II called it *hyperkinetic reaction of childhood,* which it described as "characterized by overactivity, restlessness, distractibility, and a short attention span."[326]

Following this, there was a slow shift in emphasis from the disruptive behavior associated with it to the attention problems. By 1980, DSM-III called the same pattern *attention deficit disorder* (with or without hyperactivity).[327] Now it was seen as a cognitive and developmental problem, rather than primarily a behavioral one. The ambiguity of whether this should be considered two separate disorders or one combined was resolved in 1987, when DSM-III-R presented the current *attention deficit hyperactivity disorder* label.[328]

The most recent psychiatric conception of ADHD in DSM-5 is that it consists of two basic components.[329] One is inattention, which is marked by such characteristics as (1) carelessness, (2) difficulty sustaining attention or focus for long periods, (3) distractibility, (4) lack of follow-through, (5) poor organization, (6) avoidance of tasks requiring "sustained mental effort," (7) losing things, and (8) forgetfulness. The second is hyperactivity and impulsivity, which may include (1) fidgeting, (2) leaving one's seat, (3) restlessness, (4) unable to sit quietly, (5) always "on the go" or "driven by a motor," (6) excessive talking, (7) difficulty waiting one's turn, and (8) interrupting or intruding on others. These factors may appear in different proportions, ranging from "predominately inattentive" to "predominantly hyperactive/impulsive." Furthermore, these characteristics must "interfere with or reduce the quality of social, academic, or occupational functioning."

What Is ADHD?

The psychiatric characterization of ADHD actually encompasses a triad of characteristics. The psychologist Russell Barkley described ADHD patients as "excessively active, unable to sustain their attention and ... deficient in impulse control."[330] The first questions we must ask are whether these three go together and, if so, how. If the underlying problem is one of inattention, then we might group ADHD with cognitive competence and say that over-activity and poor impulse control are secondary. If, as I see it, the primary problem is behavioral control, then the inattention is a product of social competence dysfunction.

Barkley presents a psychological theory that ADHD is not fundamentally a problem of inattention. As Barkley points out—and I have observed—the inattention of children (and adults) with ADHD is not general, as it might be with someone who sustained damage in an area of the brain directly controlling attention. A person diagnosed with ADHD can spend hours playing online video games but can't do schoolwork or chores for more than a few minutes. Studies also show that kids labeled ADHD show much less impulsive or disruptive behavior during free play, when their fathers are home, or when they are on a fun field trip. They do worst when someone else sets the task or when they have to restrain their own behavior in a public setting, such as school or church.

In Barkley's theory, the problems of ADHD are created by deficiencies in three related functions of the human brain. The first of these concerns *behavioral inhibition*, our ability to suppress an immediate response to what is occurring in the environment. There are three aspects to this inhibition. One is inhibiting the urge to act in the moment with the most readily available response. Another is inhibiting responses that proved ineffective in the past; this involves being sensitive to our errors. The last is in inhibiting responses to events that are distracting or irrelevant to the task at hand.

Lack of inhibition interferes with the development of *self-control*, the ability to direct behavior toward the future. To do that, we have to have the time to consider the best course of action, and we can't do that if we're already acting. Barkley describes *self-control* as engaging in actions that take into account future consequences. These actions need to be visualized and privately rehearsed before being expressed. Sometimes there must be time to consult with others who have a stake in what we do. Barkley writes, "sharing and cooperation depend on a capacity to wait and to sense the future implications of what a person does with others."

The third element, which depends on inhibition and self-control, is the development of *executive functions*. These involve judgment, delaying gratification, and a general future orientation. Barkley describes this process: "we see and hear ourselves (among other self-directed senses), talk to ourselves, motivate ourselves, and play with information to change ourselves for the sake of improving our future consequences."

If this constellation of abilities does not develop fully, we are limited in our ability to regulate ourselves appropriately in the social sphere. Barkley concludes, "those with ADHD have a form of temporal nearsightedness or time blindness that will produce substantial social, educational and occupational devastation via its disruption of their day-to-day adaptive functioning relative to time in the future."

Psychostimulants and ADHD

The first medication used to treat hyperactive children was accidentally discovered by a pediatrician named Charles Bradley in 1937.[331] In that era, chronically sick children were subjected to pneumoencephlograms to study their brains. This meant injecting air into their spinal columns and having them sit up, so the air would rise to their brains. This was a painful procedure, which caused vicious headaches. Bradley was looking for a medication that would help their headaches during the procedure.

One of the drugs Bradley tried was a new stimulant called Benzedrine, which was becoming a common treatment for allergies and asthma. Benzedrine did nothing for the headaches, but to Bradley's surprise, it improved children's concentration on their schoolwork. The children called it "arithmetic pills." Bradley was puzzled by the paradox that a stimulant could "subdue" children and help them study. He wrote an article describing his findings, but it attracted little attention.

Twenty years later, a new stimulant drug that was related to amphetamines came on the market as a treatment for narcolepsy. The pharmaceutical company Ciba-Geigy called it Ritalin and touted it as the safe alternative to amphetamines.[332] Psychiatrists who were aware of the Bradley article considered it a drug that could also be used to calm agitated children who were thought to be suffering from brain damage. The idea of using Ritalin to calm hyperactive children, however, was anathema to many psychiatrists and the public at large. They expressed concerns about "mind control" and "drugging our children."[333] There were also fears that prescribing it might increase illegal drug use.

Originally there was little pressure to prescribe Ritalin, because hyperactivity was seen as a form of brain disease, and the only children for whom it was considered suitable were in residential facilities or hospitals. In the 1970s, the use of Ritalin slowly grew, until perhaps 150,000 children were taking it. The numbers grew again in the 1980s, when the DSM made attention deficit an official disorder. It was in the 1990s when both diagnoses of ADHD and the drug treatment for it really took off. Robert Whitaker reports that at that time, an organization was formed called Children and Adults with Attention Deficit Hyperactivity Disorder (CHADD). It was advertised as a patient support group, but it was largely funded by Ciba-Geigy. CHADD lobbied Congress and got ADHD services covered under the Individuals with Disabilities Education Act. The number of children found to have ADHD and prescribed Ritalin and its sister drugs mushroomed.

Ritalin and other stimulant drugs are similar to the SSRI antidepressants in that they block the reuptake of a brain neurotransmitter, only in this case, the neurotransmitter is dopamine—the major transmitter in the motivational systems of the brain. It is called the "pleasure chemical" because jolts of it are highly reinforcing. It also has the effect of increasing the saliency of some stimuli to the exclusion of distracting ones. As Paul Hammerness, psychiatrist at Harvard Medical School, concludes, "It may be that these medications increase the brain's ability to attend to a task, in part by increasing the saliency of a task or increasing the sense of interest or pleasure in performing the task."

CHADD and the pharmaceutical companies worked hard to convince the public that these drugs are specific to ADHD. CHADD's website reassures us that "despite their name, these medications do not work by increasing stimulation of the person. Rather, they help important networks of nerve cells in the brain communicate more effectively with each other." The makers of Concerta, another ADHD drug, trot out the chemical-imbalance theory: "it is thought that ADHD medications restore the balance, or level, of these neurotransmitters, leading to many behavioral and academic improvements."[334]

Of course, there is no evidence for a deficit in dopamine or any other neurotransmitter related to inattention and hyperactivity. The effects of stimulant drugs are general in all people. As many a college student cramming for exams knows, stimulant drugs like Ritalin and amphetamines really help you stay up all night and focus intensely on your studies. These drugs work the same way for all of us. If you want to work harder and improve your focus, you can do so by taking them—you'll even enjoy it at the same time.

There are just a few problems with that. Most ADHD drugs are stimulants with the same mechanism as cocaine and methamphetamine. The only real difference is that illegal drugs act very rapidly, giving the feeling of a "rush" and then their effects disappear quickly. This makes drug addiction occur quickly. Tolerance to and dependence on ADHD medications builds as well, though it is less obvious. But if you take ADHD medications over an extended period of time and then stop, you will suffer withdrawal.

There is one ADHD drug, Strattera, that is said to be a non-stimulant medication. It does not directly affect dopamine, but rather another activating neurotransmitter, noradrenaline. It is true that Strattera can't get anyone high, but it has effects similar to stimulants. The jury is still out on whether it can cause dependence or has other adverse long-term effects. If not, we might soon find that we are all taking a Strattera pill along with our morning coffee.

ADHD and Autism

ADHD is, in many ways, the flip side of autism with respect to social competence. The social dysfunction of autism is related to a person's inability to perceive and understand the social signals of other people. This lack impedes their ability to form interpersonal relationships. People diagnosed with ADHD have less difficulty understanding social cues and more difficulty conforming to social requirements. Whether the problem is faulty input or control of the output, the result is dysfunctional social behavior.

ADHD and autism traits should both be distinguished from people who behave disruptively for other reasons. The dimension of social competence is different from the socialization dimension to be considered in chapter 13.

People appropriately described as ADHD or autism types are not antisocial and self-centered. They do not behave in an intentionally destructive or willful way. They do not harm other people or their property. People with either ADHD or autism issues are often frustrated and unhappy with the troubles their behavior causes them.

I want to make it clear that I see both ADHD and autism as model types on a dimension rather than as discrete conditions. With respect to ADHD, people range from the most conforming, organized, and disciplined of us to the loose cannons who seem unable to control their behavior in any social circumstances. Most of us exist somewhere in the middle. We do fine when we are interested and stimulated, but when bored or confined by the expectations of others, we can become disruptive.

There also may be no real separation between ADHD and autism traits. There do not appear to be discrete sets of characteristics, but more of a continuum between them. When we observe more of a perceptual deficit, such as seemed evident with Temple Grandin, we call it *autism*. But Grandin had a great deal of difficulty controlling her behavior as a youngster, and that could equally well have been identified with attention deficit and hyperactivity. Conversely, many children labeled ADHD could equally be seen as having an autism spectrum disorder if one looks for deficiencies in social interaction and restricted interests. In other words, there are many people in the middle who have characteristics of both ADHD and autism; how they are seen depends on what the clinician is looking for.

Positive Aspects of ADHD

Looked at through the lens of deficit, ADHD can have devastating consequences for many people. In many cases, its characteristics lead to a life of frustration and failure, with the consequent shame, low self-esteem, and unhappiness. But this occurs in particular social circumstances, and it neglects potential positive features that can be seen in many people who are labeled ADHD.

Today there is a growing reaction to the gloomy picture of ADHD as a mental disorder. Edward Hallowell is one such authority; he is a psychiatrist, former faculty member at Harvard Medical School, and the author of many books on ADHD. He considers ADHD a gift, but one that is hard to unwrap. He writes, "ADHD is a terrible term. As I see it, ADHD is neither a disorder nor is there a deficit in attention. I see ADHD as a trait, not a disability. When it is properly managed, it can become a huge asset in one's life.... As I like to describe it, having ADHD is like having a powerful racecar for a brain, but with bicycle brakes. Treating ADHD is like strengthening your brakes."[335]

Hallowell recounts his own experience as an "undiagnosed attention deficit disorder student" and how finding a mentor teacher helped him overcome his limitations and succeed.[336] He was a bright but mediocre eleventh-grader at a private school who was getting by, but unenthusiastic and underachieving. He had little belief in himself. Then one special English teacher began to "call on this quiet boy sitting in the back of the class, not to embarrass him, but to draw him out." Dr. Hallowell "discovered he had more ideas than he thought he did."

The English teacher assigned *Crime and Punishment*, which initially made him groan. But he quickly became inspired and spent the entire weekend reading it. His teacher singled him out and gave him the notebooks Dostoevsky compiled while writing his novel. "A part of the boy's mind that had lain dormant came back to life. He was brimming with curiosity and confidence." One teacher changed his life forever.

Other authorities, people who work extensively with people diagnosed with ADHD, have also described some of the positive aspects they see in such people. Deborah Estes, EdD, a former high school teacher, middle school principal, and educational consultant in Texas, has listed twenty-nine positive characteristics that she has observed in ADHD. These include being sensitive, empathic, creative, inventive, perceptually acute, spontaneous, and energetic.[337] Pete Quilly, an adult ADHD/ADD coach and blogger, has compiled an even more extensive list of assets. He writes, "ADHD is an allergy to boredom. If we ADDers are interested in something, ADHD is generally not a problem. For those of us who like the online world, it's rarely boring."[338]

My major concern is that the ADHD diagnosis is more and more being used as a means of controlling children—mostly boys and mostly by schools. As reported by political scientist Rick Mayes in the *Harvard Review of Psychiatry*, the diagnosis of ADHD is mostly driven by teacher complaints, and "only a minority of children with the disorder exhibit symptoms during a physician's office visit."[339] It is much easier for a school to request that a child be labeled ADHD and put on medication to accommodate the school, rather than for the school to accommodate the child. I understand that it is very difficult to teach a classroom full of children with different needs. Some discipline and order must be maintained. But children learn in different ways, and good teachers create an environment that suits the needs of almost all kids.

Like autism, ADHD is a negative evaluation that focuses on a child's weaknesses. It tells children that they are deficient in some way. But the traits that lead to the diagnosis may be advantageous, if channeled in a positive direction.

Final Thoughts on ADHD

I recall reading an article some years ago about a major league baseball player. What I had noticed about him was his fierce intensity when he was at the plate. I was surprised to read that he had been diagnosed with ADHD as a school child and what a difficult time he had had with it. He was put on medication after medication and still was never able to succeed. The contrast between the pathetically disabled child and the confident, accomplished superstar was striking.

Temperament, proclivities, and learning styles certainly have biological aspects underlying attainment, but psychological and social factors must be accounted for in any attempt to understand the dysfunction we call ADHD. Psychologically, children are raised in different family environments, with different expectations, conflicts, and tolerances. Socially, the resulting traits play out in a wider world of school, employment, and community. Sometimes the developed traits are rewarded, and the person thrives. In other cases, someone is mismatched to life circumstances and becomes dysfunctional in that context.

We can't all be superstars, and many of us struggle to overcome our limitations. We may need help and guidance, but we aren't disordered. We are all of different temperaments, with different mixes of assets and liabilities. When the world is right, and we learn the requisite skills, I believe we can all achieve, according to our own lights. It doesn't help to be labeled ADHD or autistic.

10

Pain and Bodily Illness

One of my favorite cartoons shows a headstone inscribed with "John Smith, 1910–2010." The epitaph: "See, I really was sick."

We humans are frail creatures. We will get sick and we will die. Health is a precarious and uncertain thing. We will all suffer illness and injury throughout our lives. As we age, we increasingly recognize that life is a terminal disease. It is natural to be concerned about our well-being and to want to protect it.

When we experience physical symptoms, it is difficult to know when we should seek medical attention. Pay too little heed, and we may miss something treatable. We do not want to suffer needlessly or find out that we could have prevented a medical catastrophe. But if we spend too much time, energy, and resources on every potential ailment, we risk becoming chronic invalids, taking too many drugs, and getting too many tests and treatments.

We are bombarded by advertisements telling us to pay more attention to our bodies and to see our doctors for the latest pharmaceuticals. Many of us have come to expect our doctors to treat any ill feeling we have. We are angry if we are told that there is nothing to do and that we will have to live with a particular problem. The paradox of modern medicine is that as its power to diagnose and cure major diseases grows, there is an increasing number of people seeking medical answers for every minor distress.

The rising tide of people looking for medical attention is revealed in the most recent statistics available from the U.S. Department of Health and Human Services.[340] In 2006, there were an estimated 1.1 billion visits to physicians' offices, hospital outpatient departments, and emergency departments in the United States: almost four visits a year for every person in the country. From 1996 to 2006, the number of emergency-room visits increased from thirty-four to more than forty for every hundred persons. There were roughly 2.6 billion prescriptions for drugs in 2006, and the percentage of doctors' visits that resulted in a prescription increased significantly between 1996 and 2006. I would imagine that when the next report comes out, this trend toward more drug prescriptions will continue.

The obvious conclusion is that we are increasingly seeing ourselves as ill and want medication to address our problems. To begin to understand this, we need to make a distinction between feeling ill and having a disease. *Feeling ill* means the subjective experience of adverse or alarming bodily sensations. *Having a disease* means having an objectively verifiable condition that has an identifiable cause, course, and outcome. Much of the time, the two go together; perceived symptoms are signs of diseases. But this connection is not always true. As James Pennebaker, psychology professor at the University of Texas, put it, "awareness of internal sensations usually does not represent a one-to-one correspondence with actual physiological change."[341]

When people go to the doctor feeling ill, they usually expect the doctor to find a biological reason for their problem. They're often dissatisfied if the physician finds nothing wrong. They can even be indignant: "Are you trying to tell me it's all in my head?" If the doctor comes up with a reasonable, benign explanation, patients are likely to still want a "cure" for what they believe to be a disease. If that doesn't work, the patient frequently wants further diagnostic testing and additional treatment. The result can be that patients develop a dysfunctional sick role that may take over their lives.

Here is one example of the dilemma. The American Autoimmune Related Disease Association (AARDA) estimates that there are eighty to one hundred autoimmune diseases (including type-1 diabetes, multiple sclerosis, and rheumatoid arthritis) and that up to fifty million Americans suffer from them. An autoimmune disease is one that causes the body's immune system to attack its own cells as if they were invaders. Some may be relatively easy to spot, but most are so difficult to identify that, according to AARDA, it takes an average of five years and five doctors to make a correct diagnosis.

Among the most frequent symptoms of autoimmune diseases are

debilitating fatigue and brain fog. Meghan O'Rourke had these symptoms for many years. Her doctors first told her that she was "a little anemic or a little bit vitamin D deficient."[342] But O'Rourke's condition continued to worsen. "I felt like a mechanism that moved arduously through the world, simply trying to complete its tasks. Sitting upright at my father's birthday party required an act of will."

Finally, O'Rourke saw a doctor who specialized in woman's health. She listened to O'Rourke's history and said, "even before I see your labs, I am highly suspicious that you have some kind of autoimmune disease." Sure enough, her labs came back showing antibodies in her thyroid gland, and she was diagnosed with a form of Hashimoto's disease.

Fine. But was a low-functioning thyroid really the cause of her subjective symptoms? If the treatment—thyroid medication—worked, her ill feelings and the objective disease could be considered one and the same. But after taking the medication for six weeks, O'Rourke felt worse and had new symptoms: headaches, itching, joint pain, and fainting. Her doctor told her to increase the thyroid medication and to avoid wheat.

People with fatigue and brain fog may have evidence of autoimmune defects, just as people with back pain may have evidence of bulging discs. But there are many people with similar physical signs who don't have the subjective symptoms, just as there are many people with the symptoms but none of the objective signs. In other words, feeling ill is a psychological and social phenomenon that exists as its own experience, whether or not objective causes can be found.

O'Rourke did eventually find solace online. "Here was," she said, "a group of people, rich and poor, who were connected by one thing: the inability of doctors to alleviate their symptoms." And many recommendations she found online gave her hope. She changed her diet to something more paleo, jumped on a trampoline to stimulate her lymphatic system, and dry-brushed her body. She spent much of her money and half her days buying and preparing food. She had "joined the First Assembly of the Diffusely Unwell" church. After a few weeks, she was almost her old self.

Alas, it was not to last, because it is "the nature of autoimmune diseases to attack in cycles." Her doctor suggested she might now be hyperthyroid and should try lowering her medication dose. When O'Rourke objected, her doctor said, "Okay, then raise the dose and see how you do." New symptoms emerged, and new autoimmune diseases were diagnosed. O'Rourke even began to recognize what professor of rheumatology Norton Hadler told her was called *negative labeling:* "When you give patients a diagnosis, they tend to feel sicker than they did without one. Focusing on symptoms, some studies suggest, can make them more severe."

Things changed for O'Rourke when she came to a realization. "I had become trapped in my identity as a sick person, someone afraid of living. If my mission in life had been reduced to being well at all costs, then illness had won. I sounded, I realized, like every other health-obsessed narcissist.... In order to become well, I would have to temper my own fanatical pursuit of wellness."

Could O'Rourke have some form of unknown biological disease? Of course she could. Might some future generation look back on us and comment on how ignorant we were about diseases? Sure. But the nature of O'Rourke's ill feelings would still not become a disease. It might be considered a type of madness.

A Case of Too Many Symptoms

Cindy was referred to me by her neurologist for an evaluation of her memory complaints. She told me, "I forget things a lot. I can't do more than one thing at once. I have to stop and think about what I am doing. I feel like my mind is slow, and I have trouble getting out what I want to say. I have to keep rereading what I put down on paper so I don't mess up." My job was to help determine whether she had some form of brain dysfunction, perhaps related to a disease such as multiple sclerosis.

Cindy had many physical symptoms as well, including dizziness, palpitations, fatigue, exhaustion upon exertion, the sense of being on a boat when she turned her head, generalized pain, sleepiness, and headaches. She also complained of urinary frequency and urgency, muscle cramps, and general weakness. She had had a large number of medical tests, including brain scans, all of which showed she was essentially normal.

She was having a great deal of difficulty carrying out the usual routines of life. She couldn't work and was on long-term disability. When she was having a bad period (which was most of the time), she spent most of her day sleeping. Her husband told me, "when she goes through her bad spells, she can't do anything. I have to do it. She can't even drive."

All these problems had started two years previously, she reported to me, "my body started changing; my mood, my personality and my mind, too." Sometime after this, she said, "[I] crashed. My body shut down. I couldn't walk down the stairs." She saw her family practitioner, who immediately sent her to the hospital by ambulance. There was no diagnosis. She was sent to a psychiatric nurse practitioner, who "ruled out" any psychiatric disorder as the cause of her symptoms.

Did any of this add up? On further questioning, I found out that she had been taking antidepressants for anxiety and depression for seven or eight years. When I asked her about her life history, she told me that she had never been abused or neglected, but that her mother treated her like a "slave-girl." She said she had to do all the household chores and care for her younger brother, while her mother "would just sit around and talk to her friends." She also told me that she had a long history of migraine headaches, sciatica, heartburn, and irritable bowel syndrome. And she added, "I would get tendinitis easily."

As I talked to her, several other pieces of information emerged. She saw herself as a caretaker: "I take care of everybody else," she said. A few years before, she and her husband almost divorced; they were living only as roommates. She began taking homeless teenagers into her home because she felt that she "had a purpose." Now, she said, things between her and her husband were much better. She denied any emotional problems, saying, "I don't worry about anything—just about what is wrong with me." Both her teenage daughters, however, went to the same psychiatric practitioner that she did, for "anxiety, panic disorder, and depression." Her seventeen-year-old daughter was pregnant.

My observation of her was that she showed no sign of physical or emotional distress throughout the interview. She also did not exhibit any deficits in her cognitive capacities when she talked to me. She was cheerful and sociable. It was very difficult, however, to get a straight story from her. She spoke rapidly and continuously and jumped from subject to subject. She was focused on her many symptoms, which she presented in an overly detailed and dramatic fashion. Her husband was pleasant, but he was solicitous and tended to speak for her.

To test whether she had any notable cognitive deficits, she was given a full battery of cognitive tests. The results were unremarkable and just where they should be—in the average range. Her intelligence, memory, language, and motor abilities were consistently average. In sum, there was no evidence of cognitive impairment.

What can we make of all this? The cognitive tests, the only part of her complaints that could be evaluated objectively, showed no sign of brain damage. All her other symptoms were subjective and, while dramatically presented, did not seem to concern her greatly. She did not exhibit any real distress. Her bodily symptoms appeared to be part of a life-long pattern, even if she had become extremely dysfunctional only more recently. There were many hints that she got a great deal of social reinforcement (what is often called a *secondary gain*) for her disability from her husband and others in her life. My conclusion was that she was converting underlying emotional conflicts and coping difficulties into physical symptoms. In actuality, she could function far better than she did and could have been leading a more productive life.

It is dysfunctional to put too much emphasis on bodily symptoms, to worry too much about health, and to expect doctors and medications to cure every complaint. When unreasonable health concerns and expectations begin to dominate our lives, they crowd out productive and enjoyable life experiences and leave us as invalids. The term we can use for this is *somatoform dysfunction,* meaning "psychological illness in the form of bodily disease."

Years ago, psychiatrist Thomas Szasz wrote an essay describing people who lead lives of chronic pain; he characterized this type of person as *l'homme douloureux,* "the painful man." This term "refers to a man whose humanity is related to, or is wholly dependent upon, his being in pain and suffering."[343] He explained that these "are individuals who have made a career out of suffering. At one time they may have been attorneys or architects, busboys or businessmen, models or maids, but when their careers fail or no longer suffice to sustain them, they become 'painful persons.'" Painful persons represent one end of a somatoform dysfunction dimension.

A Biopsychosocial Perspective on Illness

How do we know we are ill? This is a fundamental question. In the continuous flow of sensations coming from the body, how does the brain pick out pieces of information that are unusual and interpret them as something wrong? It is vital to our survival that we detect when something dangerous is occurring in our bodies. When wrongness is detected, our brain develops a plan of action. Sometimes that plan begins when a person's brain labels the wrongness as *illness.*

In our day-to-day existence, we respond to most bodily signals with little or no conscious awareness. We scratch when our skin itches and change positions when we sense stiffness. Parts of our lower brain, particularly the hypothalamus, interpret recurrent bodily signals, such as need for food and water, and initiate well-developed action plans, like motivating us to eat. Similarly, other brain structures, like the amygdala, react to bodily sensations with emotional responses, like fear. Sometimes these signals are conceptualized as illness by the highest levels of our brain.

If our perceived symptoms reach a certain threshold, we become more concerned and take more determined—and conscious—measures. It is, of course, prudent to attend to problems that disturb us. It is just as bad to ignore significant physical symptoms that might indicate serious disease as it is to overrespond to minor ones.

In his theory of physical symptoms, Pennebaker distinguishes between the awareness of symptoms and the reporting of them.[344] Whether we become consciously aware of physical sensations depends on their magnitude and on what other things we might be experiencing at the time. Awareness also depends on "our general propensity to attend internally," as well as on specific beliefs that may direct our attention to particular kinds of symptoms.

Simple awareness is only the first step, and whether we report symptoms is a different matter. People who become aware of symptoms may choose not to report them or to overreport them, or they may fall somewhere in the middle. Reporting symptoms depends on how we interpret them and on the social context of rewards and punishments for reporting them. Pennebaker notes that "self-reporting[s] of such common sensations as shortness of breath, racing heart, and tense muscles have different meanings to different people"—they perceive them differently. Furthermore, people who have experienced positive results from reporting symptoms are more likely to do so.

Pennebaker has identified two major personality factors—"attentiveness to body" and "competence and control"—that create a tendency to overreport symptoms. He cites studies that have shown that "people who chronically attend to internal states tend to report a large number of symptoms, visit physicians and take more over-the-counter medications than people who are not attentive to their bodies."

Additionally, people's sense of competence and control over their environments is a factor. According to Pennebaker, "people who do not perceive themselves as in control of their environments report more symptoms than those who feel more in control." People with low self-esteem and people who suffered major reversals in life changes or events, which caused them to feel a loss of control, reported more health-related issues.

Pennebaker summarized the studies of personality factors in those prone to report physical symptoms by describing a typical overreporter. Such a person is "self-conscious and anxious, has low-esteem and aspires (but may not be succeed in being able) to control aspects of his or her environment."

The relationship between stressful life changes and the tendency to attend to and interpret bodily sensations is particularly apparent. One dramatic example of this is what is famously called *medical student's disease*. A study of first-year medical students revealed that 70 percent of them reported symptoms of the diseases they were studying.[345] These were students under some stress, and they were generating some autonomic arousal symptoms available for interpreting. They were also studying many rare diseases, often with ambiguous symptoms. They were scrutinizing their bodies for symptoms and finding them. They could then alarm themselves by interpreting these sensations in the context of their new knowledge about disease.

A similar phenomenon has been observed throughout the ages and across cultures and has become known as *mass psychogenic illness* or *mass hysteria*. These outbreaks of physical symptoms with no obvious biological basis often occur in groups of friends or coworkers in stressful circumstances.

Mass Psychogenic Illness

Over the last millennium, there have been frequent reports of collective delusions, some of which, like the Salem witch trials or apocalyptic cults, have had tragic consequences. These group delusions often have a bodily nature. This phenomenon, which used to be called *mass hysteria* and is now known as *mass psychogenic illness,* is defined as the "rapid spread of illness signs and symptoms affecting members of a cohesive group … whereby physical complaints that are exhibited unconsciously have no corresponding organic etiology."[346] The theory is that some form of psychological distress is being channeled into physical symptoms.

Two types of mass hysteria have been distinguished.[347] *Anxiety hysteria* is usually of short duration and is triggered by something that is perceived as threatening, such as a strange odor. One modern case of it occurred in 1998, when children in Jordan were vaccinated at school for tetanus and diphtheria; 800 became sick, and 122 were hospitalized.[348] For the vast majority, no organic cause could be found. Typical complaints included nausea, headache, dizziness, and generalized weakness.

The second type is called *motor hysteria,* because its symptoms are more obvious and dramatic, including shaking, spasms, trance-like states, and what we generally recognize as histrionics. This sort of mass psychogenic illness usually develops gradually and may last for long periods of time. It has often been described in strict and rather isolated social settings, such as schools and convents.

One historical case of motor hysteria happened in medieval France, at a time when it was widely believed that people could be possessed by animals. In one large convent, a nun began to meow like a cat. Soon other nuns began meowing, and finally all the nuns began meowing together for several hours each day. This astonished and disturbed the entire town. It ended only after the nuns were informed that a company of soldiers would whip them with rods if they didn't stop.[349]

In a case of anxiety hysteria in 1944, a woman in Mattoon, Illinois, called the police saying that she and her daughter had been sprayed by a sweet-smelling gas by a mysterious stranger. They were left nauseated and dizzy, and the woman had difficulty walking. The *Mattoon Daily Journal-Gazette* published a sensational story entitled "Anesthetic Prowler on Loose." Over the next several weeks, twenty-nine victims called the police reporting that they, too, had been sprayed by the gas and had similar symptoms.[350]

Another case, one that has been extensively studied, involved drinking Coca-Cola in Belgium in 1999.[351] It began when students in one secondary school complained of nausea, vomiting, abdominal pain, dizziness, and headache after consuming Coca-Cola. Within days, students at four other secondary schools made the same complaints. The epidemic spread, until the Belgian Poisoning Call Center had received over seven hundred calls about similar symptoms.

Coca-Cola officials investigated and found that the beverages delivered to the first school had very low concentrations of hydrogen sulfide (which caused the soda to smell rotten). For the other schools, the outside of the cans had been contaminated by a chemical from the pallets used to transport them (which explained a medicinal odor that the students had described). The company, however, concluded that the low concentrations of these chemicals could not cause toxicity.

The Belgian epidemiology group studying this incident found that only a small percentage of students (13 percent) in the first school reported symptoms, and an even smaller percentage of students in the four other schools were symptomatic. The reports of illness, though, clustered in certain classrooms, and girls were much more likely to complain than boys. The study also found "evidence of unusual mental stress among those reporting illness." The authors concluded that while cases at the original school might reasonably be attributed to the Coca-Cola itself, only mass psychogenic illness could explain the majority of cases.

There is a clear gender difference in when and how men and women react to bodily symptoms. Among healthy people, the sexes report approximately equal levels of most symptoms, but they respond differently in certain stressful environments. Pennebaker's research found that women are more sensitive to cues from their external environment, while men are more likely to ignore them and depend on internal physiological sensations.[352]

The result of this gender split plays out in cases of mass psychogenic illness. Illnesses of this sort are far more likely to involve women than men; this is true across cultures. But this sensitivity to the environment may not always be a bad thing. If there are low levels of toxins in the environment that are harming people, women are more likely to detect them.

There is also a strong relationship between the tendency to experience and report physical symptoms and a personality trait called *negative affectivity*, which is defined as a tendency toward a negative mood and low self-concept.[353] It is similar to constructs like neuroticism, pessimism, and anxiety traits. People with high negative affectivity tend to report many more physical symptoms than others. Pennebaker concludes that "high negative affectivity individuals appeared to be hypervigilant about their bodies and have a lower threshold for reporting subtle bodily sensations. Because of their generally pessimistic view of the world, they are also likely to worry about the implications of their perceived symptoms."[354]

Interestingly, the negative affectivity trait seems to have a strong genetic component. The Minnesota Twins study studied more than four hundred pairs of identical and fraternal twins, some of whom had been raised apart, and found that negative affectivity had a high degree of heritability.[355] This finding has been replicated in a number of other large-scale studies. The implication is that there is a strong inborn disposition to perceive ill health, independent of any objective measures of sickness.

We report bodily symptoms in a social context. Whenever we complain of illness, we are not just describing what we feel, we are seeking something from other people. We tell our doctors because we want information about causes and consequences, as well as help relieving our symptoms. We tell our families for reasons as varied as attention, sympathy, and acknowledgment. We tell our employers, insurance companies, and government agencies in order to get benefits, such as relief from work or financial payments.

These are all forms of reward that, for vulnerable persons, can lead to the overreporting of symptoms or, in extreme cases, the adoption of a "sick role" in life. Being sick can be purposeful, whether an individual is aware of it or not. One obvious purpose for telling doctors about pain is to get medications to ease it. Doctors control the supply of narcotics, and complaining of pain is a way to get them. Having serious symptom complaints can also be a means for escaping stressful or onerous situations at home, work, or school. When doctors declare that you have a disease, it can provide a means of income through Social Security disability payments or workers' compensation.

More subtle is the effect being symptomatic can have on family and friends. Being ill elicits attention from loved ones, and who doesn't want a little TLC at times? It's harder to see, however, why some people offer a litany of complaints to any available ear. What may explain it is that most people do not wish to be rude or antagonistic and will listen with attention and sympathy.

Even less obvious are the effects an ill person can have on a stressed family. Family systems theorists have long described how an ill family member (especially a child) can bring a dysfunctional family closer together.[356] According to child and adolescent psychiatrist G. Pirooz Sholevar, "this helps regulate the internal stability of the family, but does so at the cost of reinforcing the child's psychosomatic symptoms and the dysfunctional family organization."[357]

None of what I am saying about the social context is meant as moral condemnation of ill individuals. I do mean to bring to light the usually neglected impact that these social aspects have on all of us. The emphasis on medical explanations for what ails us has profound social effects on how we perceive our physical (and mental) health, our tendency to seek medications, and the rising levels of disability. We will consider these issues further later in this book.

Before I end this section, I'll briefly give some attention to the developmental issues involved. As we grow up, life teaches us how to detect physical symptoms and when to seek medical care for them. There have been four major themes relating to the perception and reporting of these symptoms in the developmental literature.

Pennebaker described the first theme as the *attentiveness of parents*.[358] This factor "assumes that the degree to which parents are attentive to the child's health will ultimately influence the child's symptom reporting and/ or health-seeking responses." The strongest test of this hypothesis was René Dubos University Professor of Behavioral Sciences at Rutgers University David Mechanic's two studies of children, which were done sixteen years apart.[359] In the first study, he interviewed fourth- and eighth-grade children and their mothers about perception of symptoms. There was a significant, but very small, correlation between a mother's concern about symptoms and the child's reports of symptoms.

In the second study, he interviewed the same children as young adults.[360] He found that parental attentiveness and overconcern had a long-lasting effect. It contributed to a "distress syndrome"; these young adults "report more physical and psychological distress, are more upset by stressful life events, and use more medical, psychiatric and other helping services."[361]

The second theme Pennebaker reviews is *parental interpretation of sensations*. Even if parents are inattentive to a child's symptoms, they still convey their attitudes and beliefs about illness. Pennebaker concluded that "the way that the parent interprets ambiguous sensations can be adopted by the child." Mechanic's studies found that mothers who were under stress reported more symptoms both for themselves and their children and were more likely to take their children to the doctor and to give the medications.

A third theme involves the reward or "secondary gain" that comes from reporting symptoms. It is the rare adult who directly rewards a child for being sick, but there are circumstances in which being ill does produce gain. For instance, children whose parents are divorced or in conflict tend to report symptoms more frequently. The reason appears to be that a child's health problems reduce family conflict. These children tend to get sick when family discord increases. Furthermore, children with poor social relations tend to have more symptoms than children who are socially well-adjusted. The reason for this is that being symptomatic becomes a way to avoid school and other activities the child doesn't want to do as well as an excuse for failure.

The fourth theme comes from the psychoanalytic tradition: how symptom formation relates to sexuality and social insecurity. Worrying about or displaying physical symptoms reduces anxiety and is a way of calling attention to oneself. Several studies have shown a connection between sexual maladjustment and displays of physical symptoms.[362] Other data indicate that women who reported a traumatic sexual experience prior to age seventeen are much more likely to be high symptom reporters than women who did not.[363]

With these issues in mind, we now turn to four variations on the theme of pain and bodily illness. These are hypochondriasis, hysteria, somatization, and chronic pain.

Hypochondriasis
(a.k.a. Illness Anxiety Disorder)

"The hypochondriac resents the arbitrary nature of death. He wants to control it. And control comes with knowledge.... And so, when I felt light-headed for a month, I leafed through some books and determined it was multiple sclerosis."[364]

Hypochondria is an ancient term describing a part of the body, the upper abdomen, which was believed to be the cause of unexplained illness, and it retained a sense of that into more modern times. Erasmus Darwin, for example, wrote, "The hypochondriac disease consists in indigestion and consequent flatulency, with anxiety or want of pleasurable sensation."[365] In 1822, however, the French psychiatrist Jean-Pierre Falret firmly associated the term with the "morbid preoccupation with physical health,"[366] and it has retained this meaning to the present day.

Today, psychiatry has abandoned the term *hypochondriasis* for the much less colorful *illness anxiety disorder*. The meaning, however, remains the same. The major symptom of illness anxiety disorder, according to DSM-5, is, "Preoccupation with having or acquiring a serious illness." Although this fear is considered unjustified on the basis of medical evidence, for the hypochondriac, as humorist Gene Weingarten says, "Any symptom we might experience could be a sign of serious illness and impending death. You can never be sure. It is always a matter of probability."

In Catherine Belling's analysis—and I agree—the major underlying factor in hypochondriasis is doubt. It is not the overemphasis on specific symptoms or on the disability related to them, although these may occur as well. It is not about the objective presence or absence of real disease. The source of hypochondriacal suffering is "we do not know for certain either way."[367] According to Belling, "Hypochondriacs have two significant beliefs: that their bodies contain something that will kill them, and that, if they could only read their bodies closely enough, they should be able to find that lurking threat before it's too late."

The distinction between fear of illness and real disease, as well as the great irony of hypochondriasis, lies in a story Belling relates about British journalist John Diamond. Diamond wrote a great deal about his own medical anxieties in his newspaper columns. He described himself as suffering from "advanced hypochondria." In his book *Because Cowards Get Cancer Too*, he observed, "But just as being paranoid doesn't mean that they're not out to get you, so being a hypochondriac doesn't mean you're not about to die."[368]

On one occasion, Belling wrote, Diamond went to his doctor and had a blood test. The test turned out positive for an infection, and he was diagnosed with mononucleosis. He was initially quite pleased to have "a really, truly provable illness, with an incontrovertible set of blood test results signed by a real lab technician in a white coat. I've gone, as it were, legit."[369] Soon, however, his symptoms worsened, and he began to doubt. He went to a specialist, and Diamond suggested several life-threatening diseases he might have. These were "offered by way of a good-luck charm in the knowledge that the true diagnosis is never the one the hypochondriac suggests to his doctor." Diamond died at age forty-seven. As it happened, the cause of his death was nothing that he had imagined or even what his doctors thought was his malady. He had cancer.

The sad paradox is that people who are hypochondriacal may indeed die sooner than those who see their health positively. A University of Zürich study looked at data from the 1970s in which more than eight thousand people rated the state of their health from excellent through very poor. The research team then examined death records and other data to see how many of these people were still alive.[370] They adjusted for such factors as documented health problems at the start of the study, smoking, and family life. The results were startling. The better people rank their health to begin with, the more likely they were to be alive thirty years later. Women who had rated their health as very poor were 50 percent more likely to have died, and men, a whopping 330 percent, compared to people who had rated their health as excellent. Since there was no evidence that the one group started out in actual poorer health than the other, it would seem that a positive and optimistic attitude leads to better health. The implication is that closely watching your health and going to doctors at the slightest sign of illness does not protect your health. As one of the authors of the study concluded, "The results suggest that being healthy does not only mean not being sick, but also being socially, physically and mentally well. So it's rather a question of what keeps you healthy then what makes you ill."[371]

Cyberchondria

Hypochondriasis has greatly increased in recent years, and access to information has a great deal to do with it. Today, we face a constant barrage of drug advertisements and medical advice on television and in magazines, teaching us what to look for and prompting us to ask our doctor for this or that medication. Lately, the internet has become a major part of this phenomenon, so much so that the condition has been given a name of its own, *cyberchondria,* which has even been given a formal definition: "The unfounded escalation of concerns about common symptomatology, based on a review of search results and literature on the web."[372]

A 2003 survey found that more than 60 percent of Americans use the internet for medical information.[373] Many of these are reputable sites, such as WebMD, the Mayo Clinic's website, and MedicineNet, where a person can find reliable information about diseases. Even authoritative sites, however, can be alarming and can lead people to misdiagnose their symptoms in the most frightening way. Looking up a headache can bring on a brain tumor.

All this information can be particularly devastating for the person prone to hypochondriasis. As Brian Fallon, professor of psychiatry at Columbia University concludes, "For hypochondriacs, the Internet has absolutely changed things for the worse.... Hypochondriacs tend to latch onto diseases with common or ambiguous symptoms or that are hard to diagnose."[374] Such a person becomes "almost addicted to looking up information, examining himself, and getting reassurance from other people."

One major down side of this incomplete and undigested knowledge is the climate of mistrust it can breed between patient and physician. Patients often arrive with internet-generated expectations and may "get suspicious when their doctor doesn't give them a referral or a test they ask for," Fallon observes. "They can feel they are not being listened to, and so they'll go shopping for another doctor and wind up repeating the process." This second-guessing harms the relationship between doctor and patient, which is necessary for the most effective medical care.

Final Thoughts on Hypochondriasis

To a degree, hypochondriasis is adaptive. Poor health is the ultimate dysfunction. If we are dying of a serious disease, no other form of dysfunction matters very much. Protecting our health is the most important function.

In our age, the best way to keep our health is to recognize the significance of symptoms early and to seek medical attention quickly. If the symptoms turn out not to be related to a serious disease, little is lost, but if we delay and the symptoms are the sign of something malignant, effective treatment might be impossible at that point. It is also true that tests sometimes produce false negatives, and a doctor who says we are fine might be wrong. There are occasions when we should seek another opinion and more tests.

It is a matter of balance and where to strike it. At some point, obsessive worry about health and the search for medical answers is counterproductive. It leads not only to misery and the loss of a productive life but also to poorer health and perhaps an earlier death. Excessive physical vigilance and doubt do not substitute for a healthful lifestyle and satisfying pursuits.

In the face of medical uncertainty, a degree of denial is beneficial. To get on with our day-to-day existence, we must assume our health is stable and that minor variations in bodily sensations are the norm. We might be wrong, but we can't be happy if we worry constantly. Similarly, when we go to the doctor's office with symptoms, it is usually better to trust the professionals. Under most circumstances, I assume my physician has more expertise and a more objective view than I have. I trust my doctor to consider my condition more completely than I can. If I lost that trust, I would change doctors rather than try to doctor myself.

In *Minds that Came Back,* W. C. Alvarez told a story about how persistent hypochondriacal beliefs can be.[375] When Dr. Alvarez was an intern, he saw a man who said he had a frog in his stomach. Sensing an easy cure, Alvarez gave him an emetic. "While he was vomiting," he wrote, "we slipped a palmed frog into the basin." The man was thrilled and grateful. His belief was justified. Unfortunately, the cure didn't last. The next day the man returned and announced that Dr. Alvarez had been too late. "A dozen baby frogs had hatched out and were hopping about in his stomach."

Hysteria (a.k.a. Conversion Disorder)

Hysteria, more recently known as *conversion disorder,* is almost the polar opposite of hypochondria. It is all about the symptoms with none of the doubt and fear. The symptoms the hysterical person exhibits are bold, dramatic, and alarming, at least to others. The ostensible victim, however, may not seem distressed or worried by what seems a terrible affliction. The term *la belle indifference,* "the beautiful indifference," is a description frequently used to describe the person displaying conversion symptoms.

Paralyzed

If a colleague of yours didn't show up as expected, and when you went to his home, you found him lying immobile and unable to communicate, you would consider it an alarming medical emergency. That was how friends found Jeremy, a twenty-three-year-old Mormon missionary in South Africa.[376] Jeremy was an American college graduate who had been in South Africa for only three weeks when he was stricken. Doctors in Johannesburg could find no evidence of injury or infection to explain his sudden paralysis and sent him back to the United States by air ambulance.

Beverly Purdy, the young doctor who treated him in Salt Lake City, saw a healthy young man lying in bed staring at the ceiling and not replying to questions. A physical exam found nothing wrong, and tests for many possible neurological diseases proved negative. Although he appeared paralyzed, tests of involuntary reflexes showed that nerves and muscles worked properly. If it was a brain disease, it was an odd one, because both legs were paralyzed, meaning that both sides of the brain were damaged.

The doctor interviewed the young man's parents. Jeremy had always been hardworking and highly responsible. He never been involved in drugs and had no history of mental-health issues. He had volunteered for his mission. It seemed inconceivable that he could be faking his condition. What had caused this devastating illness was inexplicable.

Then a staff psychiatrist suggested the possibility of a conversion disorder. With this clue, Dr. Purdy gave Jeremy a mild sedative, reassured him that his nerves and muscles work well, and told him his paralysis was reversible. She then broached the idea that his problem might be a conversion symptom. At that point, Jeremy turned and made eye contact. Tearing up, he said, "I couldn't do it anymore. The mission. I hated being there and didn't like approaching people about religion."

Suddenly, what had seemed incomprehensible became clear. Jeremy had been caught in a classic unresolvable conflict. He had made a commitment to his parents and to God, and he couldn't break his promise. The only way out was to be demonstrably unable to continue his mission through no fault of his own. Becoming physically incapacitated was an acceptable solution. Ten days later, Jeremy was completely recovered.

The most famous case of hysteria was that of Anna O, described by Sigmund Freud and his older colleague Josef Breuer.[377] Anna O's symptoms began after she had nursed her dying father through his sickness, and they were quite dramatic, including "trance-like states, hallucinations, spasms of coughing, a refusal to eat or drink, a rigid paralysis of the extremities on the right side of her body, severely disturbed vision, outbreaks of uncontrollable anger, a failure to recognize those around her, and finally a failure of language."[378] Remarkably, while she couldn't speak or understand her native language, German, she could speak English.

Breuer treated her for two years by talking to her about her symptoms and tracing them back to their traumatic origins. He claimed that this was cathartic and caused her symptoms to disappear. Anna O called it "the talking cure." Freud's extensive discussions with Breuer led him to adopt the same methods with his hysterical patients. Breuer and Freud concluded that, "hysterics suffer mainly from reminiscences" in which repressed memories emerged in the form of physical symptoms. This was the foundation of the psychoanalytic method.

Unfortunately, the case they presented of Anna O was not the whole truth. Breuer and Freud wrote, "We found to our great surprise at first, that each individual hysterical symptom immediately and permanently disappeared when we succeeded in bringing clearly to light the meaning of the event by which it was provoked." But in truth, after Breuer abruptly terminated her treatment, Anna O was institutionalized at a sanatorium for three and one half months and was institutionalized again on three later occasions. She continued to exhibit hysterical symptoms for at least a decade after her treatment ended. This remained a secret for a hundred years.

Whatever we make of Freudian interpretations today, Freud did establish that hysteria is a psychological phenomenon, not a neurological one. Hysterical symptoms are now seen as a conversion of psychological conflict and unacceptable impulses into physical symptoms, which typically appear suddenly and often after a stressful life experience. They frequently involve the loss of bodily functions; blindness, paralysis, numbness, and the inability to speak are common.

There are three theories that attempt to explain why conversion symptoms occur. The psychoanalytic tradition focuses on unconscious drives and the internalized prohibition against their expression.[379] The physical symptoms allow forbidden wishes and urges to be expressed in a disguised way. An alternative explanation is the *learning theory model*, which argues that a person exhibits conversion symptoms because they produce reinforcing consequences.[380] The third theory, the *social-cultural hypothesis*, combines the psychoanalytic and learning models. In this formulation, conversion symptoms occur in cultures that prohibit the direct expression of intense emotions.[381] Physical symptoms are an acceptable way to express these emotions. Conversion, then, is a form of nonverbal communication of a forbidden idea or feeling. According to psychiatrist Ann Schwartz and colleagues, this suppression of prohibited ideas is strengthened by social forces such as gender roles, religious beliefs, and cultural restrictions.

There is some recent support for the idea that emotions tied to memories of stressful life events can be "converted" into physical symptoms. In one such study, psychiatrist Selma Aybec and colleagues used functional MRI brain scans to compare a group diagnosed with conversion disorder to a control group.[382] They first had both groups complete a survey of stressful life events and handed the results to an expert panel that was blind to which kind of participant completed each survey. For each survey, the panel judged which ones revealed memories of threats likely to result in conversion symptoms. In other words, threatening memories that could be "escaped" by physical symptoms. Then the participants were asked during an MRI scan to recall both the "escape" events and equally threatening control events.

The results showed distinctly different patterns of brain activity in the way the patients and the control group processed the two sorts of threatening memories. The authors concluded, "the way adverse life events are processed cognitively can be associated with physical symptoms." In some way, the relationships between "abnormal emotion and memory control are associated with alterations in symptom-related motor planning and body schema."

The general conclusion we can reach is that symptoms that seem bizarre and incomprehensible become understandable in the context of a human response to life events. All of us must find a way both to have our needs met by others and to explain ourselves to ourselves; sometimes physical symptoms are the way to achieve both goals.

A Contaminated Lady

Sometimes conversion symptoms are so unreal and threatening to a person's well-being that they can only be called delusional. This was the case with Ms. S. I evaluated her on multiple occasions when she was involuntarily committed to psychiatric hospitals over a period of five years. She was first brought to the hospital because she had excoriated her scalp with her fingernails so badly that she had lost a great deal of blood.

When I met her, she told me the wounds in her head were not self-inflicted, but were the result of ringworms coming out of her scalp. She said that her contamination by bacteria and worms had begun many years before when someone was leaving feces outside her door. "That would make worms," she said. To disinfect her apartment, she closed the windows and sprayed it with many cans of Raid. She was also using harsh chemicals on her face and hands to kill the parasites she knew were there.

Her only problem, she said, was that no one would help her get rid of her bugs. She would not believe the evidence that there were no worms or parasites on her. She even showed me a strand of hair that she claimed had bugs. I saw nothing. When I asked her why she was in a psychiatric hospital, she said, "They wanted to cover for Dr. B's neglect. I was railroaded. They were lying."

She could not return to her own apartment and was finally placed in a group home, but she did not like this solution. Even under supervision, she would find dangerous chemicals to apply to her body or would excoriate her scalp. She was psychiatrically committed several more times, and everyone remained at a loss as how to keep her safe outside a hospital setting.

It is difficult to know the origin of her delusions, but it was known that she had dropped out of college due to "heart pain." She had been married twice, in what were described as abusive relationships. After her first marriage, she had been declared an unfit mother and had been psychiatrically hospitalized for what she described as depression and being emotionally battered. I concluded that she had probably suffered delusions for most of her life, but had functioned marginally until the delusions became out of control.

Somatization
(a.k.a. Somatic Symptom Disorder)

The term *somatization* was introduced by the psychoanalyst Wilhelm Stekal in 1943 to describe bodily symptoms that arise from neurotic causes. He saw somatization as the physical expression of psychic causes, "as if the organs of the body were translating into physiopathological language the mental troubles of the individual."[383] Perhaps this is what cynical physicians have in mind when they call a patient's presentation an "organ recital."

The current DSM avoids that flowery analogy in favor of the more prosaic *somatic symptom disorder,* but the meaning is about the same. In DSM-speak, the condition involves "excessive thoughts, feelings or behaviors related to the somatic symptoms or associated health concerns."[384] This is a bit different than the hypochrondiac's belief that he has a disease, and it can manifest itself in three ways: "1) disproportionate and persistent thoughts about the seriousness of one's symptoms, 2) persistently high levels of anxiety about health or symptoms, and 3) excessive time and energy devoted to these symptoms or health concerns." Severity is judged by the number of symptoms the person complains of or "one very severe somatic symptom."

A frequent example is the patient who comes to the doctor for evaluation of headaches. There are many different types of headache, some serious and some treatable. If someone is having frequent headaches who didn't often suffer from them previously, it is quite reasonable to consult a physician and perhaps undergo tests to see if the headache is a symptom of a medical condition such as a brain tumor, stroke, or inflammation. Some, like migraines and cluster headaches, have distinct patterns that may be effectively treated. Most headaches, though, fall into that amorphous category *tension headache,* with no clear cause or treatment.

Most of us have experienced tension headaches. We associate them with times of stress, emotional conflict, and intense work. We will usually take an aspirin and rest, or, if they are persistent, try to make life changes to reduce them. We generally can be reassured that they are not serious medical conditions, and even if they are noxious, they do not tend to rule our lives.

Now take a person who had headaches for thirty years and comes to a new doctor looking for his tenth head MRI. This person has had a dozen different diagnoses, even more different medications, and he plans his daily life around his headaches and his doctor appointments. This man appears to really want to be told that he has a brain tumor.

I don't mean to imply that the symptoms are contrived. Those who fabricate symptoms for specific gain are a different category. The people I'm referring to are dysfunctional precisely because they believe so strongly in their symptoms and are so difficult to convince that a further search for physical causes and treatments will be nonproductive.

The dysfunction for these people lies in the amount of their lives and their energies are consumed by their symptoms. I have attempted to reason with them, saying, "You have spent the last ten years focused on your symptoms and looking for solutions that weren't there. Do you expect to go round again and live those years over? Why waste any more of your precious time? Why not accept your symptoms as part of the cross you bear, so to speak, and get on with your life?" We all want to lead as healthy a life as possible, but the real mission is to accept, overcome, or find ways to cope with our chronic somatic ills. In my experience with several thousand patients, to do otherwise is to lead a life of dysfunction.

The Tired Woman

Many years ago, an infectious-disease specialist called on me to do a consult on a woman whom he had admitted to the hospital. She suffered from extreme fatigue, muscle weakness, and aches and fever of unknown origin. The doctor had done every test and examined every possibility to explain her condition and had come up with nothing. He wanted me to see if there was a psychological explanation.

What I found was an attractive young woman named Janet who could barely lift her head and who needed the assistance of a nurse to get out of bed and walk a few steps to the bathroom. She was spending all her days just lying in bed, without even reading or watching television. She was not dazed or confused, and she was able to carry on a normal conversation with me. She seemed more like a person recuperating from the flu than one who had been debilitated for months on end. I did what I could, which wasn't much, but we did agree that I would see her as an outpatient.

What I learned about her history was that she had no family in the area but had moved here after college to take a job as an art teacher. She quickly fell in love with a man who came from a prominent and affluent local family. They married and had a daughter. They seemed to be a happy and successful family until her husband deserted her for another woman. Not only did this destroy the life she had built and relied on, but also, due to his ability to hire a good lawyer, he had gotten custody of their daughter.

I do not know if this trauma was the cause of her illness. During the two years I saw her, she had an up-and-down course with several more hospitalizations, but nothing physical was ever found. She was eventually given a diagnosis of chronic fatigue syndrome, and I suspect that today she might be considered to have chronic Lyme disease or an autoimmune condition. I doubt, however, that anyone would have found something objective that could be successfully treated.

What I did was help Janet slowly reestablish her life as an artist. I introduced her to another patient of mine who was also an artist, who got her to attend art shows. In time, Janet met another man, married, and moved to New Mexico. As far as I know, she is doing well. Perhaps what was wrong with her went away, but I suspect any curative factor was the change in her life circumstances.

Chronic Pain

All the issues we have discussed in this chapter come together when we consider chronic pain. In the biomedical model, pain is either biogenic (that is, it's a disease) or it is psychogenic (that is, it's imaginary). If it is biogenic, any psychosocial factors, such as depression, behaving sickly, and social disability, are secondary and should go away when the disease is cured. If the pain is psychogenic, there was no disease to begin with. Psychogenic pain is a "mental illness."

Looked at in this common-sense manner, chronic pain is perplexing. Do all the people suffering from it have an imaginary illness? If not, why does it exist at all? We can understand the biological function of acute pain as a warning sign of disease or injury. Such pain may last moments to months, but rarely more than six months. When the body heals, the damage is gone, and the perception of pain should go with it. What are we to make of pain that persists beyond the time of healing or where there was never any objective tissue damage to begin with?

Extent of the Problem

Chronic pain would be of interest only to specialists if the extent of the problem wasn't so huge. A 2003 survey of studies of chronic-pain rates around the world showed a low of about 10 percent in Israel up to about 55 percent of the population in other countries.[385] Chronic pain afflicts about 30 percent of Americans.[386] One study estimated that pain-related issues accounted for up to 80 percent of visits to doctor's offices.[387] The cost for treating pain in the United States is in the range of $562 to $635 billion a year.[388]

Beyond the raw statistics, chronic pain has a major social impact, including prescription drug abuse, disability, and the burden it puts on families. Chronic pain also extracts an emotional toll on both patients and health care providers. It is often intractable, and treatment is frustrating. Attempts at treatment often result in angry, adversarial relationships between doctor and patient.

In order to get a better handle on the persistence of the chronic-pain phenomenon, I did a telephone survey to determine the fates of three hundred patients we had evaluated in the chronic-pain program that I helped to run.[389] This was an outcome study, done four to six years after we first saw them. When we first evaluated them, these people had had chronic back pain for an average of three years, and only 8 percent were working full time or otherwise fully functional. Further significant demographics were that 78.6 percent claimed their injury was work-related, and 43.3 percent had already had one or more back surgeries prior to our seeing them. The question I sought to answer was what had happened to their chronic-pain dysfunction in the intervening years. Had they become less or more disabled by pain?

I constructed an eighteen-item scale that I called the Perception of Disability Scale. It covered a wide range of activities and perceptions related to pain dysfunction from the average amount of back pain to difficulties bending and twisting to the amount of pain medications taken. Patients were asked to rate whether they had improved, stayed the same, or gotten worse since we first saw them.

The results were discouraging. They showed how intractable chronic pain could be, especially when there were major social factors involved. Overall, only 29 percent of these patients perceived their pain disability as having improved over the years, while 40 percent saw themselves as worse. Of people who were working, 45 percent considered themselves better and 22 percent were worse. Conversely, of those who saw themselves as unable to work, 9 percent were better and 63 percent were worse. Of those receiving disability compensation, only 6 percent believed they had improved, while 61 percent were worse. On the other hand, for people who were not receiving compensation or who had settled their claims, 44 percent saw themselves as improved and only 26 percent were worse.

I also explored the benefits of ongoing treatment for chronic-pain disability. Taking narcotics or sedatives is supposed to diminish pain and make it easier for people to function. About 22 percent of my sample was still taking these types of medication on follow-up. Of these, 12 percent said they were improved and 65 percent considered themselves more disabled by pain. Even more remarkable were the results for people who had had back surgery between the time of their initial evaluation and my follow-up. Back surgery is performed only because the surgeon sees a physical abnormality that he or she believes is causing the pain. In my study, forty-eight patients had subsequent back surgery and only seven said they were less disabled. A striking twenty-nine of these (58 percent) described their disability as worse.

The take-away from studies like mine is that once pain becomes ingrained in someone's lifestyle, it is very difficult to eradicate. Treatments that try to eliminate the source of pain (e.g., surgery) or dull it (e.g., narcotics) are rarely successful and are often part of the process of increasing pain disability. To better understand why this should be, we now turn to discussing how we come to perceive pain.

Feeling No Pain

There is a rare condition called *pain asymbolia* that demonstrates how vital pain is to our survival. Pain asymbolia is an inability to feel pain. Some people are born with this inability; they rarely live beyond their teens, because they do not recognize injuries and diseases that would cause severe pain in most people.

The best-documented case is of a Canadian woman, Ms. C, who came to McGill University as a student.[390] Her father was a physician, and he alerted the doctors there to examine her. Ms. C was a very intelligent young woman who seemed normal in every way, except that she had never felt pain. As a child, she had bitten off the tip of her tongue while chewing food and suffered third-degree burns while kneeling on a hot radiator to look out the window.

She had pathological changes in her joints and had had several operations to correct them. Her surgeon attributed this to the lack of protection that usually comes with pain. She did not shift her weight while standing, turn over in her sleep, or avoid damaging postures. When she tripped or fell or pulled muscles, she didn't limp or rest her joints as she recovered. As a result, her joints became inflamed, and the tissues eroded. Eventually, the dead and dying tissues in her joints became a breeding ground for bacteria, and infection set in. The infection spread to her bones, causing osteomyelitis, which even powerful antibiotics couldn't reach. She died at age twenty-nine from the massive infections that could not be controlled. One could say that she was killed by lack of pain.

There is another curiosity about pain asymbolia that we might mention. Sometimes people who cannot feel pain respond to something like being stabbed with a needle by laughing. Neurologist V. S. Ramachandran explained that this puzzling phenomenon was related to a "false alarm" theory of laughter.[391] The evolutionary significance of laughter, he theorized, is to communicate to the group that a potentially threatening event is trivial and doesn't require a response. So, if someone merely pretends to stab us with a needle, there is no pain, and we might laugh at the "joke."

A small region of the cortex called the *insula* is the brain's threat detector. When the insula detects a threat, such as pain or a menacing sight and sound, it sends a message to the cingulate gyrus for further evaluation. In some cases of pain asymbolia, there is a disconnect between the insula and the cingulate gyrus. The pain message gets to the insula as a threat, while the cingulate gyrus determines there is nothing to worry about. In Ramachandran's hypothesis, laughter represents a resolution of this double message "threat, but no threat." Pain asymbolia, then, means that while a threatening message is detected, it is discounted and never motivates a fight-or-flight response.

What Is Pain?

If pain were a purely physical phenomenon, a sign of disease, there would be a consistent relationship between the extent of physical damage to the body and the subjective experience of pain. But this is not the case. Many studies have shown that there is only a loose connection between observable physical abnormality and measures of pain severity and disability.[392]

The classic study of just how variable pain perception can be was conducted by pioneering anesthesiologist Henry Beecher on soldiers severely wounded at Anzio Beach in World War II.[393] When these men arrived at Army hospitals, 65 percent of them reported little or no pain, and only one in three of them requested narcotic analgesics. It wasn't as if they could not experience pain. These same men would complain bitterly when inept corpsmen tried to do vein punctures.

By way of contrast, Beecher later examined the pain response of postsurgical patients in a Chicago hospital.[394] Objectively, they had similar physical damage, so that one might expect pain levels to be about equal. The pain these patients experienced, however, was much more severe, and they demanded much greater amounts of narcotics. Beecher concluded that the difference between the two groups was the meaning of the pain. For soldiers, being wounded was a relief. They had survived the battlefield. The surgical patients did not experience this sense of relief.

Our common experience of pain also challenges the biomedical explanation of pain in the other direction. What we call *tension headaches* are presumed to be caused by the over-contraction of scalp muscles, but careful studies of these muscles show no unusual contractions.[395] Similarly, migraine headaches are said to be caused by the dilation of blood vessels, but no clear evidence supports this, nor are there abnormalities in the nerves, muscles, or brain coverings that could cause the pain.[396]

The most puzzling of all is the rare head pain called *trigeminal neuralgia.* People who have this condition experience a severe, sharp pain in the face in response to light touch or a sudden breeze. Local anesthetics will abolish this pain for as long as the medication lasts, but then it will come back. Yet the nerves and tissues of the face seem perfectly normal.[397]

We might argue that in trigeminal neuralgia there is something amiss in the signal that the nerves from the face were sending to the brain. Indeed, there could be a false pain message, but that can't be the whole story. This was demonstrated by the neurologist Antonio Damasio in his discussion of a young man "who could do little but crouch immobilized whenever the excruciating pain stabbed his flesh."[398] As a last resort, the man's neurosurgeon extracted a small portion of his frontal lobes.

The results were dramatic. The day before the surgery, the young man cowered in fear, lest any movement trigger the terrible pain. Two days after surgery, he was "relaxed, happily absorbed in a game of cards." He showed no signs of pain. When asked, however, he said that his pain was the same.

The pattern of pain sensation and the recognition that it was pain remained; what was missing was the suffering. His brain was no longer able to create a feeling of pain.

What we can conclude from studies of pain is that it is not a biomedical disease, but an illness—a feeling of ill health—that is different for each person experiencing it. We have discussed the concept of illness previously, but for pain we can use Dennis Turk's description that "the diversity in illness expression (which includes its severity, duration, and consequences for the individual) is accounted for by the interrelationships among biological changes, psychological status and the social and cultural contexts that shape the patient's perceptual response."[399] In other words, pain—any pain—is a complex biopsychosocial experience.

To understand pain from a nervous-system perspective, I'll present the gate control theory of psychologist Ronald Melzack and his colleagues. The experience of pain is a three-part process.[400] The first part is the sensory-discriminative dimension. Prospective pain, called *nociceptive stimulation,* is recorded in the peripheral nerves and wends its way through the thalamus to the sensory cortex. This provides information about the location, magnitude, and qualities of the pain stimulus. The signal can be enhanced or diminished along the way by a series of "pain gates." For example, when the pain signal reaches the spinal cord, pain and touch fibers interact with touch signals tending to moderate pain signals. That's why if you hit your thumb with a hammer, you rub it. At a more complex gate, higher brain levels can release opiate-like chemicals called *endorphins* that diminish the pain signal that can get through.

The second part of the experience of pain is the motivation-affective dimension. In Melzack's conception, the pain signal travels to the brain's arousal system and to the limbic system to create "the powerful motivational drive and unpleasant affect that triggers the organism into action.... If injury or another noxious input fails to evoke aversive drive, the experience cannot be labeled as pain."[401] In other words, if it doesn't drive you to action, it isn't pain.

The third dimension is the cognitive-evaluative, which involves the highest levels of the cortex, the executive brain. How the pain signal is interpreted determines the pain response. The frontal lobes combine the incoming nociceptive information with other perceptual information and past experiences, and it weighs the "probability of outcome of different response strategies." This calculus creates both the emotional and behavioral response to pain.

Although the Melzack model has been modified in its particulars since its inception, it continues to provide a framework for the understanding of pain in general. It makes sense of the many apparent contradictions in acute pain conditions that would otherwise be inexplicable. For a more complete picture, we turn now to chronic pain.

The Biopsychosocial Picture of Chronic Pain

Chronic pain is especially difficult to understand unless we see it as a complex interaction of biological, psychological, and social factors and recognize that the relative weights of these factors change over time. For example, acute pain may start out as a predominantly biological phenomenon, although it never is completely that. Then, over time, the biological or nociceptive element of pain may fade, while the psychological and social factors become stronger and a larger determinant of a person's behavior. What begins as something we can recognize as pain from our own experience becomes something more aptly described as "suffering."

Frequently, the fear of what the pain may mean, such as further injury, leads to protective measures, like limping or disuse, which maintain the pain signals, causing a vicious cycle. Other psychological factors, such as depression and stress, may grow out of the prolonged experience of pain, sensitizing a person to pain signals and increasing the perception of pain. I should also mention here that treatment itself can directly increase pain signals. For instance, surgery that is meant to relieve a biological cause of pain may lead to scar tissue that increases nociceptive stimulation.

Conversely, pain treatment can have a beneficial psychological effect that has no real physical basis—the placebo effect. There is an old adage that one must use a placebo while it still works. This psychological phenomenon was demonstrated using a technique called *transcutaneous electrical nerve stimulation* (TENS). TENS involves placing electrodes on the skin and delivering a pattern of electrical impulses to counteract the nociceptive signals. A group of researchers administered TENS to a group of patients with intractable low back pain.[402] The patients reported substantial improvement. When the researchers performed the same procedure using sham TENS, the patients reported the same degree of relief.

The importance of social and cultural factors in influencing beliefs and expectations, as well as the behavior of patients, is often ignored, at least by health care providers. I previously discussed how children learn to perceive and interpret bodily symptoms. This is an important factor in the development of chronic pain. Even more striking are the rewards and punishments that accrue to a person in pain. One group of researchers video-recorded the behavior of pain patients and the responses of their spouses engaged in cooperative household tasks.[403] They found that the spouses of chronic-pain patients were more apt to respond solicitously to displays of pain than were the spouses of healthy controls. Other reinforcing social factors include receiving medications and disability payments, such as workers' compensation, and being able to avoid unsatisfying jobs. In my work with chronic-pain patients, I recognize that different patients exhibited different levels of biological, psychological, and social factors and that the mix in each individual was very important in predicting his or her response to treatment. I developed a typology of chronic pain that reflects the different weights of these factors:

Structural/Mechanical Syndrome

These people were seen as having a predominantly biological cause for pain with little evidence of psychological or social involvement. They tended to be well-functioning individuals who had had a specific injury with defined and localized symptoms. There were no global pain behaviors or dramatic exhibitions of disability. They had jobs or lifestyles that they wanted to return to, and they did not depend on disability payments or narcotics.

Psychosomatic Pain Syndrome

This is the predominantly psychological type. These people did not report any specific injury and had no clear physical defects. Nor did there appear to be major social reinforcing factors. They typically reported a long history of bodily complaints and often of psychological dysfunction. Increases in pain were more likely to be related to stressors than to any specific movements or activities. Their symptoms focused on complaints of pain, and they did not exhibit pronounced pain behaviors.

Manipulative Pain Syndrome

This is the predominantly social dimension. These people were the identified malingerers. They were difficult to detect, because they did not accurately report their problems. To assess this type required evidence that (1) their behavior and reports to the examiner were at marked variance to what they exhibited outside the examination, (2) there was clear evidence of social gain, and (3) there were no objective physical findings.

Disuse/Pain Protective Syndrome

These people combined biological and psychological factors with little evidence of social reinforcement. Typically, they had sustained an injury, but their rehabilitation was complicated by fear of harm, learned pain protective behavior, continuous searching for medical solutions, and depression due to loss of functioning. These people usually had rather generalized pain symptoms such as muscle spasms, diffuse painful symptoms, and numbness over large areas of the body. They were usually attempting to lead a productive life despite pain.

Chronic-Pain Syndrome

The largest group of chronic-pain patients we saw displayed equal amounts of biological, psychological, and social factors. Although they typically had been injured and exhibited the psychological factors of the pain protective syndrome, all their complaints were colored by social factors. They almost always were not working and expressed anger and bitterness at their employers, workers' compensation, and doctors. Despite repeated treatment failures, they continue to seek medical procedures, and they were very defensive about implications that the pain was "all in their head." Despite all this, they were discontent and unhappy with their circumstances and struggled to find a solution.

Chronic-Pain Lifestyle

These were usually long-term chronic-pain patients who had become accustomed to unproductive and miserable lives. Any remaining biological factors were overwhelmed by massive psychological and social factors. While such people continued to look for a cure and were even willing to submit to surgeries, they had too much to lose to ever return to a functional life. They were marked by extreme passivity and resignation to the disabled role. They usually exhibited extreme displays of their pain, such as crying, groaning, and pain posturing. They were often either alcoholics or addicted to pain medication.

Pain Disability Syndrome

A small percentage of patients appeared to have had a legitimate injury and were leading a nonproductive and pain-regulated life, but seemed to be remarkably content with and adjusted to their circumstances. There was little evidence of anger, depression, or anxiety. They seemed to enjoy their disabled lifestyle and their only motivation for treatment was to maintain their benefits. These people combined predominantly biological and social factors.

Pain Secondary to Psychological Disturbance

The final type represents only a few patients referred for chronic pain. These were people whose pain complaints appeared to represent an underlying reality dysfunction. Their pain complaints seemed highly exaggerated, inconsistent, and illogical and suggested no known medical disorder. They could be characterized as having bodily delusions.

Lost in a World of Pain

A chronic-pain patient I saw some years ago was Mr. B, a thirty-five-year-old former truck mechanic who had hurt his back three years earlier while lifting something. What happened after that injury was fairly typical. He was treated with rest and anti-inflammatories, and when he didn't get much better, he was sent for a back scan. When that didn't show anything significant, he was sent for physical therapy.

Physical therapy went on for six months, at which point his therapist told him she thought he had a disc problem and suggested an MRI. It was negative. Next, an anesthesiologist injected steroids in his back, and he saw a chiropractor. No help. He tried going back to work on limited light duty but was unsuccessful at making any gains.

Next, he insisted on a referral to a surgeon, who expected to cure him by doing a fusion surgery on his lower back, but this did not help. Then he saw a different surgeon, who (according to Mr. B) told him that the first surgeon "may have done the wrong surgery and left a disc in there that was rotted." I read the report of this second surgeon, which actually recommended an aggressive behavioral approach, not additional surgery, to help him cope with his pain and get back to work. Unfortunately, he'd been terminated from his job and had no other prospects.

When I saw him, this once vigorous man was a miserable invalid. He spent most of his days in bed, dealing with constant pain. He might get up to do a few minimal chores, but he wouldn't walk far for fear his leg would give out. He slept poorly and had no enjoyable activities. He was frustrated, discouraged, and pessimistic about his future. Despite the treatment failures, he continued to believe something was seriously wrong with his back that required additional surgery. He told me that workers' compensation should compensate him for the failed surgery and offer him a financial settlement.

I understood that this was a chronic-pain syndrome and that after three years it would be difficult to make any changes. But since he was certainly miserable and his doctors were strongly recommending a psychological approach, I felt I would give it a shot. My plan was to gradually teach him to manage his pain, overcome his fear, and function more normally despite his pain. Just how impossible this would be became apparent the next week.

Mr. B returned accompanied by his wife, who immediately challenged me, "you are the tenth doctor he has seen, what do you have to say?" Rather than help me work with him, she took over and spoke as his advocate. By the end of the session, she was accusing me of "working for the insurance company." While a degree of anger at doctors, their insurance company, and Mr. B's employer was understandable, this was not going to end well. Mr. B and his wife had more to be gained by his being sick than by getting well. Any further treatment was more likely to reinforce his dysfunction rather than to help him improve.

Final Thoughts on Chronic Pain

Here are some general conclusions that I believe apply to chronic-pain dysfunction as well as to other forms of somatization.

Acute Pain Is Different from Chronic Pain

When a person first experiences an alarming pain, it makes sense to do something about it. If you injure your back, it makes sense to rest and protect it for a few days while it heals. If pain persists, you might go to the doctor to determine if some biological cause exists and requires treatment. None of this is dysfunctional.

Over some period of time, however, the body heals, and unless you have some terrible disease, the pain becomes chronic and residual. After about six months, the likelihood of finding a medical cure is very low. In other words, pain itself becomes the problem. Chronic pain takes on a life of its own that may be either unrelated to a specific injury or caused by the patient's own pain protective behaviors. Now, continual diagnoses and treatments of presumed causes make the problem worse. They feed into the attitudes and beliefs that are keeping a patient disabled.

The More Chronic the Pain, the More Dominant the Psychological and Social Factors

Most people who sustain injuries or other acute pain conditions do not become chronic-pain patients. Even when people continue to have some physical impairment, they typically adjust. They might have intermittent pain or limit some activities, but pain doesn't rule their lives. It is when psychological and social factors intrudes that the chronic-pain condition develops.

We should make a distinction between pain and suffering. *Suffering* is the dysfunction that I am referring to here. As the pain psychologist Wilbert Fordyce once said, "People who have something better to do don't suffer as much."[404] As psychological and social issues increase over time, suffering increases and a productive life diminishes.

Psychological and Social Factors Are Different and Have Different Implications

Medical providers often lump psychological and social issues together in chronic pain, but they shouldn't. The psychological component of suffering is a direct result of an injury or disease. For instance, we may become fearful of using an injured body part or anxious about the consequences of the disease. We might become distressed or depressed about the changes in our bodies and the loss of abilities we once had. Or we might experience a posttraumatic emotional response to a frightening injury.

Social factors are the result of circumstances surrounding an injury, not due to the injury itself. They reinforce the perception of pain. Here are some common examples that lead to a life of suffering: (1) anger at an employer or insurance company that results in a person needing to prove that she is injured, (2) compensation payments that breed a sense of dependency and the belief that one needs to remain disabled in order to survive, and (3) taking drugs that are addicting, which makes the person maximize the pain she is experiencing in order to keep getting them.

11

Substance Misuse and Dependence

Substance dependence has been a major mental-health and public-policy issue for a long time. In 1996, *New York Magazine* published an article entitled "The No-Win War." It had been twenty-five years since Nixon had declared an open war on drugs, and there had been a covert war for much longer than that. Despite the intense efforts of the federal government and law enforcement, the problem kept getting worse. Arrests for drug possession in 1994 had totaled over one million people and the federal government had spent $13.2 billion fighting the drug war. The article argued that the war on drugs had been lost. There was growing support for a new direction from the both the left, in *Washington Monthly,* and from the right, in *National Review.* Even Newt Gingrich said, "Either legalize it or get rid of it."

Today, almost twenty more years have passed, and the war rages on. Not much has changed. Marijuana has been decriminalized in several states. But this has been tried before, most notably in Alaska, which decriminalized marijuana in 1975, only to recriminalized it in 1990. The names of some of the drugs in the news have changed. Today we hear a great deal about the synthetic hallucinogen Bath Salts or Monkey Dust and about prescription drugs like Oxycontin. Open any newspaper, and you'll read multiple articles about crimes committed under the influence of drugs, drug-related deaths, and the arrests of drug users and dealers.

Any objective observer must conclude that the war on drugs remains a failure and the problems related to drugs continue unabated. In fact, the overall situation is worse now than it was in 1996. We have increasingly become a society dependent on legal drugs, seeking pills to cure whatever ails us.

Drugs, legal or not, are undermining the fabric of our society. It is my belief that to address the problems that drugs present, we must look at them in an entirely different way. This chapter offers a biopsychosocial perspective on drugs and how we might change our view of them.

Historical Perspective on Drugs

In the nineteenth century, drugs including opiates and cocaine were widely used and accepted.[405] In 1868, the *Press Herald* in Portland, Maine, reported that Auburn's "resident apothecary" could count fifty opium users in that small town. They got their drugs not only from him but also from "country grocers." In June 1888, a survey of Boston drugstores found that 15 percent of all prescriptions contained opiates and that 78 percent of prescriptions refilled three or more times contained opium. Laudanum, a mixture of opium and alcohol, was a favorite patent medicine for almost anything that ailed you.

People did realize that opium and cocaine were addicting, but they just were not considered the menace to society that alcohol was. In fact, morphine (derived from opium) was seen as a substitute for alcohol. An 1889 medical paper described morphine as "less inimical to healthy life than alcohol" because "it calms in place of exciting the baser passions, and hence is less productive of acts of violence and crime." There was little appetite for outlawing drugs. "Demon Rum" was the real problem.

The first attempt to control the sale of drugs was the Harrison Narcotics Act of 1914. It was not a prohibition law, but a tax bill that required producers, importers, sellers, physicians, and even people who gave away opium or coca leaves to be licensed and pay a fee. The law, however, contained a hidden kicker. A physician could prescribe these drugs "in the course of his professional practice only." This was interpreted by law enforcement to mean that doctors could not prescribe them to addicts, because addiction was not a disease and addicts were not patients. After many doctors were arrested, they got the point. The result was that addicts were cut off from a legal supply of their drugs, and all kinds of adulterated and contaminated drugs entered the black market.

The medical response to this was immediate and prescient. Just six weeks after the law went into effect, the *New York Medical Journal* editorialized "As was expected ... the immediate effects of the Harrison antinarcotic law were seen in the flocking of drug habitués to hospitals and sanatoriums. Sporadic crimes of violence were reported, too.... The really serious results of this legislation, however, will only appear gradually and will not always be recognized as such. There will be failures of promising careers, the disruption of happy families, the commission of crimes,... and the influx into the hospitals for the mentally disordered of many who otherwise live socially competent lives."

In 1918, the secretary of the treasury appointed the first of many commissions to find out why the drug problem was not improving. It found that narcotics use had increased, that underground narcotics trafficking was about at the same level as legitimate medicinal use, and that drug smuggling was rampant. Their recommendation: sterner drug enforcement.

In the years following, there were many attempts—with new, draconian laws—to stem the tide of drug abuse. In the 1920s, the temperance movement finally won their battle to constitutionally prohibit alcohol. We are all aware of how disruptive and expensive a failure that was. Laws prohibiting marijuana use were enacted by many states, beginning in 1935, at the prodding of Harry Anslinger, the former assistant prohibition commissioner who was now commissioner of narcotics. He proclaimed, "The states and cities should rightfully assume responsibility for providing vigorous measures for the extinction of this lethal weed."

Five years after the Harrison Act, the narcotics unit of the U.S. Treasury urged Congress to fund "narcotics farms" where addicts could be both incarcerated and receive treatment, but Congress preferred to pass punitive measures rather than costly therapeutic ones. Finally, in 1935, the Public Health Service opened a hospital for narcotics addicts in Lexington, Kentucky. It had a thousand beds, and tens of thousands of addicts were treated there. In 1953, Harry Anslinger bragged about its success with statistics showing that of eighteen thousand addicts admitted between 1935 and 1952 "64 percent never returned for treatment, 21 percent returned a second time, 6 percent a third time and 9 percent four or more times. These figures should give everyone confidence that the United States Public Health Service Hospital can secure good results in one of medicine's most tremendously difficult tasks."

The flaw in this reasoning was that Anslinger only counted addicts who never returned to Lexington, but he made no attempt to determine whether they remained abstinent. An actual follow-up study in 1962 of about two thousand Lexington alumni showed only 6.6 percent remained abstinent throughout the follow-up period of one to four and a half years. Another study of 453 Lexington grads did follow-ups at six months, two years, and five years after discharge. Only twelve people were abstinent on all three follow-ups—a failure rate of 97 percent.

George Vaillant, who had been a staff psychiatrist at Lexington and was later a professor at Harvard Medical School, studied the fate of one hundred Lexington alumni admitted between 1952 and 1953. He followed them for almost twelve years. What was unusual about this group was that almost all of these patients or their families received regular contacts from a social agency. Vaillant found that "in spite of these favorable conditions, within two years all but ten of the hundred patients again became addicted." What happened to the ten who did not? Three died, two became alcoholics, and three had never used narcotics more than once a day. In addition, these hundred patients had served over 350 prison terms and had been voluntarily admitted to hospitals at least two hundred times. Despite these dreadful statistics, Vaillant declared narcotics addiction very treatable. His logic was that at one point in time in 1964, twenty-three of these patients appeared to be doing well, as far as he could tell.

The Lexington experience has been repeated many times over the years, with many different forms of abstinence treatment. At any given time, about 10 percent to 15 percent of addicts appeared to be cured, but almost all become readdicted or were imprisoned within a few years. Consumers Union, the publisher of *Consumer Reports,* attributed this finding to a "post-withdrawal syndrome" of anxiety, depression, and craving. They note that "prolonged incarceration and treatment may postpone drug-seeking behavior, but it does not alleviate the underlying syndrome."

By 1966 it had been firmly established that incarceration, incarceration plus treatment, and incarceration followed by intensive parole supervision did little to reduce opiate addiction. So, in 1966, New York State announced the largest and costliest drug program in history; it would be based on just those failed principles. Addicts were committed to rehabilitation centers for three years. In 1970, even Governor Nelson Rockefeller conceded that the program was a failure. He told a group of clergy "it is a God-damn serious situation. I cannot say we achieved success. We have not found answers that go to the heart of a problem."

Unfortunately, therapeutic communities such as Synanon, Daytop, and Phoenix House were seeing the same rate of success. The founder of Synanon conceded, "we have had 10,000 to 12,000 persons go through Synanon. Only a small handful who left became ex-drug addicts. Roughly one in 10 has stayed clean for as much as two years."

In the late 1960s a treatment program was developed that actually worked: methadone maintenance. Methadone is a long-acting synthetic narcotic developed by the Germans during World War II. Vincent Dole, a metabolic disease specialist, and Marie Nyswander, a psychiatrist, teamed up to study morphine metabolism in addicts. They planned to use methadone to detoxify their patients, but instead of reducing it immediately, they kept their first two patients on high doses for a prolonged period of time. To their surprise, both addicts became "normal, well-adjusted human beings."

Dole and Nyswander then developed a small methadone maintenance program at Manhattan General Hospital with consistently good results. One of their patients got a college degree in aeronautical engineering and was getting his master's while remaining on methadone. Methadone maintenance was a success in that it relieved the craving for morphine in almost all cases, and almost all addicts stayed on it voluntarily. They also led law-abiding and generally productive lives.

There are other advantages to methadone. It is cheap, legal, and long-acting. When an addict takes it by mouth on a daily basis, there is no rush or high. In fact, the addict feels nothing. Dole and Nyswander demonstrated this by substituting a placebo dose; the addicts did not know the difference until withdrawal symptoms appeared hours later.

There is one big downside—methadone is addicting. If it is discontinued, the craving for heroin returns. This means an addict has to remain on methadone for life. This fact was impressed on me in 1973 when I worked as a psychologist at a methadone maintenance clinic. One fellow had been on methadone for about five years and was working, supporting his family, and living an ordinary life. He was doing so well that he and the clinic decided it was safe to detoxify him to let him live a drug-free life. Within a month, he was back on heroin and had lost both his job and his family. This was a tragedy of good intentions.

The Good, the Bad, and the Ugly

When I speak of drugs, I mean all psychoactive substances—chemicals that are intentionally taken to affect the functioning of the brain. Specifically, these chemicals cross the blood-brain barrier and, once in the brain, perturb the biochemistry of the brain's synapses. Different psychoactive drugs perturb different brain systems, replacing, blocking, or altering the neurotransmitters that carry messages in that system. What all these drugs have in common is that they flood the brains synapses, for better or worse. Unlike the natural transmitters, they are not selective in the work they do.

There are no real distinctions between the drugs seen as medicines prescribed by doctors to treat mental disorders and drugs bought on the street for pleasure. Nature knows no difference. She doesn't know if the drug was derived from a plant grown in a farmer's tobacco field or in a marijuana grower's basement, in a meth lab or the lab of a big drug company. The distinctions society makes are moral ones, and I call them "the good," "the bad," and "the ugly."

Good drugs are the drugs that are manufactured and marketed by pharmaceutical companies. What makes them good is that a doctor prescribes them to you. Even if you follow the ad's advice and ask your doctor to prescribe the drug to treat your erectile dysfunction, it is only a good drug if your doctor orders it. The same drugs become bad drugs if you buy them on the street without a prescription. If your doctor prescribes Ritalin for your attention deficit disorder or Oxycontin for your chronic pain, it is treatment. If you buy them from your neighbor, they are drugs of abuse.

There is a never-ending supply of bad drugs, and street scientists are as busy searching for new ones as pharmaceutical scientists are for prescription ones. People interested in that sort of thing seem willing to take almost any mind-altering drug. The exception seems to be antipsychotic drugs, which few people take willingly.

This brings us to the class of drugs society is most ambivalent about: the ugly drugs. These are the drugs that are most commonly used by adults, but we make great efforts to prevent our children from using them. These, of course, are alcohol, nicotine, and caffeine; someday cannabis may join them. While we may concede that these drugs are addicting and cause other problems, they are neither banned nor prescribed.

There are negative consequences to the moral distinctions we make between drugs. They make us react to drug use in an emotional rather than a rational way. We usually downplay the overuse of prescribed medications and overreact to the unsanctioned use of drugs. This hamstrings our ability to objectively examine the real harm that drugs of all sorts may do. It also prevents the study of the possible beneficial effects of illicit drugs.

I suspect that all (or almost all) psychoactive drugs may be beneficial to some people in some cases and harmful in others. In fact, I have formulated three general principles about the use of all such drugs.

- When drugs are used in small quantities over short periods of time or intermittently, they are unlikely to harm us and may benefit us. For example, psychiatric drugs like Valium and opiates, street drugs like marijuana or even cocaine, and, certainly, alcohol can all help us over an emotional hump, relieve our pain, or give us more enjoyment of social activities.

- Using small amounts of a drug over a long period or intermittently bingeing on drugs is risky. You may get away with it or even benefit, but you may end up dependent and find your life revolving around the drug. For instance, many of us drink coffee or use tobacco with uncertain consequences.

- Using large amounts of a drug over long periods of time is almost sure to be detrimental. It does not matter whether the drug is crack or heroin, alcohol, or prescribed drugs—extended use leads to dependence. I used to think some of the psychiatric drugs, such as antidepressants and antipsychotics, were exempt from this principle. I no longer think so. As we will see ahead, the brain changes to adjust to all drugs. Addiction may be permanent.

In my view, the real drug problem is not that people take drugs (whatever the legality of their drug of choice), it is that too many people in our culture are using drugs to artificially solve life's problems. Drugs do not choose the course of our lives or undo foolish decisions. But many of us act as if drugs will take the place of the hard work of living life. Addiction is one consequence, but more generally, when drugs become the central focus of people's lives, those people's ability to function in the world diminishes. They lose the skills needed to cope with suffering and whatever stressors life throws at them. They use chemicals instead. It does not really matter if the drug they use is Valium or alcohol, heroin or Prozac.

Classification of Drug Use

Psychiatry and the substance-abuse treatment community views extended drug use as a disease process that develops from abuse to dependence. Abuse is defined as "a maladaptive pattern of substance use leading to clinically significant impairment or distress." Dependence adds additional elements, such as tolerance and withdrawal. I prefer a more useful and less judgmental classification system based on the biopsychosocial model. My classifications are chronic habitual use, addiction, dependence, and abuse, which are not mutually exclusive.

The vast majority of us habitually use psychoactive substances of one sort or another. We are chronic habitual users. We drink coffee, smoke cigarettes, drink wine and other alcohol and perhaps smoke pot on a regular basis. Sometimes we might overindulge or want to cut down, but by and large, we do not consider this type of substance use problematic. As George Bernard Shaw once said, "alcohol is the anesthetic by which we endure the operation of life."

When we use enough of a psychoactive substance for long enough, we become addicted to it. Addiction is the biological aspect of substance use. Addiction does not depend on the effect of the drug—you don't have to get high when you take it. The only factor that matters is that the brain's neurons adapt to the chemical perturbing their synapses. This is a process called *homeostasis*.

Consider this, however. Being addicted is not necessarily dysfunctional or even troublesome by itself. It is simply a biological fact. Many people are addicted to caffeine, nicotine, opiates, and alcohol without knowing or caring. If we can get a constant supply of the drug, and it does not have a detrimental effect on our lives, why does it matter? Cancer patients who chronically take narcotics for pain are physiologically addicted. The problems for society come when we try to prohibit people from getting the drug they are addicted too.

Addiction to Nicotine

Nicotine is one of the most addicting drugs known. Until a few years ago, conventional wisdom said that people smoked for pleasure and slowly developed an addiction over the course of many months. Research by Joseph DiFranzia has shown that the addiction process begins with the first cigarette and develops rapidly, perhaps in just days.[406]

When you smoke a cigarette, the nicotine triggers the brain to increase production of a variety of neurotransmitters. In response, the body acts to inhibit these transmitters. When a person does not smoke another cigarette, the inhibition effect is excessive and mild withdrawal symptoms occur. For the novice smoker, a single cigarette suppresses withdrawal for weeks, even though the nicotine is long gone from the body. A cigarette every few weeks suffices to keep withdrawal symptoms at bay.

As a person continues to smoke, tolerance develops, and the impact of each cigarette lessens. The time between smoking a cigarette and the onset of withdrawal decreases. According to DiFranzia, "compared with the withdrawal-related adaptations that may appear overnight, dependence-related tolerance typically develops at a glacial pace." As the brain becomes sensitized to nicotine, the withdrawal adaptation becomes stronger, and craving for another cigarette becomes greater.

DiFranzia concludes, "nicotine is addictive not because it produces pleasure but because it suppresses craving.... The first cigarette is sufficient to trigger a remodeling of the brain."

Dependence is the psychological aspect of substance use. Although dependence and addiction often go together, the person need not be *physically* addicted to become *emotionally or psychologically* dependent on drugs. Dependence is the process in which a person's life begins to revolve around the procuring and taking of his or her drug of choice. All drugs can produce dependence when they dominate and impair the lives of a vulnerable person.

There are several possible routes to substance dependence. One is the hedonic route. It is no revelation that drugs of abuse are immediately rewarding. They commandeer evolutionarily old parts of the brain, parts originally involved in our survival. We perceive this as pleasure, and adverse effects materialize only later. Addiction researcher George Koob conceptualizes the dependence process as "a disorder that progresses from impulsivity to compulsivity." Taking a drug is initially an impulsive act of pleasure, gratification, or relief. The compulsion to take drugs develops slowly, as the drug use hijacks the brain's reward and stress systems. After tolerance develops, if drug access is delayed or prevented, an emotional state of dysphoria, anxiety, and irritability appears. Pleasurable reward becomes the negative reinforcement of symptom relief. As Koob puts it, this leads to "recurrent and persistent thoughts (obsessions) that cause marked anxiety and stress, followed by repetitive behaviors (compulsions) that are aimed at preventing or reducing stress."[407]

Pleasure and the Brain

The key to drug dependence is a small area in the brain called the *nucleus accumbens* and the neurotransmitter it runs on, dopamine. The nucleus accumbens is the pleasure center of the brain, and animal studies show that the direct stimulation of it is highly rewarding—animals will readily perform tasks that trigger this stimulation. If the dopamine system is blocked or damaged, however, an animal will stop performing these tasks. The inference is that it is dopamine and stimulating the nucleus accumbens that is the source of pleasure.

Most addicting drugs appear to increase dopamine levels, either directly or indirectly. Stimulants, like cocaine, amphetamines, and Ritalin, directly increase the amount of dopamine in the synapses by both causing neurons to release more and by interfering with normal reabsorption of the dopamine. Nicotine, alcohol, and opiates have all been shown to stimulate the nucleus accumbens by less direct pathways.

A second route to dependence is what I describe as *medical expectations*. People have probably used drugs to soothe what ailed them since before the dawn of civilization. There is evidence that the opium poppy was cultivated in Mesopotamia as early as 4000 BC (in the Garden of Eden?). Laudanum, as a medical cure, was brought to Western Europe from Constantinople in 1524. But it is fair to say that the ubiquitous belief that medicines should be used to cure every distress and solve every problem is a modern one. We are bombarded by marketing messages to that effect and the true miracles of modern medicine lead us to believe it to be true.

It is not remarkable that vulnerable people will turn to drugs for relief or that doctors will continue to prescribe them. People want to believe their problems are medical and that there is some way to help them. The problem is that the drugs often work for a time. Whether the drug is a narcotic that dulls pain, an antidepressant that relieves misery, an anxiolytic that soothes anxiety, or alcohol, which makes almost anything more tolerable, a person feels better until tolerance develops—and then they don't. I've seen this process occur hundreds of times in my practice (see chapter 10 for how this relates to chronic pain). I put at least part of the blame on medical providers, who often act as drug enablers. As the humorist Tom Lehrer sang in the "Old Dope Peddler," they are "doing well by doing good." Dependency develops as the person seeks more and more drugs and does not look for other solutions.

The third route to dependency is social influence. Humans are intensely social animals. The evolutionary biologist E. O. Wilson has written extensively about the evolution of the social instinct and concludes "people must have a tribe." He points to the many social psychological experiments showing "how swiftly and decisively people divide into groups and then discriminate in favor of the one to which they belong."[408] We can see this in graphic action in the drug subcultures organized in reaction to our drug laws. Drug use has become almost a tribal ritual in groups as diverse as street gangs, motorcycle clubs, and college fraternities. My analysis is that moralistic drug laws are perceived by many people as thwarting what they want to do, and this makes the enforcers of these laws the enemy. Drugs become central to group identity, and members take pride in the drugs they take and what they do when they take them. Unfortunately, they are not immune to the laws of tolerance and drug dependence.

Before we leave drug dependence, we must consider why it is that people can be substance-free for many years and then relapse into drug use. It is a phenomenon seen over and over again in cigarette smokers, alcoholics, narcotics users, and many others. People may believe they've beaten their addiction; they've moved on. Then, suddenly, it's as if they never stopped using.

The explanation for relapse may lie in a combination of physiology and psychology. Physiologically, brains are plastic and designed to change. When a neural circuit is stimulated repeatedly, it strengthens and becomes easier to activate. That is the nature of adaptation—what we call *learning*. Once the circuit is easily activated, it tends to stay that way. I recently got back on skis after five years, and I was about as good as I ever was.

Over the course of time, drug users activate certain circuits a great many times, and those circuits strengthen. In a sense, the person learns to be an addict, and the relevant brain circuits are extremely easy to reactivate after a break. Psychologically, there are a variety of events that can trigger the addiction circuits, especially anxiety. As Avram Goldstein, a Stanford University School of Medicine pharmacologist and addiction expert, analyzed it, there is an intimate connection between anxiety and withdrawal.[409] Both states are experienced as "being sick" by an addict, and drugs of addiction dramatically relieve them. Once this connection is cemented in brain circuits, anxiety easily activates craving.

I define *drug abuse* as the social consequences of drugs, how a person's use of drugs harms others. *Child abuse* indicates physically and mentally harming a child. *Sexual abuse* means inflicting sexual harm on others. No one would describe compulsive masturbation as sexual abuse. In the same light, I believe it brings needed clarity to use the term *drug abuse* to describe deviant social behavior resulting from drug use. People can be addicted or dependent without being drug abusers. Drug abuse involves injury to society, not the individual.

A Young Drug Abuser

I evaluated seventeen-year-old Trent at the Youth Development Center—a euphemism for *juvenile jail*. The judge ordered a pre-adjudicatory evaluation, which meant that I would give the court as much information about Trent as I could gather and make dispositional recommendations. Trent freely admitted that he had robbed a taxi driver by threatening her with a knife. Here is his story.

Trent came from a generally middle-class family, and he was an active and normal child. His mother recalled, however, that he was oppositional and difficult to discipline, and Trent agreed, saying, "we feuded a whole lot. We both hate being wrong." They both said they had a close relationship. Trent thought his father was "real stubborn, real strict."

His parents divorced when Trent was twelve, and he lived mostly with his mother and his new stepfather, whom he hated. He would go to live at his father's house for a few weeks whenever he was really angry at his mother. He would also go to his father's house to steal his dad's drugs.

Trent's father had once been an alcoholic but was sober for ten years until the divorce, after which he returned to drinking. When Trent was little, however, his father injured his back and became addicted to narcotic analgesics. By the time of the divorce, Trent's father would not only get narcotic prescriptions but also buy more drugs on the street. Trent saw that his father had "a ridiculous amount" of them and could not say a thing if Trent stole some.

Trent began smoking marijuana at age twelve and began abusing the Oxycodone and Oxycontin he stole from his father. By ninth grade, he was snorting drugs so often that "[his] nose was bleeding." His life revolved around drugs "100 percent," and his mom recalled taking him to the emergency room multiple times because she was "scared and trying to get him some help." After he got in trouble for public intoxication and for damaging a storefront, Trent was admitted to a residential drug-treatment program for almost a year. After discharge, he was sober for about a month and went to Alcoholics Anonymous. Then, he said, "I slowly fell apart. I did everything AA told me not to do." Soon he was back to drinking heavily, smoking pot, abusing the Adderal that had been prescribed for his presumed attention deficit disorder, and using any other drugs he could get his hands on.

There were two sides to Trent. He was a charming, articulate, sociable, and well-intended young man. In school, his teachers were universally positive in their evaluation of him, especially recently. Their reports were glowing: "one of the most motivated students I've worked with"; "incredibly motivated to do well,"; "a very caring and likeable young man"; and "remarkable emotional intelligence and honesty."

Yet, there was what his rehab program called a "dark side" to Trent. He admitted he had been in many fights and that he initiated them "for fun." He was frequently suspended from school for breaking the rules, including bringing alcohol to school and smoking pot in school. At age fifteen he had gotten intoxicated, "borrowed" his stepfather's truck, and smashed it up in the driveway. His criminal activities culminated in the taxicab robbery. Trent explained to me how it came about.

After his discharge from drug treatment, Trent was on probation and was supposed to live with his mother, stay away from drugs, and meet his probation officer regularly. Instead, he began spending much of his time with a girlfriend and doing drugs. Just before the robbery, he was living with another girl he had just met. He had a probation meeting coming up, but said, "I knew I was going to fail the drug test and go to jail, and I also wanted something new." His plan was to run away to Florida with the girl; she agreed to go with him. But first, they hatched a plan to get some money. Trent said, "I got really drunk, and we did Klonopin [a drug similar to Valium and alcohol]." He told me it was the girl's idea to call a taxi and rob it and that she gave him the knife to use. Whether this is true or not, Trent did admit to doing it: "I was hammered and very willing to do what she said. When she gave me the idea, I ran with it. This will help me get to Florida."

Today, Trent has very good intentions. He says, "I know where I screwed up and I can move forward from it." He wants to be sober and return to rehab "to complete the program again. I didn't feel I fully completed last time." He wants to graduate from high school and go to college to be a drug counselor in the future. The big question is whether good intentions and drug treatment are enough to alter the path of drug abuse Trent is on. Or are much stronger measures needed?

Two major factors associated with drug abuse are disinhibition and desperation. Disinhibition means that the usual constraints placed on behavior related to emotions and motivations are suppressed, freeing the person to act in ways she ordinarily wouldn't. Alcohol and related sedative drugs (such as barbiturates, benzodiazepines, and sleep medications) are disinhibiting; they enhance the effect of the major inhibiting neurotransmitter GABA (gamma-amino butyric acid). Enhancing GABA suppresses brain activity from the top down. This means that before you lose consciousness, the newest parts of the brain—the forebrain, which provides judgment and restraint—are turned off. You then lose the constraints on your drives and can act on your impulses.

A little bit of disinhibition may be fine. When you come home after a tense day, a glass of wine or a cocktail loosens you up, and you feel good. Going to a party and having a little more to drink may help you be happy, sociable, and flirty. The problems start when you have too much and become too disinhibited. Perhaps a novice drinker will just pass out or make an ass of himself, but the tolerant drinker has the capacity to remain on his feet and do antisocial things.

Stimulants like amphetamines can disinhibit antisocial behavior in another way. The flood of dopamine they produce can cause paranoia and vivid hallucinations called *amphetamine psychosis*. Psychiatric researchers Burton Angrist and Samuel Gershon demonstrated this in a series of experiments in which volunteers took large hourly doses of amphet-amines.[410] One subject heard a gang coming to kill him and believed the experimenter had set up the trap. He would not believe explanations that his feelings were induced by the amphetamines. Some people act violently to their paranoia.

Lately, the news has been full of stories of people who have become irra-tionally violent on a synthetic stimulant called Bath Salts or Monkey Dust, and I have evaluated several of them. Bath Salts was actually first synthesized in 1910 but remained obscure until the last decade. Its effect is similar to that of amphetamines, and people have told me that they can become paranoid and violently out-of-control on it. There have been an increasing number of bizarrely aggressive crimes committed under the influence of Bath Salts.

Narcotics, from heroin to Oxycontin, are not disinhibiting and being high on them does not directly lead to antisocial behavior. Addicts suffering from withdrawal, however, become increasingly desperate for the next dose. This craving builds, and addicts who can't get their drug will behave in irrational ways to get relief. Recently, this has led to an increasing number of addicts robbing pharmacies and demanding prescription narcotics. I recently evalu-ated a young pharmacist for psychological trauma after she had been held up four times over the previous nine months. One addict even handed her a list of the precise narcotics he was demanding.

Public Policy

One hundred years after the Harrison Narcotics Act, the warnings of the *New York Medical Journal* have come to pass. Despite all of the legal efforts to suppress illicit drug use in this country, the drug problem continues to disrupt our communities and undermine our democracy. We learned noth-ing from the failure of alcohol prohibition of the 1920s. We cannot success-fully prohibit things people desire to do. We seem to have learned this in the case of sexual behavior, but why can't we apply the same reasoning to drugs?

The United States incarcerates a quarter of the world's prisoners. We have seven times as many people in prison now as we did in 1965. Senator James Webb remarked that "with so many of our citizens in prison … there are only two possibilities.... Either we are home to the most evil people on earth or we're doing something ... vastly counterproductive!" A huge percentage of these people are incarcerated for crimes connected with drugs or alcohol—selling, possessing, or using drugs, as well actions committed under the influence of drugs and crimes committed to procure drugs.

We have tried incarcerating people for drug use and made the problem worse. We prohibit people under the age of twenty-one from purchasing alcohol and tobacco products, but they continue to drink and smoke. We exhort people not to use drugs with public health messages and slogans like "just say no." They make little impression. We offer drug and alcohol treatment based on abstinence and have not improved the drug picture. What should we do differently?

First, we might consider the purpose of our criminal code. It should be to protect us from predators and maintain an orderly society. Our laws should not be an emotional or aspirational expression. They should preserve our freedoms, be consistent, be effective, and, above all, be laws that most people would choose to follow. When a significant portion of the populace will not accept certain kinds of laws as legitimate, the social contract breaks down.

Our drug laws aspire to prohibit what a large segment of society wants to do. As a result, our criminal justice system often becomes fractured and incoherent. We have difficulty knowing what we are holding people accountable for. Is it their actions, when they cause injury to others, or is it their appetites that we wish to control?

We are also sending a double message about drugs, particularly to our children: it is desirable to take drugs to feel good if it is defined as "medical," but it is terrible to use the same drugs for the same purpose without a doctor's approval. A great number of people, especially the young, will not accept this. Why listen to a society that promotes drugs that profit and are controlled by powerful interests, while condemning people who want to use similar drugs as they choose? One result is that teachers, doctors, and law enforcement cannot engage people in a reasonable discussion about the dangers of drug use. They are dismissed as hypocrites.

Drug laws have helped create a split between an aboveground and an underground society. The covert society includes not only drug cartels and street gangs but also high school and college students who smoke pot and use phony IDs to purchase alcohol and tobacco. There are also a large number of adults—including Hollywood types, business executives, and even doctors—who use illicit drugs with impunity. In fact, they form their own sets of social rules counter to society's rules.

What we reap is that the more dysfunctional kids, often from unstable and fractured environments, form peer groups or gangs that center on drug use. As I have witnessed multiple times, these kids will try any drug they are offered in order to get high. For them, drug use becomes a point of pride. Many of them resort to crime to support the habits that develop. Unfortunately for us, a portion of them become violent predators.

Schools' zero-tolerance-for-drugs policies compound the problem. Even young teens who bring alcohol or drugs to school are automatically expelled and end up in the juvenile justice system. School may be the one stable place in these kids' lives. Expelling them means there is no place for them but the streets. They join the army of throw-away kids for whom drugs become a way of life.

Our drug laws of the past hundred years have amounted to a failed experiment in social engineering. What was intended as a way to protect us from ourselves has had serious unintended consequences and few benefits. So what do we do now? Here are a few suggestions.

- Gradually eliminate criminal penalties for drug possession and personal use. This has already started with marijuana in some states, and this is a good first step. Next we should start making safer, long-acting drugs available in pharmacies or drug dispensaries without prescription. In time, we can decide whether to simply allow the open sale of almost any drug and regulate it as we do alcohol.

- Slowly remove most psychoactive medicines from prescription status. There is little real justification for limiting access to these drugs when we can simply ask a doctor for prescriptions for them. The principle should be that any drug that can be advertised to the general public cannot be a prescription drug. It is certainly better for society if people can walk into a pharmacy and buy Oxycontin rather than heroin from the street. Reasonable people should want to take most drugs only under a medical provider's guidance. But that should be the message, not prohibition. I am in agreement with methadone maintenance as the best choice for those addicted to narcotics, and I think it best that medical providers dispense it. There is no need, however, for people to go daily to expensive clinics when they could just check in with a nurse practitioner every few weeks.

- The age for buying alcohol and tobacco should be rolled back to eighteen. We have accomplished nothing by raising the age to twenty-one except create a demand for a phony IDs. People must learn how to responsibly and safely use psychoactive drugs, and it has to start in adolescence. We should not encourage a culture of fraud and deceit among our young.

- The legal system should focus on substance abuse. Medicine should be concerned with addiction. And mental-health providers' province should be substance dependence. Morality should be left to other institutions.

12

Controlling Impulses and Desires

It is something of a paradox that our basic drives and appetites are the source
of so much human dysfunction. It is hard to conceive of early humans being
distressed by erectile dysfunction, bulimia, pathological gambling, or the
myriad other impulse-control difficulties that plague us. Something about
the complex modern world creates these problems.

Large, organized societies require rules to function; some of these are
explicit, some implicit. Many of them concern the appropriate expression
and direction of our ancient needs. Civilized society places great emphasis
on the inhibition and control of certain impulses, especially those involving
sexuality and anger. There are some specific laws that regulate what we can
and cannot do. Frequently, however, control is achieved by socially induced
emotions such as guilt and shame.

We might say that indulging our impulses is the spice of life. Eating a
modest, healthy meal may satisfy our needs, but filet mignon and a decadent
dessert are a true pleasures. Paying bills is necessary, but buying a frivolous
luxury is more fun. Even the expression of anger has an important place as
an emotional release. Impulse-driven behaviors, performed in moderation
and in appropriate circumstances, are healthy and rewarding. But when they
are excessive, repetitive, or socially inappropriate, they produce misery and
dysfunction. As most of us recognize, at the extremes, impulsive behavior
can become self-destructive and injurious.

Overcontrol of impulses can become just as self-defeating. Impulse-
control dysfunction is bidirectional. Both binge eating and anorexia can create major problems. Loss of sexual drive can be distressing, while compulsive

sexual behavior can be life-distorting and dangerous. Good functioning demands a balance between expressing our impulses and controlling them. Too much or too little control causes dysfunction.

Some of the motivational problems involve basic biological drives, such as hunger and sex. Anger and rage are less pleasurable, but are also universal human emotional impulses that can become problematic. Other impulse-driven behaviors, like hoarding, internet addiction, and compulsive gambling, are more mystifying but are prominent sources of dysfunction in modern society.

Sexuality

The four motivations commonly recognized as drives—breathing (or "air hunger"), thirst, hunger for food, and sex—have a great deal in common and one notable distinction. All are recurrent, and after each is sated, there is a period of rest. Then motivational tension builds again, and the desire to perform the behavior increases. Satisfying the drive is immediately pleasurable and relieves the tension. Although the increasing desire can cause distress, we often seek the build-up because it can enhance the reinforcing pleasure. The model for all this is the artificial drive of drug addiction, with its endless cycle of withdrawal, craving, and consumption.

Now, the big difference. The four drives differ in how long satisfaction of them can be denied. Breathing is extremely demanding and the drive cycle repeats several times a minute. Even with breathing, however, we can experience the reward of a big gulp of air after swimming underwater. Thirst is less demanding, but still difficult to postpone, and when we are thirsty, drinking a glass of cold water is pleasurable. Hunger for food can be postponed still further. We can survive a long time without eating, but it is also more richly rewarding than either breathing or drinking. Sexual consumption can be postponed indefinitely but remains incessantly demanding. It is the only drive whose consumption earns its own label, an orgasm.

The conclusion I draw is that the more you can postpone a drive, the more dysfunction is related to it. Breathing and thirst are rarely responsible for much dysfunction. Food is a much greater source of problems. Sex, however, is the drive that causes the most distress and dysfunctional social behavior.

Sexuality follows the pattern exhibited by the other drives. Tension builds, and the need becomes preoccupation. The tension of sexual arousal is usually desirable, at least to a point. The greater the arousal, the more ecstatic the consumption. That is why sex has become the basis of so much advertising and popular culture. Titillation sells. But mounting sexual arousal can be distressing if it cannot be appropriately relieved. It can be particularly painful to be repeatedly sexually aroused and not achieve an orgasm.

Despite the loosening of strictures on sexuality in much of society, sex remains a source of conflict. Sexual expression for teenagers, even masturbation, is condemned in most circles. Some expressions of sexuality remain subject to harsh punishment. In some religious corners of our society, any sexual activity outside heterosexual marriage—and many acts within it—are considered taboo.

The peculiar ambivalence we have toward sexuality is highlighted by a thought experiment I enjoy doing. Imagine that public attitudes toward sex and hunger were reversed. Eating would be expected to be done in private and only with approved others, but not alone. We could get pleasure from some ways of eating and certain foods, but not others. On the other hand, sex could be engaged in openly and in sextaurants, which we would rate with stars. It wouldn't matter if you masturbated or had anal sex or sex in groups. If this reversal of roles were possible, isn't it likely that far more guilt and shame would be attached to eating than sex and, therefore, much more dysfunction.

Sex in the Brain

The sexual drive must have roots in the brain, but where is it located? Attempts to answer this question have an interesting beginning. In 1944, one Dr. Erickson reported the case of a woman who at age forty-three began waking at night feeling "hot all over," as though she were having sex.[411] Over the next few years, she started having similar sexual spells during the day. Erickson initially diagnosed nymphomania and destroyed her ovaries with x-rays, but that didn't help. Finally, he connected these spells with seizures she was also having. Surgery revealed she had a slow-growing tumor pressing on her brain. When it was removed, the seizures and the sexual spells disappeared.

In 2004, there was a report of a Taiwanese woman who complained that an orgasm swept over her when she brushed her teeth. This had been occurring for four years, and she finally sought medical attention when she also started losing consciousness. It was finally determined that, for reasons unknown, brushing her teeth was triggering epileptic seizures in her brain's temporal lobes. Twenty such cases of spontaneous orgasm have been reported, and 80 percent of them were found to have temporal lobe epilepsy.[412] Clearly, sexual arousal is related to activation of areas of the brain's temporal lobes.

Studying the brains of normal people having orgasms is not so easy. However, using fMRI and fancy EEG studies of people looking at erotic pictures, researchers have begun to get a picture of the brain regions involved in sexual arousal. These are areas of the temporal brain that are also involved in other basic drives, including the amygdala (which orchestrates powerful emotions), the hippocampus (which manages memories) and the insula (which is part of the system for the awareness of the state of our own bodies). Activity in these areas can be considered the source of libido, so it shouldn't be surprising that the electrical storm of a seizure in the temporal lobes might produce uncontrollable sexual arousal and orgasm.

Most interesting from our perspective is a brain-scan study of two groups of men exposed to erotic pictures.[413] One group (the controls) was sexually ordinary. The experimental group reported they rarely had sexual desires or fantasies. The main difference between the two groups was that in the desire-impaired group, a part of the frontal lobe called the *medial orbitofrontal cortex* was especially active.

The orbitofrontal cortex is a major player in the formation of social emotions like guilt, shame, embarrassment, and pride. It keeps primitive impulses from getting out of control by suppressing desires. So, if the orbitofrontal cortex kicks in when men (or women) are exposed to erotic stimuli, they don't respond with sexual arousal. An overactive orbitofrontal cortex, then, may be the biological source of many sexual dysfunctions such as erectile dysfunction and low sexual desire.

Conversely, if the orbitofrontal cortex is underactive, perhaps because of injury, underdevelopment, or intoxication, people may become hypersexual.

302

Knock out the inhibition afforded by social emotions, and people may have limited ability to control and direct sexual actions.

Sexual Dysfunction

People inherently have greater or lesser sexual drives, and it is not dysfunctional to have strong or weak desires. People with a weak drive may be lacking an important source of pleasure, but there are other satisfying alternatives. People with stronger desires must align their sexual expression to social realities to achieve a healthy sex life.

A form of sexual attraction that can become highly dysfunctional is called *sexual paraphilia*. It is not that unconventional sexual attractions are, in themselves, dysfunctional. We are all entitled to our own fantasies, and such fantasies can enrich our sex lives. Even acting on many of these fantasies with a willing partner is not a dysfunction. In some cases, however, acting out sexual fantasies can become socially unacceptable and dysfunctional.

Unnatural Love

One of the most unusual (to our eyes), yet benign forms of sexual attraction has taken root in Japan. Young men are falling in love with female body-pillow dolls and treating them just as they would a woman, forming an intense romantic relationship. Often these "relationships" have a sexual nature, but they are much more than just sexual release. In Japan, the phenomenon is called "2-D love."

Lisa Katayama describes this Japanese subculture and the young men who occupy it.[414] One such man, Nisan, "met" his true love at a comic-book convention. It was love at first sight; he "found himself staring into Nemutan's bright blue eyes." Nemutan is actually a large pillow with a cartoon character printed on the front, a prepubescent girl wearing a bikini and ribbons in her hair.

Nisan knows she isn't real, but he takes her everywhere he goes, including the beach and restaurants. He responds to questions with, "Of course she is my girlfriend. I have real feelings for her." He even says, "When I die, I want to be buried with her in my arms."

Nisan is not alone. He is part of a large subculture, called *otaku,* of young people of both sexes who have formed fanatic relationships with characters in video games, anime, and manga. People with 2-D lovers are a segment of that population large enough to have their own slang term, *moe.* In a *moe* relationship, "a man frees himself from the expectations of an ordinary human relationship and expresses his passion for a chosen character, without fear of being judged or rejected."

Moe seems to grow out of the facts of recent Japanese romantic life. More than 25 percent of men and women in their early thirties are unmarried virgins. Fewer than 50 percent of them have friends of the opposite sex. A guidebook called *Health and Physical Education for over Thirty,* which prepares people for the journey of first meeting someone, having sex, and marrying, is a bestseller. When that doesn't work, many men find their love in *moe.*

Nisan is a typical example. At thirty-seven, he is balding and diabetic and still lives in his parents' home. He did have a girlfriend once, but she dumped him, and he has no other prospects. While some men have sexualized their *moe* relationships, Nisan's is chaste. When he positions Nemutan in his car or a restaurant booth, he is careful not to touch her "private parts." He still wishes to get married someday, but he hopes his prospective wife will accept Nemutan. "She is my life's work," he says. "I would be devastated if that was taken away from me."

What is considered a paraphilia is subject to change as social conventions change. Homosexuality, masturbation, and sex out of wedlock were once considered taboo but are now considered normal in most advanced societies. There are, however, a set of sexual fixations that remain unacceptable, at least in most circumstances.

One such paraphilia that most of us would consider the most destructive is pedophilia, defined as having "recurrent, intense, sexually arousing fantasies, sexual urges, or behaviors with a prepubescent child or children."[415] Pedophilia is most dysfunctional when it involves the sexual exploitation of children, especially when it is incestuous. Collecting and viewing child pornography is also destructive because it is so hurtful to the children involved.

We can debate whether private fantasies and urges involving pedophilia are dysfunctional, but they certainly can become so when they cause shame or guilt or preoccupy the person.

There are many less invasive paraphilias that become increasingly dysfunctional as they go from occasional fantasy to obsession or antisocial action. Some are common enough to be named. Voyeurism involves becoming sexually aroused by spying on an unsuspecting person who is naked or engaged in sex. Exhibitionism is the unwelcome exposing of one's sexual parts, especially to children. Frotteurism is sexual arousal caused by rubbing against or touching a non-consenting person. Other sexual activities that are usually lumped with paraphilias can be part of healthy sex play but can become socially dysfunctional include sexual sadism and masochism, fetishism, and cross-dressing.

Gender Identity

Psychological dysfunction related to gender identity is based in the strong social pressures to assume characteristics typically associated with one's sexual anatomy. Although biological gender may (usually) be dichotomous, gender traits do not fall neatly into boy and girl. There is a range of traits associated with gender, with more boys at the masculine end and more girls at the feminine, but there is considerable overlap, and most of us fall somewhere in the middle. Society, however, forces us to define ourselves as male or female, gay or straight. The psychiatrist Michael Quadland of Mount Sinai's Human Sexuality Program suggests that psychological gender difficulties are due to "society's intolerance of ambiguity."[416] He says, "acceptance of human complexity, with all its wonders and fascination, would obviate the need to narrowly define gender or resort to surgery to 'correct' it."

The crux of the matter is whether gender identity is defined more by genetic and biological factors or by psychological and social factors. Most people follow their sexual anatomy in identifying themselves as female or male. In the Western world, this identity is less and less determinant of gender role. Some factors are inescapable—only women get pregnant and bear children. But social roles, from sexual attraction to vocational preferences to interpersonal behavior, are increasingly gender nonspecific and highly variable across sexes. It is no longer possible to identify a dominant, aggressive truck driver as male or a fashion-conscious nurse as a female. We are heading toward a society in which males and females can adopt almost any conceivable social role.

What then constitutes gender dysfunction? The current psychiatric classification calls this form of dysfunction *gender dysphoria,* "a strong desire to be of the other gender or an insistence that he or she is the other gender."[417] These desires cause distress and functional impairment. In other words, it is not the simple fact of gender identity that causes dysfunction, but the "marked incongruence between one's experienced/expressed gender and assigned gender."

For some, this incongruence is resolved by accepting a compatible gender role and finding a supportive social environment for that role. For other people, the discrepancy between anatomy and social role is not acceptable. Many attempt to resolve their sexual confusion by sexual reassignment. This may begin with hormonal treatments, followed by surgical procedures.

Whether sexual reassignment is beneficial remains controversial. One skeptic is Paul McHugh, former psychiatrist-in-chief at Johns Hopkins Hospital, who believes that "sex misalignment is simply a mistake—it does not correspond with physical reality."[418] He says sex reassignment procedures "can lead to grim outcomes." He describes the transgendered as suffering from a "disorder of assumption" similar to anorexia, "where the assumption that departs from physical reality is the belief by the dangerously thin that they are overweight."

McHugh sees being transgender as a form of "body dysmorphic disorder" in which the individuals "have come to believe that some of their psychosocial conflicts or problems will be resolved if they can change the way that they appear to others." He became involved with the issue in the 1960s, when Johns Hopkins became the first American medical center to perform sex reassignment surgery. In the 1970s, the hospital began a study comparing the outcomes for people who underwent surgery with people who did not. Although most of the surgically treated reported that they were satisfied with it, it was found that they made no better psychological adjustments than the others. McHugh came to believe that this surgery was inappropriate treatment, and Johns Hopkins stopped doing it.

McHugh's position is supported by a long-term outcome study of 324 people who had sex reassignment surgery in Sweden.[419] This study found that ten years after surgery, both male-to-female and female-to-male patients had significantly more psychological dysfunction than a similar sample of transgendered people who had not had surgery. Death by suicide was more than twenty times greater among them, and there were far more instances of psychiatric hospitalization and substance misuse.

McHugh concludes that changing sex is "biologically impossible." Surgery does not change a person's true gender, but produces "feminized men or masculinized women." This is an argument worth considering, and the better route may be the psychological one of helping people adjust to their gender confusion and learn to accept who they are.

Anger

Charles Darwin believed that all human emotions could be observed in lower animals, because they served the same purpose for all. For Darwin, rage was the universal response to threat that arouses an animal to defend itself. "Unless an animal does this act or has the intention or at least the desire to attack its enemy," he wrote, "it cannot properly be said to be enraged."[420] For him, anger was a form of this instinctive aggressive reaction that "differs from rage only in degree."

Human anger, however, is much more than a lesser rage reaction. It is a product of the human cognitive apparatus of decisions and learned responses. The experience and expression of anger is influenced by cultural and family rules. Anger is preceded by a complex, almost instantaneous, series of judgments about the intentions and culpability of another person, the social position of that person, the potential consequences of expressing anger, and what the culture says is justifiable. Psychology professor James Averill summarized the dual nature of anger, calling it "an emotional state that involves both the attribution of blame for some perceived wrong and an impulse to correct the wrong or prevent its recurrence."[421]

Perhaps the last time most of us experience true uncontrollable rage is in infancy. Soon children learn how to control and display their anger. Children and some adults may exhibit sudden, explosive anger that appears to be rage, but it is almost always expressed in the context of learning and culture. As social psychologist Carol Tavris colorfully observed, "Parents scrutinize each flounce of a fist, each hearty cry, for its emotional meaning, and in so doing they are rehearsing their own culture's customs about emotion and preparing to instruct their baby."[422] Most of us learn how to channel anger in culturally approved directions.

Massacre of the Innocents

In December 2012, nineteen-year-old Adam Lanza shot his mother and then mowed down twenty children and six adults at Sandy Hook Elementary School in Connecticut. Andrew Solomon, author of *Far from the Tree,* tried to make some sense of this tragedy by interviewing Adam's father.[423] I will not try to portray Adam as typical of mass murderers—there is no such thing—but I will use his story to illustrate how festering anger can get out of control and lead to unspeakable actions.

According to Peter Lanza, Adam's father, his son showed social dysfunctions from an early age. Adam did not speak until he was three, though he could understand a great deal of language. He was hypersensitive to sensory stimuli. He said he smelled things no one else could, and he incessantly washed his hands. He was so sensitive that his mother had to Xerox his textbooks because he could not tolerate the color graphics.

He was highly imaginative, but in odd ways. His father recalled him as, "always thinking differently. Just a normal, little, weird kid." His imaginings, though, tended toward the violent. In fifth grade, he and another boy wrote a tale, "The Big Book of Granny," in which an elderly woman killed people with a gun in her cane. In one chapter, Dora the Berserker said, "I like hurting people ... especially children." A later teacher described Adam as "intelligent but not normal, with anti-social issues."

He did not know how to express emotions. In one telling incident in grade school, he was in a school play and had to show feelings. His mother, Nancy, wrote, "Adam has taken it very seriously, even practicing facial expressions in a mirror."

In adolescence, he became increasingly odd. He had a "difficult, lumbering gait," could not adjust to changing classes in school, and made no friends. At age 13, his parents took him to a psychiatrist, who diagnosed Asperger's syndrome and recommended homeschooling.

His parents took him to Yale's Child Study Center, where a clinician described him as a "pale, gaunt, awkward young adolescent, standing rigidly with downcast gaze and declining to shake hands." He displayed "relatively little spontaneous speech, but responded in a flat tone with little inflection and almost mechanical prosody." He had obsessive-compulsive traits, such as not touching metal objects for fear of contamination. If his mother walked in front of him into the kitchen, he made her enter again, walking behind him. His mother found his behavior increasingly onerous and was "almost becoming a prisoner in her own house."

Adam's parents and mental-health professionals were distracted by the Asperger's diagnosis and did not recognize any signs of impending violence. In retrospect, however, it was seen that he'd begun to be preoccupied by mass murder, which he only expressed online. In the end, he left an electronic spreadsheet on mass murder and a photo of himself with a gun pointed at his head.

He did show signs of increasing distress. For instance, Nancy once emailed Peter, "He had a horrible night…. He cried in the bathroom for 45 minutes and missed his first class." Peter, who was separated from Nancy, became more distant from Adam, while Nancy "would build the world around him and cushion it." She tried to make his days the best possible by indulging his isolation. She also indulged his fascination with guns by taking him on trips to a shooting range.

By his late teens, Adam was increasingly estranged from both his parents and spent much of his time on Wikipedia, editing entries on mass murders. He couldn't concentrate on schoolwork and described himself as "such a loser." He would not talk to his mother about what he was feeling. Still, he had big aspirations, such as applying to Cornell University, even though this was entirely unrealistic.

Two years before the murders, Adam started avoiding meetings with his father, and Peter was never to see him again. Nancy discouraged Peter from coming to see him, and according to Peter, she "controlled the situation." Adam and his mother became so isolated that workers on the property were never allowed to enter the house or even ring the doorbell. In the year before the murders, Adam even stopped responding to his father's emails. Nancy told Peter, "I will talk to him about that but I don't want to harass him. He has had a bad summer and has actually stopped going out." In fact, Adam had ceased talking to his mother, and they were communicating only by email.

His mother tried to keep up appearances, but about a week prior to Adam's rampage, she confessed to a friend, "I'm worried about losing him." She did not consider that he could become violent, and she continued to keep guns in her house. Meanwhile, Adam wrote an essay describing women as inherently selfish, despite his mother's constant attempts to accommodate him.

On the morning of December 14, 2012, Adam shot his mother four times. His father speculated, "The reason he shot Nancy four times was one for each of us: one for Nancy, one for himself, one for Ryan [his older brother], one for me." Then, for unknowable reasons, Adam went to his old elementary school and murdered twenty-six of the children and teachers. Then he shot and killed himself. In Solomon's opinion, "the link seems clear: the more Adam hated himself, the more he hated everyone else."

For me, the key to Adam's murderous behavior is not Asperger's or any other type of mental disorder. It is anger. Anger may have been the only true social emotion that he was capable of comprehending. He was bright enough to know he was not succeeding in life and had no future. From the clues he left behind, anger alternated with despair. It seems reasonable to speculate that his final act was to take the life of his mother, whom he blamed for his problems, and then the lives of children who had the promise that he could never realize.

Anger can be a productive emotion when it is properly deployed. It can get the results we want when kindness and calmness do not. It can energize us to compete and succeed. It can forcefully assert our rights and warn people who are violating them. And it can force others to pay attention to us. There are times in life when anger is necessary and effective. Expressing anger can also relieve tension and even be pleasurable. Verbally attacking someone and settling a grievance can be satisfying, giving you a sense of victory or power. Even hating a lover who wrongs you feels better than "helplessly [enduring] the pangs of rejected love."[424]

Much distress and dysfunction, however, comes from the maladaptive expression or suppression of anger. Social organization requires that anger be controlled, and people who violate those rules bring harm to others and often to themselves. Some of these rules are simply good manners. In a social conflict, courtesy allows both parties to retain dignity and respect. Apologies and keeping angry expressions within bounds makes it possible to dispel anger before it destroys relationships.

Biology of Rage and Anger

Psychologist and neuroscientist Jaak Panksepp described RAGE as one of the seven primary emotional systems characteristic of all mammals.[425] Each mammalian brain has a hierarchical RAGE system in the midbrain. Electrical stimulation of these areas causes nonhumans to attack and bite objects in front of them. Such stimulation makes humans clench their teeth and feel intense anger.[426] A deep, primitive brain region, called the *periaqueductal gray*, appears to produce the rawest, most incoherent rage. This rage response is refined and elaborated as it passes to the medial hypothalamus and up to the medial amygdala.

Rage becomes anger when it reaches the higher brain regions of the cortex, where decisions are made about expressing, suppressing, or redirecting it. Areas of the frontal lobes, such as the dorsolateral region, factor in social and strategic variables, along with past learning, to decide whether to inhibit anger or vent it. We know that these higher brain regions feed this information back to the primitive RAGE system.

Thoughts can trigger or sustain a rage reaction as well as master it. As Panksepp and Bevin note, "The neocortex is always concerned with ideas about what may increase rewards and life satisfactions and how punishments will reduce well-being." When the cortex perceives an injustice or irritation and judges that the benefits outweigh the risks, it can precipitate an angry reaction. "But is catharsis good for you?" Panksepp asks. "That, no doubt, depends on whether it brings you what you wanted."

On rare occasions, explosive rage can be triggered by brain pathology, such as epilepsy or a brain tumor or injury. Most of the time, however, there is some understandable provocation that the person is responding to. Like a two-year-old's temper tantrums, explosions occur in some social circumstances and not in others. Learning to control and modulate anger is the key to long-term well-being.

Psychotropic Drugs and Mass Murder

There is a highly controversial association between mass shootings and the use of psychotropic medications. The facts are these. Attorney General Eric Holder reported that mass shooting incidents tripled between 2009 and 2013. At the same time, there had been a rapid increase in the number of psychotropic drugs prescribed. It is estimated that as many as 90 percent of shooters during that period were taking (or were suspected of taking) psychiatric medications.[427]

Correlations do not prove cause, but the association is troubling. Studies have shown that acts of violence may be "a genuine and serious drug event" with several classes of drugs, especially the antidepressants that affect serotonin levels (SSRIs).[428] Daren Savage compiled a list of twenty-six individuals who either committed or attempted mass murder and were taking psychotropic drugs at the time. The list begins with John Hinckley, who attempted to kill President Ronald Reagan in 1981. It also includes Kip Kinkel, who killed his parents and opened fire at his school in Oregon the next day; Eric Harris, one of the shooters in the Columbine High School massacre; Andrea Yates, who drowned her five children; Seung-Hui Cho, the Virginia Tech shooter; and Adam Lanza, the Sandy Hook shooter.[429]

As of this writing, the most recent mass murderer was Andreas Lubitz, the Germanwings copilot who locked the pilot out of the cockpit and intentionally crashed the plane into the Alps. Newspaper reports indicate that Lubitz had a history of psychiatric treatment, and SSRI antidepressant drugs were found in his home.[430] Lubitz is suspected of trying to hide his psychiatric treatment, and it may never be known if he was taking the drugs at the time of the crash. Nonetheless, it is within the realm of possibility that taking an SSRI contributed to his suicidal action, which killed so many others.

There is a model for drug-influenced action that we are all familiar with, and that is alcohol. Drinking does not directly make anyone violent, but it does disinhibit emotional constraints. Sometimes this allows people to become funny or sexually aroused, and sometimes it is anger or hatred that they reveal. People under the influence often do things they would be unlikely to do when sober. Antidepressants and other psychiatric drugs may have an analogous effect on some people.

Currently, we cannot definitively connect psychotropic medications to homicidal behavior, because people with violent tendencies may just be more likely to be prescribed them. However, such a strong association raises red flags. Today, SSRIs are prescribed with almost no thought about potential consequences. Should doctors be handing them out so cavalierly, assuming that they do no harm?

Anger and Culture

Feeling angry is universal, but when and how it is expressed is determined by the rules of each culture. Anthropologists have documented this in tribe after tribe, as have sociologists in our industrialized versions of tribes. What arouses anger depends on how a particular society thinks people should behave. "Anger, with its power of forcefulness and its direct threat of retaliation, helps regulate our everyday social relations in family disputes, neighborly quarrels, business disagreements, whenever the official law is too cumbersome, inappropriate or unavailable (which is most of the time)."[431]

One striking example of what can cause anger in husbands in different cultures was offered by psychologist Ralph Hupka. The question he asked was when would a man get angry if a stranger seduced his wife? An Ammassalik Eskimo would, as a proper host, invite a male guest to have sex with his wife, but he would be angry if the guest decided to help himself without the husband's knowledge. The Toda people of southern India practiced what we might call "open marriage." Both husbands and wives were allowed to take lovers if certain rules were obeyed. A man would first have to get a married woman's permission and then negotiate a yearly fee with her husband. Any Toda would be furious if a man tried to start an affair without playing by the rules. Contrast this with Muslim Arab or middle-class American males, most of whom would be enraged at the very thought of sharing their wives.

The expression of anger also differs between cultures. This is most apparent in small, close-knit societies, where the cohesiveness of the tribe is necessary for survival. In those societies, anger is typically expressed conventionally and almost never aggressively within the tribe. In some, anyone who loses his or her temper is ostracized. In others, a person expressing anger will feel shame, avert his or her eyes, and walk away.

Suppressing Anger

There is a myth perpetuated by our culture that suppressing anger has adverse psychological consequences. Suppressed anger is held responsible for all kinds of psychosomatic illnesses, as well as depression. This assumption is not borne out by the evidence. People with illnesses from headache to heart disease are not more or less likely to suppress or express anger. Living in stressful environments may make people prone to both anger and illness, but there is no causal connection between the two. Similarly, distressing life events may make us angry and depressed, but we will be depressed whether we express the anger or not.

Many people accept the notion that, if we don't release our anger, it becomes a dangerous internal force—expressing anger is cathartic and drains the emotional cesspool. This idea is based on a misinterpretation of the

Freudian concept of repression, but Freud's repression is not the same as suppression.[432] He saw the suppression of anger and other emotional "instincts" as not only beneficial to the individual but also necessary for the survival of society. The preferred outcome of analysis was developing conscious insight, not catharsis.

Much of the problem in understanding anger stems from the way we think about it as a physical object or force. We talk about anger residing within us, something that can be swallowed, displaced, or turned inward. It can become a storm or a fever raging inside us. The British psychiatrist John Bowlby characterized this way of speaking as a tendency to "reify emotions, especially unpleasant ones."[433] "Instead of describing the situations in which a person becomes angry, he is said to 'have' a bad temper." The consequence is that "once emotions are reified the speaker is spared the task of tracing what is making the person in question afraid or angry." Metaphor is not explanation.

Expressing our feelings of anger through verbal aggression usually does not make us feel less angry, but more so. Most researchers would agree that, although we believe that venting our anger will "clear the air," it can have the opposite effect. Psychologist Leonard Berkowitz writes, "Frequently, however, when we tell someone off, we stimulate ourselves to continued or even stronger aggression."[434] Furthermore, when we chronically express anger, people close to us will fight back and escalate the situation, tune us out, or become intimidated and depressed. These are not beneficial results.

But isn't long-term inhibition of negative emotions, especially anger, stressful? Can't it have deleterious effects on physical well-being? If so, would this not mean that frequent ventilation of anger is helpful, as some therapists want their patients to believe? Might expressing your angry feelings be necessary to reduce rage? "Letting off steam is a wonderful metaphor and seems to capture exactly how angry outbursts work," Tavris points out, "but people are not teapots."[435] But what we are really doing when we continually vent our anger is practicing anger. "You are acquiring a cathartic habit," Tavris explains. You do not become less angry; you are learning to use anger as a means for solving interpersonal problems. Instead of applying reason and a calm discussion to resolve differences, anger becomes a habitual response that precludes understanding what the other person wants.

Some people see anger as inextricably linked to aggression. Become furious, and you are liable to attack someone, without regard to the consequences. Angry people can indeed act without inhibition, just as a person can respond to sexual desire or fear with socially destructive behavior. The connection between anger and aggression, however, is not inevitable. We can use our ability to think and decide what to do before anger is expressed in a violent way. We can suppress it, postpone it until we can find an effective way to express it, or redirect it to chopping wood.

Beneficial Anger

Expressing anger can be an effective means of social communication, when it meets a person's goals. There are occasions when you may wish to "use anger for retaliation and vengeance, for improving a bad situation, or for restoring your rights," Tavris writes.[436] She offers five conditions under which expressing anger are most effective.

- Anger "must be directed at the target of your anger." Displacing it toward a safer target does nothing to diminish it.

- Anger "must restore your sense of control over the situation and your sense of injustice; it must inflict appropriate harm on the other person." In other words, it must accomplish a social goal.

- "The expression of anger must change the behavior of the target or give you a new insight." Anger must either change the way the recipient acts toward you or teach you that you do not perceive the target's behavior correctly.

- "You and your target must speak the same anger language." You must express your anger in a manner that the recipient gets the message. We need to "tailor our communications to fit the purpose."

- "There must be no angry retaliation from your target." When your anger leads to an angry response from the other person, the situation only escalates, with no resolution.

As Aristotle observed more than two millennia ago, "Anybody can become angry, that is easy, but to be angry with the right person, and at the right time, for the right purpose, and in the right way, that is not within everybody's power and it is not easy."[437]

Hoarding

Compulsive hoarding is a newly defined mental disorder in DSM-5, and the distress it causes has been the subject of reality-television shows. Hoarding is a natural response of humans and other mammals; we accumulate food and other necessities to prepare for times of scarcity. Like anger, it can be seen as self-protective behavior, something important to our survival. It becomes increasingly dysfunctional, however, when it comes to dominate a person's life and is divorced from the actual value of the objects collected.

Many people enjoy the pastime of collecting things. There can be social and educational rewards for collecting things as diverse as stamps and dolls. I would imagine that many biologists got their start by following in the footsteps of Darwin and amassing a collection of butterflies or stuffed birds. I know that I tend to save books and back issues of magazines on the off chance I may want to read them again.

Fugen Neziroglu, director of the Bio-Behavioral Institute in New York, wrote about the difference between collecting and compulsive hoarding.[438] Collectors generally take pride in their collections. They enjoy displaying them and talking about them. They organize what they collect, add to it selectively, and keep their collection within financial and time limits. Hoarders, on the other hand, are usually embarrassed by what they collect and do not want others to see it. They tend to feel sad or ashamed when they add to the clutter. They may buy things that they can't afford and go into debt.

Saving things becomes compulsive hoarding when it becomes self-destructive. Hoarders may accumulate such a quantity of clutter that they cannot use parts of their homes for their intended purposes. They may fill bathtubs, kitchens, and bedrooms so full of old newspapers, clothing, or furniture that they can't bathe, cook, or even walk into a room. The clutter can be bad enough that it causes unsanitary or unsafe conditions.

Over and above the physical dangers, hoarding is accompanied by a great deal of psychological and social distress. Hoarders suffer severe anxiety when they attempt to throw things away. They are obsessively worried about running out of a supply of something, needing an item in the future, or accidentally discarding something in the trash. They may compulsively buy unnecessary "bargains" or constantly search for items they think are unique or perfect. They may not allow other people into their homes due to embarrassment or the fear that others might touch their things.

Socially, hoarding interferes with relationships. It often causes resentment, anger, or worry among people close to the hoarder. It can lead to divorce or loss of child custody. Neziroglu quotes one hoarder: "My husband is upset and embarrassed, and we get into horrible fights. I'm scared when he threatens to leave me. My children won't invite friends over, and I feel guilty that the clutter makes them cry. But I get so anxious when I try to throw anything away."

Hoarding reaches the point where it may be considered compulsive in a surprising 2 to 5 percent of adults.[439] Its early manifestations can often be traced to childhood, but it becomes much more evident as people age. It can usually be kept in check during the years of child rearing and working, but takes over in older people, when family members who might help control the clutter begin to move away or die. One study of self-reported hoarders found that 70 percent of them began hoarding before age twenty-one and that it became more prominent after the age of forty.[440]

Perhaps the saddest and most troubling form of hoarding is animal hoarding. These people accumulate large numbers of cats, dogs, and even horses, more than they can take care of or properly house. We periodically read about police or animal control officers finding a house overrun with starving pets and with animal feces and even dead animals littering the floors. The stench may be unbearable, but the owner continues to live there and collects more animals.

Animal hoarders aren't deliberately cruel. They care deeply about their pets, believe they are taking good care of them, and can't imagine giving them up. Their lack of understanding can be so far from reality as to reach the level of delusional thinking.

One theory offered to explain animal hoarding—and perhaps other types of hoarding as well—is poor early-life bonding between parent and child.[441]

The thought is that accumulating animals or other possessions may fill the need for loving relationships. Although recollections are not necessarily reliable, animal hoarders frequently reported a history of childhood domestic trauma.

Internet Addiction

Internet addiction is a modern form of compulsive behavior that substitutes fantasy for real life. The compulsive use of the internet and related phenomena like texting, social media, and internet gaming has led to addictive behaviors across the world. These electronic interactions replace face-to-face contacts and may impede the development of intimate social relationships and reduce long-term satisfaction. These activities may even be causing undesirable rewiring of the prefrontal cortex.

Until the twentieth century, our principal means of escaping everyday reality was to watch plays or to read fiction—a pleasant escape into a social drama outside our own. In the last century, we developed new technology—first movies, then radio and television. Each advance made escape into an alternative reality easier, more involving, and more artificial. Still, it was a limited escape, and most of us quickly returned to our real lives and real social interactions.

In the twenty-first century, however, internet technology hit us, and our evolutionary heritage was unprepared. We can now be wired 24/7, and our social networks have become increasingly shallow and divorced from the nitty-gritty of real social interactions. We have friends without social bonds and become involved in the electronic lives of people we don't even know.

All of this is highly reinforcing. It takes no sustained effort, and if we aren't immediately satisfied, we just cut the connection. This novel kind of relationship began with sex, because internet sex is so antiseptic, free of lasting commitment and apparent consequences. Pornography and chat rooms became the new intimacy. Now it extends to social interactions of all types. As journalist Tony Dokoupil observed, "Every ping could be a social, sexual or professional opportunity and we get a mini-reward, a squirt of dopamine, for answering the bell."[442]

For some people, preoccupation with the internet becomes so all-encompassing as to rival the effects of alcohol and drugs. It may occupy all of a person's waking hours, crowding out productive activities and leading to job loss and divorce. Some people have even died when they developed blood clots after sitting in front of the computer playing video games for days on end.

One young man named Alexander reported that when he was introduced to World of Warcraft, he began playing it a couple of hours a day but soon was up to sixteen or seventeen hours a day.[443] He had aspired to become a biologist, but he flunked out of college in his second semester. "School wasn't interesting," he said, and being online was "an easy way to socialize and meet people."

Making Money

Finally, there is our most prevalent form of impulse-control dysfunction, making money. This is a chronic habitual activity that adults engage in for most of their lives for good reason. Since money represents goods and services that we need and desire, spending time and energy to make it is a rational thing to do. But when does acquiring money cease to be a productive activity and more of an emotional dependency that crowds out other life goals? In other words, when does it become more like drug dependence, sexual paraphilia, or binge eating?

The reasonable motivation for making more money is to in some way increase our life satisfaction. At some point, however, compulsively struggling to earn even more of it interferes with, rather than enhances, our lives. Columnist Daniel Gross described the case of Wall Street bankers.[444]

"Just as Tiger Woods was placed on this earth to whack the dickens out of dimpled balls, Wall Streeters were placed on this planet to dispense and receive bonuses.... But betting on the direction of currencies and enriching the already rich is not a particularly edifying pursuit. Bankers toil like maniacs not because they like working in creative teams, but because they like getting paid. Throughout December, tense dramas play out in office suites in Greenwich, Connecticut, and Manhattan as bonuses are negotiated. Traders and bankers plead their cases, threaten to leave, profess undying loyalty and complain of the betrayal."

This sounds a lot like addictive behavior to me. Why stockpile great hordes of money, more than a person can sensibly use, to the detriment of actually living.

In an interview with *Discover* magazine, the behavioral economist George Loewenstein describes greed as a form of desperation.[445] It is "the antithesis of self-interest because you're so motivated to achieve some goal that you do it at the expense of other things that might be more important to you." In the case of greed, the motivation is more "loss aversion" than pleasurable acquisition. The hyper-acquisitive, especially financial swindlers like Bernie Madoff, see a group of richer people they must compete with, and they become desperate to catch up. Lowenstein believes that "much cheating occurs not because cheating people just want more, but because they feel 'in a hole' that they can get out of only by cheating."

Dysfunction in the realm of money—from compulsive gambling to stock market speculation and financial fraud—can be seen as having a similar dynamic to drug addiction. Winning the jackpot is exciting and rewarding, but the high doesn't last. Victims chase the high, but tolerance builds, and they require more and more money to achieve it. When they don't feel like they are winning, they suffer pangs of desperation similar to withdrawal.

People chasing money persuade themselves that they are acting rationally, but their behavior is self-destructive. They mistake acting on primitive emotional responses for good sense, and they do the same foolish things over and over in the same form as an addiction. Here is my list of paradoxes seen in dysfunction regarding money.

- Many people consider money their most valued possession. Yet it isn't tangible, only symbolic. Excess money does not make you happy.

- Many people work hard to make more money even when they already have more than they need. They may spend all their time at it even if they find what they do isn't interesting, gratifying, or useful.

- Compulsive gamblers are the most obvious example of people who pursue money in a repetitive and exhausting manner. Most of them end up losing all the money they have.

- Most paradoxically, having too much money has a tendency to reduce happiness, not increase it. Research shows that having fewer choices is more satisfying than endless ones. Too much money, like too much sex, dulls the thrill.

A Biopsychosocial Perspective on Impulse Control

All impulse-control dysfunction begins in the biological imperatives of the human condition. To survive and thrive, we must satisfy, yet control, our needs, desires, and emotions. We can assume that, like all things human, the strengths of these drives vary widely. Those of us with weaker ones will have an easier time controlling and directing them, and those with the strongest will be most prone to dysfunction.

Weak or strong, however, it is life experience that teaches us when and in what manner it is appropriate to express our drives. The strategies and habits we learn to control our impulses may be effective or inadequate on the social stage on which they play out. We suffer distress and dysfunction when we can't find an appropriate and productive way to satisfy our desires and needs or when we act on them in a way that is destructive in our lives.

A key to well-being lies in the development of self-control. People with inadequate self-control typically succeed poorly in life. As social psychologist Roy Baumeister expressed it, "Given that most of us lack kingly power to command others to do our bidding and that we need to enlist the cooperation of others to survive, the ability to restrain aggression, greed and sexual impulses becomes a necessity."[446]

13

Socialization Dysfunction

We are born narcissistic creatures. This fact should surprise no one. As dramatically stated by *Time* magazine writer Jeffrey Kluger, "Small children by their very nature are moral monsters. They're greedy, demanding, violent, selfish, impulsive and utterly remorseless."[447] He bolsters his argument by quoting developmental psychologist Mark Barnett's characterization: "it's an evolutionary imperative for babies to be selfish and narcissistic at birth in order to get their needs met. Life is set up so that they get what they have to get to survive."

Luckily, we don't stay that way. Evolution also provides an out. As we mature, we become socialized. Our need to cooperate with others forces us to learn impulse control, empathy, tolerance, remorse, and other social emotions. We generally become less self-absorbed and egocentric.

But some of us do have deficiencies in socialization that interfere with our ability to coexist with others. Before we describe types of socialization dysfunction, it is interesting to consider why humans are social creatures at all. From the genetic perspective, the point of existence is to survive and pass our genetic inheritance on to the next generation. Evolution requires that animals operate on the "selfish gene" principle. Biologist Richard Dawkins has called the living organism a "survival machine" and a "vehicle for the genes to ride inside."[448] The vast majority of animals lead individual lives with little or no connection to other members of their species. Even those mammalian species that form cooperative groups can be explained by selfishness, called *kin selection*. They cooperate with others because "the group is an alliance of related individuals that cooperate with one another because

323

they are related."[449] If relatives survive, more of the individual's genes will survive.

What are we to make of the very few groups that have achieved a level of cooperation that biologist E. O. Wilson calls *eusocial* or "super-cooperators?" Humans join ants, bees, termites, and naked mole rats as eusocial creatures. Wilson defines a eusocial colony as one where multiple generations live together and where there is a division of labor among group members. This division is altruistic, in that some members will sacrifice themselves so that other members may live and reproduce. Wilson contends that eusociality is a social instinct that creates a survival advantage for the group. This trait has allowed eusocial animals to dominate the world (except for naked mole rats). Human beings are actually late to the party, since social insects have been around for hundreds of millions of years.

The social trait that is being inherited by humans is reciprocity. Individuals who act reciprocally earn favor from the group. To receive survival benefits from the group, one must demonstrate a degree of altruism. Even sacrifice of oneself is rewarded, because the group itself survives.

Here is a dilemma. There is eternal conflict between the forces of individual self-preservation and of group selection. Even in the most cooperative societies, it still benefits the individual to act selfishly and get away with it. According to Wilson, there is always the pressure of individual interest favoring "selfishness, cowardice and unethical competition." These traits will win out if an individual finds them more favorable than group membership.

On the other hand, when a society is structured so that individuals perceive a large benefit from group membership (or severe punishments for transgressions), "the members will be prone to altruism and conformity." Group adherence is usually highest during times of war, as Wilson observes: "Group-selected traits typically show the fiercest degree of resolve during conflicts between rival groups."

To translate evolutionary theory into psychology, we can consider group pressure to act cooperatively and altruistically the process of socialization. This is not necessarily a beneficial thing, because people can become maladaptively socialized when, as Wilson notes, "selfish leaders" are able to "bend the colony to serve their personal interests." Socialization is a double-edged sword, making humans the most cooperative and the most dangerous animals on the face of the earth.

Bringing us back to our subject, we can create a dimension of socialization, in which the most successful level of functioning is the person who cares about others' feelings, is considerate and thoughtful, is able to maintain intimate interpersonal relationships, and is socially integrated. Perhaps we can describe this as the *mature adult model.* To the extent that people deviate from this model, their social interactions become increasingly restricted and ineffectual. I should note that some of the characterizations I will describe are ones that can be highly successful in some areas of life (often politics and business) but are limiting and unrewarding in others.

People who are inadequately socialized can be described in a number of broad types. These types range from the most destructive people in society to the merely noxious. We will begin with the most deviant type, the predatory person, often called the *psychopath.*

Predatory People

People act in socially destructive ways for all sorts of reasons. Many of us (perhaps most of us) have acted on impulse in ways that violated or harmed others. We fail to inhibit our urges, often aided by alcohol or other drugs, and regret our actions afterward. Some people convince themselves or are convinced by others that harmful actions are the right and proper thing to do. Terrorists act that way. Most of us try to consider our effects on others.

The most frighteningly harmful people, however, are those that act without conscience, those who are called *psychopaths* by some and *sociopaths* by others. Psychopathy is actually the extreme end of a dimension, with relatively benign con artists and charmers at the mild end.

The first clinical reference to such people was by the French psychiatrist Philippe Pinel who, writing in the period just after the French Revolution, called the condition *insanity without delirium.* Others at the time used a more judgmental label: *morally insane.* The argument about whether people who acted without remorse or restraint were sick or evil came up sporadically over the next 150 years but took on new urgency with the advent of World War II.

Emerging information about Nazi atrocities, in particular, made the public aware that a whole nation could follow one man down a path of cruelty and horror. It focused attention on those among us who behave in this manner and the societal havoc they could create. The psychiatrist Hervey Cleckley offered the first detailed view of this type of person, whom he called the *psychopathic personality*, in his classic book *The Mask of Sanity*, first published in 1941.[450]

Cleckley described a young man named Gregory, who attempted to kill his mother but failed when his gun malfunctioned. Cleckley wrote that Gregory's "repeated antisocial acts and the triviality of his apparent motivation as well as his inability to learn by experience to make a better adjustment and avoid serious trouble that can be readily foreseen, all make me feel that he is a classic example of psychopathic personality." Writing in general about psychopaths, Cleckley observed, "It is impossible for him to take even a slight interest in the tragedy or joy or the striving of humanity as presented in serious literature or art. He is indifferent to these matters in life itself."

The Psychopathic Pharmacist

Eric Larson's *The Devil in the White City* details the exploits of the psychopath H. H. Holmes against the backdrop of the Chicago World's Fair in 1893.[451] Holmes was a doctor who came to Chicago in 1886 and convinced one Mrs. Holton to hire him to run the family pharmacy, E. S. Holton Drugs, and to help her with her husband's serious medical condition. After Mrs. Holton mysteriously disappeared (Holmes told people she was visiting relatives in another state), he acquired the business and changed its name.

Holmes was actually born Herman Webster Mudgett, and his early life foreshadowed the clever Chicago serial killer he later became, including the seemingly accidental death of a childhood friend and episodes of conning women out of their money. Larson describes him as a good-looking charmer whom women found irresistible. The tumultuous city of Chicago, where people could go to disappear, was the perfect venue for Holmes to ply his trade.

Prior to the opening of the fair, Holmes built an elaborate building near the fairgrounds that he specially designed for his purposes. The first floor housed his pharmacy and shops in which he conducted other fraudulent activities. The top two floors had rooms that he rented to women. These floors had secret passages and chutes to the basement, so that Holmes could enter women's rooms secretly, enjoy torturing and murdering them, and then conveniently slide their bodies down to the basement. He also built a soundproof vault into which poison gas could be introduced and a kiln in the basement to dispose of the corpses.

As Holmes's fraudulent financial dealings slowly came to light and his creditors closed in, he fled. He was finally arrested and jailed in Philadelphia for insurance fraud. A Philadelphia detective named Frank Geyer was assigned to investigate the case and suspected there were more crimes to uncover, including the murder of the three children of an associate of Holmes's, who were missing. As Geyer traced Holmes's path across the Midwest, he uncovered a trail of murder. The exact number of women and children Holmes killed will never be known, but it was somewhere between twenty-seven and two hundred.

Holmes had an incredible ability to find vulnerable people and manipulate them. He was intelligent and convincing, and he did not hesitate to cheat and lie or to swindle and ruin other people to achieve his ends. He was cleverly ghoulish. At one point, a woman he seduced, Julia, became pregnant and pushed him to marry her. He agreed on the condition that she allow him to give her an abortion. He then chloroformed and killed her, but instead of burning her body in his kiln, he had another plan. He asked a friend who knew how to strip the flesh off bodies to help with a corpse he said he had been using for research and to send him back the skeleton, which he then sold to a medical school that needed skeletons and didn't ask questions.

In prison in Philadelphia, Holmes gloated about his increasing fame and began a memoir of his life. Geyer's search for the missing children excited him, and he reveled in the charade. Even after evidence of his many murders was uncovered, Holmes continued to play his game of manipulation and distortion. He found a willing journalist to publish his memoir and the book came out after his conviction for murder. During his trial, he proudly confessed on three occasions to different numbers of murders. He was sentenced to death, but his only concern was that his body be encased in cement so that it could not be used for science.

The psychologist Robert Hare took up the work of defining the characteristics of the psychopathic type.[452] Hare began his work in the 1960s, when he happened to get a position at the British Columbia Penitentiary and met such a person, Ray, on his first day there. Ray told Hare he wanted help with a problem and, once in the office, pulled out a knife and waved it in Hare's face. Ray didn't stab him, but Hare soon recognized that Ray had caught him in a trap. "I had shown myself to be a soft touch who would overlook clear violations of fundamental prison rules in order to develop 'professional' rapport with inmates."

Hare began to see the psychopath as "a self-centered, callous and remorseless person, profoundly lacking in empathy and the ability to form warm emotional relationships with others: a person who functions without the restraints of conscience." Description is all well and good, but Hare wanted to know how could he objectively identify which inmates were true psychopaths. The usual psychological tests and interviews were useless. Psychopaths, he saw, were experts at "distorting and molding the truth to suit their purposes. Impression management was definitely one of their strong suits."

Using Cleckley's work as a basis, Hare and his group of clinicians found they could identify psychopaths by examining prison records and conducting long, detailed interviews. Over the course of ten years, Hare refined an instrument, which he called the "Psychopathy Checklist" for determining who the psychopaths were in a highly reliable way, without relying on self-report. This checklist is now used around the world to identify psychopaths from other sorts of social deviants and criminals.

Hare's checklist is designed to rate twelve patterns of personality traits and life experiences that collectively define the psychopathic personality. As will become clear, a psychopath will have an aggregate of these features, and very few people will have all of them. To be labeled a psychopath, one must achieve a high score on the checklist as rated according to a scoring manual. Hare estimates that only one in two hundred serious criminal offenders will receive a maximum score. Conversely, as Hare explicitly states, "Be aware that people who are not psychopaths may have some of the symptoms described here. Many people are impulsive, or glib, or cold and unfeeling, or antisocial, but this does not mean they are psychopaths." Here, briefly described, are Hare's "symptoms."

The checklist divides the characteristic patterns of psychopathy into two major divisions. The first describes emotional and interpersonal traits typically observed in psychopaths.

- *Glib and superficial.* Psychopaths are often witty, articulate, and charming. They know how to flatter you and present themselves in the best possible light. But on closer examination, "they seem too slick and smooth, too obviously insincere and superficial." They may act as if they have expert knowledge in many fields, and they may even claim degrees and credentials that they don't have. Amazingly, they show no concern if they are found out, and they smoothly change the subject.

- *Egocentric and grandiose.* When listening to psychopaths, you quickly realize that they have an astonishingly inflated view of their own worth and accomplishments. They have an immense sense of entitlement, because they are "superior beings who are justified in living according to their own rules." In circumstances where they can't be the "center of the universe" (such as in a courtroom), they may come across as "arrogant, shameless braggarts."

- *Lack of remorse or guilt.* Psychopaths exhibit a total lack of concern for their victims or remorse for their actions. They are concerned with only themselves. They may see a victim as the one to blame, as deserving of it or as having learned a hard lesson in life, even if they murdered this victim. When it is to their advantage, they will claim remorse or, more likely, some form of insanity or memory loss. Even psychopathic serial killers may present themselves as the real victims with an absolutely straight face.

- *Lack of empathy.* The logical continuation of the above characteristics is a lack of empathy for other people. Psychopaths just do not connect with the emotions of other people, whether they are victims or not. Misfortunes that befall family members or victims of environmental catastrophes leave them indifferent. If they have children, they see them as possessions, like their cars, that they can take care of or neglect as they will.

- *Deceitful and manipulative.* Hare states that, "lying, deceiving and manipulation are natural talents for psychopaths." They are proud of their imaginative abilities and enjoy putting something over on people. They often lie when it isn't necessary, just for the pleasure of it. Being found out means nothing. They simply shift gears, sometimes with a series of contradicting lies that confuse the listener. For the psychopath, that is fun. Hare says, "it is as if the words take on a life of their own, unfettered by the speaker's knowledge that the observer is aware of the facts."

- *Shallow emotions.* When a psychopath displays emotion, it is likely to be dramatic and short-lived. They seem incapable of what we would call *feeling* and experience only a momentary raw emotion. As Hare expresses it, "they equate love with sexual arousal, sadness with frustration and anger with irritability." Emotions are so shallow that they appear to be playacting. The psychopath "knows the words, but not the music."[453] This lack of feeling even extends as far as their own selves. They lack the capacity for anxiety or grief. When Saddam Hussein was on the scaffold about to be hung, he noticed a nervous physician in attendance. "Do not be afraid doctor," he said, "this is for men."[454]

Hare's second section of psychopathic characteristics are behavioral and lifestyle observations. Hare summarizes this facet of the psychopathic picture as reflecting "a chronically unstable and aimless lifestyle marked by casual and flagrant violations of social norms and expectations."

- *Impulsive.* Psychopaths tend to act on impulse rather than by weighing pluses and minuses and possible consequences. Their goal is "to achieve immediate satisfaction, pleasure or relief." They never seem to learn how to delay pleasure or to modify their behavior in accordance with social rules. They give little thought to the future and may change plans frequently. If they make a calculation, it's about what they think they can get away with.

- *Poor behavioral controls.* In addition to a live-for-the-moment approach to life, psychopaths tend to lack inhibitory controls. When most of us feel slighted or irritated, we control and conform our behavior to the social circumstances. We think before we act. Psychopaths often do not do this. They appear hot-headed and are likely to respond to criticism or frustration with violence or verbally abusive outbursts. These interruptions are short-lived, however, and afterword, they act as if nothing had happened.

- *Need for excitement.* What motivates a psychopath above all is excitement. Perhaps excitement is the only legitimate feeling such a person has. In situations in which you or I might feel apprehensive or scared, the psychopath feels alive. Doing novel or dangerous things—sometimes the riskier the better—gives their life meaning. Crimes, violence, and living on the edge may give them the "adrenaline rush" they need. In their constant search for new experiences, many psychopaths abuse many kinds of drugs. For some, the search for a thrill extends to torture and murder.

- *Lack of responsibility.* Psychopaths do not learn from experience. They are recurrently irresponsible and unreliable. If they work, they tend to be untrustworthy and erratic in their performance. If they are parents, they are neglectful, abusive, and indifferent to their children's welfare. They do not honor commitments and think little of exploiting family and friends. The fact that their actions may cause hardship or harm to others means nothing to them. When they get in trouble, they are frequently successful in talking their way out of it by convincing others of their good intentions and trustworthiness.

- *Early behavior problems.* Psychopathic behavior usually shows up early in life. Children who later become psychopaths often show a pattern of disruptive behaviors. Looking back at the early records of psychopathic offenders frequently reveals the triad of disruptive behavior diagnoses: conduct disorder, oppositional-defiant disorder, and attention deficit/hyperactivity disorder. We have to be careful with this prediction, however, because the large majority of children who get these diagnoses do not become psychopaths. There are, however, certain patterns of behavior in children that are associated with psychopathy. These include torturing animals; cruelty to other children, including siblings; setting fires, persistent lying and threatening, and precocious sexuality.

A Youthful Offender

Society hesitates to call a young person a "psychopath," as well we should. Adolescents are not fully formed, and many life paths are yet open to them. The executive areas of their brains, which control processes of inhibition and judgment crucial to social behavior, will continue to develop until they are in their mid-twenties. Still, some youths raise much cause for concern about what will become of them. Dylan was one such youth.

When I met Dylan he was seventeen and was in a youth detention center, awaiting my recommendation to the court. He had been charged with two different crimes. First, he and his brother had broken into the home of a kid whom they believed had stolen a friend's golf club and their marijuana. He said they had snuck in to retrieve the items when they thought no one was home, because, he explained, "his dad is a psycho and would kill us." He was seen exiting a rear window. The second charge was for unlawful sexual contact, which occurred three weeks later. He blamed this on the girl, who had been living at the same youth shelter where he was still living. He said that she called him twice to tell him she was in town. The first time she asked him to meet her outside, he refused, because he knew it would get him expelled from the shelter and it violated his conditions of release from detention. The second time he relented, but he said he was only "going to stop by for a little bit." He told the staff that he was going out to look for job applications.

He explained to me that when he and the girl both lived at the shelter, she had tried to initiate sexual contact several times. He said, "[Once she] grabbed me by the crotch and didn't even look out for the staff." When they met outside, she took his hand, and he decided to lead her to a more private place. According to him, she then "gave me a hand job." His actual charge was having "pushed her to the ground and touched her in her private area."

Dylan's parents had never married, and he and his three brothers were initially raised by their mother with little contact with his father. He said that his mother was "mentally unstable," and when he was seven, she "locked herself in her room and cried all the time." For the next three years, the boys mostly took care of themselves. His mother became increasingly abusive to him and his brothers, and Dylan said she went "from a belt to broomsticks." Other than beatings, she had no control over him or his brothers. When he was ten, his mother left to move in with her boyfriend, because she "couldn't handle four boys." In her place, his grandfather's ex-wife moved in to care for them. After about a year, however, there were allegations of sexual abuse by an older brother, and the state took custody of the boys. Dylan still considers this woman the only real parent he ever had. From kindergarten on, Dylan had "a little bit of anger problems," and they got worse. In third grade, he was transferred to a special behavioral-impairment program, where he became increasingly disobedient. After he and his brothers were taken by the state, he and one brother, Michael, were put in a residential treatment program, where he stayed for five years. He told me that he had still hoped to return to his mother, but when she "chose Michael instead," he was disappointed and angry and acted out more.

According to his state guardian, when he was first at the residential program, "he was very aggressive and oppositional and he assaulted staff." After many ups and downs, his behavior started to improve, but after his brother left, he became even more oppositional. He wanted out, and at sixteen, a foster home with a single male was found for him. He thought this was the "perfect placement" for him, but the situation quickly deteriorated and in a six-month period, "there were over 30 incident reports regarding his actions." His foster guardian wanted him out, and an independent-living group home was found for him, but he ran away and was found living with the family of a friend. After he became homeless for a time, his mother took him in temporarily, but he began "swearing at his mother, right in her face, and was physically intimidating to her."

Meanwhile, Dylan got into mounting conflicts with the law, including burglary of cars, selling marijuana on school grounds, criminal mischief, and public intoxication. Six months before his most recent charges, he was suspended from high school for having sex with a female student on school grounds. His state guardian expressed the concern that "he is developing a criminal mentality, justifying his actions and feeling he is above the law."

When I evaluated him, Dylan was initially quite pleasant and cooperative. But as the interview progressed, he became disenchanted with its direction. He became irritated and increasingly unwilling to let me direct the interview or to answer my questions. He was obviously struggling to maintain control and challenged me, saying, "I was under the impression this psychological evaluation was to help me out with placement." He wanted to be sent to a psychiatric hospital so that he could get out of detention and, as he put it, "help me with my anger."

In my report, I concluded that Dylan was "an extremely demanding, impulsive and self-centered young man who has been unable to delay gratification or accept responsibility for his actions." He expressed good intentions, but he always seemed to act out if he couldn't get his own way, and he couldn't follow the rules for any period of time. Until his recent incarceration, he had never really experienced the consequences of his own actions. My concern was that "the more he gets away with his behavior, the worst his future chances become."

Adult Antisocial Behavior

There are many behaviors that the community finds antisocial and distasteful that do not qualify as psychopathic. Many people exhibit elements of Hare's Checklist without reaching the threshold of psychopathy. Psychopathy should be considered the bottom of an anti-social dimension with an estimated four percent of the population reaching that extreme.[455] Antisocial behavior is not necessarily criminal and people who exhibit it may never be publicly exposed.

In fact, psychological researchers have described a number of different personality types that fall somewhere on an antisocial dimension. The personality theorist Theodore Millon has described ten such subtypes of psychopathy: covetous, unprincipled, disingenuous, risk-taking, spineless, explosive, abrasive, malevolent, tyrannical, and malignant.[456] The psychologist Martha Stout gives an example of a covetous psychopath named Doreen. Stout describes the covetous psychopath as one who "thinks that life has cheated her somehow, has not given her nearly the same bounty as other people, and she must even the existential score by robbing people, by secretly causing destruction in other lives."

Doreen is a psychologist at a psychiatric hospital. At least, everyone thinks she's a psychologist. Actually, it is a charade. She has a bachelor's degree in psychology, but she seduced two prominent professors and blackmailed them into writing letters of recommendation calling her a doctor. She managed to gain a postdoctoral position, which qualified her as a clinical psychologist, and then got a job at the hospital, all without anyone questioning her credentials. She was an expert at playing the expected role, and who was going to find out any differently?

She was extremely vain and insecure and exceptionally deceitful, but she hid it well. To nonthreatening people who could help her maintain her disguise, she was courteous and pleasant and presented herself as a very nice, caring, and hard-working person. She secretly hated women who had attributes she desired, however, and she would do cruel and vicious things to harm lower-ranking women without raising suspicion in any one that mattered.

One such woman was Jackie, a new employee at the hospital. Jackie was smart, beautiful, good-natured, and a highly effective therapist. Doreen hated her and wished to destroy her. Her hospital had a peculiar system in which a patient had both a therapist and an administrator who monitored the patient's progress. Jackie was Dennis's therapist, but as Doreen was his administrator, she saw an opening to harm Jackie.

When Dennis came into the hospital, he was highly paranoid, but Jackie had done good work with him and wanted to see him discharged. Doreen was going to undermine that. In her most compassionate tone, she told Dennis that Jackie did not intend to discharge him and had told her that he was sicker than he had been when he came in. She also told him that Jackie would not see him as an outpatient, because he was much too dangerous. Dennis became still as a statue as he processed all this. Doreen then called the guards to take him to a locked ward, saying that he'd become acutely psychotic. She knew that Jackie would assume that she had failed and blame herself.

People like Doreen are not dangerous psychopaths. They may never be caught and prosecuted. Yet Doreen had little conscience. She had no compunction about harming a helpless patient in order to damage someone who had qualities she coveted.

Abusers and Bullies

Even in the most genteel and civilized societies, there is room for competition. It is hard to imagine a successful society without it. Competition pushes people to maximize their capabilities and allows culture to progress.

Competition is also conflict. Sports competition is a form of stylized warfare. There are winners and there are losers. Fans line up to root for their favorite combatants, and as vicarious participants in the battle, they become winners and losers, too. The analogy can be stretched to include competition in school, on the job, and in life in general. Competition plays an important role in preparing us for a productive and satisfying life.

In a civilized society, however, competition is carried out within social rules of fairness. These rules may be ambiguous, but they are important. We know we assert ourselves only so far, and we do not intentionally harm or attempt to ruin other people. We don't compete with people who are weaker or more vulnerable than we are; we care for them. We trust and cooperate with people who are allies and do not attack or undermine them. We play fair.

We learn these rules as we grow up. We are taught them by our parents, teachers, and other authorities, and eventually we internalize them as conscience and ethics. As adults, most of us try to live within these constraints as we vie for position and favor.

Abusers and bullies transgress these rules. They physically or psychologically harm others who are weaker or are in their control. Bullies are not the destructive outliers that psychopaths are. They are the sort of people who may conform to society's rules in most circumstances and may never be recognized as harmful by the community. In selected circumstances, however, and when they believe they can get away with it, they cheat and harm others to gratify their own needs and desires.

Sexual predators are particularly destructive. They prey on the vulnerable to gratify their own sexual desires. Sex is, of course, a natural human expression, and one that is usually bound by cultural conventions involving mutual attraction and consent. Most of us recognize that in the game of sexual competition, certain sexual objects and behaviors are off-limits. Children, for example, are not to be used to gratify adult desires. Likewise, well-socialized people do not sexually abuse adults who do not or cannot give consent. Internalized social rules prevent most of us from sexually abusing people who are too intoxicated or mentally impaired to consent. Similarly, we do not take sexual advantage of people we have power over, such as students, employees, and patients. People who do these things are violating trust.

Bullies are similar to sexual abusers and often are the same people. Bullies exercise power and control over people weaker than they are. Bullying has been conceptualized as "strategic behavior motivated by a desire to gain social dominance in the peer group."[457] This may be so, but I believe the idea of bullying can be extended to any social group, including the family, the office, and social organizations—any place where people of different levels of power meet.

Sometimes bullying is direct physical aggression, as happens with the schoolyard bully or with a physically abusive parent. Often the abuse is more psychological, involving humiliation or verbal attacks. At other times, bullying is more abstract, such as cases of people discriminating against others or depriving them of their rights. The common factor seems to be that one individual asserts dominance over another in a manner that is socially destructive.

Human societies are hierarchical, and social institutions usually function best when individuals recognize their place in them. Some people are leaders—by role, position, or personality—and others are not. Families in which parents abdicate their dominant role do not produce socially effective children, and groups without heads do not solve problems very efficiently. When hierarchy is not balanced by equality and empathy, however, the social group becomes dysfunctional, with the powerful individuals dominating weaker ones. The results of excessive dominance can be seen in totalitarian societies, domestic violence, and bullies.

A recent study by psychologist Silvia Postigo and colleagues from Universidad de Murcio reviewed the principal theories that attempt to explain bullying behavior and its origins.[458] The first such explanation, in 1939, was a frustration-aggression model—aggressors compensate for real or imagined insults by victimizing others.[459] Today, these kinds of bullies are seen as a small but high-risk group for engaging in school bullying.[460]

There are also "restorative" models, which explain bullying behavior on the basis of compensation for personal characteristics of the bully. One is the shame management theory, which holds that bullies compensate for deficiencies, such as low academic achievement or a poor self-esteem "by projecting their own shame onto the victim."[461] The bully then blames the victim.

Other models of bullying focus on developmental and social-learning factors. One of these highlights the kind of bully who has learned how to infer the mental state of potential victims (called *theory of mind*) in order to damage them but has not developed the emotional empathy needed to control these impulses.[462] Such people experience what has been called *moral disengagement*—feelings of pride and satisfaction from aggression, but no sense of guilt or shame. Another developmental and social-learning theory proposes that the bully has learned that violence is an effective means of achieving what he wants—this is called *instrumental behavior*.[463] These bullies learn aggressive behavior through exposure to violence and family models of aggression. For these individuals, bullying is unprovoked, intentional, and deliberate.

To sum up these theories, bullying may be either reactive or proactive. Reactive bullies are compensating for personal deficiencies or perceived insults and threats. Proactive bullies gain satisfaction from their aggression.

Tar Babies

At a lesser degree of dysfunction, there are many people whose behavior creates significant problems for people who get too close to them and ultimately for the individuals themselves. Such people are often described as having personality disorders, and we are all familiar with some of these types—the narcissistic, paranoid, dependent, histrionic, and the like.

Under some circumstances, these traits can be instrumental in a person's success. Rock musicians, actors, and politicians, for example, may benefit from narcissistic and histrionic traits. Bond traders and, again, politicians may find the charm and lack of remorse of antisocial traits helpful. Academics and computer programmers may be assisted by obsessive-compulsive and schizoid traits.

There is a range of personality traits that can be beneficial at times and at other times dysfunctional. What may work in the world at large can be particularly destructive in close interpersonal relationships. I use the metaphor of the Tar Baby to describe the problems they create. Get too close to them and you get stuck and the more involved you get, the more a trapped you become.

In the famous Uncle Remus story, "Br'er Rabbit and the Tar Baby," Br'er Fox wants to take the bossy Br'er Rabbit down a peg or two. He makes a doll out of tar, puts a straw hat on its head and sits his Tar Baby in the middle of the road. Soon, Br'er Rabbit comes along and says, "Good morning, how are you feeling this morning?" The Tar Baby says nothing. Br'er Rabbit gets irritated and says, "You're stuck-up, that's what's wrong with you. And I'm going to cure you."

He gets so angry that he hits Tar Baby in the jaw. His fist sticks. "If you don't let me loose, I'm going to hit you again," says Br'er Rabbit. That fist sticks, too. He kicks and head butts Tar Baby until Br'er Fox comes out from behind the bushes and says, "Howdy Br'er Rabbit. You look kind of stuck-up this morning."

Tar Babies aren't intentionally destructive people. They do not want to harm or exploit or dominate others. Under certain circumstances, they may be attractive, interesting, and pleasant, and their personalities may serve them well. But their egocentric traits can make intimate relationships with them a miserable experience.

What I call Tar Baby types come in a variety of forms. Before I describe these types further, I want to be clear that I am talking about patterns of traits, not the moral character of people. All people are a mixture of traits, and calling someone a paranoid person, for instance, is only shorthand for the extreme expression of that pattern.

The classic illustration of a Tar Baby is the borderline personality. In earlier chapters, we discussed the borderline person in the context of both reality distortion and mood dysregulation. Now we will consider the interpersonal problems presented by such people. Borderline people form unstable and intense relationships that can go from love to hate in a moment. They are emotionally volatile and impulsive. They constantly fear abandonment and lack a clear sense of self-identity. This pattern makes them highly manipulative. Psychoanalyst Helen Deutsch once described them as "people who, because they lack a consistent sense of self-identity, are parasitic on the emotional experiences of people they become dependent on."[464] People who try to help or love them become stuck in uncomfortable binds.

Paranoid people form difficult relationships in another way. They are hypersensitive, suspicious, and mistrustful. In intimate relationships, they doubt the sexual fidelity of their partners and the loyalty of their friends. They are always on guard and look for hidden meanings in even the most benign remarks and events. Paranoid people generally have difficulty getting along with others or being close to anyone. They're angry, hostile, and frequently at odds with others. Despite this, some can be quite successful. President Richard Nixon was able to hide his paranoia or use it effectively to forge a successful political career, until he was undone by Watergate. Being the spouse or intimate of a paranoid person is often distressing or even dangerous.

Histrionic people need to be the center of attention and feel unappreciated if they are not. They can initially be charming and flirtatious, but they can also be sexually provocative and manipulative. Their emotions are shallow and shift rapidly. They're often undependable and embarrassing. If they are attractive enough, like Marilyn Monroe, histrionic people can be successful actors. But getting too close to them can be like riding a bucking bronco. Eventually you get thrown on your head.

Like the character of Greek myth, Narcissus, narcissistic people are in love with themselves. They think they are special and superior and require other people to admire them. Yet their self-esteem is fragile, and they constantly need other people to give them positive attention. They have a sense of entitlement and unreasonable expectations for favorable treatment. Like histrionic people, such people can be superficially charming, but very wearing on others. They can be very successful if they are big-time athletes, politicians, or rock stars. Some pedophiles, like Penn State coach Jerry Sandusky, are likely to be narcissists. Bill Clinton seems to have some narcissistic traits. Getting too close to a narcissistic personality means constantly massaging his ego and bearing his fickleness.

People with dependent personalities are unassertive and submissive and need others to take care of them. They have difficulty making even minor decisions without a great deal of advice and reassurance. They don't take the initiative or assume responsibility for most major areas of their lives. Dependent traits can be adaptive when such people are attached to dominant personalities, such as being married to a successful businessperson. But if you expect a mature and reciprocal relationship with a dependent person, you will suffer disappointment.

Obsessive-compulsive people attempt to maintain a sense of control through excessive attention to rules, trivial details, lists, and schedules. They exhibit "a preoccupation with orderliness, perfectionism, and mental and interpersonal control, at the expense of flexibility, openness, and efficiency."[465] Some mild obsessive-compulsive traits can be quite productive. Many successful scientists, accountants, computer scientists, and writers need to be obsessive-compulsive to a point. But taken to an extreme, these people cannot make decisions, and they often get lost in the details of what they are trying to do. Interpersonal relationships with such people are often frustrating and unrewarding, especially when one expects some sort of decisive action from them.

Asocial People

I include asocial people in this chapter because making any sort of relationship with them is so difficult. Psychiatry includes them among the personality disorders. One doesn't necessarily need to have close interpersonal relationships to lead a satisfying life, but such people can be socially difficult, and when they attempt to get close to others, the result can be unhappy and conflicted for both parties. I include in this category personality patterns called *schizoid, schizotypal,* and *avoidant.*

People who are labeled *schizoid* are loners who get little satisfaction from intimacy and would rather be by themselves. They are typically seen as distant, cold, and aloof. They're often insensitive to the feelings of others and oblivious to the normal subtleties of human interactions. The schizotypal type is similar, but with the addition of eccentricity. They are also loners, with no close friendships or confidants, but they are also seen as odd or strange. From the community perspective, they exhibit distortions in reality and magical thinking.

Avoidant people are socially inhibited, hypersensitive to criticism, and having marked feelings of inadequacy. Socially, they are shy and anxious and will try to avoid interpersonal contact. They are the kinds of people who seem to assume other people are critical and disapproving.

It is important to emphasize once again that these descriptions represent points on a dimension. We can recognize that people range from gregarious to introverted and that there can be many reasons for this. Similarly, people can vary from logical, skeptical, and hard-headed to more idiosyncratic and emotional thinkers, as well as from assertive to hesitant actors. What forms of personality styles are most effective varies according to time and place.

What also strikes me about these personality designations is how hard they are to distinguish from entirely different categories of psychiatric disorders. Where does one draw the line between schizoid, schizotypal, and avoidant types and people on the autistic or schizophrenic spectra? The diagnosis given by a mental-health clinician derives from that clinician's belief system and the attributes he or she chooses to observe more than any objectively defined criteria condition.

Empathy

The psychological construct that underlies mature social functioning is empathy. Empathy involves our ability to both appreciate another person's feelings and to respond appropriately to them. As Tonya Singer, director of social neuroscience at the Max Planck Institute for Human Cognitive and Brain Sciences, put it, "when assessing the world around us and our fellow human beings, we use ourselves as a yardstick to project our own emotional state on to others."[466] Well-functioning people are able to empathize with others and respond appropriately, yet recognize that they are separate from others. Deficiencies in empathy help explain dysfunction in both social competence and socialization, but also the differences between them.

We can look at empathy as having two facets: cognitive and affective. Cognitive empathy is the ability to recognize another person's inner state. It is the act of "putting oneself in somebody else's shoes."[467] This has been described as a theory of mind function of the frontal lobes by which we learn how to be aware of and anticipate others' perceptions, feelings, thoughts, and motives.

Emotional empathy is the ability not just to know but also to *feel* what another is feeling—and with it, to "respond with sensitivity and care to another's suffering."[468] It is a function of the limbic system and is particularly communicated by facial expressions. For instance, observing someone with a fearful expression activates our own amygdala and informs us that "a novel situation is aversive" and we best avoid it.[469] Seeing a disgusted face activates our own insula and tells us to avoid eating whatever that person ate. There is evidence that the emotional aspect comes first and is seen in infants and toddlers, while the "explicit cognitive perspective-taking"—the "standing in another's shoes"—develops later in childhood.[470]

People lacking social competence have a deficiency in cognitive empathy. They have difficulty creating a theory of mind and translating their own self-conscious awareness to the mental state of other people. They do not have a deficit in emotional empathy. People described as autistic do show an automatic response to distress in others; their "basic emotional empathic response is intact."[471]

343

On the other hand, people with degrees of socialization dysfunction have little difficulty recognizing another person's emotional state, but it is the emotional response that is aberrant. Psychopathic types—at the extreme end of the dimension—may have highly developed cognitive empathy, but an inability to respond with sympathy and sensitivity to the feelings of others. Instead, they may use the distress of others to their own advantage. At less malignant levels, bullies and abusers may experience emotional empathy in some circumstances, but they often lack care and compassion for people they associate with.

Some psychologists, such as Daniel Bateson, distinguish between two forms of emotional empathy.[472] One he calls *empathic concern*—the feelings of sympathy and compassion evoked by another's distress. This kind of emotional empathy generates prosocial responses like being helpful and supportive. The other kind of empathy is what he calls *personal distress*. It is focused on oneself, the "state of distress evoked by witnessing another person's distress." The motivation for a person experiencing personal distress is to alleviate his or her own suffering, not to help the other person. Bateson writes, "This distress may not lead one to respond with sensitivity to the suffering of another, especially if there is an opportunity to relieve one's own distress without having to relieve the other's distress."

In some circumstances, the tendency to react to the distress of others with personal distress may be a cause of antisocial behavior. A study of parents at risk for abusing a child evaluated the subjects for the two kinds of emotional empathy.[473] Parents at a higher risk of child abuse were the ones who reported higher levels of distress when they saw a child cry. Their motivation was to prevent the child from crying. Low-risk parents reported feelings of sympathy and compassion rather than increased personal distress. They wanted to console the child.

Our ability to adequately modulate our empathic emotions demands a capacity to respond to another's emotion while also separating ourselves from the other person. The studies of Tonya Singer and her colleagues show that this ability might be located an area of the brain called the *right supramarginal gyrus,* which "ensures that we can decode our perceptions of ourselves from that of others."[474] When this area is disrupted, people can't make that separation. Some deficiency in this area may be at the root of narcissistic, borderline, and other "Tar Baby" types of people. These people may exhibit a self-centered deficiency in true compassion that can harm people to whom they come too close.

Empathy is the psychological mediator of social consciousness. It aligns our conceptions of ourselves with the emotional needs of others. As they do with all other traits, people are likely to vary biologically in their capacity for empathy of both the cognitive and the emotional kind. But life experience is more important than biology in the development of functional empathy. As Temple Grandin demonstrates, even people who have major deficiencies in perceiving another's mental state can learn ways to function well in society. Once she recognizes another person's needs, Grandin has no deficit in responding to them.

Conversely, people who grow up in environments that do not teach caring and concern for others or do teach people to hate and misuse others may never learn emotional empathy. Any innate capacity for empathy in such people may be twisted, diverted to obtaining personal gratification from others, despite the harm it does them. They become the antisocial people in society.

PART III

TREATMENT AND OTHER ISSUES

14

Dimensional Treatment

Allow me to start with a disclaimer. This is not a chapter to teach clinicians how to do therapy or any other mental-health treatment. Nor is it a self-help guide for troubled people. Nor is it exhaustive; it doesn't try to discuss treatment for every kind of problem people may have. What I intend is to provoke thought about what might be appropriate and effective treatment when we look at problems in a dimensional way.

In this complex world, we are bombarded with information, manipulation, and marketing, and it is difficult to hang on to simple truths. To me, a basic truth is that the goal of life is to survive and thrive. In mental-health terms, *surviving* means making decisions and following plans of action that improve our chances of leading healthy and productive lives. *Thriving* means working to build an emotionally satisfying life. Helping people achieve these general goals is the definition of *treatment*.

Put more directly in the terms of this book, the goal of any mental-health treatment is to assist people in moving in a positive direction along one or more dimensions of dysfunction, or at least to prevent movement in a nega-tive direction. Describing treatment in functional terms makes it easier to judge the efficacy and legitimacy of any form of treatment. No matter how well it is marketed or how many adherents it has, if a particular form of treat-ment doesn't improve functioning, it should not be considered treatment.

There are several tricky questions that need to be addressed before we consider the specifics of treatment. Does describing dysfunction as "men-tal disorders" assist in evaluating treatment outcomes? Does treatment that offers short-term improvement but possible long-term harm constitute legitimate treatment? Above all, who gets to define what effective treatment is: the patient, the clinician, families, the payer of the bills, or independent outside auditors?

The first question comes down to whether describing psychological dysfunction in medical terms can lead to effective treatment. In principle, at least, medical treatment is grounded in the existence of diseases. Although there is a blurring of boundaries between disease and disorder throughout medicine, much of the time medical treatments are those that are intended to prevent, cure, or slow the progression of a specific disease. With diseases, the success of treatment can be judged by objective standards. Real or more effective treatments continue to be used, while false ones eventually are dropped.

The problem for mental health is that since mental disorders are only metaphorical diseases, they cannot be defined by objective standards. They may be described by consensus opinion as in the DSM, but that does not solve the treatment issue. There can be no cure for an opinion.

The only true value in using diagnostic labels in mental health is when they guide treatment. Otherwise, labeling is of no real benefit. I am not convinced that telling people they have a mental disorder helps them lead a better life. It is commercial demands, not therapeutic ones, that direct professionals toward using these diagnostic terms. Insurance carriers insist on a medical diagnosis before they will pay, and pharmaceutical companies market their wares as specific to psychiatric disorders. Many patients, too, want to be told what is wrong with them. But I don't see that being told a diagnosis leads to a better life.

The second concern is that there are many things we can do in life that makes us feel better for a short time. We can get drunk or high and feel less anxious and depressed. We can engage in a sexually exciting, but ultimately unhealthy, relationship and feel better about ourselves for a time. In either case, however, we are not benefited in the long run.

Translate this to treatment, and we have two major therapeutic dilemmas involving dependency. One involves the use of psychoactive drugs that may provide short-term benefits but create an addiction-like need and make a person more dysfunctional after a time. As the medical model has taken hold in mental-health treatment, the use of psychiatric medications has greatly increased. Many people have come to see these drugs as the only effective treatment for their problems. There is little emphasis on the negative effects of their chronic use. We must question whether this is legitimate treatment.

The second dilemma surrounding short-term benefits is when a therapeutic relationship becomes a dependency rather than an agent of change. It is to a therapist's advantage to keep the patient coming, for reasons of ego or profit. To do this, a therapist may take on the role of an enabler. Psychiatric providers are the source for drugs that patients like to take or are addicted to. Other clinicians become overinvolved in their patient's lives. Many clinicians become advocates when they should be objective observers.

The final major question is who gets to decide whether treatment is needed, and if so, what that treatment should consist of. Most of us would agree that for an intervention to be considered treatment, either medical or mental health, it must be something the patient desires and agrees to. Most medical care requires informed consent before any procedure is undertaken. The patient is told in detail what the treatment entails and what its risks and benefits are. Unless a patient is found incompetent and someone else is appointed to decide what is in the patient's best interests, the patient should be allowed to make these decisions for himself or herself.

Anything else, no matter how beneficial we might think it is, is social control. The trouble is that in the field of mental health, true treatment and social control are often conflated. Often the patient is not the one who is asking for treatment and assessing the benefit—some external agency is. Such interventions may be necessary to protect the patient or society, but in those cases, I question whether it should be called "treatment."

With these thoughts in mind, I will discuss treatment from a biopsychosocial perspective. Biological treatments mostly concern psychiatric drugs, but there are a few other brain interventions that I will mention briefly. Psychological treatment includes psychotherapy and counseling. Social treatment includes psychiatric hospitalization and some alternatives.

Psychiatric Drug Treatment

The world's first and still most successful psychiatric concoction was the herbal remedy Theriac. The second-century Greek physician Galen is reported to have prescribed it as treatment for unbalanced bodily humors. For 1,500 years, it was the best-selling pharmaceutical for the relief of nervousness. As psychiatrist David Healy points out, the commercial importance of Theriac was probably a major reason Galenism survived for so long.[475] It is unlikely, he suggests, that "the merchant classes of the late Roman period or the Middle Ages would have welcomed a new science of disease any more than the pharmaceutical companies and physicians of today would welcome a new way to view psychiatric drugs."

In the nineteenth century, people of all sorts used patent medicines containing opium in order to improve their well-being. Another "miracle drug" used by many, including Sigmund Freud, was cocaine. A variety of drugs were used in the psychiatric hospitals in the first half of the twentieth century, but they were considered chemical restraints, not treatments. These drugs were classified as sedatives or stimulants and were recognized to have only crude effects.

This use of drugs for mental conditions was to change in the 1950s and 1960s with the dawning of the psychiatric drug revolution. Psychiatric drugs began to be seen as specific medications for mental diseases. Psychiatry and drug companies collaborated to produce classes of "magic bullet" drugs that were said to treat different classes of mental disorders. The reasons for this revolution had less to do with science than with three major political factors:

- Psychiatry was highly motivated to be seen as a legitimate medical specialty that treated real diseases.
- Pharmaceutical companies saw an opportunity to sell blockbuster drugs and had the power to market them.
- There was an intense public desire to find a cure for mental illness and to get people out of mental hospitals.

Four kinds of medication were identified as miracle drugs. These drugs came to be labeled major tranquilizers (antipsychotics), minor tranquilizers (anxiolytics), psychic energizers (antidepressants), and mood stabilizers. Nobody really knew what these drugs did or whether they worked, but the drug industry teamed up with psychiatry to market them, and they quickly became accepted by the public.

There are many similarities between modern psychiatric drugs and Theriac. The makers and providers of today's Theriacs have just as strong an investment in them. We no longer believe that black bile is the cause of mental problems, but the psychiatric establishment continues to push the notion that they are caused by chemical imbalances in the brain. When it was learned that these drugs acted by interfering with or enhancing the action of different neural transmitter molecules, they were promoted as addressing abnormalities in neurotransmitters in the brain. This gave rise to the chemical-imbalance theory of psychiatric disorders. The new drugs were then presented as specific to these pathological imbalances that caused mental disease.

As Healy noted, "appearances and rhetoric can deceive. Like Theriac, psychoactive drugs act on a multiplicity of brain systems and receptors and are better thought of as cocktail compounds rather than as specific magic bullets." To understand what these drugs really do, we can follow a distinction that British psychiatrist Joanna Moncrieff makes between disease-centered and drug-centric medications.[476] Disease-centered medications target a specific disease pathology. These drugs usually have a positive effect on people who suffer from the disease and have no effect or an adverse one on those who do not. We measure the efficacy of such drugs based on how they change the disease process, not just symptoms. Obvious examples are antibiotics, which treat bacterial infections, or insulin for diabetes.

Drug-centered medications do not differ in their effects on patients and non-patients. They produce a "global state" in all. Any therapeutic effect derives from how well this "drug-induced state" improves the well-being of the individual. These drugs do not affect an underlying disease. For instance, opiates may have the effect of reducing pain, but they create the same state for all people, whether they are in pain or not, and they will not cure an injured back. Narcotics may be a useful treatment at times, but pain is not an endorphin-imbalance disease.

The way psychiatric drugs are classified implies that they are disease-centered. Antipsychotics, antidepressants, anxiolytics, and mood stabilizers are all named on the presumption that they address an underlying pathology in the relevant brain transmitter. So antipsychotics presumably correct a dopamine imbalance, and antidepressants correct a serotonin or norepinephrine imbalance. In order to make this claim, however, you must first have a convincing theory of disease to explain how the drug corrects it. Then you must prove that your drug treats that specific disease.

Moncrieff argues that neither of these requirements is met by research and that the disease-centered model for psychiatric drugs is a myth. She writes, "The disease-centered model of drug action has been adopted, and recently widely publicized, not because the evidence for it is compelling, but because it helped promote the interests of certain powerful social groups, namely the psychiatric profession, the pharmaceutical industry and the modern state." Instead, all psychiatric drugs have only a drug-centered effect. They produce an altered mental state that we consider intoxication when applied to recreational drugs. These states "may be useful or desirable in certain social and interpersonal situations, including the situations that are brought to the attention of psychiatrists and called mental disorders," Moncrieff concludes. We can take advantage of these drug-induced states as treatment in certain circumstances, but they do not return people to normal.

There is a small group of psychiatrists who go much further than Moncrieff in condemning psychiatric drugs, and their views should not be dismissed. One of them is psychiatrist and one-time consultant to the National Institute of Mental Health (NIMH) Peter Breggin. Breggin wrote, "Psychiatric drugs don't correct biochemical imbalances—they cause them."[477] The paradox of these drugs is that they create a chemical imbalance in normal brains. They flood the brain with excess biochemical transmitters or block ones that are there.

This contention first came from a surprising source. Steven Hyman was the director of NIMH when, in 1996, he concluded that psychiatric drugs, "create perturbations in neurotransmitter functions."[478] The brain adapts to these perturbations with a homeostatic response "that attempts to maintain equilibrium in the brain in the face of environmental changes in the internal milieu." Over time, flooding the brain with these chemicals causes "substantial and long-lasting alterations in neural functioning"—an abnormal brain. The tragic irony is that chronic use of psychiatric drugs creates something like an addiction. The now-altered brain requires continued administration of an artificial substance in order to be normal.

Moncrieff argues that these drugs have a potential benefit if they are used for short periods of time and with a whole different philosophy—a drug-centered approach. Her view is that "the drug-centered model of drug-action implies a different sort of relationship between psychiatric service users and providers. Instead of acting like a medical doctor, telling the patient what diseases they have and what is the appropriate treatment, the psychiatrist or prescriber needs to act more as a pharmaceutical advisor."[479]

She advocates a collaborative approach between doctor and patient in which the key is "the user's experience of a drug's effects." This means the doctor has to be candid about drug tolerance and potential side effects, particularly with long-term use of the drug. The doctor must be clear that psychiatric drugs do not cure an underlying disease state. The patient can then help decide whether the benefits of the drugs in controlling their symptoms outweigh the negatives.

This change in treatment philosophy fits well with a dimensional approach. When used in modest doses for short periods, drugs may set the stage for the psychological and social changes necessary for long-term improvements in a patient's functioning. But when they are overused, as is often the case today, they can become detrimental to the person's long-term functioning.

Antipsychotics

The first type of antipsychotic drugs, called *phenothiazines,* has been around for more than half a century. In 1949 a French naval surgeon named Henri Laborit began administering one to some of his patients. He noticed that it created a "euphoric quietude."[480] He began using it as an anesthetic cocktail to induce "artificial hibernation" in surgical patients, and he suggested its use in psychiatry to produce "a veritable medicinal lobotomy." By the early 1950s, use of one such drug, chlorpromazine, had spread through asylums throughout Europe. It made the wards quieter and the patients easier to control. A U.S. drug company marketed it as Thorazine.

Thorazine and its kin became termed *neuroleptics,* which literally means "taking hold of the nerve." It was soon recognized that the effects of these drugs were similar to those of the disease *encephalitis lethargica* (sometimes called "sleepy sickness") and that the "symptoms progressed from reversible somnolence to all types of dyskinesia and hyperkinesia, and finally to parkinsonism."[481] Another contemporary psychiatrist frankly stated, "We have to remember that we are not treating diseases with this drug. We are using a neuropharmacologic agent to produce specific effects."[482]

When Thorazine came into use, no one had any idea how it worked. Then, in 1957, the neurotransmitter dopamine was discovered. It was soon learned that drugs like Thorazine blocked dopamine by occupying its receptors. Soon, a killer marketing idea was born: schizophrenia was caused by an excess in dopamine. There were two lines of research that supported this idea. First, it became known that amphetamines created a dopamine excess and that people taking them frequently experienced paranoia and visual hallucinations. Second, there was an odd similarity in the effect of taking a neuroleptic drug and Parkinson's disease, and there was also the fact that L-dopa (a dopamine enhancer used to treat Parkinson's) sometimes caused hallucinations and delusions. An "irresistible conclusion" was born, as British psychologist Richard Bentall put it, "that overactivity of the dopamine system causes psychosis."[483]

The problem is that no research has ever shown an excess of dopamine in patients described as schizophrenic. Nor has any study ever shown a connection between a neurotransmitter imbalance and a mental disorder. With neuroleptics, the disconnect became clear with the advent of PET scans of the brain, which showed evidence contrary to an excess-dopamine hypothesis. Then came a problem with the new generation of antipsychotics, which were said to be more effective. Paradoxically, they don't have the same affinity for dopamine as the more dopamine-focused first generation. The newer drugs affect several different transmitter substances, and it is difficult to say they are all out of balance.

Therapeutic Effects of Neuroleptics

Although the dopamine-excess hypothesis has been effectively debunked, we can still ask whether neuroleptics are the best drug-centered treatment for reality dysfunction—or even if they are effective at all. Most of us would agree that people in the throes of acute psychosis need the best available treatment, as do the long-term functional problems of people labeled schizophrenic. Is the long-term administration of neuroleptic drugs the best solution?

The question of effectiveness was asked in a large study conducted by NIMH in 1967. It was a one-year follow-up study comparing a randomized group of hospitalized patients treated with antipsychotics to a placebo control group.[484] The startling result was that the rehospitalization rate for the placebo group was lower than for the antipsychotics group.

A later NIMH study asked how patients who received antipsychotic medication fared if they were later taken off the drugs.[485] This study compared a placebo group, which had never taken antipsychotics, to groups that took different doses of chlorpromazine, which was then discontinued. They found that the drug groups did somewhat better while on the drug, but when the drug was withdrawn, they fared worse, and the higher the dose, the greater the probability of relapse. The relapse rate for the placebo group was only 7 percent, while the group that had been treated with the highest doses of antipsychotics relapsed at a rate of 65 percent.

Even worse was an observation that exposure to antipsychotics, whether discontinued or not, made psychotic patients more vulnerable to relapse. A 1977 study found that "relapse is greater in severity during drug administration then when no drugs are given."[486] As medical journalist Robert Whitaker commented, "Initial exposure to a neuroleptic seems to be setting patients up for a future of severe psychotic episodes."[487]

Despite these studies, today almost every patient hospitalized for psychosis is immediately put on antipsychotic medication. In fact, standard-of-care guidelines recommend that these patients remain on these drugs for at least one to two years.[488] Recent studies have appeared to support this practice. For instance, a recent compilation of 116 studies involving 6,493 patients calculated the benefits of continuing patients on antipsychotics after they were stabilized compared to a group of patients who were changed from an antipsychotic to a placebo.[489] The focus was on what percent of each group relapsed over the next year. There was a big difference. Of those who stayed on medication, 27 percent relapsed and 10 percent were readmitted to a hospital, while for patients whose drugs were discontinued, 64 percent relapsed and 26 percent were readmitted. In general, the medicated groups seem to have a much better quality of life.

There are notable limitations to studies like this one. It did not have a control group of patients who had never taken antipsychotics, because that would be impossible in today's world. This sort of study can tell us nothing about whether antipsychotic drugs are the best treatment for psychosis. The only conclusion we can draw from it is that patients who had previously been habituated to antipsychotics did worse when the drugs were withdrawn, at least in the short term.

Moncrieff has determined that all these studies confound withdrawal symptoms with true relapse. Her own study of relapse indicated this. "The pharmacological stress placed on the body by withdrawal may induce a relapse and a small proportion of people may experience an episode of psychosis that is part of the withdrawal syndrome and may have nothing to do with their original condition."[490] There remains a distinct possibility that if the initial storm of psychosis could be weathered without resorting to drugs, these patients might fare much better.

A Psychiatrist Speaks

The position of the great majority of psychiatrists on the primacy of psychiatric drug treatment is well presented by Edward Drummond in *The Complete Guide to Psychiatric Drugs: Straight Talk for the Best Results,* which is aimed at a general audience.[491] The book adopts a disease-specific model and advocates a comprehensive psychiatric assessment prior to being prescribed the right medication. "It's important that you know that there are really good treatments if you have a psychiatric problem," he writes. "Our understanding of psychiatric problems like depression, anxiety, schizophrenia, and bipolar disorder and the treatments that have been developed for them are vastly superior to what we had 50, 20 and even 10 years ago."

He credits advances in the diagnosis and treatment of psychotic disorders as a major reason for the great reduction in long-term institutionalization of people previously seen as "hopeless." Of antipsychotic drugs, he says, "They are quickly effective for inappropriate, agitated, or aggressive behavior. After some days, the inappropriate expression of emotion is generally improved. The disorganized thinking begins to improve within a matter of days, but the full benefit may not be seen for many weeks, or even months. The intensity of delusions and hallucinations usually diminishes within days or weeks, but rarely go away entirely."

He goes on to discuss the negative effects of the "standard" or older generation of antipsychotics. These dopamine-blocking drugs caused "a variety of unpleasant day-to-day side effects" as well as serious irreversible ones like tardive dyskinesia, a condition that involves involuntary and repetitive movements. He then describes drugs of the new generation of "atypical" antipsychotics. These drugs are called *atypical* because they are much less specific than the older ones in that they block several other neurotransmitters in addition to dopamine. The psychiatric opinion is that they are preferable, because "some people find them more effective" and "they cause fewer muscular side effects" with "a much lower rate of tardive dyskinesia."[492]

Drummond concludes that "most people find that medication significantly improves the ability to function." He recommends starting with one of the atypical antipsychotics and possibly supplementing it with a standard one. He advises, "Although the side effects may seem scary and unpleasant, you may find the improvement in your thinking and functioning worth the trouble."

What he does not address (and this is common among almost all psychiatrists) is any connection between what these drugs do in the brain and the psychiatric disorders they are designed to treat. He asserts the psychiatric definition that "schizophrenia is a life-long illness characterized by a waxing and waning of psychotic symptoms." But he

359

also admits, "There is no accepted etiology or pathogenesis of schizo-phrenia." Yet schizophrenia is construed as an entity to be specifically treated by medications whose true mechanism of action is unknown and which presumably have to be continued for life.

Neuroleptic Side Effects

Almost from the start, researchers recognized that the miracle neuroleptics had side effects resembling Parkinson's disease.[493] When Van Rossum first proposed that the action of neuroleptics was that they block dopamine receptors, he also suggested that Parkinson's-like effects "are a prerequisite for neuroleptic action."[494] To complete the picture, three American neuroleptic researchers described a set of "side effects" very similar to Parkinson's: "a lessening of spontaneity, paucity of gestures, diminished conversation and apathy."[495]

Peter Breggin has described this drug-related phenomenon as a "deactivation syndrome" with symptoms of "disinterest, indifference, diminished concern, blunting, lack of spontaneity, reduced emotional activity, reduced motivation or will, apathy and in the extreme, a rousable stupor."[496] These effects are markedly unpleasant both for many patients and for others who take them. Two Israeli physicians who tried Haldol injections remarked, "The effect was very similar in both of us. Within 10 minutes, a marked slowness of thinking and movement developed, along with a profound inner restlessness."[497] Bentall described what happened when he took a different neuroleptic, droperidol. "[I] became restless and dysphoric to the point of being very distressed. I burst into tears and, for some reason, I felt compelled to tell David [a psychiatrist colleague] everything I ever felt guilty about."[498]

Although these effects may be transient, long-term administration can cause much more serious and irreversible effects. Among the worst is tardive dyskinesia, a condition whose symptoms includes "abnormal, involuntary, repetitive movements, most commonly involving the face and mouth, but which can involve the limbs and trunk as well."[499] Additionally, cognitive deficits, such as memory impairment and executive dysfunction, have been documented with tardive dyskinesia.

The new generation of atypical antipsychotics has been said to reduce or eliminate the side effects, but research has contradicted this claim. In

The Myth of the Medical Cure, Moncrieff reports that some of them cause Parkinson's symptoms at the same rate as the older drugs, while others do so only at high doses. Some atypical antipsychotics have been shown to cause memory and other cognitive impairments, and many are sedating and cause increased appetite and diabetes. Patients often describe feeling like zombies, emotionally flat and unable to accomplish their normal routines. All of the atypicals can still cause tardive dyskinesia, although at possibly lower rates.

Elevating Mood

Much the same story I tell about antipsychotics can be repeated for other psychiatric drugs. All perturb synaptic transmission, and they gradually become the brain's new normal. None of them is a specific medication for anything. Some of them are not notably different from drugs of abuse, like alcohol and cocaine. I once thought that antidepressants were different. No one seemed to become addicted to them or suffer real harm from them. I now think otherwise.

The majority of modern antidepressants, selective serotonin reuptake inhibitors (SSRIs), work by keeping serotonin around in the synapses for an extended period of time.[500] The problem is that there is a reason that transmitter substances are quickly cleared from the synapse. Staying around blurs the message that is sent to the next neuron. The built-in adaptive response to lingering serotonin is for the neuron sending this message to decrease the amount of serotonin it squirts into the synapse and for the number of serotonin receptors to decrease.[501] After some time, these changes become semipermanent, and the brain needs excess serotonin to keep the balance.

There is also an adverse psychological effect from reliance on these drugs to alleviate depression, panic, or other mood dysfunction. As Moncrieff suggests, "the idea that your emotional state has been caused by a biochemical imbalance in the brain is profoundly disempowering."[502] It discourages people from searching for life changes that may help them resolve their own symptoms. Whenever they are confronted with problems in life, they think drugs are the only solution.

Summing-up Psychiatric Drugs

I am highly critical of the way modern Western medicine uses psychiatric drugs, but when used appropriately, they have benefits and, at times, may be lifesaving. To me, the old adage "desperate times demand desperate solutions" applies. When people are in crisis or miserable, and no other remedy is at hand, then even problematic solutions must be tried. To my mind, medication and other biological solutions can be part of the biopsychosocial intervention model, with the following principles in mind.

- Psychiatric medications should be the last resort, not the first line of treatment. The drugs we have now should not be used routinely or commonly. This principle is the opposite of the situation today, with untold millions of people given psychotropic drugs with little consideration of the consequences. In 2008 an estimated 11 percent of American women and 5 percent of men were taking antidepressants,[503] and 3.5 million American children were taking stimulants for ADHD.[504]

- These drugs should be prescribed for the shortest time possible. As with narcotics, the longer psychotropics are used, the higher the chance of addiction and the lower the chance of a positive effect. For some drugs, like neuroleptics, there is an increasing probability of irreversible adverse effects.

- Psychiatric drugs should be used in the lowest doses possible. Like alcohol and most other psychotropic drugs, taking these medications in small amounts even over a long time may have few or no bad effects. We might even find that a small dose of daily Prozac or Seroquel is as good for you as a glass of red wine. But until we find out what the safe limits are, it is best to keep use to a minimum.

Stimulating the Brain

There are a number of biological interventions that directly stimulate the brain in order to reduce symptoms. The oldest and most widely used is electroconvulsive therapy (ECT). ECT has been used since 1938 and is now considered the gold standard for "treatment-resistant depression" (that is, the 20 percent to 30 percent of patients with severe depression who don't seem to respond to any other form of treatment).[505] Studies say that 60 percent or more of these patients show an immediate improvement after a course of ECT. Unfortunately, 65 percent of them relapsed to their old state within six months.[506]

ECT passes an electric current through the brain, causing a generalized seizure. No one knows why this should help anyone. The procedure used to look gruesome, with the shaking of a seizure, but now it is done under general anesthesia and with a paralytic agent. Even so, ECT still has some big drawbacks. The worst seems to be cognitive impairment, especially memory deficits. These are usually temporary, but for some people they can be permanent. It is also very expensive; a usual course of ten treatments costs between $10,000 and $15,000.

Some psychiatrists contend that ECT "is more acceptable as an acute treatment than a chronic one." I can see its usefulness for people who are so debilitated by severe mood dysfunction that they can't take care of their basic needs. This is especially true for the elderly, who don't have enough time left to wait depression out. What concerns me is when ECT is used repeatedly on people who are chronically depressed due to poor life decisions.

Other kinds of brain stimulation techniques are still at the experimental stage, and their effectiveness has not been proven. One is Transcranial Magnetic Stimulation (TMS), which uses a strong magnetic field to induce an electric current in the brain—often the frontal lobes. TMS doesn't cause a seizure, so there is no cognitive impairment. On the other side, it is not so clear that it does much good.

Two other types I might mention are Vagus Nerve Stimulation (VNS) and Deep Brain Stimulation (DBS). VNS involves surgically rapping electrodes around the Vagus nerve in the neck and putting a battery in the chest. The Vagus nerve is continuously pulsed and that stimulation goes up to the brain. In DBS, electrodes are implanted deep in the brain to provide stimulation. It is a technique sometimes used for Parkinson's disease. Needless to say, surgical measures are rather extreme and need a lot more validation before they should be recommended.

Psychotherapy and Counseling

The major form of psychological intervention is called *psychotherapy* or sometimes *counseling*. I believe we should make a distinction between the two terms, but I will get into that later. There are two general issues about therapy I will discuss first, before I get to specifics: what is it and what are its effective ingredients.

Psychotherapy is based in something humans have been doing since the beginning of recorded history and perhaps since the origin of consciousness: using language to influence other people. Since time immemorial, people with power or special social designations (such as parents, chiefs, teachers, priests, and shamans) have wielded this influence without the use of physical force (although force is not excluded). In modern societies, we have created many categories of people who are publicly certified to exert influence in their areas of expertise. Among them are that group of talkers we collectively call *therapists*.

What distinguishes therapists is that their job is to help people who are in emotional distress or difficulty of some kind. As psychoanalyst Franz Alexander remarked in 1946, "Everyone who tries to console a despondent friend [or] calm down a panicky child in a sense practices psychotherapy.... Methodologically, psychotherapy to a large degree is nothing but a systematic, conscious application by which we influence our fellow man in daily life."[507]

How Therapy Works

There are hundreds of schools of psychotherapy. These brands differ in language, approach, and procedures. Like religions, they seem incompatible with each other, and it is impossible to compare and contrast them all. Should we throw up our hands in despair and, like the Dodo in *Alice in Wonderland*, yell, "Everybody has won and all must have prizes"? Or, despite superficial differences, do the effective forms of psychotherapy have elements in common by which we can judge them?

In the 1960s, the psychiatric thinker Jerome Frank asked this very question. He believed that despite the "multitude of conflicting theories and methods," all psychotherapies had similarities in their goals and essential ingredients.[508] The common goal was "to induce changes in patients' attitudes and behavior which, it is believed, will diminish their suffering." The core method is persuasion, which psychotherapies of all types share with "healing in primitive societies, miracle cures, religious revivalism, communist thought reform, the so-called placebo effect in medical practice, and experimental studies of persuasion." The power of psychotherapy relies "primarily on the healer's ability to mobilize healing forces in the sufferer by psychological means."

The common conditions that therapy addresses are those that lead to distress and disability. The particular source of that distress is demoralization, "a sense of powerlessness to affect oneself and one's environment." All psychotherapies "combat demoralization not only by alleviating (a patient's) specific symptom, but also, and more importantly, by employing measures to restore his self-confidence and to help him find more effective ways of mastering his problem." Although not explicitly mentioned by Frank, this attitude is the opposite of trying to correct chemical imbalances through biological means.

Frank believed that each person needed to "impose an order and regularity on the welter of experiences impinging upon him." Doing this requires people to develop individual systems of assumptions about themselves, their actions, and the world about them. If our systems of assumptions are unhealthy, they lead to internal conflict and create feelings of insecurity and distress. Frank argued, "much psychotherapy consists of supporting patients through crises until they can regain their previous state of equilibrium. Small changes produced by psychotherapy in one's assumptive system may initiate a train of events that eventually produce changes in many others."

The success of any therapy begins with the therapist's ability to form a therapeutic relationship with the patient. A patient must hold the "conviction that the therapist cares about him and is competent to help him." The ideal therapeutic relationship is one in which the therapist is "able to participate completely in the patient's communications, understand that patient's feelings and convey his ability to share them." The ideal therapist is someone who is "empathetic, genuine, and warm."

Frank concludes that despite their differences in their apparent aspects, all beneficial therapies have five essential common elements:

- All provide patients with "new opportunities for learning at both cognitive and experiential levels."
- All "enhance the patient's hope of relief."
- All "provide success experiences which enhance the sufferer's sense of mastery, interpersonal competence or capability."
- All "help the patient overcome his demoralizing sense of alienation from his fellows."
- All "arouse the patient emotionally." Frank saw strong emotional arousal as "prerequisite to all attitudinal change."

The therapeutic process relies on our human ability to think using language and imagery. Thinking allows us to solve problems and make choices before we act. Using the words of Julian Jaynes, we use our incredible thinking capacities to create an "analog I" or self.[509] This mini-me represents who we think we are and what we wish to be, how we believe others perceive us and what we fear we are, what we love and cherish and what we loathe and avoid. It is an enduring sense of person, and it appears continuous and real to us.

Our thoughts create a metaphorical world, "mind-space," for the self, this "me," to inhabit, which extends in time and space. It is populated by the people, places, and things we recall—which we may or may not have actually experienced. It also contains the things we desire and those we fear. The self travels through this mind-space. It can travel back in time and try to explain why things are the way they are for us. The self can also appraise what we did in the past and place value on the results. The self can try out different ways to think, feel, and act in present-day mind-space and then travel to the future to see the imagined consequences. This projection can be more or less accurate and more or less desirable.

Once we create a coherent self, it is resistant to change. We seek to maintain a consistent perspective on the world, inside and out. It is very disconcerting when we receive information we cannot incorporate into the self and its mind-space. Negative experiences like traumas and losses and positive ones like successes can force us to change the self, for better or worse. But without external input, it is very difficult to change the way we picture ourselves and the world we inhabit.

The role of the therapist is to provide that input in a manner powerful enough that the patient must alter aspects of the self and its mind-space. Every effective psychotherapy pushes patients toward a revised sense of self and a more realistic view of the world it occupies. It is the job of the therapist to guide patients toward seeing themselves and their problems in a more benign light. The therapist ferrets out and challenges erroneous and maladaptive ways of thinking and offers ways to reimagine self and solve problems.

There are three factors that help define a psychotherapeutic process. First, there is a therapist, a healer who is formally entitled to offer advice and counsel to sufferers. Second, therapists, no matter their professional title, promise to use their knowledge and competence to help patients improve their lives for no rewards other than payment for service. Therapy is not for the personal gratification or aggrandizement of the therapist. Third, there must be a suffering patient, who comes to the therapist and voluntarily lends the therapist the power of influence, with the expectation that the therapist can improve his or her life.

There are some important implications of these elements that we should take a moment to consider. The first is the therapist is not there to tell people how to lead their lives or to intervene beyond their expertise. There are professionals who are entitled to directly intervene in people's lives—lawyers, accountants, physicians, and some social workers. They are not therapists. It offends my ethical sense when I find therapists who lose their objectivity and act as advocates or tell patients how to live.

It is easy for therapists to become arrogant. The people coming to a therapist are often confused, dependent, and emotionally overwhelmed. Therapists may believe that they can take over for patients and tell them what they should do. This is wrong. It is not the therapist's place to tell patients what their goals should be or to control their patients' lives. The legitimate role of the therapist is to remain as objective as possible while helping patients to define their own goals, to see the adverse consequences of their current thoughts and actions, and to find their own solutions.

Psychotherapy and Counseling

Not everybody or every problem is suitable for psychotherapy. Many, if not most, people with psychological and behavioral dysfunctions are more likely to benefit from different sorts of interventions. These include guidance and instruction, advocacy and help in living, or direct supervision. None of these are psychotherapy. They are all forms of counseling.

The fundamental requirement for psychotherapy is that the sufferer voluntarily comes to the therapist in distress. The patient must be willing to lend the therapist the power of influence with the expectation that it will improve the patient's life. It is not a process that can be imposed by courts, parents, or spouses. It can't be undertaken for a special benefit, like supporting a claim for disability payments or helping a divorce case. Real therapy is a difficult and often painful process that puts demands on patient and therapist alike. It is much more than having a friend or a confidante. It is never easy to change habits of thought and behavior, so therapy must begin with a motivated patient.

The term *counseling* implies a more specific and directed process. There are many kinds of counseling professionals who give advice in their areas of competence. I go to my lawyer for legal help and my stockbroker for financial help. I do not expect them to go beyond the boundaries of their expertise. A mental-health counselor should be similar. When a person comes to a marital or substance-abuse counselor, the subject should be defined and limited. The counselor has specific expertise and information to impart and performs like a coach or a teacher. Counselors should not stray into areas beyond their specific role.

The distinction between psychotherapy and counseling is important, because many clinicians fill both roles. It is unfair when a clinician tries to do both at the same time. Psychotherapy offers a protected environment where it is safe to reveal secrets and concerns without fear of censure or embarrassment. The patient determines the problems to be addressed, and the therapist does not give direct advice. The therapist is allowed to use manipulation and interpretation because the patient gives permission.

While counselors are expected to keep most interactions confidential, they may be accountable to others in addition to their clients. For instance, counselors may report to the courts about sex offenders' or drunk drivers' treatment or to human-service agencies about child abuse or neglect cases. Counseling is often a major part of social interventions, as I will describe later in this chapter. From the dimensional perspective, counseling is the treatment of choice for most problems related to reality misperception, cognitive competence, social competence, chronic pain and other bodily disorders, and socialization dysfunction. Psychotherapy is most appropriate for distress caused by anxiety and mood problems, as well as some impulse-control problems.

Change

The first step in therapy is helping the patient to understand which of life's problems can be solved and which have to be accepted. This distinction is well expressed by the Serenity Prayer attributed to the theologian Reinhold Niebuhr and made famous by its use in Alcoholics Anonymous. One version of it is as follows:

> Oh God, give us the serenity to accept what cannot be changed,
> The courage to change what can be changed
> And the wisdom to know the difference.

Adapted for the therapy process, it means that patients must understand that there are many things they cannot change. They can't change their upbringing, traumas they may have experienced, or their past actions. These things can only be accepted with serenity. People can change the way they think about themselves and how they act in the future.

The fundamental purpose of therapy is change. A group of clinicians and theorists connected to the Mental Health Institute in Palo Alto, California, considered the problem of change some years ago. This group greatly influenced my thinking as a young psychologist and was a major force in the cognitive-therapy movement. Their thesis, as presented by psychologist

Paul Watzlawick and his colleagues, was that there are two kinds of change.[510] Change of the first sort is movement within a set of assumptions, or a "frame." Second-order change is change that breaks free of those assumptions and reframes the problem. First-order change operates within a system and is powerless to change that system. Changing the system means changing the rules of the frame, so it is change of change. A simple example is a person having a nightmare. She might change many actions within the dream, such as run, fight, or scream, but she still remains within the nightmare. The only way out is to change the rules and wake up.

In the emotional sphere, Watzlawick and his coauthors offer an example of what happens if a friend, relative, or therapist tries to alter the mood of another person. Say someone is feeling sad and depressed. The natural inclination is to try to cheer him up by offering advice. When the advice doesn't work, the well-meaning "therapist" redoubles the effort "to make him see the silver lining around every cloud." The "patient" perceives this as a demand that he replace feelings of sadness and pessimism with others of joy and optimism. This compounds the sufferer's problems, because not only does he continue to feel sad but he now also feels like a failure.

Sadness becomes badness. What may have started as a temporary and harmless emotional difficulty is now complicated by guilt. As Watzlawick and his coauthors observed, "Clinical experience shows that the individual will eventually apply the depression-engendering 'solution' to himself and thereby become fit to be labeled a patient."

An effective solution involves a second-order change, reframing the problem. Perhaps being depressed is the logical outcome of life circumstances and the way the person thinks about them. If the helper can challenge the person's assumptions and help him not to see his situation as a disaster, the depressed person can see his difficulties in a new light and no longer need to feel depressed.

To summarize this, effective therapy helps people make real changes in the way they think and act. It challenges faulty assumptions and old ways of thinking. Therapy often uncovers hidden emotions and conflicts, which the patient can then resolve. Making these changes allows patients to make wiser decisions, gain acceptance of themselves, and follow a better life course.

Cognitive Therapy

The therapeutic approach that makes the connection between ways of thinking and dysfunctional action most explicit is termed either *cognitive therapy* or *cognitive behavioral therapy*. *Cognitive therapy* is the more appropriate term, because, except under unusual circumstances, the only behavior that the therapist has access to is what the patient says and does in the office.

Cognitive therapy deals primarily with what a patient says, and the patient is considered truthful, although not free of distortions. For this to work, the patient must be willing to reveal beliefs, emotions, and fantasies. Bringing these to light allows the therapist to expose illogical and unreasonable patterns of thought as well as maladaptive behaviors. The patient can be taught new ways of solving problems and then practice them. I will briefly highlight the general ideas of cognitive therapy and then provide some specific examples.

Albert Bandura was one of the founders and foremost theorists of cognitive therapy. He emphasized the human ability to use thought to control emotion. "To the extent that people can regulate what they think," he said, "they can influence how they feel and behave.... Many human distresses are exacerbated by failures of thought control."[511] The principal benefit of psychotherapy is to help people exert that control by directing them toward "the sociocognitive tools needed to deal effectively with whatever situations might arise."

He introduced the term *self-efficacy* to describe a person's sense of control. He formally defined it as "beliefs in one's capacities to organize and execute the courses of action required to manage prospective situations." When people see themselves as ineffectual but see others around them as successful, it fosters "self-disparagement and depression." Despondency is a product of seeing others working and succeeding in getting what they desire, while we fail and are powerless. When we see those around us as equally powerless, we tend to become apathetic and resigned, but not depressed.

A related source of depression lies in the beliefs people develop about their ability to control their own consciousness.[512] He illustrates this idea with a proverb: "You cannot prevent the birds of worry and care from flying over your head. But you can stop them from building a nest in your hair." It is not just having disturbing thoughts and ruminating about failures that makes us depressed and anxious. It is the sense that we cannot turn the thoughts off. People with a high sense of self-efficacy believe they can treat even the most difficult life circumstances as challenges. On the contrary, with a low sense of control, even minor failure causes strong negative emotions. A key component of cognitive therapy, then, is to help the patient establish and strengthen a sense of self-efficacy.

Albert Ellis was the most accessible and popular of the cognitive therapists and the charismatic founder of Rational Emotive Therapy. He brought terms like *self-efficacy* to life with graphic ones like *catastrophizing* (obsessively thinking about the worst) and *musterbations* (believing that desirable outcomes are musts). Like so many of his era, Ellis was initially a Freudian analyst, but because analysis was interminable, he lost faith in it. He took the un-analytic approach of actively engaging with his patients and found that they progressed much faster. In 1955, he gave up psychoanalysis entirely for his new form of treatment. His premise was that the therapist could help the patient change behavior by exposing and challenging irrational beliefs and persuading the patient to accept rational ones.[513]

Ellis came to believe in describing people's problems in the active voice.[514] He would not say that a person "suffers from depression" but that "he depresses." He might tell a patient, "You largely constructed your own depression. It wasn't given to you. Therefore, you can deconstruct it."[515] For Ellis, that meant that we have the ability to "control our own emotional destiny." As he expressed it, "The best years of your life are the ones in which you decide your problems are your own. You do not blame them on your mother, your ecology, or the president. You realize you can control your own destiny."

In Ellis's formulation, it is not the experience of adverse events that make us depressed, but the irrational beliefs we hold about them. Ellis writes, "People have healthy, and often strong desires, goals, and values that they raise to absolute musts, shoulds, demands and necessities." These give rise to self-statements such as, "Because I strongly want to be achieving and winning significant others' approval I absolutely must keep fulfilling these goals!" or "Because I greatly prefer that people and conditions treat me considerately and fairly, they absolutely must do so." When people fail to achieve what they hope to or when others don't comply with their demands, they depress themselves.

A second form of irrational belief is "overgeneralization." People often judge themselves globally and conditionally: "I am a good person when I do good things; and I am a bad person when I do bad things." This kind of thinking "puts people's entire worth, instead of their performances, on the line."

Awfulizing is a third ticket to misery. Here "humans take something that they wish were not happening and claim therefore that it absolutely must not happen and therefore it is horrible if it does." The result is that they conclude, "This unfortunate condition (e.g., not getting something I want) is completely bad, is the end of the world, is totally devastating, is the worst possible thing that could happen, and it makes my life totally devoid of all possible pleasure."

The goal of psychotherapy is to "help clients disturb themselves less emotionally and to enable them to leave happier and more fulfilling lives." It is not just feeling better that counts, but actually getting better. That is, the goal is making changes and learning strategies that will help people experience less distress and disturbance in the future.

Ellis's premise is that "humans are innately problem solvers" who look for and try to rectify "conditions they consider 'bad' or inimical to their basic interests." Unfortunately, we "are innately predisposed to act sloppily," and we often do not see the difference between functional and dysfunctional behaviors. As a consequence, people "frequently wind up with inaccurate or self-destructive thinking, emotions and behaving."

The crux of Ellis's method lies in the development of "unconditional self-accepting," that is, teaching patients to respect themselves as worthy people "whether or not they perform well and whether or not you or anyone else favors them." If people "unconditionally accept themselves as 'good' humans even when they are performing badly and relating poorly, they can minimize what Ellis called their *anxietizing* and depressing.

Overcoming Panic

The Australian physician Claire Weekes developed a technique for overcoming anxiety attacks that remains relevant today.[516] She described four simple, yet effective, ideas we can all practice: *facing, accepting, floating,* and *letting time pass.*

Facing means that your effort is required and you must confront the situations and experiences you fear. Others can guide you, but they cannot do it for you. Facing means not shying away from the experience of your symptoms because you fear that will make them worse.

Accepting, in Weekes's terms, is "letting the body loosen as much as possible and then going toward, not withdrawing from, the feared symptoms, the feared experiences." It is learning that one can experience highly unpleasant feelings without dreading them or being overwhelmed by them. "Acceptance means throwing away the gun and letting the Tiger in, if he wants to."

Floating is the concept of going with and not fighting your anxiety. It is a sense of rising above and observing your anxiety rather than struggling against it. "Where fighting is exhausting, floating—by removing the tension of forcing—makes repeated effort less daunting."

Weekes's last point, *letting time pass,* points to the fact that anxious people become "sensitized," in the sense that they have had long exposure to being anxious and to reacting to it maladaptively. Therefore, it takes a long time and much relearning to be able to adequately control anxiety. "Recovery is built on repeated experiences of discovering that symptoms no longer matter." Be patient and let time pass.

Once anxious people learn that they can control their fear and that it will not overwhelm them, kill them, or make them crazy, they can cease perceiving it as an enemy. They can recognize it as part of themselves and not as an alien invader; they can begin to accept it as just a feeling. They may even benefit from the experience.

Mindfulness

One of the most talked-about new brands of psychological intervention is called *mindfulness*. It is typically described as a melding of modern psychology with an ancient Buddhist form of meditation called *anapanasti,* which means "mindfulness of breathing."[517] The psychotherapeutic use of this kind of meditation was popularized in the West by Jon Kabat-Zinn in his description of the Mindfulness-based Stress Reduction Program for the chronically ill at the University of Massachusetts.[518] His program combines meditation with a technique he called the *body scan* for body awareness, and even yoga to help people reduce stress.

As Buddhist philosophy and meditation practices have become more popular, they have gained a presence in the business world and have even been incorporated into the school curriculum in Los Angeles. Mindfulness has also increasingly become a component of cognitive behavior therapy. The goal has been described as interrupting autonomic processes that lead to depression and other kinds of psychological distress. It teaches people to shift from automatically reacting to incoming information to observing and accepting it without judging it.[519]

Rebecca Crane, who directs the Centre for Mindfulness Research and Practice at Bangor University, describes the condition of mindfulness as "the awareness that emerges when we pay attention to experience in a particular way: on purpose (the attention is deliberately placed on particular aspects of experience); in the present moment (when the mind slips into the past or the future, we bring it back to the present); and nonjudgementally (the process is infused with acceptance of whatever arises)."[520] Mindfulness teaching incorporates three broad elements: (1) the "systematic development of awareness" through formal practice of meditation and informal "cultivating present-moment awareness in daily life"; (2) the cultivation of an attitude of "kindness, curiosity and a willingness to be present with the unfolding of experience"; and (3) acquiring an "embodied understanding of human vulnerability," which means learning that "although suffering is an inherent part of experience, there are ways that we can learn to recognize and step out of patterns of habitually collaborating to perpetuate it, add to it and deepen it."

A recent meta-analysis of more than two hundred studies of the outcomes of mindfulness-based therapies concluded that these treatments were "especially effective for reducing anxiety, depression and stress."[521] They had not, however, proved more effective than traditional behavior therapy or even pharmacological treatment.

I and a number of other clinical psychologists began using techniques similar to mindfulness in the 1970s. We did not see them as based in Eastern philosophy or mystical in any way. As I described earlier, my strategy combined biofeedback, relaxation training, and imagery. Biofeedback is a means of calling patient's attention to the present state of their bodies and learning to consciously control that state. Relaxation training is similar to meditation in its calming and present focus. And the use of vivid imagery, engaging all the senses, takes people far away from their cares and worries.

I describe mindfulness as a form of therapy designed to enhance executive or cognitive control of negative emotions. It promotes a way of thinking that is incompatible with habitually overresponding to negative states like anxiety, depression, anger, and chronic pain. The message is one of acceptance and focus on the present. With consistent practice of relaxation or meditative techniques, we are less likely to dwell on problems and troubles of the past or make terrible predictions about the future. The practice interrupts the habits of misperception and false assumptions that generate so much of our distress.

Recent evidence shows that a consistent practice of meditation has real and beneficial physiological effects on the brain.[522] Brain-scan studies show that there are actual changes in both the structure and function in the brains of experienced meditators. These changes correlate with a reduced stress response and an enhanced sense of well-being. Meditation practice may even "diminish inflammation and other biological stresses that occur at the molecular level."

Parenting

Many mental-health clinicians specialize in treating distressed children by psychiatric drugs or psychotherapy. These interventions may be appropriate and beneficial, but they come with a major concern. Young children do not choose to enter treatment. They are referred by parents, pediatricians, or schools. They have little or no say in whether to take the drugs or to engage in the therapy.

Since the child is referred to therapy by adults, it is common for people to identify the child as the source of the problem. It is difficult to look beyond the child to the parents, family system, or the school as the source of the child's problems. This practice is unfair to the child and ethically questionable.

There are, however, forms of family therapy and parenting counseling that avoid these problems and have proven extremely effective. One of the most comprehensive and well-researched counseling systems designed to teach parenting skills is the Incredible Years training plan developed by Carolyn Webster-Stratton.[523] The effectiveness of this system as a violence-prevention program has been established in independent outcome studies.[524]

Webster-Stratton's book, *The Incredible Years,* which describes her system, is detailed in its recommendations and how to achieve the desired results. The following are some of the major principles:

- Play is an extremely important part of parenting. It builds a relationship and attachment. It teaches problem solving and communication skills. It helps parents become sensitive to a child's needs in a way that promotes self-worth and competence.

- Positive attention and encouragement should be used without delay and without mixed messages to improve a child's social behavior.

- Tangible rewards, incentives, and celebrations should be used to reinforce positive behavior.

- Parents learn to give appropriate commands and set limits.

- Parents learn to ignore certain negative behaviors while paying attention to positive ones.

- Timeouts are used to calm the situation and to avoid any ineffective punishment.

- Parents teach responsibility and good decision making by providing age-appropriate consequences. Consequences should be as natural and logical as possible.

- Parents learn to discuss problems with the children and help them come up with solutions. This helps the child become an independent problem-solver.

- Parents learn effective ways to help children regulate their emotions.

- Finally, parents learn to teach children how to be friends and how to cope with problems with their peers.

Perhaps the greatest benefit of programs such as Webster-Stratton's is that they do not see the child as mentally disordered but instead see that the child is responding to a psychosocial system. In an age when so many children are medicated for ADHD, bipolar disorder, and anxiety disorder, this attitude changes everything. It may be expensive, time-consuming, and difficult for some parents to swallow, but it is better than victimizing the children.

Psychotherapy for Schizophrenia

The type of madness labeled *schizophrenia* is seen by many as an unlikely candidate for psychotherapy. It is the most stigmatized form of dysfunction and is typically seen as a serious mental disease that must be immediately medicated. But if schizophrenia is thought of as a set of problematic attributes (call them *symptoms* if you like) that interfere with a person's life, these problems can be addressed just as any other human dysfunction. We can't cure something that is not a disease, but we can help people better understand and control their symptoms, just as we do with other problems in people's lives.

This is the attitude taken by cognitive therapists who work with this population. In this section, I'll talk about the approach of two British psychiatrists, David Kingdon and Douglas Turkington, who cowrote a guide to this practice.[525] They begin by adopting a vulnerability-stress model—the view that schizophrenia is a normal way for vulnerable people to break down under stress. "The precise symptoms (e.g., voices or delusions) and any combination of symptoms ... that are produced will be determined by the nature of the vulnerabilities and stresses experienced. These symptoms, though, are just as understandable as any other psychological problem." Their message is that "given sufficient or specific types of stress, most individuals—maybe everybody—could develop the symptoms the person is experiencing."

They call this message "normalizing." A simple example is of a person experiencing disturbed sleep due to pressures at work. The man thinks he hears someone calling his name, and in his heightened state of anxiety, he fears he is going mad. His train of thought runs out of control. "Maybe I will be put in a mental hospital.... I will be locked up and injected.... Life will be unbearable." He becomes frightened, and his increasing anxiety and sleep deprivation convince him that he really is mad.

Teaching him that feeling crazy is something that many people would experience under similar circumstances might prevent him from externalizing his problem (that is, seeing his problems as something that exists outside of his mind). Normalizing has two major therapeutic effects: "it draws meaning from confusion, which is reassuring and destigmatizing," and "it provides the basis for specific interventions that can alleviate the distressing and disabling symptoms."

There are four types of symptoms that are usually designated as schizophrenic: delusions, hallucinations, thought disorder, and a set of negative symptoms (such as emotional flattening, lack of drive, lack of pleasure, cognitive impairment, and social withdrawal). Delusion is the core problem, according to Kingdon and Turkington. They define *delusion* as "a shorthand term for strongly held beliefs that distress the person or interfere with his or her life." Rather than delusions being seen as pathological or even false, they should be seen as something to be "understood and their consequences explored." With this perspective, "delusions may explain situations or relationships that are confusing to the person and give order and meaning to his or her life."

Hallucinations are a particular form of delusion. They are the beliefs held by the person that her own thoughts are generated outside her mind—that is, externalized. Hallucinations are very similar to obsessions. In both phenomena, "ideas, thoughts and images are involuntarily produced" and they occur "recurrently and persistently and are experienced as senseless and repugnant." The only distinction is that the hallucinating person fails to recognize that these are her own thoughts.

Even at their most bizarre, hallucinations are really a commentary on the person's life situation. For instance, some hallucinations may originate in an earlier trauma. People who have been sexually assaulted may hallucinate derogatory and demeaning comments in the voice of the attacker, and these voices may even command them to kill themselves. When a therapist engages with the patient, and they search for an understanding of the meaning of the hallucinations, it helps normalize the perception.

Thought disorder can be reconceptualized as a communication disorder. A person who is highly agitated by inner concerns may speak in a convoluted, fragmented, and nonsensical manner. But beneath the strange and frustrating expressions, the patient is trying to communicate something important. "The driving theme is usually one of threat, fear or distress, and once this is identified a focus on relevant events and beliefs allows a reduction in arousal and increased coherence of speech."

The collection of so-called negative symptoms can be seen as surface appearances in response to the turmoil occurring underneath. They may represent the person acting as if he is "in shock." For instance, what we see as flattening of affect "may be a direct reaction to abusive, derogatory voices or thoughts, and the 'frozen' expression, a 'front' to the world." It "may be an attempt to cope with seemingly overwhelming disturbance." Similarly *anhedonia* (the lack of pleasure), "may be related to demoralization, hopelessness or feeling numb" and social withdrawal is a "way to cope with overstimulation."

When a patient deemed schizophrenic can be engaged in therapy and his problems normalized, the work of reducing symptoms and developing an effective life can begin. Many specific cognitive-therapy techniques have been developed over the years and have proven successful. One early example was the work that Aaron Beck did with a person with a paranoid delusion.[526]

Beck began by helping the patient clearly identify his persecutors. The patient wrote down how they looked and dressed, their behavior, and their demeanor. Beck then undertook a systematized reality-testing program in which he examined the evidence with the patient. As the patient began to feel safer, he was able to realistically examine the behavior of people he took to be government agents. He gradually began to decrease his suspicions, until they were gone. He did not become depressed or anxious as his delusions abated, and his paranoia did not return.

Cognitive therapy with severely disturbed people is time-consuming and difficult, but studies have shown that when done well, it is cost-effective and leads to long-term improvement. Unfortunately, the immediate application of antipsychotic medication has made its use a dying art.

Effective Decision Making

The principal job of a therapist, in my view, is to help people make better decisions and then act in accordance with them. This starts with understanding the role of our emotions in how we think. Most of the time, making decisions on an emotional basis works just fine. In the course of our lives, we develop values, ethics, and morals, which are based in our emotional systems and which guide us to do what feels right and what has worked for us in the past. Without them, we would be paralyzed by analysis and unable to get through the day productively. People whom we call obsessive-compulsive types don't trust their emotional guides and spend their time second-guessing and redoing their actions.

Emotions, however, are not always a reliable guide. Many people who come to therapy have not learned effective emotional habits (such as over-reacting to perceived threats) and they keep repeating the same maladaptive behaviors over and over. Their values are full of shoulds and musts that make them miserable. Other people are inadequately socialized and respond to urges and desires impulsively, with negative consequences. Strong emotions, particularly negative ones like fear and anger, tend to narrow our focus and cause us to respond in self-defeating ways.

When our emotional habits do not work effectively, we must engage our executive brains to channel or sometimes suppress our emotions. To be successful, we must think rationally. We need to broaden our perspective and consider what courses of action are in our long-term best interests.

In my way of thinking, therapy is all about helping people learn how to achieve this self-interest. Therapy is not about the decisions themselves, but about how we make them and how we judge their potential consequences. It is about challenging faulty emotional assumptions and planning more effective behaviors. A therapist might ask a patient, "What are the benefits you hope to achieve by this course of action? What are the possible risks? Do short-term benefits outweigh longer-term costs?"

For me, the two achievable goals of therapy are to improve both perspective and control. *Perspective* is roughly equivalent to terms like *insight* and *judgment*. It means gaining as accurate an understanding of ourselves in relation to the world around us as we can. It means distinguishing our own emotions, desires, impulses, and beliefs from those of others in our social world. It also means being fully aware of what kind of future we wish to have and what the consequences of our current actions are most likely to be.

I begin with what I flippantly call the Gallon Theory of Enlightened Self-Interest. We go around only once in this life, and we might as well build the most satisfying one we can. We ought to act in our own best interests, within the limits imposed by our talents and abilities as well as by social boundaries. We are not placed on this earth to satisfy other people's expectations, desires, and beliefs.

By *self-interest*, I don't mean self-centeredness. For most of us, good interpersonal relationships are important to life happiness. Protecting, nurturing, and caring for people we love are vital goals for most of us. But, ultimately, we do these things because they enhance our own lives, not, in actual fact, for the other. *Perspective* means we should examine what we choose to do or wish to do in light of our own long-term interests.

Part of perspective is an acceptance of what is. To live a successful life, we must understand and accept our own history and the world around us (the things we cannot change), while working to change what we can. I take my cue from the book of Ecclesiastes, which I learned from the classic Pete Seeger folksong.

"*To everything there is a season, and a time for every purpose under heaven.*"

Almost every human experience has its time and place in our lives. If we can view these experiences without distortion or denial, we can use them to our own benefit. Almost any dysfunction included in my dimensions can have an upside, if used correctly. So one major job of a therapist is to help a patient gain a benign perspective on himself or herself and a forward-looking plan.

Perspective must be accompanied by learning appropriate control of one's emotions and behaviors. A great deal of human misery and dysfunction comes from people responding to their emotions without carefully considering the consequences. For instance, people who respond to sexual temptation by having an affair and later come to regret it. This is not to say that we should squelch all our emotions and desires. It means that we must learn to control or redirect actions we might take in response to them. How we respond to our feelings and desires is a strategic choice and needs to be made prudently.

Here are some examples of how I might apply these principles. Take reality misperception first. Suspension of reality can be both entertaining and productive. Fantasy is fundamental to both creativity and fun. In its time and place, we can welcome it, no matter how insane it seems. Fantasy becomes dysfunctional when it dominates a person's life, is confused with reality, or is frightening. Appropriate therapy can help that person understand the distinction between imagination and the outer world and learn to keep them separate. As I discussed in the last section, the important step is to test imaginings against the reality of the outside world and to decide when to allow them free reign and when to control them.

Depression, with its sadness and withdrawal from the world, also has its place in our lives. It is an important part of the healing process that follows loss or failure. It is beneficial for us to acknowledge and accept depression, but not to let it consume our lives. The role of therapy is to help people to understand their depressed feelings and to express them fully and directly— and then to move on.

Anxiety is also to be seen as an important part of effective functioning. At times, it is a warning that should be heeded. Anxiety is often a potent motivator that results in long-term satisfaction. I wouldn't have been able to persist in writing this book if it didn't make me anxious not to. The job of therapy is to help people realistically appraise circumstances that appear threatening and then to respond to them proportionately. There is a time to let anxiety (and guilt) inhibit our behavior and there is a time to be bold. Therapy should help people to accept anxiety as natural and to use it productively.

Finally, what I have described as *socialization* is an important dimension for healthy human functioning. We have a right to the personality we have, but therapy can help people be perceptive about their impact on others. We can learn how to adapt our personality traits in order to build strong, mutual relationships. We can also learn that there is a time to be self-interested and to negotiate our way in this world to our own advantage.

In summary, here are a few of my therapeutic principles:

- There are no shortcuts. Real change takes effort, persistence, and, often, emotional pain. Drugs can't take the place of real work.

- Poor, emotionally driven decisions have consequences. To make a better life, a person must learn to make better decisions, no matter how difficult.

- Since every journey begins with the first step, effective change requires taking action in the real world. For a person to say they are trying isn't good enough.

- Very few things in life are "I must," "I should," or "I can't." Mostly it's "I won't" or "I fear the consequences." Erroneous beliefs are to be challenged.

- Many things in life can't be changed. They have to be accepted, and we need to move on. The past is over.

Psychiatric Hospitalization and Some Alternatives

The modern psychiatric institution is not the human warehouse of yesteryear. Mental hospitals that once held thousands of patients today have less than a tenth that number. Length of stays that once measured in years (or a lifetime) now last weeks or months. And in my experience, psychiatric patients are generally treated with respect and compassion.

There is a clear need for these institutions in society. Without them, jails and streets become the de-facto mental facilities. A civilized society needs to provide a safe haven and a means of controlling those of its citizens who are too distressed and unable to survive in the community or whose behavior cannot be tolerated. Hospitals also remove people in crisis from the stressors in their lives and place them in a therapeutic environment.

A large percentage of people admitted to psychiatric hospitals are referred to them from the emergency departments of general hospitals.[527] Most are brought in by the police, mental-health caseworkers, or family in a state of reality crisis we call *psychotic*. This may be an acute breakdown or an exacerbation of a chronic condition. There are pressing issues of safety for the person and the community. Sometimes there are concerns that the breakdown was caused by a medical condition.

At this stage, people have to be taken care of, even against their will. In a civilized society, they can't be ignored and thrown out on the street. The ones who are too psychotic to cooperate have to be put in secure facilities. There aren't a lot of options for supervised and controlled settings outside of psychiatric hospitals.

The question, however, is whether these institutions need to be or even should be called *hospitals*. The primary intervention in a psychiatric hospital is a social one, since it takes people in crisis out of the community environment, stabilizes them, and returns them back. The reason they are called *hospitals* is because psychological dysfunction has been redefined as *mental illness*. And also because older terms like *asylum* and *refuge* have become unacceptable euphemisms.

The Psychiatric Hospital

As psychiatry medicalized, the procedures of these institutions became increasingly hospital-like. But these are hospitals where the patients are locked in, often involuntarily, and sometimes treated against their will. The treatment is focused on medication management—getting patients on psychiatric drugs and adjusting their medications until they are judged fit to be returned to the community, either to resume their usual lives or to be placed in a structured environment like a group home. Psychological treatment usually revolves around convincing patients that they have a mental illness and that they need to stay on their meds.

Involuntary Hospitalization and Involuntary Treatment

The most ethically fraught issues in mental health involve involuntary commitment and treatment of people defined as mentally ill. We value our freedom to chart our own life course. We want to choose where we live, where we go, and what we are able to do. For most of us, this freedom extends to seeking mental-health treatment. We may choose to seek therapy, take medications, or even go to a hospital if we are desperate. This is not the case, however, for people who are involuntarily hospitalized. They can be locked in institutions for extended periods of time and sometimes forced to take psychiatric medications. All fifty states and the District of Columbia have laws that allow people who are judged at serious risk of harm to be placed in specified psychiatric hospitals against their will. Forty-two states also have an outpatient commitment procedure of some form.

Here is how it works in my state. A person who is initially evaluated as mentally ill and harmful can be "blue-papered" for an emergency commitment on the signature of a judge. *Risk of harm* means that the person might cause harm to himself (as indicated by suicidal attempts or threats) or physical harm to others (as shown by violent behavior or threats) or that the person is unable to avoid or protect himself from physical or mental impairment or injury. This blue-paper starts a clock; the patient can be held for a short period of time, but then the hospital needs to apply to the court for a longer period of commitment.

When the hospital applies for commitment, a hearing is scheduled before a judge. An independent mental-health expert is appointed to examine the patient and to be a witness at the hearing. An attorney is appointed for the patient, and the state attorney represents the hospital. On the appointed day, all gather before a judge. I have participated in a large number of these hearings, so I know the procedure well.

I, as an outside examiner, will be called first. I will be asked to testify if I believe the patient is mentally ill, which is defined as any condition "which substantially impairs his mental health" with the exception of "mentally retarded or sociopathic persons." I will then be asked if there is a reasonable certainty of harm and if hospitalization is the least restrictive setting to prevent this harm. I will also be asked for an estimate of how long a commitment should be ordered, with a limit of four months for a first commitment. Following me, a hospital psychiatrist testifies to the same issues. The attorneys for both the hospital and the patient have opportunities to question each of us in turn, and the judge can also question either of us. Following this, the patient and any family members present have a right to testify, if they so choose. As in any court, the attorneys can then make closing arguments, and finally, the judge makes a final decision.

I have continuously grappled with the commitment process and my role in it. On the one hand, it is a confinement very like incarceration, but without any wrongdoing. Do we have a right to take away a person's liberty without a charge? On the other hand, as a society we do not want to see psychotic people harm themselves or others. I have concluded that it is justified to take seriously impaired people out of society and place them in a protective environment for reasons of safety, as long as there are appropriate legal constraints. I wish these institutions were not called "hospitals," but they are all we have at present. It is better to take away people's freedom for a few months, after due process, than to allow them to harm themselves or others.

I feel very differently about involuntary treatment, which is allowed in most states. Involuntary treatment means that a person who is involuntarily committed (and sometimes people who are not hospitalized) can be forced to take psychiatric medications. There is a judicial procedure for this as well, in which a judge must affirm that the patient "lacks the capacity to make an informed decision regarding treatment" and would not voluntarily "comply with recommended treatment."

Involuntary treatment goes far beyond commitment, because it forces a person to take potentially dangerous drugs or be injected with them or perhaps even be subjected to ECT. Since the patient is already confined, a safety argument does not apply. As we have seen, these drugs are not benign and do not treat disease. Forcing people to take them violates their right to informed consent and may harm them. Besides, forcing people to take them is the worst possible strategy if a hospital psychiatrist wants the patients to keep taking these drugs after they are discharged.

The hospital model can be beneficial when it helps patients through an acute crisis, but paradoxically, it can be harmful to those who become chronic patients. Hospital treatment is centered on the immediate, with little effort or resources applied to a transition back to the community or to long-term rehabilitation. When any future planning is done, the focus is on medication. The result is, as I have frequently observed, that the same patients are repeatedly admitted, stabilized, and discharged again. It is a psychiatric merry-go-round.

One of the reasons for this vicious cycle is the fact that a great many patients reject taking antipsychotic medications and discontinue them as soon as they can. For the reasons I discussed earlier (the effects of stopping drug treatment), they become psychotic again and need to be readmitted. Since the common attitude of after-care is that patients must take these drugs for life, no effort is made to help them adjust to a life without the drugs.

Given all of these facts, there are some important questions about psychiatric hospitalization that society needs to think hard about:

- Is there really a legitimate medical purpose that requires all the trappings and procedures of a hospital? Or should these institutions be considered places of refuge and rehabilitation that see patients through a crisis and then transition them back to the community with strong social supports?

- Should psychiatric drugs be the chief means of stabilizing these patients, or are there alternatives with more satisfactory long-term outcomes?

- Should psychiatric patients be effectively incarcerated in locked units and treated without their consent? Should we continue to treat psychotic people as if they were dependent children with few rights and no responsibilities?

Alternatives to Hospitalization

There are alternatives to the psychiatric model of hospitalization and medication management for the most of the psychiatrically impaired. Earlier in this book, I described the nineteenth-century Moral Therapy movement, which provides a successful model for nonmedical social institutions for these people. After the demise of this movement, there was little attempt to offer this form of treatment until the Scottish psychiatrist R. D. Laing came along in the 1950s.

Laing explicitly challenged the Kraepelinian idea that the behaviors of psychotic people are signs of disease. Instead, he argued that they were attempts to communicate. He referred to a Kraepelin case description of a young man in "catatonic excitement." Rather than seeing this as a symptom of mental illness, Laing argued, "One may see his behavior as expressive of his existence."[528] Madness of the schizophrenic form represents an existential crisis for a psychologically desperate person, according to Laing.

In 1965, Laing founded an experimental community for psychotic people at Kingsley Hall in London. It was designed to allow people the room to work through their madness and internal chaos without the use of drugs or restraints. Residents were treated with kindness and respect. The program was described in a brochure at the time: "Behavior was feasible which would have been intolerable elsewhere. It was a place where people could be together and let each other be."[529] Kingsley Hall closed in 1972, when neighbors objected to it and its lease ran out.

Laing was easily dismissed by psychiatry, because he was a renegade who did not speak the language of medicine. Loren Mosher, on the other hand, was not so easily dismissed. Mosher was an establishment psychiatrist with a medical degree from Harvard; he served as the first chief of NIMH's Center for Studies of Schizophrenia from 1968 to 1980.

Mosher established the Soteria Project, which was essentially a social rehabilitation residence for psychotic people, based on Moral Therapy principles and "loosely fashioned" after Kingsley Hall. It ran from 1971 to 1983. Soteria operated two small refuges in the San Francisco Bay area of California. It admitted mostly young adults who were referred from two county-hospital emergency psychiatric screening centers and were diagnosed schizophrenic. It was designed as an experiment. The aim was to compare the outcome of Soteria's alternative treatment to that of typical inpatient psychiatric treatment.

The guiding philosophy of Soteria was that schizophrenia was not a disease, but was an "altered state of consciousness in response to crisis.... The affected person's state usually involves personality fragmentation with the loss of sense of self."[530] Treatment was conceived of not as a "doing to" the patient, but as a face-to-face "being with" the person. At Soteria, "the disruptive psychotic experience was neither aborted nor forced into a compromise, but was seen as having potential for reintegration and reconstitution." The major function of Soteria's staff was to help to "provide an atmosphere accepting strange states of mind and facilitating their integration into resident's lives." It was a nonprofessional staff, and they acted much like "trip guides" for people taking LSD by staying close to the patients and keeping them safe.

In the comparison study, all the hospitalized patients received antipsychotic drugs, while only 24 percent of the Soteria group received any (and those amounts were mostly minimal). Yet at six weeks, both groups exhibited similar improvements. Mosher concluded that "the Soteria environment proved to be as powerful as antipsychotic drugs for acute symptom reduction."[531]

At a two-year follow-up, the Soteria group had better overall outcomes than the psychiatrically hospitalized group. On a standard measure of psychopathology, the Soteria group had a 48 percent higher likelihood of showing good or excellent improvement and a 40 percent higher chance of being employed. Soteria graduates had fewer readmissions, and 43 percent of them had received no further antipsychotic medication. Only one of the psychiatrically hospitalized patients was discharged drug-free.

Like the Moral Therapy asylums before it, Soteria was extremely successful in helping people work through their psychoses and return to effective social functioning. Continued maintenance on psychiatric medications was not necessary. As Mosher explained, Soteria showed that "acute psychosis, in a properly designed environment, can be dealt with interpersonally, without medical and chemical controls used routinely in most settings."[532]

The response of traditional psychiatry to Soteria was predictable and attacking. Speaking for their profession, psychiatrists William Carpenter and Robert Buchanan asserted that, "Schizophrenia is a disease syndrome, and afflicted patients should be treated by clinicians who are informed about all relevant treatment interventions. It is improper to withhold an effective treatment based on ideology."[533] In response to such criticism, Mosher and his colleague, Voyce Hendrix, observed, "A study that implicitly calls into question the medical model, the need for psychiatric hospitalization, sometimes even the mental-health professionals themselves, is unlikely to be popular."[534]

In America, the ethos of Soteria died, but it lived on in Finland. Its beginnings there can be traced to 1969, when a psychiatric hospital in Turku, Finland, under the leadership of Yrjö Alanen initiated a psychotherapy-based program for schizophrenic patients. The aim was not to treat psychotic symptoms, but to strengthen the patients "grip on life."[535] Over the years, the Turku system was refined and outcomes continuously improved. A five-year follow-up of patients admitted in 1983 and 1984 found that 61 percent were asymptomatic and only 18 percent were disabled.

In the 1990s, most Finnish hospitals reverted to the biological model, but one in western Lapland continued a non-medication approach, called Open-Dialogue Therapy. The hospital followed the outcomes of their first-episode psychotic patients admitted between 1992 and 1997. After five years, 79 percent were asymptomatic and 67 percent had never suffered a relapse; 73 percent were working or were in school. With regard to medication, 67 percent had never taken an antipsychotic and only 20 percent were taking antipsychotics chronically.[536] Professor of psychotherapy Jaakko Seikkula reported, "There are patients who may be living in a quite peculiar way, and they may have psychotic ideas, but they still can hang on to an active life. But if they are medicated, because of the sedative action of the drugs, they lose their 'grip on life'; and that is so important."

15

The Present and the Future

This chapter deals with a number of issues in mental health and health care in general that have broad impact on society in the United States and in other industrialized countries. Specifically, the way we conceive of and deliver mental-health care is insupportable and needs to change. A number of questions must be asked:

- Is the current medical model of mental health valid and reasonable?

- Are current treatment approaches effective in relieving suffering and reducing mental-health disability?

- What could our future mental-health care system look like?

The Present System

We expect our health care, including mental health, to be based in the best science available and to be directed toward our best interests as patients. We want to trust our doctors and therapists to know and do what is right for us, not what benefits them the most. We want to believe that the drugs that pharmaceutical companies produce are real treatments for genuine medical problems. What we have, however, is a health care system often dominated by commercial interests and political power.

We are constantly bombarded by messages about the importance of being diagnosed and the power of psychotropic drugs to treat us. Biological psychiatry has been a miracle of marketing, and this story has been successfully sold to us by drug companies, mental-health providers, hospitals, and health insurers.

Advertising Drug Cures

I open up my *Sports Illustrated* and within a few pages, ads for Viagra and Cialis catch my eye. We know what kind of medical problems magazine readers have. Viagra tells me that I never back down from a challenge. What kind of challenge might that be? Cialis tells me I should be ready any time the moment is right. I wonder if that means I have to have a partner. Of course, I have to ask my doctor if these drugs are right for me. It has me wondering what I have to do to show my doctor that I have erectile dysfunction.

A few pages later, I see a big ad for Abilify. An innocuous name, that. At first I might think its purpose is to Abilify me to have an erection, but I know it's not. What it is going to do is make my depression go away when used as "adjunct" treatment along with the antidepressants I'm supposed to take. Of course, I'm supposed to ask my doctor whether Abilify is right for me.

What I am not supposed to ask is what kind of drug Abilify is. It sounds so mild, sort of like a baby aspirin. I'm not supposed to know that it is a potent antipsychotic that blocks dopamine receptors, among others, in my brain. If I take it long enough and in high enough doses, I too might get tardive dyskinesia or some other serious side effect. Perhaps, if I stopped taking it abruptly, I'll become psychotic due to a withdrawal syndrome.

In none of this drug advertising is there any suggestion that I should first try to work on any psychological and social problems that might be causing sexual dysfunction or other misery. Nowhere does it say that the drugs should be a last resort. Nor that I should use them for as short a time as possible. No, I have a brand-name disease, so I need a brand-name drug to cure it.

Psychiatry, followed by most other mental-health professions, has the trappings of science, but without the substance. Science is tentative and depends on the slow accumulation of knowledge, not dogma. Science changes with new evidence, no matter how invested scientists might be in older theories. Science must be a skeptical and open process. Faith, on the other hand, is certain and unchanging. What we have today in mental health is more faith and less science. The DSM is called "psychiatry's bible" for good reason. It was created by elite groups of psychiatrists by consensus opinion. Mental disorders were not developed as scientific hypotheses that were objectively tested. Mental disorders are what psychiatry chooses them to be.

The great problem with mental-disorder diagnoses is that they are opinions masquerading as fact. No matter how tightly the criteria for them are written, they are always malleable and subject to bias. Psychiatrist Daniel Carlat observed, "Our diagnoses are subjective and expandable, and we have few rational reasons for choosing one treatment over another."[537] What one clinician may categorize as major depression, another might call dysthymia, bipolar disorder, or something else. Making definitive diagnoses may serve the clinician well, satisfy an insurance company, and lead many patients to believe they have a complete explanation for what is wrong with them, but it is not what we should expect from a field based in science.

We, as patients, also have strong incentives to see our psychological difficulties as mental disorders. It seems so much easier to believe that we have a chemical imbalance called *depression* or *anxiety disorder* that explains why we feel bad. We can then take medications for it rather than doing the hard work of changing our lives. Having a diagnosis also legitimizes our problems in the eyes of society. It is the road to insurance payments and disability benefits. Who can hold a person accountable if they have bipolar disorder or PTSD?

It is eye-opening to recall a previous, not so distant, era when psychiatry was dominated by a belief system that seemed the polar opposite of the current one. For more than half a century, psychoanalytic concepts explained why we felt and acted the way we did. The cure then for our emotional problems was analytic therapy. When I was young, almost every sentient human I knew seem to accept it as scientific gospel. All this changed with remarkable speed with the successful marketing of psychiatric drugs and the new politics of biological psychiatry.

Has the Psychiatric Model Been Successful?

In this book, I've tried to demonstrate that there is a better way to look at people's psychological difficulties than as quasi diseases. My argument would have little practical relevance if the psychiatric model were truly beneficial for patients. Few would care if diagnosing patients with mental disorders and medicating them was curing or diminishing those disorders. Why should we bother with a complex dimensional model if medical psychiatric treatment was really decreasing suffering across the world? But has it been successful?

To determine whether the psychiatric emperor is wearing any clothes, we need to examine some objective measures of treatment efficacy. There are no biological markers of illness to look at, and these data must be gathered independently of professional self-interest. A good place to start is the statistics for mental-health disability. Disability determinations certify that people are unable to function economically in society. Successful mental-health diagnosis and treatment should lead to a decrease in disability. Has it?

Social Security Administration data compiled by Robert Whitaker indicate that in 1987 (the year Prozac was approved), the mental illness disability rate was one in every 184 adult Americans.[538] Despite all the presumed psychiatric advances, the disability rate doubled, to one in seventy-six, by 2007. The rise in disability for children is even more startling. In 1987, 16,200 children under age eighteen received disability payments for mental disorders. By 2007, there was thirty-five times that number, or more than 560,000. Further, as the use of psychiatric drugs in young children increased, the rate of disability dramatically increased.

There may be many economic and cultural shifts contributing to the enormous increase, but it cannot be that there is an epidemic of mental illness sweeping the nation. What it most likely represents is an epidemic of mental-health diagnoses founded upon political and financial reasons. Similarly, it is a stunning paradox that the vastly increased use of psychiatric drugs has gone hand-in-hand with a rising tide of psychiatric disability in children. How do we reconcile the trumpeting of psychiatric advances with these grim statistics of failure?

Another possible measure of the psychiatric model's success is to evaluate it across cultures. Those developed countries with the most access to modern psychiatric treatment should have much better outcomes for people with severe mental conditions such as schizophrenia than less developed ones. The most extensive and credible studies that looked at outcomes around the world were done by the World Health Organization (WHO).

In a study reported in 1992, WHO researchers identified patients at twelve sites around the world who were diagnosed as having a first episode of a psychotic breakdown, as diagnosed by Western standards.[539] These patients were assessed again two years later, and there were striking differences in the outcomes. More than twice as many patients in the developing countries were found to have made a complete recovery (37 percent), compared to those in the developed world. Only 16 percent of the patients from developing countries continued to show impairments in social functioning, compared to 42 percent of the patients from rich countries. When WHO followed up these same patients at intervals of fifteen and then twenty-five years, the difference in outcome remained just as large.[540]

What these results mean is that people who become psychotic in countries with the least access to psychiatric care have the highest likelihood of coming out of it successfully. This isn't due to differences between how the patients were diagnosed, because they were all evaluated in the same way. Nor was the benefit from not getting psychiatric treatment temporary. There were two major differences in treatment between the two kinds of societies. One was use of antipsychotic drugs. In the poor countries with little psychiatric care, only 16 percent of patients received regular medication, while 61 percent of the rich-country patients did. In Agra, India, only 3 percent of patients were found to be taking psychiatric medication after two years. This group had the best recovery of all the sites.

This finding suggests that patients' chances of recovery from a psychotic episode improve the most if they discontinue antipsychotics or never take them in the first place. Explain this as we may, it is the reverse of what we would expect from a successful medical model. How long would we tolerate it if we found that the lack of access to cancer treatments in the developing world improved outcomes?

The second big difference between the two kinds of cultures is social. Poor societies are simply much more accepting of people whose behavior may be bizarre and whose thinking may be eccentric. Families are more supportive, less willing to turn their loved ones over to strangers and hospitals. Aberrant behavior is not so readily stigmatized and feared. Accepting societies allow people the space and time to adjust and recover. Drugs and hospitals seem to truncate this process. It is hard to see a benefit to a medical model.

As a final issue that relates to the psychiatric medical model, we can look at the treatment of depression. The great majority of published articles show that treatment of depression by a variety of antidepressants is successful. But publication is selective. Most of the research is funded by drug companies, and there is a strong publication bias toward positive results. The truth came out when psychiatrist Erick Turner was able to ferret out all the studies drug companies had to submit to the FDA to get their drugs approved.[541] Turner tracked down seventy-six company-sponsored studies submitted for twelve new antidepressants that were approved from 1987 to 2004. Of these, thirty-eight showed the antidepressant beating a placebo, but the other thirty-six showed the same or worse results for the antidepressant. If you just read the published literature, you wouldn't know that only about half the studies showed that an antidepressant was better than nothing. Of the thirty-eight positive studies, thirty-seven were published, while of the thirty-six negatives, twenty-two were suppressed, and only three were accurately presented as negative results.

Results of this sort led the *British Journal of Psychiatry* to editorialize that there was "limited valid evidence" for using antidepressants.[542] Daniel Carlat concluded, "If I relied on the published medical literature for information (and what else can I rely on?), it would appear that 94 percent of all antidepressant trials are positive. But if I had access to all the suppressed data I would see that the truth is that only about half—51 percent—of the trials are positive."[543]

An even more damning result demonstrated what happened when people taking antidepressants discontinued them. A meta-analysis of the literature showed that half the depressed people who stopped taking antidepressants relapsed over the next fourteen months.[544] The longer patients were on the drugs, the greater the rate of relapse.

Another revealing study compared the outcomes of treatment by the newer generation of antidepressants with cognitive behavior therapy.[545] The authors randomly assigned 240 depressed patients to either drug treatment or therapy. After sixteen weeks of treatment, both groups responded equally well, with a little more than half improving. The patients who showed a positive response were divided into three groups. Those responding well to medication were either continued on their drugs or switched to a placebo, while the CBT group discontinued therapy except for three booster sessions over the next year. The result was that 76 percent of the medicated patients who were switched to a placebo relapsed into depression over the next year, as did 47 percent of those who remained on an antidepressant. However, only 31 percent of patients who received CBT relapsed. Even brief CBT had a long-lasting positive effect for many more patients than did antidepressants.

My objection to the present medical model of mental disorders is not just theoretical. It is that diagnosing and treating people as if they were sick is not beneficial and is often harmful. Psychiatric diagnosis gives a deceptive message: "there is something wrong with you, and I, the psychiatrist, will fix it with my medication." This is not a message that teaches the person to make appropriate life changes, control their behaviors, or accept the circumstances of their lives. Psychotropic drugs may have their place, but a biomedical model cannot be relied upon to relieve suffering.

The Profit Motive

Competent science imposes a discipline on all health care professions. When economic and political interests hold sway, the credibility of the science diminishes. The effect of this infection extends beyond the mental health to all areas of health care. The harm it does was ably documented by the noted oncologist Otis Webb Brawley.[546] Brawley says, "We doctors are paid for services we provide, a variant of 'piece work' that guarantees we will err on the side of selling more, sometimes believing we are helping, sometimes knowing we are not, and sometimes simply not giving a shit."

Health care (both the physical and mental kind) can be likened to an incredibly complex game with a large pot of gold at stake for the participants. The participants are numerous, and no one knows what positions they all play or what they all do. Players range from large institutions, like hospital networks, pharmaceutical companies, and medical insurers to individual providers in a multitude of professional specialties. The referees, such as they are, are entirely inadequate to enforce what rules exist.

This is how the game is played. The institutions and the professionals influence the public and politicians to authorize and legitimize their product. Patients (i.e., customers) represent pieces of gold for the providers, but the customers typically pay little or nothing individually. Instead, the players vie to get the entire community, as represented by insurance companies and the government, to pay them the highest possible amount of money. Paradoxically, the insurers have little incentive to keep costs down, because the more they spend, the more they can get from all of us.

As most of us are aware, this game is breaking down. The pot of gold cannot expand forever. There cannot be an unlimited number of professions operating by their own rules and charging the public what they like. Society must appoint powerful referees to decide what is and is not effective health care, how much can be charged for it, and how the system must be organized.

For all the money they make, even physicians are becoming increasingly dissatisfied with their profession. Thus cardiologist Sandeep Jauhar opens his recent memoir, *Doctored,* with this revelation, "When I look at my career midlife, I realized that in many ways I have become the kind of doctor I never thought I would be: impatient, occasionally indifferent, at times dismissive or paternalistic."[547]

The reason for this, as expressed by family physician Philip Caper, is that an increasing number of doctors view their work as a job rather than a profession. They have made a deal with the devil: "More and more of us become corporate employees subject to pressure to meet financial goals that are often different from what is best for our patients."[548]

We are all legitimately self-interested and wish to be rewarded for our skills and efforts. Just as individuals look out for themselves, it is entirely rational for professional groups to look out for the interests of their members.

But we all tend to believe what it is in our best interest to believe. Groups create a culture that defines how members think and behave. Financial interest is a major incentive for almost any culture, and members rarely challenge the rules of the group. Whether you are an investment banker or a mental-health professional, you will tend to hold firm beliefs that support the legitimacy of what brings in the money.

Listen to Dr. Brawley describe his experience in oncology: "Doctors who own labs have been shown to order more tests than doctors who don't. A doctor at a for-profit practice is more likely to prescribe treatments that benefit him the most. I've heard of community oncology practices that hold regular meetings to inform doctors about treatment techniques that maximize billing."[549]

I do not accuse health and mental-health professionals of any greater avarice than anyone else. Most of those I know adhere closely to the standards of their professional groups. But unless the public demands independent and untainted science, these groups may merely reinforce the group's self-interest. Speaking of the harmful overtreatment of a cancer patient, Brawley remarked, "The oncologists who gave Lilla these drugs were practicing medicine in accordance with widely accepted standards. The problem was, these standards sucked."

We must take profit motives out of the game—as much as possible—so that both individual patients and society as a whole can rely on the objectivity and judgment of health professionals. This demands that there be independent bodies on a national or international scale that set standards and practice guidelines to which the professionals can be held accountable. Brawley describes the process by which these bodies would operate as a "clinical epidemiology," which, he says, "is about cleansing yourself of prejudice, asking questions broadly and getting reliable advice from people who have no financial stake in the process." There is a partial model that attempts to do this for general medical practice called the United States Preventive Services Task Force (USPSTF). Brawley notes that USPSTF created a panel to set standards for breast cancer screening. This panel excluded radiologists in order "to rise above medical practice, self-interest and self-delusion."

USPSTF has similar guidelines in place for alcohol misuse, cognitive impairment, and depression, but only for general medical practices. In this country, the only treatment guidelines for mental health are those promulgated by the American Psychiatric Association. There is nothing like a national panel with a clinical epidemiology orientation for mental health, but there needs to be.

A New Model for Mental Health

A dimensional model for mental-health dysfunction already partially exists in our understanding of cognitive competence. Until recent years, low intelligence was termed *mental retardation*. It was relabeled *intellectual disability* because the negative connotation of calling a person *mentally retarded* was seen as too stigmatizing. This is because the term *mental retardation* categorizes people as having a specific mental disorder. We understand there is no such thing.

Intellectual disability implies a continuum. There is no cut-off point, only a professional determination based on what can be learned about a person's functional abilities, supplemented by cognitive testing. It is accepted that it is an opinion that a person is intellectually disabled and that opinion is used to qualify the person for psychological and social services and determines the level of help necessary.

Intellectual disabilities range from mild to profound, and these labels are merely descriptions that point to levels of impairment in certain sorts of functional abilities. We recognize that there is likely to be a biological component to intellectual disability, which might be based in genetic anomalies or brain damage, and most of the time, we understand that it is simply part of life's variability. No one would posit a chemical imbalance. Even the most ardent biological psychiatrist would not believe that someday we will have a chemical cure for intellectual disability. But even though intellectual disability is not a medical disease, that does not mean that we should stop looking for treatable or preventable causes, and this is so for all types of dysfunction. A specific search for the biological causes of mental disorder diagnoses, however, is unlikely to be productive.

If we went back to using categorical terms like mental retardation, it would inevitably be stigmatizing, because it suggests that certain people are different from other human beings. They either have a disease or are somehow not quite human. I have often heard people argue that we must destigmatize mental illness, but the very same people call others "schizophrenic." The only way to legitimize people who exhibit functional deficits is to stop calling them names.

There are many reasons for characterizing people's problems, but I see little valid purpose in categorizing them. There are two important pieces of information we might wish to know about a person's dysfunction. The first is qualitative—what sort of dysfunction it is. The second is quantitative—how severely dysfunctional the person is. These are judgment calls that should only be made after all available information about an individual is obtained and weighed. I do not think that assigning a mental disorder diagnosis adds anything to this process, and in fact, it truncates it. It is far too easy to listen briefly to a patient, then pigeonhole him or her with a label, and think you are done. My model is to gather as much biological, psychological, and social information as possible before characterizing an individual's most significant dimension of dysfunction. Labels only help to characterize the pattern of dysfunction.

The Proliferation of Mental Help Professions

The current profusion of mental-health professions works against any attempt to rationalize the system. There is a Tower of Babel of professional tribes competing with one another. Each has its own rites of passage, theories, and even language. Each profession fights to improve its status in the hierarchy of providers. The battle is over prestige and economic gain. Each group looks to be licensed—not to inform the public, but to gain economic advantage.

It is a marketing process controlled by emotion and salesmanship, not logic and results. Psychiatry is at the top of the heap. It got there through its association with the rest of medicine and because it had the powerful backing of drug companies and hospitals. Only psychiatrists and nurse practitioners can prescribe psychiatric medications. Nurse practitioners are now horning in on psychiatry as a cheaper alternative. I do not believe that either profession can continue into the future in its present form. Psychiatry is not the same as the rest of medicine. The core of medicine is the treatment of disease, not a disease metaphor.

Clinical psychology is the other major doctoral-level mental-health profession. It is backed by a science of psychology, just as physical medicine has biology. Psychology is the science of human behavior and has developed an extensive and valid literature. Psychologists have often been the innovators of new forms of psychotherapy. Unfortunately, my experience is that many clinical psychologists have a limited acquaintance with science and prefer to ignore it. Even those well versed in psychological science usually have little knowledge of medical science. This prevents them from working effectively with medical professionals.

Sub-doctoral professionals have taken on much of the duties of therapy and counseling. The profession of social work, as the name implies, began by helping the poor find resources, but most social workers now have become independent therapists. Priests and ministers have always been counselors for their flocks, but now they have also morphed into pastoral counselors and have hung out their shingles. There are also a variety of function-specific counselors, such as substance-abuse and marital counselors and whoever else can get legislatures to license them. I have seen mental-health clinicians with fifteen letters after their names. I suppose they specialize in alphabet soup.

I recognize that there are many caring, competent, and thoughtful clinicians in every one of these professions. But I do not see how this profusion of mental-health professions makes any sense. In order to have a credible mental-health system in the future, we must develop a new set of professions with consistently defined standards of training and competence. These should be parallel to, but not part of, the medical system.

To start with, I suggest we replace psychiatrists and psychologists with one combined profession that we might call *doctor of behavioral health*. This new profession would not be trained either in medical schools or departments of psychology. They would be independent, as schools of pharmacy are. The basic education would be a combination of psychological and medical science. There would be a heavy emphasis on neuroscience, because the advancing knowledge of how the brain works will become increasingly important in mental-health evaluations. The clinical component of this new doctoral training would not be organized around mental disorders, but on an understanding of the dimensions of dysfunction. Clinical teaching would emphasize therapeutic techniques that help patients more successfully function in the world and mitigate their distress.

These new doctors would be able to work in both medical and behavioral settings. They would interact with all other health care providers in a true team effort that addresses all a patient's biological, psychological, and social needs in a unified manner. In this health care utopia, the other mental-health professions—including social workers and counselors—would have specific roles as well, but they would need to be carefully defined.

Final Thoughts

The paradox of the present health care system (or lack thereof) is that it encourages a separation between mind and body. It diverts patients onto two tracks. When the patient comes through the medical track, there is an emphasis on medical tests and procedures, with little regard to psychological and social factors. But when physicians suspect a nonphysical component, such as depression or anxiety, they send the person over to mental health in a separate silo. These parallel systems are a cumbersome process that rarely leads to a team effort.

An exclusively physical or exclusively mental approach may be appropriate in acute or crisis situations. If someone is having a heart attack or has a broken leg, psychological and social factors don't immediately matter. But as health needs become more complex or chronic, psychological and social factors—along with the physical—must be addressed for a successful outcome. What is needed is an integrated health care system that properly addresses people's needs at the level required.

I have experienced both ways of doing health care. In the years when I was part of a chronic-pain program, we attempted a true interdisciplinary team approach. A rehabilitation medicine physician, an anesthesiologist, a physical therapist, and I evaluated each new patient to see what we could offer. We met as a team to form a joint impression and a treatment plan that we thought would benefit the patient the most. While other team members worked on physical exercise and pain management, my job was to run psychosocial pain groups and to see some patients individually to help change self-defeating beliefs and attitudes toward their pain.

The pain program was a model for an integrated treatment, but it ran into the headwinds of the prevailing health care system. For one thing, purely medical interventions, such as steroid injections or even surgeries, were far more lucrative to the providers and got much less resistance from both patients and insurance companies then did a tedious multidisciplinary approach. The hospital that owned us saw the numbers and supported what paid the best. It became a pain procedure clinic with a little psychological tail that could occasionally wag. I got out.

The other big problem that we encountered in the pain program was the multitude of players in our fragmented health care system. The patients who were referred to our pain program were also seeing a parade of family physicians, orthopedic surgeons, psychiatrists, and others who each had a finger in the pie. They prescribed pain medications, a host of psychiatric drugs, and often recommended surgical procedures that were usually antithetical to our program's functional goals. The sad result was a local example of what happens with increasing regularity in our dysfunctional system. Only a minority of chronic-pain patients could be successfully extracted from the pain disability system.

Since my days in the pain program, I have been asked to do hundreds of independent evaluations of patients disabled by either chronic pain and/ or psychiatric disorders. Reviews of these patients' records open another discouraging window. Most of these records are hundreds if not thousands of pages long and contain treatment notes from scores of providers. Each provider had his or her own pet diagnoses to explain the patient's subjective experiences. If it was a medical specialist, I would read diagnoses such as reflex sympathetic dystrophy, fibromyalgia, or degenerative disc disease. If the provider was a psychiatrist or other mental-health professional, the diagnoses routinely included major depression, anxiety disorder, and post-traumatic stress disorder.

It was apparent as I read through these records that those offering new evaluations and treatment rarely read anybody else's reports. Each of them did their own thing, as if no one else was involved or had attempted any treatment before them. Few of them, especially the mental-health providers, seemed concerned about the long-term outcomes of their patients. What seemed to matter most was that the patient accepted the doctor's diagnosis and kept coming. It was no surprise to me that these patients became increasingly disabled and that each new treatment made their problems more intractable.

The health care system does not need to be this way. It would not be if we, the public, insisted on an integrated and rational system that had to evaluate whole persons and make them more functional, not less.

Notes

Preface

1 Tonya Lurhmann, *Of Two Minds: The Growing Disorder in American Psychiatry* (New York: Knopf, 2000).

2 Ethan Watters, *Crazy like Us: The Globalization of the American Psyche* (New York: Free Press, 2011).

3 Robert Whitaker, *Anatomy of an Epidemic: Magic Bullets, Psychiatric Drugs, and the Astonishing Rise of Mental Illness in America* (New York: Broadway, 2011).

4 Thomas Szasz, *Psychiatry: The Science of Lies* (Syracuse, NY: Syracuse University Press, 2008).

5 By a dimension, I mean a range without any breaks. Familiar examples are height and weight. There are unusually short people and very tall ones, but height forms a continuous dimension and who is short and who is tall as a matter of opinion.

1: Introduction and Some Definitions

6 B. F. Skinner was a Harvard professor; his name became synonymous with the behaviorist school of psychology.

7 Robert L. Gallon and Christina Herring, "A Treatment Program for Headaches," in *The Psychosomatic Approach to Illness*, ed. Robert L. Gallon (New York: Elsevier Biomedical, 1982).

8 Alexander Lowen, *The Betrayal of the Body* (New York: Macmillan, 1967).

9 E. O. Wilson, *The Social Conquest of Earth* (New York: Liveright Publishing, 2012).

10 *Dorland's Illustrated Medical Dictionary*, 32rd ed. (Philadelphia: Saunders, 2011), *s.v.* "disease."

11 As recounted in Szasz, *Psychiatry: The Science of Lies.*

2: How Madness Became Medical

12 Quotes in this section and other information about the ancient under-standing of madness are described in Roy Porter, *Madness: A Brief History* (Oxford: Oxford University Press, 2003).

13 The early history of psychiatry in America described here is reported in detail in Robert Whitaker, *Mad in America: Bad Science, Bad Medicine, and the Enduring Mistreatment of the Mentally Ill* (Cambridge, MA: Basic Books, 2002).

14 For an authoritative biography of Freud, see Peter Gay, *Freud: A Life for Our Time* (New York: W. W. Norton, 1988).

15 For a brief and readable description of Freudian theory, see Calvin S. Hall, *A Primer of Freudian Psychology* (New York: Mentor Books, 1955).

16 *Libido* meant the sexual energy of life, and *thanatos* was the death instinct.

17 For an extensive discussion of Kraepelin, see German E. Berrios and Roy Porter, eds., *A History of Clinical Psychiatry: The Origin and History Psychiatric Disorders* (New York: New York University Press, 1995).

3: The Rise of Psychiatric Diagnosis

18 German E. Barrios and Roy Porter, *A History of Clinical Psychiatry: The Origin and History of Psychiatric Disorders* (New York: New York University Press, 1995).

19 Richard P. Bentall, *Madness Explained: Psychosis and Human Nature* (New York: Penguin Books, 2003).

20 This is the original usage of the term *autism;* psychiatry now uses *autism* to describe a disorder.

21 Bentall, *Madness Explained.*

22 Barrios and Porter, *A History of Clinical Psychiatry.*

23 Bentall, *Madness Explained.*

24 Bentall, *Madness Explained.*

25 Bentall, *Madness Explained.*

26 Gerald Klerman, "The Evolution of a Scientific Nosology," in *Schizophenia: Science and Practice,* ed. J. C. Shershow (Cambridge, MA: Harvard University Press, 1978).

27 Robert L. Spitzer, "On Pseudoscience in Science, Logic in Remission, and Psychiatric Diagnosis: A Critique of Rosenberg's 'On Being Sane in Insane Places,'" *Journal of Abnormal Psychology* 84, no. 5 (1975): 442–52.

28 J. E., Cooper et al., *Psychiatric Diagnosis in New York and London* (Oxford University Press, 1972).

29 American Psychiatric Association, *Diagnostic and Statistical Manual of Mental Disorders*, 4th ed., 1994.

30 J. Cloud, "What Counts as Crazy? This Is the Book Doctors Use to Define Mental Illness—and It's All About to Change," *Time*, March 3, 2013, 42–45.

31 L. Cosgrove and S. Krimsky, "A Comparison of DSM-IV and DSM-5 Panel Members' Financial Associations with Industry: A Pernicious Problem Persists," *PLoS Medicine* 9, no. 3 (2012).

32 Allen Frances, "DSM-5 Is a Guide, Not a Bible: Simply Ignore Its 10 Worst Changes," *Huffington Post*, December 12, 2012.

4: An Alternative Model

33 These quotes are from the introduction to *Diagnostic and Statistical Manual of Mental Disorders*, 4th ed.

34 Joanna Moncrieff, *The Myth of the Chemical Cure: A Critique of Psychiatric Drug Treatment* (New York: Palgrave Macmillan, 2008).

35 A. Schwartz and S. Cohen, "ADHD Seen in 11% of U.S. Children and Diagnoses Rise," *New York Times*, March 31, 2013.

36 Stuart L. Kaplan, "Mommy, Am I Really Bipolar?" *Newsweek*, June 27, 2011.

37 Marcia Angell, "The Epidemic of Mental Illness: Why?" *New York Review of Books*, June 23, 2011.

38 Jordan W. Smoller, "The Etiology and Treatment of Childhood," *Journal of Polymorphous Perversity* 2, no. 2 (1985): 3–7.

39 Davis J. Kupfer, Michael B. First, and Darrel A. Regier, eds., *A Research Agenda for DSM-V* (Washington, DC: American Psychiatric Association, 2002).

40 N. Craddock, M. C. O'Donovan, and M. J. Owen, "Psychosis Genetics: Modeling the Relationship between Schizophrenia, Bipolar Disorder and

Mixed (or Schizoaffective) Psychoses," *Schizophrenia Bulletin* 35, no. 3 (2009): 482–90.

41 Daniel J. Luchins, "At Issue: Will the Term *Brain Disease* Reduce the Stigma and Promote Parity for Mental Illness?" *Schizophrenia Bulletin* 30, no. 4 (2004): 1043–48.

42 Ronald W. Pies, "Psychiatry and the Myth of 'Medicalization,'" *Psychiatric Times*, April 18, 2013.

43 Sally Satel, "Why the Fuss over the DSM-5?" *New York Times*, May 12, 2013, Sunday Review.

44 S. Nassir Ghaemi, "DSM-5: If You Don't Like the Effects, Look at the Causes," *Mood Swings* (blog), *Psychology Today*, January 9, 2013.

45 Thomas Insel, "Transforming Diagnosis," *Director's Blog* (blog), *National Institute of Mental Health*, April 29, 2013, www.nimh.nih.gov/about/director/2013/transforming-diagnosis.shtml.

46 Jamie Doward, "Psychiatrists under Fire in Mental Health Battle," *Guardian*, May 11, 2013.

47 George L. Engel, "The Need for a New Medical Model: A Challenge for Biomedicine," *Science* 196, no. 4286 (1977): 129–36.

48 Gerald M. Edelman, *Neural Darwinism: The Theory of Neuronal Group Selection* (New York: Basic Books, 1987).

49 Irving I. Gottesman, *Schizophrenia Genesis: The Origins of Madness* (New York: W. H. Freeman, 1991).

50 Elkhonon Goldberg, *The New Executive Brain: Frontal Lobes in a Complex World* (New York: Oxford University Press, 2009).

51 Antonio Damasio, *Looking for Spinoza: Joy, Sorrow, and the Feeling Brain* (Orlando, FL: Harcourt Books, 2003).

52 Joseph LeDoux, *Synaptic Self: How Our Brains Become Who We Are* (New York: Penguin Books, 2002).

53 Antonio Damasio, *Descartes' Error: Emotion, Reason, and the Human Brain* (New York: Penguin Books, 1994).

54 John J. Ratey, *A User's Guide to the Brain: Perception, Attention and the Four Theaters of the Brain* (New York: Vintage Books, 2002).

55 Goldberg, *The New Executive Brain.*

56 Goldberg, *The New Executive Brain.*

57 R. Davidson, "Cerebral Asymmetry, Emotion and Affective Style," in *Brain Asymmetry,* ed. R. Davidson and K. Udall (Cambridge, MA: MIT Press, 1995), 361–88.

58 Jaak Panksepp, *Affective Neuroscience: The Foundations of Human and Animal Emotions* (New York: Oxford University Press, 1998).

59 These definitions are as formulated by Jaak Panksepp and Lucy Bivan, *The Archaeology of Mind: Neural Evolutionary Origins of Human Emotions* (New York: W. W. Norton, 2011).

60 Ratey, *A User's Guide to the Brain.*

61 E. F. Torrey, *Surviving Schizophrenia* (New York: HarperCollins, 2001).

62 Ratey, *A User's Guide to the Brain.*

63 Helen Fisher, *Why We Love: The Nature and Chemistry of Romantic Love* (New York: Henry Holt, 2004).

64 Peter R. Breggin, *Medication Madness: The Role of Psychiatric Drugs in Cases of Violence, Suicide, and Crime* (New York: St. Martin's Griffin, 2008).

65 Albert Bandura, *Self-Efficacy: The Exercise of Control* (New York: Worth Publishers, 1997).

66 Albert Bandura, ed., *Self-Efficacy in Changing Societies* (Cambridge: Cambridge University Press, 1995).

67 Philip Zimbardo, *The Lucifer Effect: Understanding How Good People Turn Evil* (New York: Random House, 2007).

5: Reality Misperception

68 What psychiatry means by *reliability* is agreement. The challenge is whether psychiatry can define a diagnostic term so that a group of psychiatrists (with the same training) can evaluate a patient and come to the same diagnosis. Reliability is important, but it is not the same as validity. Validity requires an objective standard, such as a brain scan or an autopsy result.

69 Sigmund Freud, Letter to Martha Bernay, 1882, quoted in Earnest Jones, *Sigmund Freud: Life and Work* (London: Hogarth Press, 1953).

70 Daniel C. Javit and Joseph T. Coyle, "Decoding Schizophrenia" *Scientific American* 290, no. 1 (2004): 48–55.

71 E. Fuller Torrey, *Surviving Schizophrenia*, 4th ed. (New York: Harper Paperbacks, 2001).

72 J. Elkes and Charmian Elkes, "Effects of Chlorpromazine on the Behavior of Chronically Overactive Psychotic Patients," *British Medical Journal* 2 (1954): 560–65.

73 The National Institute of Mental Health Psychopharmacology Service Center Collaborative Study Group, "Phenothiazine Treatment in Acute Schizophrenia," *Archives of General Psychiatry* 10 (1964): 246–61.

74 J. M. Van Rossum, "The Significance of Dopamine Receptor Blockade for the Action of Neuroleptic Drugs," in *Neuro-psycho-pharmacology*, ed. H. Brill (Amsterdam: Excerpta Medica Foundation, 1966).

75 S. Matthysse, "Antipsychotic Drug Actions: A Clue to the Neuropathology of Schizophrenia," *Federation Proceedings* 32, no. 2 (1973): 200–25.

76 Herbert Y. Meltzer and Stephen M. Stahl, "The Dopamine Hypothesis of Schizophrenia: A Review," *Schizophrenia Bulletin* 2, no. 1 (1976): 19–76.

77 Nancy C. Andreasen, "Understanding Schizophrenia: A Silent Spring," *American Journal of Psychiatry* 155 (1998): 1657–59.

78 Studies reported by Daniel B. Smith, *Muses, Madmen, and Prophets: Rethinking the History, Science and Meaning of Auditory Hallucinations* (New York: Penguin Books, 2007).

79 T. B. Posey and M. E. Losch, "Auditory Hallucinations of Hearing Voices in 375 Normal Subjects," *Imagination, Cognition and Personality* 2, no. 2 (1983): 99–113.

80 Molly Worthen, "A Great Awakening," review of When God Talks Back: Understanding the American Evangelical Relationship with God, by T. M. Luhrmann," New York Times, April 27, 2012.

81 Cited in Smith, *Muses, Madmen and Prophets*.

82 Results reported by Bentall, *Madness Explained*.

83 E. Peters et al., "Delusional Ideation in Religious and Psychotic Popula-
tions," *British Journal of Clinical Psychology* 38 (1999): 83–96.

84 Nancy Andreason, "Thought, Language and Communication Disorders: Diagnostic Significance," *Archives of General Psychiatry* 36 (1979):
1325–30.

85 Richie Poulton et al., "Children's Self-Reported Psychotic Symptoms and
Adult Schizophreniform Disorder: A 15 Year Longitudinal Study," *Archives
of General Psychiatry* 57 (2000): 1053–108.

86 This historical discussion is based on the review in Bentall, *Madness
Explained.*

87 George E. Vaillant and J. C. Perry, "Personality Disorders," in *Comprehensive Textbook of Psychiatry,* 4th ed., ed. H. I. Kaplan and B. J. Sadock (Baltimore: Williams and Wilkins, 1985).

88 R. D. Laing, *The Divided Self* (New York: Penguin Books, 1965).

89 Jerold J. Kreisman, *I Hate You, Don't Leave Me: Understanding the Borderline Personality* (New York: Avon, 1991).

90 P. S. Holzman and S. Matthysse, "The Genetics of Schizophrenia: A
Review," *Psychological Science* 1, no. 5 (1990): 279–86.

91 K. S. Kendler and S. R. Diehl, "The Genetics of Schizophrenia: A Current, Genetic-Epidemiologic Perspective," *Schizophrenia Bulletin* 19, no. 2
(1993): 261–85.

92 Pekka Tienari, "Interaction between Genetic Vulnerability and Family
Environment: The Finnish Adoptive Study of Schizophrenia," *Acta Psychiatrica Scandinavica* 84 (1991): 460–65.

93 Wendy Kates et al., "Neuroanatomic Predictors to Prodromal Psychosis in
Vellocardiofacial Syndrome (22q11.2 Deletion Syndrome): A Longitudinal Study," *Biological Psychiatry* 69, no. 10 (2011): 945–52.

94 A. M. MacIntosh et al., "Longitudinal Volume Reductions in People with
High Genetic Risk of Schizophrenia As They Develop Psychosis," *Biological Psychiatry* 69, no. 10 (2011): 953–58.

95 Brian Miller, "Never Quite As It Seems: An Apparently Chance Association May Explain a Lot about Schizophrenia," *Psychiatric Times,* April 11,
2013.

96 D. R. Weinberger and K. F. Berman, "Speculation on the Meaning of Cerebral Metabolic Hypofrontality in Schizophrenia," *Schizophrenia Bulletin* 14 (1988): 157–68.

97 D. R. Weinberger, K. F. Berman, and R. F. Zec, "Physiologic Dysfunction of Dorsolateral Prefrontal Cortex in Schizophrenia: I. Regional Cerebral Blood Flow Evidence," *Archives of General Psychiatry* 43 (1986): 114–24.

98 Julian Jaynes, *The Origins of Consciousness in the Breakdown of the Bicameral Mind* (New York: Houghton Mifflin, 1976).

99 Peter R. Breggin, *Toxic Psychiatry* (New York: St. Martin's Press, 1991).

100 Manfred Bleuler, *The Schizophrenic Disorders* (New Haven, CT: Yale University Press, 1978).

101 D. Holowka et al., "Childhood Abuse and Dissociative Symptoms in Adult Schizophrenia," *Schizophrenia Research* 60 (2003): 87-90.

102 John Read et al., "Childhood Trauma, Loss and Stress," in *Models of Madness: Psychological, Social and Biological Approaches to Madness,* ed. John Read, Loren R. Mosher, and R. P. Bentall (New York: Routledge, 2004): 223–52.

103 Gregory Bateson et al., "Toward a Theory of Schizophrenia," *Behavioral Science* 1 (1956): 251–64.

104 Gregory Bateson et al., "A Note on the Double Bind," *Family Process* 2 (1962): 154–61.

105 D. Miklowitz and D. Stackman, "Communication Deviance in Families of Schizophrenic and Other Psychiatric Patients," *Progress in Experimental Personality and Psychopathology Research* 15 (1992): 1–46.

106 M. Annet Nugter et al., "Parental Communication Deviance," *Acta Psychiatrica Scandinavica* 95 (1997): 199–204.

107 M. J. Goldstein, "The UCLA High-Risk Project," *Schizophrenia Bulletin* 13 (1987): 505–14.

108 D. Kavanaugh, "Recent Developments in EE and Schizophrenia," *British Journal of Psychiatry* 160 (1992): 601–20.

109 Goldstein, "The UCLA High-Risk Project."

110 Robert Whitaker, *Mad in America: Bad Science, Bad Medicine, and the Enduring Mistreatment of the Mentally Ill* (New York: Basic Books, 2002).

111 N. Jablonsky et al., "Schizophrenia: Manifestations, Incidence and Course in Different Cultures," *Psychological Medicine*, supplement 20 (1992): 1–97.

112 R. P. Bentall, *Madness Explained: Psychosis and Human Nature* (New York: Penguin Global, 2005).

113 Tonya Luhrmann, "Hallucinatory 'Voices' Shaped by Local Culture, Stanford Anthropologist Says," *Stanford Report*, July 16, 2014.

6: Depression and Mood Dysfunction

114 Antonio Damasio, *The Feeling of What Happens: Body and Emotion in the Making of Consciousness* (Orlando: Harcourt Books, 1999).

115 D. J. Bauman, R. B. Cialdini, and D. T. Fendrick, "Altruism as Hedonism: Helping and Self-Gratification as Equivalent Responses," *Journal of Personality and Social Psychology* 40 (1981): 1039–46.

116 David Healy, *Mania: A Short History of Bipolar Disorder* (Baltimore: The Johns Hopkins University Press, 2008).

117 G. D. Berrios, "Mood Disorders," in *A History of Clinical Psychiatry*, ed. G D. Berrios and R. Porter (New York: New York University Press, 1995).

118 Quoted in Berrios, "Mood Disorders."

119 Moncrieff, *The Myth of the Chemical Cure.*

120 Quoted in Whitaker, *Anatomy of an Epidemic.*

121 Jonathan Cole, "Therapeutic Efficacy of Anti-Depressant Drugs," *Journal of the American Psychiatric Association* 190 (1964): 122–30.

122 D. Schuyler, *The Depression Spectrum* (New York: Jason Aronson, 1974), 47.

123 Quoted in Moncrieff, *The Myth of the Chemical Cure.*

124 D. Henderson and R. D. Gillespie, *Henderson and Gillespie's Textbook of Psychiatry*, 9th ed. (New York: Oxford University Press, 1962).

125 W. Eaton, "The Burden of Mental Disorders," *Epidemiological Reviews* 30 (2008): 1–14.

126 J. P. Feighner et al., "Diagnostic Criteria for Use in Psychiatric Research," *Archives of General Psychiatry* 26 (1972): 57–63.

127 P. J. Clayton, J. A. Halikos, and W. L. Maurice, "The Bereavement of the Widowed," *Diseases of the Nervous System* 32 (1971): 597–604.

128 *Diagnostic and Statistical Manual of Mental Disorders*, 3rd ed. (Washington DC: American Psychiatric Association, 1980).

129 J. C. Wakefield et al., "Extending the Bereavement Exclusion for Major Depression to Other Losses: Evidence from the National Comorbidity Survey," *Archives of General Psychiatry* 64 (2007): 433–40.

130 American Psychiatric Association, *Diagnostic and Statistical Manual of Mental Disorders, 3rd ed.,* 1980.

131 Quoted in K. Lamb, R. Pies, and S. Zisook, "The Bereavement Exclusion for the Diagnosis of Major Depression," *Psychiatry* 7, no. 7 (2010): 19–25.

132 Sonali Deraniyagala, *Wave* (New York: Alfred A. Knopf, 2013).

133 Gary Greenberg, *Manufacturing Depression: The Secret History of a Modern Disease* (New York: Simon and Schuster, 2010).

134 Caroln A. Walter and Judith L. M. McCoyd, *Grief and Loss Across the Lifespan: A BioPsychoSocial Perspective* (New York: Springer, 2009).

135 Sigmund Freud, "Mourning and Melancholia," In *The Standard Edition of the Complete Works of Sigmund Freud,* ed. J. Stracher, vol. 14 (London: Hogarth, 1957 [1917]).

136 Robert A. Neimeyer, *Meaning Reconstruction and the Meaning of Loss* (Washington, DC: American Psychological Association, 2001).

137 Kenneth Doka, *Introduction to Disenfranchise Grief: New Directions, Challenges, and Strategies for Practice* (Champlain, IL: Research Press, 2000).

138 Colin M. Parkes, *Bereavement: Studies of Grief in Adult Life,* 3rd ed. (New York: Routledge, 2001).

139 Nathan S. Kline, "Monoamine Oxidase Inhibitors: An Unfinished Picturesque Tale," in *Discoveries in Biological Psychiatry,* ed. F. Ayd and B. Blackwell, 194–204 (Philadelphia: Lippincott, 1970).

140 Ronald Kuhn, "The Imipramine Story," in *Discoveries in Biological Psychiatry,* ed. F. Ayd and B. Blackwell, (Philadelphia: Lippincott, 1970), 205–217.

141 Peter D. Kramer, *Listening to Prozac* (New York: Penguin Books, 1993).

142 J. W. Maas, "Pretreatment Neurotransmitter Metabolite Levels and Response to Tricyclic Anti-Depressant Drugs," *American Journal of Psychiatry* 141 (1984): 1159–71.

143 David Healy, "Ads for SSRI Anti-Depressants Are Misleading," *PLOS Medicine* (news release), November 2005.

144 A. Caspi et al., "Influence of Life Stress on Depression: Moderation by a Polymorphism of 5-HTT Gene," *Science* 301 (2003): 386–89.

145 Turhan Conli and Klaus-Peter Lesch, "Long Story Short: A Serotonin Transporter in Emotional Regulation and Social Cognition," *Nature Neuroscience* 10 (2007): 1103–9.

146 Albert Ellis, *Overcoming Destructive Beliefs, Feelings, and Behaviors: New Directions for Rational Emotive Behavior Therapy* (Amherst, NY: Prometheus Books, 2001).

147 Aaron T. Beck and Brad A. Alford, *Depression: Causes and Treatment*, 2nd ed. (Philadelphia: University of Pennsylvania Press, 2009).

148 Albert Bandura, *Self-Efficacy: The Exercise of Control* (New York: W. H. Freeman, 1997).

149 Neil Burton, "Depressive Realism: Wisdom or Madness?" *Psychology Today*, June 12, 2012.

150 Rachel Aviv, "The Imperial Presidency," *The New Yorker*, September 9, 2013.

151 David Healy, *Mania: A Short History of Bipolar Disorder* (Baltimore, MD: Johns Hopkins University Press, 2008).

152 Healy, Mania: A Short History of Bipolar Disorder.

153 Joseph Schildkraut, "The Catecholamine Hypothesis of Affective Disorders: A Review of the Supporting Evidence," American Journal of Psychiatry 122 (1965): 519–22.

154 R. L. Spitzer, J. Endicott, and E. Robbins, "Research Diagnostic Criteria (RDC) for a Selected Group of Functional Disorders," *New York State Department of Mental Hygiene*, Biometrics Branch, 1975.

155 D. L. Dunner, J. L. Fleiss, and R. R. Fieve, "The Course of Development of Mania in Patients with Recurrent Depression," *American Journal of Psychiatry* 133 (1976): 905–8.

156 Healy, *Mania: A Short History of Bipolar Disorder.*

157 Quoted in Healy, *Mania: A Short History of Bipolar Disorder.*

158 M. Zimmerman, C. J. Ruggero, I. Chelminski, and D. Young, "Is Bipolar Disorder Overdiagnosed?" *Journal of Clinical Psychiatry* 69 (2008): 935–40.

159 James Phelps, "Overdiagnosis: Examine the Assumptions, Anticipate New Bipolar Criteria," *Psychiatric Times* 30, no. 3 (2013).

160 Joshua W. Shenk, "Lincoln's Great Depression," *The Atlantic,* October 2005.

161 S. Nassir Ghaemi, *A First-rate Madness: Uncovering Links between Leadership and Mental illness* (New York: Penguin Books, 2011).

162 Cited in Ghaemi, *A First-rate Madness.*

7: Anxiety and Its Consequences

163 Quoted in Scott Stossel, *My Age of Anxiety: Fear, Hope, Dread, and the Search for Peace of Mind* (New York: Knopf, 2014).

164 Aaron T. Beck and Gary Emery, *Anxiety Disorders and Phobias: A Cognitive Perspective* (New York: Basic Books, 1985).

165 Quotes from Beck and Emery, *Anxiety Disorders and Phobias.*

166 Joseph LeDoux, *The Emotional Brain: The Mysterious Underpinnings of Emotional Life* (New York: Simon and Schuster, 1996).

167 This discussion follows the review by Margaret Wehrenberg and Steven M. Prinz, *The Anxious Brain: The Neurobiological Basis of Anxiety Disorders and How to Effectively Treat Them* (New York: W. W. Norton, 2007).

168 LeDoux, *The Emotional Brain.*

169 Ratey, *A User's Guide to the Brain.*

170 Wehrenberg and Prinz, *The Anxious Brain.*

171 LeDoux, *Synaptic Self.*

172 Beck and Emery, *Anxiety Disorders and Phobias.*

173 Albert Ellis and Robert A. Harper, *A Guide to Rational Living* (New York: Institute for Rational Living, 1961).

174 Beck and Emery, *Anxiety Disorders and Phobias.*

175 Wehrenberg and Prinz, *The Anxious Brain.*

176 Wehrenberg and Prinz, *The Anxious Brain.*

177 S. Reiss, W. Silverman, and C. Weems, "Anxiety Sensitivity," In *A Developmental Psychopathology of Anxiety,* ed. M. W. Vesey and M. R. Dobbs, 92–111 (New York: Oxford University Press, 2001).

178 Beck and Emery, *Anxiety Disorders and Phobias.*

179 Wehrenberg and Prinz, *The Anxious Brain.*

180 A. T. Beck, R. Laude, and M. Bohnert, "Ideational Components of Anxiety Neurosis," *Archives of General Psychiatry* 31 (1974): 319–25.

181 G. A. Hibbert, "Ideational Components of Anxiety: Their Original Content," *British Journal of Psychiatry* 144 (1984): 618–24.

182 Raeann Dumont, *The Sky Is Falling: Understanding and Coping with Phobias, Panic, and Obsessive-Compulsive Disorders* (New York: W. W. Norton, 1997).

183 Beck and Emery, *Anxiety Disorders and Phobias.*

184 Dumont, *The Sky Is Falling.*

185 Beck and Emery, *Anxiety Disorders and Phobias.*

186 Dumont, *The Sky Is Falling.*

187 D. Mataix-Cols, A. Pertusa, and J. F. Leckman, "Issues for DSM-V: How Should Obsessive-Compulsive and Related Disorders Be Classified?" *American Journal of Psychiatry* 164 (2007): 1313–14.

188 D. Mataix-Cols, "Deconstructing Obsessive-Compulsive Disorder: A Multidimensional Perspective," *Current Opinion in Psychiatry* 19, no. 1 (2006): 84–89.

189 R. H. Bloch et al., "Meta-Analysis of the Symptoms Structure of the Obsessive-Compulsive Disorder," *American Journal of Psychiatry* 165 (2008): 1532–42.

190 J. F. Lechman, M. H. Bloch, and R. A. King, "Symptom Dimensions and Subtypes of Obsessive-Compulsive Disorder: A Developmental Perspective," *Dialogues in Clinical Neuroscience* 11, no. 1 (2009): 21–33.

191 DSM-5, *s.v.* "Tourette's Syndrome."

192 Jaynes, *The Origins of Consciousness in the Breakdown of the Bicameral Mind.*

193 Y. A. Aderibigbe, R. M. Bloch, and W. R. Walker, "Prevalence of Depersonalization and Derealization in a Rural Population," *Social Psychiatry and Psychiatric Epidemiology* 36 (2001): 63–69.

194 Elizabeth F. Howell, *The Dissociative Mind* (Hillsdale, NJ: Analytic Press, 2005).

195 David H. Gleaves, "The Sociocognitive Model of Dissociative Identity Disorder: A Re-Examination of the Evidence," *Psychological Bulletin* 120, no. 1 (1996): 42–59.

196 J. L. Lynn et al., "Dissociation and Dissociative Disorders: Challenging Conventional Wisdom," *Current Directions in Psychological Science* 21, no. 1 (2012): 48–53.

197 T. Giesbrecht et al., "Cognitive Processes in Dissociation: An Analysis of Core Theoretical Assumptions," *Psychological Bulletin* 134 (2008): 617–47.

198 Nicholas P. Spanos, "Multiple Identity Enactments and Multiple Personality Disorder: A Sociocognitive Perspective," *Psychological Bulletin* 116, no. 1 (1994): 143–65.

199 Flora R. Schreiber, *Sybil* (New York: Warner, 1973).

200 Debbie Nathan, *Sybil Exposed: The Extraordinary Story Behind the Famous Multiple Personality Case* (New York: Free Press, 2011).

201 Spanos, "Multiple Identity Enactments and Multiple Personality Disorder: A Sociocognitive Perspective."

202 S. J. Lynn et al., "Dissociation and Dissociative Disorders: Challenging Conventional Wisdom," *Current Directions in Psychological Science,* 21 (2012).

203 DSM-5, *s.v.* "Posttraumatic Stress Disorder."

204 M. J. Friedman, "PTSD History and Overview," *U. S. Department of Veterans Affairs,* undated.

205 Friedman, "PTSD History and Overview."

206 Gerald M. Rosen and Scott O. Lilienfeld, "Posttraumatic Stress Disorder: An Empirical Evaluation of Core Assumptions," *Clinical Psychological Review* 28, no. 5 (2008): 837–66.

207 N. Breslau, "Epidemiologic Studies of Trauma, Posttraumatic Stress Disorder and Other Psychiatric Disorders," *Canadian Journal of Psychiatry* 47, no. 10 (2002): 923–29.

208 G. M. Rosen, R. L. Spitzer, and P. R. McHugh, "The Problems with the Posttraumatic Stress Disorder Diagnosis and Its Future in DSM-5," *British Journal of Psychiatry* 192, no. 1 (2008): 3–4.

209 C. S. North, A. M. Suris, M. Davis, and R. P. Smith, "Toward Validation of the Diagnosis of Posttraumatic Stress Disorder," *American Journal of Psychiatry* 166, no. 1 (2009), 34–41.

210 David Dobbs, "The Post-Traumatic Stress Trap," *Scientific American,* April 2009, 64–69.

211 This and the following quotations are cited in Steve Bentley, "A Short History of PTSD: From Thermopylae to Hue, Soldiers Have Always Had a Disturbing Reaction to War," *The VVA Veteran,* January 1991.

212 Brett T. Litz et al., "Moral Injury and Moral Repair in War Veterans: A Preliminary Model and Intervention Strategy," *Clinical Psychology Review* 29 (2009): 695–706.

213 Panksepp, *Affective Neuroscience.*

8: Cogntive Competence

214 A U.S. federal statute (Public Law 111-256) called Rosa's Law mandated this change.

215 E. D. Brenner et al., "Plant Neurobiology: An Integrated View of Plant Signaling," *Trends in Plant Science* 11, no. 8 (2006): 413–19.

216 David Wechsler, *The Measurement of Adult Intelligence,* 3rd ed. (Philadelphia: Williams and Wilkins, 1944).

217 J. P. Das, "A System of Cognitive Assessment and Its Advantage over IQ," In *Human Information Processing: Measures, Mechanisms and Models,* ed. D. Vickers and P. Smith (Amsterdam: Elsevier, 1989).

218 Muriel D. Lezak, *Neuropsychological Assessment,* 3rd ed. (New York: Oxford University Press, 1995).

219 Elkonon Goldberg, *The Executive Brain: Frontal Lobes and the Civilized Mind* (Oxford: Oxford University Press, 2001).

220 David Wechsler, "Intelligence Defined and Undefined: A Relativistic Appraisal," *American Psychologist* 30 (1975): 135–39.

221 John B. Caroll, *Human Cognitive Abilities: A Survey of Factor-analytic Studies* (Cambridge: Cambridge University Press, 1993).

222 Charles Darwin, *On the Origin of Species by Means of Natural Selection: The Preservation of Favored Races in the Struggle for Life* (New York: Penguin Books, 1982).

223 Francis Galton, "On the Anthropometric Laboratory at the Late International Health Exhibition," *Journal of the Anthropological Institute* 14 (1884): 205–18.

224 Charles Spearman, "General intelligence: Objectively Determined and Measured," *American Journal of Psychology* 15 (1904): 201–93.

225 This discussion is based on Raymond E. Fancher, *The Intelligence Men: Makers of the IQ Controversy* (New York: W. W. Norton, 1985).

226 Alfred Binet, and Theodore Simon, "Applications of a New Method of Diagnosing the Intellectual Level of Abnormal People," *L'Annee Psychologique* 11 (1905): 191–244.

227 Alfred Binet, "New Research on the Measurement of Intellectual Level of Schoolchildren," *L'Annee Psychologique* 17 (1911): 145-201.

228 William Stern, *The Psychological Method of Intelligence Testing,* trans. by G. M. Whipple (Baltimore, MD: Warwick and York, 1914).

229 Lewis Terman, *The Measurement of Intelligence: An Explanation of and a Complete Guide for the Use of the Stanford Revision and Extension of the Binet-Simon Intelligence Scale* (New York: Houghton Mifflin, 1916).

230 Stephen Murdoch, *IQ: The Smart History of a Failed Idea* (Wiley, 2007).

231 Fancher, *The Intelligence Men: Makers of the IQ Controversy.*

232 David Wechsler, "On the Influence of Education on Intelligence as Measured by the Binet-Simon Test," *Journal of Educational Psychology* 17 (1926): 248–57.

233 Murdoch, *IQ: The Smart History of a Failed Idea.*

234 David Wechsler, *The Measurement and Appraisal of Adult Intelligence,* 4th ed. (Baltimore, MD: Williams and Wilkins, 1958).

235 John L. Horn, and Raymond B. Cattell, "Age Differences in Fluid and Crystallized Intelligence," *Acta Psychologica* 26 (1967): 107–29.

236 Howard Gardner, *Frames of Mind: The Theory of Multiple Intelligences* (New York: Basic Books, 1983).

237 Howard Gardner, *Intelligence Reframed: Multiple Intelligences for the 21st Century* (New York: Basic Books, 1999).

238 John White, "Multiple Invalidities," in *Howard Gardner Under Fire: The Rebel Psychologist Faces His Critics*, ed. J. A. Schaler (Chicago: Open Court, 2006).

239 Gardner, *Frames of Mind.*

240 Nicholas M. Allix, "The Theory of Multiple Intelligences: A Case of Missing Cognitive Matter," *Australian Journal of Education* 44 (2000): 272–88.

241 Richard J. Herrnstein and Charles Murray, *The Bell Curve: Intelligence and Class Structure in American Life* (New York: Free Press, 1996).

242 David Wechsler, *WAIS-IV Technical and Interpretive Manual* (NCS Pearson, 2008).

243 Herrnstein and Murray, *The Bell Curve.*

244 Francis Galton, *Hereditary Genius: An Inquiry into Its Laws and Consequences* (Horizon Press, 1952).

245 Francis Galton, *Inquiries into Human Faculty and Its Development* (London: Dutton, 1907).

246 Herrnstein and Murray, *The Bell Curve.*

247 H. Goddard, *The Kallikak Family: A Study of the Heredity of Feeble-mindedness* (New York: Macmillan, 1912)

248 Carl C. Brigham, *A Study of American Intelligence* (Princeton, NJ: Princeton University Press, 1923).

249 Herrnstein and Murray, *The Bell Curve.*

250 Walter Lippmann, "The Great Confusion," *New Republic,* January 23, 1923, 145–46.

251 B. F. Skinner, *Beyond Freedom and Dignity* (New York: Alfred A. Knopf, 1971).

252 Herrnstein and Murray. The Bell Curve.

253 Arthur Jensen, "How Much Can We Boost IQ and Scholastic Achieve-ment?" *Harvard Educational Review* 39 (1969): 1–123.

254 William Shockley, "Jensen's Data on Spearman's Hypothesis: No Artifact," *Behavior and Brain Sciences* 10 (1987): 512.

255 Quoted in Herrnstein and Murray, *The Bell Curve.*

256 James R. Flynn, *What Is Intelligence? Beyond the Flynn Effect* (Cambridge: Cambridge University Press, 2007).

257 Alexander Luria, *Cognitive Development: Its Cultural and Social Founda-tions* (Cambridge, MA: Harvard University Press), 1976.

258 Nathaniel Weyl, *The Creative Elite in America* (New York: Public Affairs Press, 1966).

259 The following discussion is based on James R. Flynn, *Asian Americans: Achievement Beyond IQ* (Philadelphia: Erlbaum, 1991).

260 The following discussion is based on Linda Gottfredson, "Why G Matters: The Complexity of Everyday Life," *Intelligence* 24, no. 1 (1997): 79–132.

261 Flynn, *What Is Intelligence? Beyond the Flynn Effect.*

262 DSM-5, 19–22.

263 P.M. Visscher et al., "Assumption-Free Estimation Of Heritability from Genome-Wide Identity-By-Descent Sharing Between Full Siblings," *PLoS Genetics* 2, no. 3 (2006): e 41.

264 R. Plomin et al., "Model-Fitting Analyses That Simultaneously Analyze All Family, Adoption, and Twin Data," *Behavioral Genetics* (2012): 195–96.

265 These data come from Alan S. Kaufman and Elizabeth O. Lichenberger, *Assessing Adolescent and Adult Intelligence,* 3rd ed. (Hoboken, NJ: Wiley, 2006) and from Alan S. Kaufman, *IQ Testing 101* (New York: Springer, 2009).

266 M-C. Chaing et al., "Genetics of Brain Fiber Architecture and Intellectual Performance," *Journal of Neuroscience* 29, no. 7 (2009): 4184–208.

267 Thomas J. Bouchard, "Genetic Influence on Human Psychological Traits—A Survey," *Current Directions in Psychological Sciences* 13, no. 4 (2004): 148–51.

268 R. Plomin and F. M. Spinath, "Intelligence: Genetics, Genes and Genomics," *Journal of Personality and Social Psychology* 86, no. 1 (2004): 112–29.

269 Flynn, *What Is Intelligence? Beyond the Flynn Effect.*

270 E. Turkheimer et al. "Socioeconomic Status Modifies Heritability of IQ in Young Children," *Psychological Sciences* 14, no. 6 (2003): 623–28.

271 M. Dayme, A.-C. Dumeret, and S. Tomkiewicz, "How Can We Boost IQs of 'Dull Children'? A Late Adoption Study," *Proceedings of the National Academy of Sciences* 96, no. 15 (1999): 8790–94.

272 K.-J. Kan et al., "On the Nature and Nurture of Intelligence and Specific Cognitive Abilities: The More Heritable, the More Culture Dependent," *Psychological Sciences,* 24 (2), (2013), 2420–28.

273 Scott B. Kaufman, "Heritability of Intelligence: Not What You Think," *Beautiful Minds* (blog), *Scientific American,* October 17, 2013.

274 Kan et al., "On the Nature and Nurture of Intelligence and Specific Cognitive Abilities."

275 Kaufman, "Heritability of Intelligence."

276 W. T. Dickens and J. R. Flynn, "Black Americans Reduce the Racial Gap: Evidence from Standardized Samples," *Psychological Science* 17 (2006): 913–20.

277 Kaufman, "Heritability of Intelligence."

278 These statistics are cited in "Alzheimer's Facts and Figures," Alzheimer's Association, www.alz.org.

279 This and descriptions of other dementias are reviewed in "The Dementias: Hope through Research," *National Institute of Neurological Disorders and Stroke,* www.nimds.nih.gov/disorders/dementias.

280 P. Chen et al., "Patterns of Cognitive Decline in Presymptomatic Alzheimer Disease," *Archives of General Psychiatry* 58 (2001): 853–58.

281 These studies and the ones below are reviewed in "Alzheimer's Testing Advances," *Alzheimer's Association,* www.alz.org/research/science/earlier_alzheimer's_diagnosis.

282 B. Reisberg, S. H. Ferris, and M. J. de Leon, "The Global Deterioration Scale for the Assessment of Primary Degenerative Dementia," *American Journal of Psychiatry* 139 (1982): 1136–39.

283 C. B. Frey and M. A. Osborne, "The Future of Employment: How Susceptible Are Jobs to Computerisation?" *Oxford Martin School*, September 17,
2013, www.oxfordmartin.ox.ac.uk.

284 Eric Brynjolfsson and Andrew McAfee, *The Second Machine Age: Work,
Progress, and Prosperity in a Time of Brilliant Technologies* (New York:
W. W. Norton, 2014).

9: Social Competence

285 Leo Kanner, "Autistic Disturbance of Affective Contact," *Nervous Child* 2
(1943): 217–50.

286 Lorna Wing, "Asperger's Syndrome: A Clinical Account," *Psychological
Medicine* 11 (1981): 115–30.

287 Oliver Sacks, *An Anthropologist on Mars: Seven Paradoxical Tales* (New
York: Alfred A Knopf, 1995).

288 Laura Schreibman, *The Science and Fiction of Autism* (Cambridge, MA:
Harvard University Press, 2005).

289 L. Waterhouse et al., "Diagnosis and classification in autism," *Journal of
Autism and Developmental Disorders* 26, no. 1 (1996): 59-86.

290 Schreibman, *The Science and Fiction of Autism*.

291 American Psychiatric Publishing, "Autism Spectrum Disorder," www
.dsm5.org, 2012.

292 Ferris Jabr, "Redefining Autism: Will the New DSM-5 Criteria Exclude
Some People?" *Scientific American*, January 2012.

293 Lindsey Tanner, "Autism Definition: Doctors Want to Redefine; Parents
Worried," *Huffington Post*, April 5, 2012.

294 T. W. Frazier et al., "Validation of Proposed DSM-5 Criteria for Autism
Spectrum Disorders," *Journal of the American Academy of Child and Adolescent Psychiatry* 51, no. 1 (2012): 28–40.

295 Ari Ne'eman, "Will New DSM-5 Autistic Criteria Impact Services?" *Simon
Foundation Autism Research Initiative*, May 2013.

296 Temple Grandin, "Observations of Cattle Behavior Applied to the Design
of Cattle Handling Facilities," *Applied Animal Pathology* 6 (1980): 19–31.

297 Temple Grandin and Richard Panek, *The Autistic Brain: Thinking across the Spectrum* (New York: Houghton Mifflin Harcourt, 2013).

298 Temple Grandin and Margaret M. Scariano, *Emergence: Labeled Autistic* (Novato, CA: Arena Press, 1986).

299 Sacks, *An Anthropologist on Mars.*

300 Grandin and Scariano, *Emergence: Labeled Autistic.*

301 Gerald Edelman and Giulio Tononi, *A Universe of Consciousness: How Matter Becomes Imagination* (New York: Basic Books, 2000).

302 M. V. Johnston and M. E. Blue, "Neurology of Autism," in *Autism: A Neurological Disorder of Early Brain Development*, ed. R. Tuchman and I. Rapin (London: MacKeith Press, 2006).

303 Ratey, *A User's Guide to the Brain.*

304 Grandin and Scariano, *Emergence: Labeled Autistic.*

305 Schreibman, *The Science and Fiction of Autism.*

306 S. Baron-Cohen, A. M. Leslie, and U. Firth, "Does the Autistic Child Have a Theory of Mind?" *Cognition* 21 (1985): 37–46.

307 H. Wimmer and J. Perner, "Beliefs about Beliefs: Representation and Constraining Function of Wrong Beliefs in Young Children's Understanding of Deception," *Cognition* 13 (1983): 103–28.

308 Roberto Tuchman, "The Social Deficit In Autism," in *Autism: A Neurological Disorder of Early Brain Development*, ed. R. Tuchman and I. Rapin (London: Mac Keith Press, 2006).

309 M. Tomasello and M. J. Farrar, "Joint Attention and Early Language," *Child Development* 57, no. 6 (1986): 1454–63.

310 R. Bakeman, L. B. Adamson, M. Konner, R. G. Barr, "Kung Infancy: The Social Context of Object Exploration," *Child Development* 61, no. 3 (1990): 794–809.

311 R. P. Hobson, "The Autistic Child's Appraisal of Expressions of Emotion," *Journal of Child Psychology and Psychiatry and Allied Disciplines* 27, no. 3 (1986): 321–42.

312 G. Rizzolatti, L. Fogassi, and V. Gallese, "Mirror Neurons in the Mind," *Scientific American,* November 2006.

313 V. S. Ramachandran and L. M. Oberman, "Broken Mirrors: A Theory of Autism" *Scientific American,* November 2006, 62–69.

314 Vilaynur S. Ramachandran, *A Brief Tour of Human Consciousness* (New York: Pearson, 2004).

315 Penny Spikins, "Autism, the Integration of 'Difference' and the Origins of Modern Human Behavior," *Cambridge Archaeological Journal* 19, no. 2 (2009): 179–201.

316 Penny Spikins, personal communication, 2013.

317 Laurent Mottron, "The Power of Autism," *Nature* 479 (2011): 33–35.

318 Mottron, "The Power of Autism."

319 L. Bachan, "When Geeks Meet," *Nature* 479 (2011): 25–27.

320 C. F. Garfield et al., "Trends in Attention Deficit Hyperactivity Disorder Ambulatory Diagnosis and Medical Treatment in the United States, 2000–2010," *Academic Pediatrics* 12, no. 2 (2012): 110–16.

321 H. Hoffman, "The Story of Fidgety Philip," from Struwwelpeter, www.germanstories.vcu.edu.

322 William James, *Principles of Psychology* (reprinted by Encyclopaedia Britannica, 1992).

323 George F. Still, "Some Abnormal Psychical Conditions in Children," *Lancet* 1 (1902).

324 M. Laufer, E. Denhoff, and G. Solomons, "Hyperkinetic Impulse Disorder in Children's Behavior Problems," *Psychosomatic Medicine* 19 (1957): 38–49.

325 Stella Chess, "Diagnosis and Treatment of the Hyperactive Child," *New York State Journal of Medicine* 60 (1960): 2379–85.

326 DSM-II, 1968.

327 DSM-III, 1980.

328 DSM-III-R, 1987.

329 DSM-5, 2013.

330 Russell Barkley, *ADHD and the Nature of Self-Control* (New York: Guilford Press, 2005).

331 Charles Bradley, "The Behavior of Children Using Benzedrine," *American Journal of Psychiatry* 94, no. 3 (1937): 577–85.

332 Whitaker, *Anatomy of an Epidemic.*

333 Paul G. Hammerness, *ADHD* (Westport, CT: Greenwood Press, 2009).

334 Quoted in Moncrieff, *The Myth of the Chemical Cure.*

335 Edward Hallowell, www.drhallowell.com.

336 Edward Hallowell, "The Importance of Mentors: One Special Teacher Can Turn a So-So Student ADHDer into a Lifelong Learner," *ADDitude Magazine*, 2005.

337 Deborah Estes, www.deborahestes.com.

338 Pete Quilly, www.adultaddstrengths.com.

339 Rick Mayes, "ADHD and the Rise in Stimulant Use among Children," *Harvard Review of Psychiatry* 16 (2008): 151–66.

10: Pain and Bodily Illness

340 M. A. Schappert and M. S. Rechtsteiner, "Ambulatory Medical Care Utilization Estimates for 2006," *National Health Statistics Reports* 8 (2008).

341 James W. Pennebaker, *The Psychology of Physical Symptoms* (Berlin: Springer-Verlag, 1982).

342 Meghan O'Rourke, "What's Wrong With Me?" *The New Yorker*, August 20, 2013, 32–37.

343 Thomas S. Szasz, "The Psychology of Persistent Pain: A Portrait of *L'Homme Douloureux*," in *Pain*, ed. A. Soulaivac, J. Cahn, and J. Charpentier (New York: Academic Press, 1968).

344 Pennebaker, *The Psychology of Physical Symptoms.*

345 S. Woods, J. Natterson, and J. Silverman, "Medical Student's Disease: Hypochondriasis in Medical Education," *Journal of Medical Education* 41 (1978): 785–90.

346 R. E. Bartholomew and S. Wessley, "Protean Nature of Mass Sociogenic Illness: From Possessed Nuns to Chemical and Biological Terrorism Fears," *British Journal of Psychiatry* 180 (2002): 300–306.

347 R. E. Bartholomew and E. Goode, "Mass Delusions and Hysterias: High-lights from the Past Millennia," *Skeptical Inquirer* 24, no. 3 (2000): 1–15.

348 S. Khrabsheh et al., "Mass Psychogenic Illness Following-Diphtheria Vaccination in Jordan," *Bulletin of World Health Organization* 79, no. 8 (2000): 764–70.

349 Bartholomew and Goode, "Mass Delusions and Hysterias."

350 Bartholomew and Goode, "Mass Delusions and Hysterias."

351 A. Gallay et al. "Belgian Coca-Cola-Related Outbreak: Intoxication, Mass Sociogenic Illness, or Both?" *American Journal of Epidemiology* 155, no. 2 (2002): 140–47.

352 T. A. Roberts and J. W. Pennebaker, "Women's and Men's Strategies in Perceiving Internal State," In *Advances in Experimental Social Psychology,* ed. M. Zanna, vol. 28, 143–76. (New York: Academic Press, 1995).

353 D. Watson and L. A. Clark, "Negative Affectivity: The Disposition to Express Aversive Emotional States," *Psychological Bulletin* 96 (1984): 465–90.

354 Pennebaker, *The Psychology of Physical Symptoms.*

355 A. Tellegen et al. "Personality Similarity in Twins Reared Apart and Together," *Journal of Personality and Social Psychology* 54 (1988): 1031–39.

356 G. Pirooz Sholevar, "The Role of the Family in Psychosomatic Disorders," in *The Psychosomatic Approach to Illness,* ed. R. L. Gallon (New York: Elsvier Biomedical, 1982).

357 S. Minuchin, B. Rosman, and I. Baker, *Psychosomatic Families: Anorexia Nervosa in Context* (Cambridge, MA: Harvard University Press, 1978).

358 Pennebaker, *The Psychology of Physical Symptoms.*

359 David Mechanic, "The Influence of Mothers on Their Children's Health Attitudes and Behaviors," *Pediatrics* 33 (1964): 444–53.

360 David Mechanic, "Development of Psychological Distress among Young Adults," *Archives of General Psychiatry* 36 (1979): 1233–39.

361 David Mechanic, "The Concept of Illness Behavior: Culture, Situation and Personal Predisposition," *Psychological Medicine* 16 (1986): 1–7.

362 H. Merskey and M. Trimble, "Personality, Sexual Adjustment, and Brain Lesions in Patients with Conversion Symptoms," *American Journal of Psychiatry* 136 (1979): 179–82.

363 J. W. Pennebaker and J. Skelton, "Psychological Parameters of Physical Symptoms," *Personality and Social Psychology* 4 (1978): 524–30.

364 Gene Weingarten, *The Hypochondriac's Guide to Life. And Death* (New York: Simon and Schuster, 1998).

365 Erasmus Darwin, *Zoomania; or, The Laws of Organic Life* (1818).

366 F. E. Kenyon, "Hypochondriasis. A Survey of Some Historical, Clinical and Social Aspects," *British Journal of Medical Psychology* 38 (1965).

367 Catherine Belling, *A Condition of Doubt: The Meaning of Hypochondria* (New York: Oxford University Press, 2012).

368 John Diamond, *Because Cowards Get Cancer Too: A Hypochondriac Confronts His Nemesis* (New York: Random House, 1998).

369 John Diamond, "Something for the Weekend," *Times* (London), May 25, 1996.

370 M. Bopp et al., "Health Risk or Resource? Gradual and Independent Association between Self-Rated Health and Mortality Persists over 30 Years" *PlosOne*, February 9, 2012.

371 Fiona Macrae, "Hypochondriacs May Have a Point! They Don't Live as Long as Research Suggests a Person's Outlook Affects Life-Span," *Daily Mail*, February 11, 2012.

372 R. W. White and E. Horvitz, "Cyberchondia: Studies of the Escalation of Medical Concerns in Web Search," *ACM Transactions on Information Systems* 27, no. 4 (2009).

373 B. W. Hesse et al. "Trust and Sources of Health Information. The Impact of the Internet and Its Implications for Healthcare Providers: Findings from the First Health Information National Trends Survey," *Archives of Internal Medicine* 165, no. 22 (2005): 2618–24.

374 WebMD, "Internet Makes Hypochondria Worse," www.webmd.com.

375 W. C. Alvarez, *Minds That Came Back* (Philadelphia: J. B. Lippincott, 1961).

376 Recounted in Beverly Purdy, "Paralyzed by Faith," *Discovery Magazine,* June 2012.

377 Josef Breuer and Sigmund Freud, *Studies in Hysteria,* trans. by A. A. Brill (Boston, MA: Beacon Press, 1961 [1895]).

378 Andrew Scull, *Hysteria: The Biography* (New York: Oxford University Press, 2009).

379 M. Hollander, "The Case of Anna O: A Reformulation," *American Journal of Psychiatry* 137 (1980): 797–800.

380 P. R. McHugh and P. R. Slavney, *The Perspectives of Psychiatry,* 2nd ed. (Baltimore, MD: Johns Hopkins University Press, 1998).

381 Ann C. Schwartz et al., "Treatment of Conversion Disorder in an African American Christian Woman: Cultural and Social Considerations," *American Journal of Psychology* 158 (2001): 1385–91.

382 Selma Aybec et al., "Neural Correlates of Recall of Life Events in Conversion Disorder," *JAMA Psychiatry* 7, no. 1 (2014): 52–60.

383 L. E. Hinsie and R. J. Carmichael, *Psychiatric Dictionary,* 4th ed. (New York: Oxford University Press, 1970).

384 DSM-5.

385 Crista Harsall, "How Prevalent Is Chronic Pain?" *International Association for the Study of Pain Clinical Update* 11, no. 2 (2003).

386 C. B. Johannes et al., "The Prevalence of Chronic Pain in U.S. Adults: Results of an Internet-Based Survey," *Pain* 11, no. 11 (2010): 1230–39.

387 S. A. Ryder and C. F. Stannard, "Treatment of Chronic Pain: Antidepressant, Antiepileptic and Anti-Rhythmic Drugs," *Continuing Education in Anesthesia Critical Care Pain* 5, no. 1 (2005): 18–21.

388 Institute of Medicine, "Relieving Pain in America: A Blueprint for Transforming Preventive Care, Education and Research," 2011.

389 Robert L. Gallon, "Perception of Disability in Chronic Back Pain Patients: A Long-Term Follow-Up," *Pain* 37 (1989): 67–75.

390 Ronald Melzack and Patrick D. Wall, *The Challenge of Pain,* 2nd ed. (New York: Penguin Books, 1996).

391 V. S. Ramachandran and Sandra Blakeslee, *Phantoms in the Brain* (New York: HarperCollins, 1998).

392 G. Waddell and C. J. Main "Assessment of Severity in Low Back Disorders," *Spine* 9 (1984): 204–8; W. E. Shankland, "Factors That Affect Pain Behavior," *CRANIO: The Journal of Craniomandibular Practice* 29, no. 2 (2011).

393 Henry K. Beecher, "Pain in Men Wounded in Battle," *Annals of Surgery* 123, no. 1 (1946): 96–105.

394 Henry K. Beecher, *Measurement of Subjective Responses* (Oxford: Oxford University Press, 1959).

395 Howard Pikoff, "Is the Muscular Model of Headache Still Viable? A Review of Conflicting Data," *Headache* 24 (1984): 186–98.

396 J. Oleson, "The Pathophysiology of Migraine," in *Handbook of Clinical Neurology*, ed. F. C. Rose, vol. 48, rev. series, 59–83 (Elsevier, 1986).

397 John D. Loeser, "Tic Douloroux and Atypical Facial Pain," In *Textbook of Pain*, ed. P. D. Wall and R. Melzack, 3rd ed. (London: Churchill Livingstone, 1994), 699–710.

398 Damasio, *The Feeling of What Happens.*

399 Dennis C. Turk, "Biopsychosocial Perspective on Chronic Pain," In *Psychological Approaches to Pain Management,* ed. R. J. Getchell and D. C. Turk (Guilford Press, 1996), 3–32.

400 R. Melzack and K. L. Casey, "Sensory, Motivational, and Central Control Determinants of Pain," in *The Skin Senses,* ed. D. R. Kenshalo (Springfield, IL: Charles C. Thomas, 1968), 423–43.

401 Melzack and Wall, *The Challenge of Pain.*

402 R. O. Dayo, N. E. Walsh, and D. Martin, "A Controlled Trial of Transcutaneous Electrical Nerve Stimulation (TENS) and Exercise for Chronic Low Back Pain," *New England Journal of Medicine* 322 (1990): 1627–34.

403 J. M. Romano et al., "Sequential Analysis of Chronic Pain Behaviors and Spouse Responses," *Journal of Consulting and Clinical Psychology* 60 (1992): 777–82.

404 Wilbert Fordyce, "Pain and Suffering: A Reappraisal," *American Psychologist,* 43, no. 4 (1988): 276–83.

11: Substance Misuse and Dependence

405 This history is adapted from Edward Brecher, *Licit and Illicit Drugs, The Consumer's Union Report on Narcotics, Stimulants, Depressants, Inhalants, Hallucinogens, and Marijuana—Including Caffeine, Nicotine, and Alcohol* (Boston: Little, Brown, 1972).

406 Joseph R DiFranza et al., "Initial Symptoms of Nicotine Dependence in Adolescents," *Tobacco Control* 9 (2000): 313–19.

407 George Koob, "Neuroadaptive Mechanisms of Addiction: Studies on the Extended Amygdala," *European Neuropsychopharmacology* 13 (2003): 442–52.

408 Wilson, *The Social Conquest of Earth.*

409 Avram Goldstein, *Addiction: From Biology to Drug Policy* (New York: Oxford University Press, 2001).

410 Burton Angrist and Samuel Greshon, "The Phenomenology of Experimentally Induced Amphetamine Psychosis: Preliminary Observations," *Biological Psychiatry* 2, no. 2 (1970): 95–107.

12: Controlling Impulses and Desires

411 This and the next case and related material were reported by Carl Zimmer, "The Brain: Where Does Sex Exist in the Brain? From Top to Bottom," *Discover Magazine,* October 2009.

412 F. Bianchi-Demichelli and S. Ortigue, "Toward an Understanding of the Cerebral Substrates of Woman's Orgasm," *Neuropsychologica* 45 (2007).

413 S. Stoleru et al., "Neuroanatomical Correlates of Visually Evoked Sexual Arousal in Human Males," *Archives of Sex Behavior* 28, no. 1 (1999): 1–21.

414 Lisa Kataymaya, "Love in 2-D," *New York Times,* July 21, 2009.

415 DSM-5, *s.v.* "pedophilia."

416 Michael C. Quadland, letter to the editor, *The New Yorker,* April 8, 2013.

417 DSM-5.

418 Paul McHugh, "Transgender Surgery Isn't the Solution: A Drastic Physical Change Doesn't Address Underlying Psycho-Social Troubles," *Wall Street Journal,* June 12, 2014.

419 C. Dhejue et al., "Long-Term Follow-Up of Transsexual Persons Undergo-
     ing Sex Reassignment Surgery: Cohort Study in Sweden," *PlosOne* 6, no. 2
     (2011).

420 Charles Darwin, *The Expression of the Emotions in Man and Animals* (Chi-
     cago: University of Chicago Press, 1965).

421 James Averill, cited in Panksepp and Biven, *The Archaeology of Mind.*

422 Carol Tavris, *Anger: The Misunderstood Emotion,* rev. ed. (New York:
     Simon and Schuster, 1989).

423 Andrew Solomon, "The Reckoning," *The New Yorker,* March 17, 2014.

424 Panksepp and Bivan, *The Archaeology of Mind.*

425 Panksepp, *Affective Neuroscience.*

426 T. H. Mark, F. R. Ervin, and W. H. Sweet, "Deep Temporal Lobe Stimula-
     tion in Man," *The Neurobiology of the Amygdala,* ed. E. B. Eleftheriou
     (New York: Plenum, 1972), 485–507.

427 Kelly P. O'Meara, "Dramatic Increase of Mass Shooting in America: The
     Role of Prescription Psychiatric Drugs," *Global Research News,* November
     21, 2013.

428 T. J. Moore, J. Glenmullen, and C. D. Furberg, "Prescription Drugs Associ-
     ated with Reports of Violence towards Others," *PlosOne,* December 15,
     2010.

429 Daren Savage, "A Brief History of Psychotropic Drugs Prescribed to Mass
     Murderers," *Los Alamos Daily Post,* January 16, 2013.

430 Mike Adams, "Psychiatric Medications Found in the Home of German-
     wings Pilot Andreas Lubitz, Who Underwent 18 Months of Psychiatric
     Treatment," *Global Research,* March 31, 2015.

431 Ralph Hupka, "Cultural Determinants of Jealousy," *Alternative Life Styles* 4
     (1981): 310–56.

432 Sigmund Freud, *A General Introduction to Psychoanalysis,* American ed.
     (New York: Washington Square Press, 1924).

433 John Bowlby, *Attachment and Loss,* vol. 2 (New York: Basic Books, 1973).

434 Leonard Berkowitz, "Experimental Investigations of Hostility Catharsis,"
     Journal of Consulting and Clinical Psychology 35 (1970): 1-7.

435 Tavris, *Anger: The Misunderstood Emotion.*

436 Tavris, *Anger: The Misunderstood Emotion.*

437 Aristotle, *Nicomachean Ethics,* 2.1109.a27.

438 Fugen Neziroglu, "Hoarding: The Basics," www.adoa.org.

439 A. Pertusa et al., "Refining the Boundaries of Compulsive Hoarding: A Review," *Clinical Psychology Review* 30 (2010): 371–86.

440 D. F. Tolin et al., "Course of Compulsive Hoarding and Its Relationship to Life Events," *Depression and Anxiety* 27 (2010): 829–38.

441 Randy Frost, "People Who Hoard Animals," *Psychiatric Times* 17, no. 4 (2000).

442 Tony Dokoupil, "Is the Onslaught Making Us Crazy?" *Newsweek,* July 12, 2012, 24–30.

443 Nicholas K. Geranios, "Internet Addicts Treated at Washington Center," *Bangor Daily News,* September 21, 2009.

444 Daniel Gross, "Pay Up! Why Wall Street Bonuses Won't Go Away," *Slate,* October 23, 2009.

445 K. McGowan, "Economist George Loewenstein," *Discover Magazine,* January 25, 2010.

446 Roy F. Baumeister, "Conquer Yourself, Conquer the World," *Scientific American,* April 2015, 61–65.

13: Socialization Dysfunction

447 Jeffrey Kluger, *The Narcissist Next Door: Understanding the Monster in Your Family, in Your Office, in Your Bed—in Your World* (New York: Riverhead, 2014).

448 Richard Dawkins, *The Selfish Gene* (New York: Oxford University Press, 2006).

449 Wilson, *The Social Conquest of Earth.*

450 Hervey Cleckley, *The Mask of Sanity,* 5th ed. (Buellton, CA: Mosby, 1976).

451 Eric Larson, *The Devil in the White City: Murder, Magic, and Madness at the Fair that Changed America* (New York: Vintage Books, 2004).

452 Robert Hare, *Without Conscience: The Disturbing World of the Psychopaths among Us* (New York: Guilford Press, 1999).

453 J. H. Johns and H. C. Quay, "The Effect of Social Reward on Verbal Conditioning in Psychopathic and Neurotic Military Offenders," *Journal of Consulting Psychology* 36 (1962): 217–20 (and quoted in Hare, *Without Conscience*).

454 Quoted in Kevin Dutton, *The Wisdom of Psychopaths* (New York: Farrar, Strauss and Giroux, 2012).

455 Martha Stout, *The Sociopath Next Door: The Ruthless Versus the Rest of Us* (New York: Broadway Books, 2005).

456 Theodore Millon and Roger Davis, "Ten Subtypes of Psychopathy," in *Psychopathy, Antisocial, Criminal and Violent Behavior,* ed. T. Milan et al. (New York: Guilford Press, 2002).

457 A. Reijntjes et al., "Peer Victimization and Internalizing Problems in Children: A Meta-Analysis of Longitudinal Studies," *Child Abuse and Neglect* 34, no. 4 (2013): 244–52.

458 Silvia Postigo et al., "Theoretical Proposals in Bullying Research: A Review," *Anales de Priscologia,* 29, no. 3 (2003): 413–25.

459 John Dollard et al., *Frustration and Aggression* (New Haven, CT: Yale University Press, 1939).

460 L. R. Burk et al., "Stability of Early Identified Aggressive Victim Status in Elementary School and Associations with Later Mental Health Problems and Functional Impairment," *Journal of Abnormal Child Psychology* 39, no. 2 (2011): 225–38.

461 Eliza Ahmed, "Understanding Bullying from a Shame Management Perspective: Findings from a Three-Year Follow-Up Study," *Educational and Child Psychology* 23, no. 2 (2006): 25–39.

462 V. Sanchez et al., "Emotional Competence of Aggression and Victims of Bullying," *Anales de Priscologia,* 28, no. 1 (2012): 71–82.

463 Albert Bandura, *Aggression: A Social Learning Theory Analysis* (New York: Prentice-Hall, 1973).

464 Helen Deutsch, "Some Forms of Emotional Disturbance and Their Relationship to Schizophrenia," *Psychoanalytic Quarterly* 11 (1942): 301.

465 DSM-5

466 Tonya Singer, "I'm Okay, You're Not Okay: The Right Supra Marginal Gyrus Plays an Important Role in Empathy," *Max Planck Institute Research News*, October 9, 2013.

467 Jennifer H. Pfeifer and Mirella Dapretto, "Mirror, Mirror, in My Mind: Empathy, Interpersonal Competence, and the Mirror Neuron System," in *The Social Neuroscience of Empathy*, ed. J. Decety and W. Ickes (Cambridge, MA: MIT Press, 2009).

468 C. Daniel Bateson, "These Things Called Empathy: Eight Related but Distinct Phenomena," in *The Social Neuroscience of Empathy*, ed. J. Decety and W. Ickes (Cambridge, MA: MIT Press, 2009).

469 R. J. R. Blair and K. S. Blair, "Empathy, Morality, and Social Convention: Evidence from the Study of Psychopathy and Other Psychiatric Disorders," in *The Social Neuroscience of Empathy*, ed. J. Decety and W. Ickes (Cambridge, MA: MIT Press, 2009).

470 Pfeifer and Dapretto, "Mirror, Mirror, in My Mind."

471 Blair and Blair, "Empathy, Morality, and Social Convention."

472 Bateson, "These Things Called Empathy."

473 J. S. Milner, L. B. Halsey, and J. Fultz, "Empathic Responsiveness and Affective Reactivity to Infant Stimuli in High- and Low-Risk for Physical Child Abuse Mothers," *Child Abuse and Neglect* 19, no. 6 (1995): 767–80.

474 Singer, "I'm Okay, You're Not Okay."

14: Dimensional Treatment

475 Healy, *Mania: A Short History of Bipolar Disorder*.

476 Moncrieff, *The Myth of the Chemical Cure*.

477 Breggin, *Medication Madness*.

478 Steven Hyman, "Initiation and Adaptation: A Paradigm for Understanding Psychotropic Drug Action," *American Journal of Psychiatry* 153 (1996): 151–61.

479 Moncrieff, *The Myth of the Chemical Cure*.

480 Whitaker, *Anatomy of an Epidemic*.

481 Pierre Deniker, "Introduction to Neuroleptic Chemotherapy into Psychiatry," In *Discoveries in Biological Psychiatry*, ed. F. Ayd and B. Blackwell (Philadelphia: Lippincott, 1970), 155–64.

482 E. E. Parson, Symposium Proceedings, *Chlorpromazine and Mental Health* (Philadelphia: Lea and Febiger, 1955), 132.

483 Bentall, *Madness Explained.*

484 Nina Schooler et al., "One Year after Discharge," *American Journal of Psychiatry* 123 (1967): 986–95.

485 Robert F. Prien, "Discontinuation of Chemotherapy for Chronic Schizophrenics," *Hospital and Community Psychiatry* 22 (1971): 20–23.

486 George Gardos and Jonathon Cole, "Maintenance Antipsychotic Therapy: Is the Cure Worse Than the Disease?" *American Journal of Psychiatry* 133 (1977): 32–36.

487 Whitaker, *Anatomy of an Epidemic.*

488 National Institute for Health and Clinical Excellence, *Schizophrenia: Core Interventions in the Treatment and Management of Schizophrenia in Primary and Secondary Care,* Guideline Number 23 (National Institute for Health and Clinical Excellence, 2002).

489 S. Leucht et al., "Antipsychotic Drug Versus Placebo for Relapse Prevention in Schizophrenia: A Systematic Review and Meta-Analysis," *Lancet* 379 (2012): 2063–71.

490 Joanna Moncrieff, "Does Antipsychotic Withdrawal Provoke Psychosis? Review of the Literature on Rapid Onset Psychosis (Super Sensitivity Psychosis) and Withdraw Rural-Related Relapse," *Acta Psychiatrica Scandinavia,* 114 (1), (2006): 3–13.

491 Edward Drummond, *The Complete Guide to Psychiatric Drugs: Straight Talk for Best Results* (Hoboken, NJ: Wiley, 2000).

492 According to Moncrieff's review of the literature in *The Myth of the Medical Cure,* this latter point is highly debatable. Studies sponsored by drug companies find that atypical antipsychotics have a better side-affect profile, but government-funded studies show no difference. Newer research shows that people on the atypicals also developed tardive dyskinesia.

493 H. Steck, "The Extrapyramidal and Di-Encephalic Syndrome During Treatment with Largactil and Serapsil," *Annales Medicopsychologiques* 112 (1954): 737–43.

494 J. M. Van Rossum, "The Significance of Dopamine Receptor Blockade for the Mechanism of Action of Neuroleptic Drugs," *Arch. Int. Psychopharmaco. Ther.* 160, no. 2 (1966): 492–94.

495 A. Rifkin, F. M. Quitkin, and D. F. Klein, "Akinesia: A Poorly Recognized Disorder," *Archives of General Psychiatry* 32 (1975): 672.

496 Breggin, *Toxic Psychiatry.*

497 R. H. Belmaker and D. Wald, "Haloperidol in Normals," *British Journal of Psychiatry* 131 (1977): 222–23.

498 Bentall, *Madness Explained.*

499 Moncrieff, *The Myth of the Chemical Cure.*

500 There are also several that block the reuptake of both serotonin and norepinephrine, called SNRIs.

501 J. K. Wamsley, "Receptor Alterations Associated with Serotonergic Agents," *Journal of Clinical Psychiatry* 48 (suppl.), (1987): 19–25.

502 Moncrieff, *The Myth of the Chemical Cure.*

503 Charles Barber, "The Medicated Americans," *Scientific American* (February/March 2008), 45–51.

504 Whitaker, *Anatomy of an Epidemic.*

505 C. Cusin and D. D. Dougherty, "Somatic Therapies For Treatment-Resistant Depression: ECT, TMS, VNS, DBS," *Biology of Mood and Anxiety Disorders* 2, no. 14 (2012).

506 Scott T. Aaronson, "Neural Stimulation For Mood Disorders," *Psychiatric Times,* September 5, 2014.

507 Franz Alexander, "Individual Psychotherapy," *Psychosomatic Medicine* 8 (1946): 110–15.

508 Jerome Frank, *Persuasion and Healing: A Comparative Study of Psychotherapy,* rev. ed. (Baltimore: Johns Hopkins University Press, 1973).

509 Jaynes, *The Origins of Consciousness in the Breakdown of the Bicameral Mind.*

510 P. Watzlawick, J. Weakland, and R. Fisch, *Change: Principles of Problem Formation and Problem Resolution* (New York: W. W. Norton, 1974).

511 Albert Bandura, *Self-Efficacy: The Exercise of Control* (New York: W. H. Freeman, 1997).

512 Albert Bandura, "Exercise of Personal and Collective Efficacy in Changing Societies," in *Self-Efficacy in Changing Societies,* ed. A. Bandura (New York: Cambridge University Press, 1995).

513 C. G. Boeree, "Personality Theories," www.webspace.ship.edu/cghoer/ellis.

514 This idea originated with William Glasser, *Reality Therapy* (New York: Harper and Row, 1965).

515 Ellis, *Overcoming Destructive Beliefs, Feelings, and Behaviors.*

516 Claire Weekes, *More Help for Your Nerves* (New York: Bantam Books, 1987).

517 Bhikkhu Analayo, *Saltipatihana: The Direct Path to Realization* (Birmingham, AL: Windhorse Publications, 2000).

518 Jon Kabat-Zinn, "An Outpatient Program in Behavior Medicine for Chronic Pain Patients Based on the Practice of Mindfulness Meditation: Theoretical Considerations and Preliminary Results," *General Hospital Psychiatry* 4, no. 1 (1982): 33–97.

519 J. N. Felder, S. Dimidjian, and Z. Segal, "Collaboration in Mindfulness-Based Cognitive Therapy," *Journal of Consulting Psychology* 68, no. 2 (2012): 179–86.

520 Rebecca Crane, *Mindfulness-Based Cognitive Therapy* (London: Routledge, 2009).

521 B. Khoury et al., "Mindfulness-Based Therapy: A Comprehensive Meta-Analysis," *Clinical Psychology Review* 33, no. 6 (2013): 763–71.

522 M. Ricard, A. Lutz, and R. J. Davidson, "Mind of the Meditator," *Scientific American,* November 2014, 39–45.

523 Carolyn Webster-Stratton, *The Incredible Years: A Trouble-shooting Guide for Parents of Children Aged 2-8 Years,* rev. ed. (Incredible Years Publishing, 2005).

524 Carolyn Webster-Stratton, *The Incredible Years: Parent, Teacher and Child Training Series,* in D. S. Elliott, ed., *Blueprints for Violence Prevention,* 2001.

525 David G. Kingdon and Douglas Turkington, *Cognitive Therapy of Schizo-phrenia* (New York: Gilford Press, 2005).

526 Aaron T. Beck, "Successful Outpatient Therapy of a Chronic Schizo-phrenic with a Delusion Based on Borrowed Guilt," *Psychiatry* 15 (1952): 305–12.

527 M. Ziegenbaum et al., "Possible Criteria for Inpatient Psychiatric Admissions: Which Patients Are Transferred from Emergency Services to Inpatient Psychiatric Treatment?" *BMC Health Services Resources,* June 2006.

528 R. D. Laing, *The Divided Self: And Existential Study in Sanity and Madness* (Harmondsworth, UK: Penguin Books, 1962).

529 Philadelphia Society, "Kingsley Hall," www.philadelphia-association.org /Kingsley Hall.

530 Loren R. Mosher and Voyce Hendrix, *Soteria: Through Madness to Deliverance* (Bloomington, IN: Xlibris Corporation, 2004).

531 Loren R. Mosher, "Non-Hospital, Non-Drug Intervention with First-Episode Psychosis," in *Models of Madness: Psychological, Social and Biological Approaches to Madness,* ed. J. Read, L. R. Mosher, and R. P. Bentall (New York: Routledge, 2004).

532 Mosher and Hendrix, *Soteria.*

533 William T. Carpenter and Robert W. Buchanan, "Commentary on the Soteria Project: Misguided Therapeutics," *Schizophrenia Bulletin* 28, no. 4 (2002): 577–79.

534 Mosher and Hendrix, *Soteria.*

535 Whitaker, *Anatomy of an Epidemic.*

536 Jaakko Seikkula, "Five-Year Experience of First-Episode Nonaffective Psychosis in Open-Dialogue Approach," *Psychotherapy Research* 16 (2006): 214–28.

15: The Present and the Future

537 Daniel J. Carlat, *Unhinged: The Trouble with Psychiatry: A Doctor's Revelations about a Profession in Crisis* (New York: Free Press, 2010).

538 Whitaker, *Anatomy of an Epidemic.*

539 N. Jablensky et al., "Schizophrenia: Manifestations, Incidence and Course in Different Cultures," *Psychological Medicine,* supplement 20 (1992): 1–97.

540 Kim J. Hopper, "Revisiting the Developed Versus Developing Country Distinction in Course and Outcome in Schizophrenia," *Schizophrenia Bulletin* 26 (2000): 835–46.

541 Erick Turner, "Selective Publication of Antidepressant Trials and Its Influence on Apparent Efficacy," *New England Journal of Medicine* 358 (2008): 252–60.

542 Gordon Parker, "Antidepressants on Trial," *British Journal of Psychiatry* 194 (2009): 1–3.

543 Carlat, *Unhinged.*

544 Adele C. Viguera,"Discontinuing antidepressant treatment in major depression," *Harvard Review of Psychiatry* 5 (1998): 293–305.

545 S. D. Hollon et al., "Prevention of Relapse Following Cognitive Therapy Vs Medications In Moderate To Severe Depression," *Archives of General Psychiatry,* 62, no. 4 (2005): 417–22.

546 Otis W. Brawley, *How We Do Harm: A Doctor Breaks Ranks about Being Sick in America* (New York: St. Martin's Press, 2011).

547 Sandeep Jauhar, *Doctored: The Disillusionment of an American Physician* (New York: Farrar, Strauss and Giroux, 2014).

548 Philip Caper, "How ACA Fuels Corporatization of American Health Care," *Bangor Daily News,* November 21, 2014.

549 Brawley, *How We Do Harm.*

Index

Drug abuse
defined, 290
disinhibition and desperation in,
293
young drug abuser, 291–293
Drug-centered medications, 353, 355
Drugs. *See also* Drug abuse; Psychoactive drugs; Psychiatric drugs;
Psychotropic drugs
advertising cures, 394
the good, the bad and the ugly,
283–286
historical perspective on, 280–284
prescribed, 285–286
principles of use, 285–286
psychoactive, 284, 285, 297, 350,
353
sedative, 293
use, classification of, 286–294
Drummond, Edward, 358, 359
DSM, 4, 24
areas of specific phobias, 153
diagnoses, 47–48
disorders in, 32
intellectual disability, 177
new, 33–35
pluses and minuses of system,
38–40
product of, 36
as "psychiatry bible," 395
use of the term disease, 41
DSM-5
acute and posttraumatic stress,
170–171
acute stress in, 169–170
ADHD, 233
autism, 214, 215, 229

bipolar disorder, 132
British Psychological Society and, 48
compulsive hoarding, 317
development of, 35–38
domains of impairments, 195–196
illness anxiety disorder, 254
DSM-I, 32
DSM-II, 32, 233
DSM-III, 33, 34–35, 115, 131, 213,
233
DSM-III-R, autism in, 213
DSM-IV, 34, 35, 38, 42–43
Dubos, René, 253
Dumont, Raeann, 150, 154, 155, 156,
159–160
Dunner, David, 131
Dykeman, Arthur, 102
Dysfunctional anxiety
anxiety defenses, 158–169
chronic anxiety, 146–153
forms of, 145
phobia, 153–157
psychological and social origins of,
143–156
social anxiety, 157–158
Dysfunctional memories, 65

E
Early-stage AD, 206
Ecological model, 52–53
ECT. *See* Electroconvulsive therapy
(ECT)
Edelman, Gerald, 54, 221, 222
Egocentric and grandiose traits, in
psychopaths, 329
Egocentric traits, in psychopaths, 329
Einstein, Albert, 230

Index

About the Author

Robert L. Gallon, PhD, has taught in the Department of Psychiatry and was a psychologist at the Psychosomatic Medicine Clinic at the Thomas Jefferson University Hospital. As Chief Psychologist at Eastern Maine Medical Center he worked with the Rehabilitation Medicine Department to found a Chronic Pain Program. He is a psychological examiner for the court for involuntarily committed psychiatric patients and a consulting psychologist for the State Forensic Service. Over the course of his career, has evaluated more than 5,000 individuals in a wide variety of circumstances. Dr. Gallon is also the tuba player in the Bangor Symphony Orchestra in Maine.